THE SKEPTICAL SUBLIME

THE
SKEPTICAL SUBLIME

Aesthetic Ideology
in Pope and
the Tory Satirists

James Noggle

OXFORD
UNIVERSITY PRESS

2001

OXFORD
UNIVERSITY PRESS

Oxford   New York

Athens   Auckland   Bangkok   Bogotá   Buenos Aires   Cape Town
Chennai   Dar es Salaam   Delhi   Florence   Hong Kong   Istanbul   Karachi
Kolkata   Kuala Lumpur   Madrid   Melbourne   Mexico City   Mumbai   Nairobi
Paris   São Paulo   Singapore   Taipei   Tokyo   Toronto   Warsaw

and associated companies in
Berlin   Ibadan

Copyright © 2001 by Oxford University Press

Published by Oxford University Press, Inc.
198 Madison Avenue, New York, New York 10016

Oxford is a registered trademark of Oxford University Press.

Library of Congress Cataloging-in-Publication Data
Noggle, James.
The skeptical sublime : aesthetic ideology in Pope
and the Tory satirists / James Noggle.
p.   cm.
Includes bibliographical references and index.
ISBN 0-19-514245-4
1. English poetry—18th century—History and criticism. 2. Verse satire,
English—History and criticism. 3. Pope, Alexander, 1688–1744—Criticism and
interpretation. 4. Politics and literature—Great Britain—History—18th century.
5. Sublime, the, in literature. 6. Skepticism in literature. 7. Aesthetics in literature.
8. Great Britain—Intellectual life—18th century.   I. Title.
PR565.S25 N64 2001
821'.509384—dc21   00-045652

1 3 5 7 9 8 6 4 2

Printed in the United States of America
on acid-free paper

To Ferrell Mackey

Preface

This book is about a current in British satire, starting in the Restoration and culminating in the final *Dunciad,* in which writers attain a peculiar kind of literary authority by facing the possibility of radical skeptical doubt. These confrontations seem especially literary because of the connection between skepticism and the incipient discourse of the sublime, as it is used to characterize an essentially unknowable or anomalous quality of aesthetic experience noted at the Enlightenment's beginnings and well beyond. It would be possible to write a book on this tradition without devoting as much of it as this one does—four of seven chapters—to Pope. This emphasis stems in part from my own interest in him and from the development of my project backward from an account of the sublime in the final *Dunciad* to its roots in the epistemological and more general ideological battles of the Restoration. But I do think that Pope's poetry explores the aesthetic uses of skeptical uncertainty with a force and range unique in the literature I am discussing, especially in the striking trajectory from the optimism of *An Essay on Man* to the final *Dunciad*'s apocalyptic vision. The complexity of the tradition of epistemological satire in which Pope's poems participate demands, I think, the attempt to describe its philosophical and general historical background offered in chapter 1, and the sketches of its unique, earlier appearances in the work of Rochester, Dryden, and Swift in chapters 2 and 3, as well as the contrasts proposed throughout between its strongly skeptical sublime and the mitigated skeptical approach to aesthetic experience represented by what must be seen as the Whiggish mainstream of early British criticism.

The threat of skepticism is a much more culturally significant and widespread phenomenon in the post-Restoration period than the notion of the sublime is, and this fact accounts for the stretches of the following discussion when the latter seems a secondary concern, or merely a way to illustrate or dramatize the psychological and cultural pressure that the former unleashes. In this dimension my discussion could be seen to follow the trend of criticism since the 1970s to use the idea of the sublime as a tool to understand larger, deeper, or at least more urgent cultural phenomena, including the Oedipus complex, patriarchy, the national debt, overpopulation, the atomic bomb, or the proliferation of literary criticism itself. But even in chapters 5 and 6, where my attention mostly falls on the influence of Montaignean Pyrrhonism on the philosophical problems of personal identity and of knowing others in Pope's Horatian poetry, I propose that such epistemological radicalism can seem poetically valuable to him because it feeds the rising sublime tradition, and that the skepticism entertained in these poems eventually motivates the *Dunciad*'s quasi-Miltonic vision of sublime catastrophe. The linkage of skepticism and the sublime in this book is based, I am convinced, on a deep homology between them, between the subjective crisis engendered by extreme doubt and the place of sublime experience at the limits of human language, reason, and perception. Furthermore, the sublime's origins in the late seventeenth century, when various areas of intellectual endeavor were not nearly as compartmentalized as they are today, make it easy to find concrete references to and resonances of it not just in epistemological treatises but also in natural science, history, political controversy, theology and sermons, and other types of discourse to which the threat of skepticism applies.

The methodology of this book will, I hope, come across as eclectic, in the attention I pay to philosophical problems, intellectual history, aesthetic theory, and political and cultural ideology. But the preponderance of close readings of poetry here, as well as of other kinds of texts, does announce my commitment to literary criticism and to the kind of history that literary criticism, broadly defined, can do perhaps uniquely well. Radical skepticism's mode of historical existence in the period, its appearance not as part of anybody's intentions or agenda but as a threat, responded to, evaded, disowned, and employed with all the subtlety at the most subtle writers' disposals—none of whom could profitably or comfortably avow themselves as Pyrrhonists—demands a kind of reading attuned not just to stances but also to ironies and moments of tension, not to articulated ideas but to implied or hidden ones, often ones of which writers must be imperfectly aware, or even unconscious, for them to be expressed at all. If radical skepticism is seen as a widespread, important motivation of the early modern intellectual culture of Britain, it must be seen as a displaced and unacknowledged one. But for just this reason it belongs in the kind of history to which this book aspires, a history of inexplicit ideological maneuvers, visibly related to actual historical conflicts but all the more potent for being resistant to univocal articulation. Thus the writers treated here employ what they cannot embrace, imply what they cannot and do not want to state, to serve as well as to resist, at times, the pressures of a given historical moment. The status of skepticism as a scarcely controllable force in this period, at once a part of and beyond subjective intention, constitutes perhaps its profoundest connection to the notion of sublimity, though also perhaps the one least available to the consciousness of its subjects.

Acknowledgments

The completion of this book was made possible in part by a grant from the American Council of Learned Societies as well as by generous leave support from Wellesley College. I would like to thank the librarians of the Bancroft Library at Berkeley, the Beinecke Library at Yale, the Houghton Library at Harvard, and Wellesley College Special Collections for helping me to materials necessary for me to see this book's argument through. Chapter 5 appeared in different form in *1650–1850: Ideas, Aesthetics, and Inquiries in the Early Modern Era,* and chapter 7 appeared in different form in *The Eighteenth Century: Theory and Interpretation.* I thank both publications for permission to use this material.

It is dizzying to me to think of all the friends and colleagues who helped me work on the ideas presented in this book and the many different times and ways they helped. At its beginnings, the project benefited from the indispensable advising of Richard Feingold, Steven Knapp, and John Traugott. The criticisms, suggestions, and intellectual guidance given at later stages by William Cain, David Ferry, Yoon Sun Lee, Beth McGroarty, Timothy Peltason, Lawrence Rosenwald, Margery Sabin, Vernon Shetley, Susan Staves, Luther Tyler, Blakey Vermeule, and Jimmy Wallenstein helped me immeasurably in finding the final contours of the book I wanted to write. I owe a special debt of intellectual and personal gratitude to Scott Dykstra and Andrew Norris, each of whose distinctive, rigorous, and brilliant sense of what makes questions interesting and arguments worth pursuing has for many years given me something to aspire to, work on, and, when I'm lucky, enjoy in friendship into the late hours. Barbara Noggle has given me a lifetime of encouragement and thoughtful friendship and love. Affection and pleasant distraction have been unstintingly supplied by C. Noggle. And my feelings of loving gratitude to Ferrell Mackey, for her wit, coolness, patience, and inspiration as I worked on this book, have grown far beyond my capacity to express them.

Contents

1. Introduction: The Skeptical Sublime—Aesthetic
   Ideology in Pope and the Tory Satirists, 3

2. The Abyss of Reason: Rochester, Dryden, and
   the Skeptical Origins of Sublimity, 33

3. Civil Enthusiasm in *A Tale of a Tub*, 71

4. The Public Universe: *An Essay on Man* and
   the Limits of the Sublime Tradition, 97

5. Pope's *Imitations of Horace* and the Authority
   of Inconsistency, 129

6. Knowing Ridicule and Skeptical Reflection
   in the *Moral Essays*, 157

7. Modernity and the Skeptical Sublime
   in the Final *Dunciad*, 181

Notes, 209

Bibliography, 245

Index, 261

THE SKEPTICAL SUBLIME

I

Introduction: The Skeptical Sublime
Aesthetic Ideology in Pope and the Tory Satirists

The sublime converges with various types of skepticism in late-seventeenth- and early-eighteenth-century British thought to disrupt or trouble the period's aesthetics, epistemology, and ideology in ways that have not been fully recognized. After Boileau's French translation of Longinus's *On the Sublime* brings the idea into European criticism in 1674, British writers attuned to the sublime's skeptical implications produce an account of it different not only from that of Longinus but from those of Burke and Kant later in the eighteenth century, as well as from the major theories of sublimity developed in literary studies from the 1970s to today. The convergence of skepticism with the sublime exposes instabilities in the dominant epistemology of the post-Restoration period, which the leading intellectual histories have usually characterized as securely grounded on procedures of probability, sociable collaboration, and "moral certainty": for a group of important writers, the skeptical sublime notes and dramatizes the occasional instability, alienation, and doubt that attend the age's cultural projects. It also helps grant the aesthetic ideology of Dryden, Swift, and Pope its peculiar character. The so-called Tory satirists have been seen, in a sometimes muddled way, as both political reactionaries and supporters of new models of taste and civil society associated with the liberal-Whig ascendancy. While these satirists appeal to the protoaesthetic category of the sublime—alongside their Whig associates and enemies— to help stabilize British culture after the traumas of the Civil War and Revolution, they also use it to remark the uncertainties attending such means of stabilization and so to express their ambivalence about the emerging social order.

3

I

A principal similarity between sublime and skeptical discourses lies in their discovery of how excessively powerful external objects draw forth the special powers of the mind. Sublime experience, in Boileau's translation of Longinus, shows us that "le monde entier ne suffit pas à la vaste estenduë de l'esprit humain":[1] the prospects of "le Danube, le Nil, le Rhin, & l'Ocean sur tout" (73) or the "fournaizes du mont Ætna" (74) occasion the spirit's sense of its own grandeur and divinity. The sublime poetry or oratory of another may also draw forth the subject's sense of his own power: "the Mind is naturally elevated by the true Sublime, and so sensibly affected with its lively Strokes, that it swells in Transport and an inward Pride, as if what was only heard had been the Product of its own Invention."[2] This economy of power between subject and object, self and other, undergoes innumerable refinements and revisions in the sublime tradition, but from its inception in modern European discourse in 1674, sublimity articulates and magnifies the mind's power in relation to powers that are external (and often seem threatening) to it, whether of nature, of a poem or oration, or of some supernatural being.[3] In Neil Hertz's words, sublime discourse originally and repeatedly sets out "knowingly to override certain conventional lines of demarcation—between writers and their subject matter, between text and interpretation . . . between sublime language and its author . . . or between sublime poet and his audience."[4]

The mind lost in radical skepticism similarly finds its doubts both occasioned and illustrated or figured by vast, powerful, external objects. The immeasurable universe causes Pascal to doubt the capacity of reason and the senses to resolve any question with certainty: "We are placed here in a vast and uncertain Medium, ever floating between Ignorance and Knowledge."[5] But in the face of vastness, the subject's own power to doubt is correspondingly magnified, as when Rochester's "misguided follower" of reason plunges into "doubts boundless Sea" in the Satyr [Against Reason and Mankind] (16,19).[6] The portrayal of doubt as itself an overwhelming force, though produced in the beset mind of the doubter, frequently appears in contests for cultural authority in the period: as English Catholic John Sergeant puts it in Solid Philosophy Asserted (1697), skepticism "creeps by insensible Degrees into even the most Learned Societies, infects the best Wits of our Nation, threatens to bear down all true Philosophy, to extinguish the Natural Light of Men's Understandings, and drown their best Faculty [reason] in a Deluge of Profound Ignorance."[7] The doubting subject discovers his destructive power in the alienating objectification of his own thought, which assumes the impersonal, "natural" dimensions of an ocean at once inside and engulfing him. Writers repeatedly describe skepticism in its extreme form as the overriding of boundaries between the subject and the world he tries to know, in all its vastness, complexity, and inconsistency, which confers its sublime power on reason or the senses by drowning them in themselves. Appalling as they are, such portrayals of skeptical doubt merely exaggerate the alienation implicit in the orthodox Longinian account of sublimity—as when the unthinkable thought of infinity at once enlarges and belittles our comprehension, or belittles it by enlarging it. In such paradoxical exchanges lie the very thrill and glory of sublime experience for its promoters: in Mark Akenside's *Pleasures of the Imagination* (1744), to be "soon o'erwhelm'd and swallow'd up / In that immense of being"[8] is simply a way to "Expand the blooming soul" (226). But similar disproportions stimulate and characterize skepticism, as the mind finds itself hopelessly exceeded by the universe and in turn produces doubts that engulf *"true Philosophy,"* reason, and the possibility of knowledge.

This darker view distinguishes the writers examined in this study from happy Shaftesburyans like Akenside. Key moments in Augustan satire explicitly associate sublime elevation with the baleful action of skepticism. For Swift, Pope, and others, skeptical doubt and sublimity both chart the same intellectual motion, in which the mind tries to ascend to extraordinary levels of thought or perception only to fall into a doubtfulness that wipes out higher truths and common sense alike. Such reversals in epistemological contexts of post-Restoration literature typically attend dogmatic efforts to reach "infallible certainty," to assert the sufficiency of human reason, or to penetrate the fundamental structure of nature underlying all appearances. The epistemological ambiguities of such reversals link them in the minds of the Tory satirists with Longinus, who describes the sublime's natural tendency to lapse into its opposite throughout his treatise. In the words of Leonard Welsted's translation (1712), "the Sublime of it self, and by its own natural Force, is Lubricous and full of Danger"[9]—whence in part derives its appeal, as the dedication of John Hall's translation (1652, antedating Boileau's)[10] puts it: "how easie and willing we are to adventure and transgresse, in things which nature seems of herself to teach us" (dedication). The subject enticed by this lubricity risks not just slipping into bombast but snuffing out thought itself, as Longinus tells us melodramatically: "so *flaming* oftentimes above the measure of their *fewell* [our thoughts] *extinguish* and miserably *decay*" (Hall, 42). Samuel Werenfels, Protestant theologian of Basel, similarly describes the danger of elevation in his *Dissertation Concerning Meteors of Stile, or False Sublimity* (1711): "of all *Meteors*, none have a greater appearance of Sublimity, than those which *Quintilian* calls *præcipita*, and others *tumida, turgida, inflata*, which are swollen, and flatulent, and full of Tumor," defined as "a certain excess of Elevation, into which all are betray'd, who possess a Strength of Imagination rather than of Judgment."[11] The correlation in Longinus of rising and falling, mental "Strength" and self-betrayal, flaming and extinguishing, thus enters the mainstream of the sublime tradition: as Steven Knapp remarks, "Kant, along with Burke and the English satirists, was aware of the intriguing proximity of *hypsos* to bathous, of subjective 'freedom' to a mad or comical inflation of the self."[12] If falling into risible bathos is the opposite of sublimity, the danger of doing so has been seen to be a feature of it.

The sublime's skeptical implications, its erosion of grounded, purposive thought in its very effort to secure for thought a transcendent status, encourage satirists to find its ironic reversals not just in rhetorical grandiosity but in all manner of destructively pretentious expression, in philosophy, religion, science, and politics. Werenfels's *Dissertation* is published in a single volume with his *Discourse of Logomachys, or Controversys About Words* because, the preface says, "as it is a common Error in Logical Disputes to confound a mere Verbal Difference with a Real; so in *Rhetorick,* they who affect *Sublimity,* are frequently betray'd *into* Meteors of Stile"—confusions that for Werenfels only promote skepticism about everything, as well as its socially deleterious effects.[13] While the Hack in *A Tale of a Tub* vows to "descend to the very *bottom* of all the *Sublime* throughout this Treatise,"[14] Swift discovers the Longinian reversal of height into depth in the efforts of ancient and modern dogmatic philosophers, quacks, Dissenters, Papists, and tyrannical princes, whose self-inflation jeopardizes not just their own thought but reason and sanity itself, as well as the fragile, post-1688 social order.[15]

Recent theoretical and historical critiques have argued that ironic reversal plagues the epistemology of modernity with particular intensity. Of course philosophy's tendency to inadvertently make a mockery of its pretensions has long been noted, from Aristophanes' portrayal of abstracted Socrates falling into a ditch to Saint Paul's remark in Romans concerning intellectual sophisticates: "Professing themselves to be wise, they became fools" (1:22). But the early modern skeptical tradition, beginning with Montaigne's rediscovery of Pyrrhonism in the sixteenth century in the *Apology for Raimond de Sebonde,* identifies the Pauline reversal as endemic to epistemology: "Of what is the most subtile Folly made, but of the most subtile Wisdom?"—a sentence that Alexander Pope doubly emphasizes in the marginal notations of his copy of the *Essays.*[16] An increasingly prevalent view of knowledge as all or nothing emerges from Montaigne's skeptical challenge: "Either we can absolutely judge, or absolutely we cannot" (vol. 2, 384—another passage highlighted by Pope). Our efforts to do the former, Montaigne implies, teach us the truth of the latter. This polarization reaches an early climax when Descartes undertakes his quest for absolute certainty by subjecting all his knowledge to absolute doubt at the beginning of the *Meditations* (1641). His successors, dissatisfied with his resolution of skepticism, seek some higher ground of certainty in turn, again to bequeath little more than doubt to thinkers after them. Wittgenstein sees the restless drive toward pure, indubitable certainty besetting the modern philosophical tradition as embroiled in just this irony: when we have philosophically purified ordinary thought and language, "We have got on to slippery ice where there is no friction and so in a certain sense the conditions are ideal, but also, just because of that, we are unable to walk."[17] Against such groundless idealizations, Wittgenstein works in the *Investigations* "to bring words back from their metaphysical to their everyday use" (sec. 116).

Wittgenstein's critique has been most widely applied in recent years by Stanley Cavell, who finds the philosophical and literary endeavors of modernity, from Shakespeare's tragedies to German Romanticism to the American Transcendentalists, to be haunted by "the quest of traditional epistemology,"[18] exemplified for him in Descartes's skeptical dissatisfaction with the "everyday" and his subsequent effort to achieve metaphysically ideal conditions of certainty. As Cavell notices,[19] Wittgenstein consistently figures such impulses to elevate or purify thought as sublime: they express, as he puts it in the *Investigations* (sec. 38), "a tendency to sublime the logic of our language" (einer Tendenz her, die Logik unserer Sprache zu sublimieren), or "even to try to purify, to sublime, the signs themselves" (das Satzzeichen selber reinigen, sublimieren, zu wollen, sec. 94), and in the surrounding sections Wittgenstein describes the urge to treat logic as "something sublime" (sec. 89). Be they never so dogmatic, such efforts for him both emerge from and result in a kind of skepticism, an alienation from "everyday" or ordinary standards of belief and practice, rising to the "frozen emptiness of sublimity," as Cavell puts it.[20] But while the sublime philosopher's implied slip and fall on the ice in the *Investigations* to Cavell suggests a "connection between romanticism and skepticism" (57), it also resonates with the Augustans' satire of Cartesianism and related dogmatisms that turn certainty into doubt and hupsous into bathos. The satirical dimension of Wittgenstein's work, stressed by Richard Rorty among others,[21] also helps clarify how such comic reversals in post-Restoration literature develop the incipient aesthetic tradition of sublimity according to the epistemological ironies animating modern thought.

This sublime economy appears especially in Augustan satire's more serious aspects, its recognition that those whom it attacks represent not just simple vice, stupidity, or selfishness but enormities that defy conventional appeals to reason or morality. This enhanced critique is demanded by the engulfing power of skeptical doubt that Pope, Swift, and other writers of the period address: for instance, Pope writes in the *Dunciad* that the dunces "explain a thing till all men doubt it, / And write about it, Goddess, and about it" (IV, 251–2).[22] They unknowingly reverse their own intent to explain and infect not only each other but "all men," all culture, with desta-bilizing doubt. Cavell identifies a similarly expanding failure of intention-ality as the action of skeptical doubt in post-Cartesian thought, where "the effort to deny skepticism is itself an expression of skepticism" (38). Such de-nials in late-seventeenth- and eighteenth-century British discourse take many forms: the "high Priori Road" of religious rationalism in the *Dunciad* (IV, 471), the "Oracular *Gusts*" of Æolian inspiration in the *Tale of a Tub* (157), the schemes of projectors and scientists satirized through the period, and at times even the moderate, probabilistic procedures of the Royal Society and Latitudinarian theology. "How can answering skepticism be tanta-mount to skepticism?" Hilary Putnam asks, commenting on Cavell's posi-tion. It can because "answers" like scientific positivism and metaphysical realism "*concede the correctness of almost everything the skeptic says,*" accept-ing the premise that ordinary, everyday knowledge and practice require in-dubitable justification or grounding and would fail us if such grounds could not be theoretically established. Putnam concludes: "skepticism, as Cavell sees it, is a perpetual dissatisfaction with the human position, a de-mand for a God's Eye View or Nothing, that degrades the only perspective that is actually available to us. It is this downgrading of the human posi-tion, this aspiration to be outside our own skins (nothing else would be good enough), that Cavell calls 'skepticism.'"[23] The power of departures from the natural human position lies in their seeming irreversibility once begun: the grip of doubt holds "all men," as Pope says, whether theorizing for or against it.

The Augustans satirically reject such doubt even as they accept and even exaggerate its engulfing, sublime danger, its genuine signification of our in-tellectual frailty. As Bolingbroke puts it in his *Letters, or Essays Address'd to Alexander Pope*, describing the excursions of philosophers, "every glittering apparition that is pointed out to them, in the vast wild of imagination, passes for a reality: the more distant, the more confused, the more incom-prehensible it is, the more sublime it is esteemed."[24] Even as he mocks fatu-ous self-inflation, Bolingbroke reminds us of the depths of doubt, the "vast wild of imagination" waiting to humble our intellectual pride. One recent commentator has noted that our "contemporary debate about the sublime revolves around two positions: the sublime provides either a way out of skepticism or a way into it."[25] The special force of the sublime in the Au-gustan satirists lies in its conflation of the two: the way out of skepticism is the way in, as they see it, the "high Priori" solutions to skeptical doubt the generation of doubt, and this reversal itself amounts to the darkest, least controllable version of sublimity imaginable, in which all positions are lost, ambiguously defined by self-opposition or reversal, and all theo-retical exits from uncertainty lead back to a centerless fog of sublime incomprehension. The Augustans' satirical depictions of these vast wilds and boundless seas indicate their own investment in ungraspable religious and metaphysical absolutes: Pope, Swift, and Dryden still believe there is some absolute truth out there, to which only the God's-eye view is adequate, even as they deny that any human perspective may grasp it. It is this very split between the absolute end and imperfect means of knowledge that animates the post-Cartesian epistemological tradition, as Cavell repeatedly argues. Thus while the Augustans' satirical views of doomed rationalism resemble some of the most potent twentieth-century critiques of epistemology's absurdly self-defeating procedures, they remain, of course, embroiled in the metaphysical traditions that Wittgenstein and his heirs, including Cavell, Putnam, and Rorty, have diagnosed and attempted to end.

The uniquely combined renunciations and assumptions of skepticism's power in Tory satire distinguish its version of the sublime from the recent theoretical accounts of it. Power has been the crucial term that each theory has described differently, its transfers, investments, losses, gains—the methods by which the subject, at first intimidated, reduced, or terrified by a power external to him, recuperates a sense of his own power or dignity. Some of the most influential theorists take Kant's account in the *Critique of Judgment* (1790) as paradigmatic. In Kant, the initially traumatic experience of vastness in the Mathematical Sublime or of natural power in the Dynamical Sublime uncovers special subjective powers: in the latter, our "physical impotence . . . reveals in us at the same time an ability to judge ourselves independent of nature, and reveals in us a superiority over nature that is the basis of a self-preservation quite different in kind from the one that can be assailed and endangered by nature outside us"[26]—our "vocation," our "highest principles" (121), or, earlier, regarding the Mathematical Sublime, "reason's ideas" (113). Thomas Weiskel's *Romantic Sublime* (1976) describes this recuperation in Kant, "the very moment in which the mind turns within and performs its identification with reason,"[27] as a method of subjecting the mind, in the apparent assertion of its autonomy, to reason's authority. For Weiskel, this event, staged by reason, links Kant's account of subjectivity to others, particularly Freud's: "the sublime moment recapitulates and thereby reestablishes the oedipus complex, whose positive resolution is the basis of culture itself" (94). The Dynamical Sublime teaches the subject that the "power within" is superior to the external power of nature, the superego superior to the threat of brute force, imparting a pleasure that functions to get the subject to embrace his subservience to the law of the father, the "Thou shalt," in his identification with his rational vocation. Neil Hertz similarly argues that the sublime object, in all its disruptive power, always acts as "the guarantor of the self's own integrity as agent," "a confirmation of the unitary status of the self": "A passage to the limit may seem lurid, but it has its ethical and metaphysical uses" (53). For both Weiskel and Hertz, then, the disorder and fear met in the sublime is a cannily selected "way out of skepticism" into a more intimately powerful rule of law and order.

The view of sublime crisis as factitious, as staged by authority, whether rational, metaphysical, patriarchal, or more vaguely cultural, has been questioned by those who see the experience as a form of genuine instability. Steven Knapp insists that in Kant's account, the subject explicitly fails to identify fully with reason, and this incompleteness prevents him from ever fatuously seeing himself as the personification of his own rational vocation: the sublime "signifies the partial or temporary coincidence of reason and the empirical agent," a signification "which depends as much on difference as it does on identity" (79). Paul de Man's grimmer view expressly criticizes the sublime of Weiskel and Hertz, turning to Hegel's sublime as the antidote to the pleasing compromise or identification with authority seen in Kant: according to Hegel, de Man says, "the definitive loss of the absolute experienced in the sublime puts an end to such an economy of value and replaces it with what one could call a critical economy: the law (*das Gesetz*) is always a law of differentiation (*Unterscheidung*), not the grounding of an authority but the unsettling of an authority that is shown to be illegitimate."[28] In de Man's austere, Hegelian refusal of all self-legitimizing, usurped authority, the only "politically legitimate and effective" discourse of the sublime is one that puts its subject in the position of the unreconstructed slave: "Poets, philosophers, and their readers lose their political impact only if they become, in turn, usurpers of mastery" (118). Jean-Luc Nancy, in "The Sublime Offering," less austerely insists on the sublime subject's avoidance of such usurpations: "The offering offers, carries, and places before . . . but it does not install in presence. What is offered remains at a limit, suspended on the border of reception, an acceptance—which cannot in its turn have any form other than that of an offering."[29] Definitive of sublime experience is the subject's inability to grasp, embody, or personify the power or authority offered to it. The sublime on Jonathan Lamb's account avoids metaphysically reinstalling authority not by withholding it but by passing it around ceaselessly according to the verve of rhetoricians, who practice "independently of rule or principle in a temporality dominated by the instant, uncommitted to ontology, teleology or truth, and dedicated to the libidinal pursuit of power by means of words that have the quality of a public gesture, something which transpires rather than an idea that is communicated."[30] Different as these definitions are, all question the view that the sublime aggrandizes the subject only in order to subject him to some stable authority. They see in sublimity "a way into skepticism," broadly defined, because it disrupts the happy subjection, described by Weiskel, Hertz, and others, of the mind in its dignified union with reason.

This sketch of some of the available accounts—there are many more[31]— reveals the uniqueness of the power relations in the skeptically riven sublime scene presented by the satirists discussed here, before the Burkean and Kantian models later in the eighteenth century more rigidly determine possible positions in the discussion. The subject of the skeptical sublime, in the effort to ascend (in Swift's words) "to Idea's of what is most Perfect, finished, and exalted" (157), finds himself alienated from the authority of these ideas. But his desolation at "the very *bottom* of all the *Sublime*" subserviently testifies to the height of what he fails to grasp: it is not uniting with the sublime object but the explicit failure to do so that compels submission. The subject sinks into unregenerate alienation from truth, less "suspended on the border of reception" of it than cast out from its influence—yet this very outcast state signifies truth's authority. As Swift puts it in the sermon "On the Trinity," "*Reason* itself is true and just, but the *Reason* of every particular Man is weak and wavering, perpetually swayed and turned by his Interests, his Passions, and his Vices."[32] The subject does not, as in Weiskel's applications of Kant, discover his coherence and destiny in his union with "reason's ideas": rather, the very link to "true and just" reason inevitably divides and alienates the mind from it; it wields its authority by being not fully graspable, beyond "personification" in Knapp's sense. The mind's cleaving to and from the sublime object determines its skeptical predicament, finding itself alienated from the very rational standards it seeks to uphold: the rational idealization of thought makes thought necessarily uncertain, like the ice on which Wittgenstein's satirized philosopher tries to walk. Sublime experience neither snugly enlists the subject under the aegis of rational authority nor permits him to defy such authority from a de Manian position of utter servitude: authority is asserted by its very refusal to gratify the subject with an image of his completeness.

Yet this alienated condition does not entirely diminish or enfeeble the mind. On the contrary, it is the source of the skeptical intellect's sublimely destructive potential, unwelcome as it is. The very distance discovered between the uncertain subject and reason unleashes a subjective power that can demolish reason itself. In Hume's political metaphor in the *Treatise of Human Nature* (1739), skepticism at once enacts and subverts reason's authority:

Reason first appears in possession of the throne, prescribing laws, and imposing maxims, with an absolute sway and authority. Her enemy, therefore, is oblig'd to take shelter under her protection, and by making use of rational arguments to prove the fallaciousness and imbecility of reason, produces, in a manner, a patent under her hand and seal. This patent has at first an authority, proportion'd to the present and immediate authority of reason, from which it is deriv'd. But as it is suppos'd to be contradictory to reason, it gradually diminishes the force of that governing power, and its own at the same time.[33]

This articulation of reason's authority by its own subversion is more drastic than Swift's account of "*Reason* in every particular man" ever alienated from the "true and just" authority of "*Reason* itself." But it describes the same structure, occurring again and again in pictures of the skeptical dilemma from the period: skepticism asserts reason's prerogatives only to expose its debility (whether in general as in Hume or in the particular case as in Swift). The Kantian model of reason as lawgiver ironically collapses in Hume in the skeptical turn that convinces reason to legislate the end of its empire. The individual subject must be demoralized by this collapse, but the process still invests the mind with the power to extend its self-subversion to include the subversion of all that philosophy could promise: "the understanding, when it acts alone, and according to its most general principles, entirely subverts itself, and leaves not the lowest degree of evidence in any proposition, either in philosophy or common life" (267–8). For Hume, as so often in accounts of skepticism, the extravagant consequences of skeptical doubt force a return to the unreflective, secure state of ordinary consciousness, but such a return does not rationally solve or answer skepticism. It occurs only because skepticism is unanswerable. His sublime narrative at the "*Conclusion of this book*" (book I of the *Treatise*)— as he ventures "upon that boundless ocean, which runs out into immensity" (264) and finally fancies himself "in the most deplorable condition imaginable, inviron'd with the deepest darkness" (269)—magnifies the dramatic powers of the individual's philosophical imagination in order to demand its heavy, utterly nonrational burial in common sense. Like other images of boundless seas and bottomless pits of doubt in the period, these emphasize the mind's sublime power, even at the height of its fear and weakness, to bring reason down.

But such descents from the heights of reason in the period are commonly seen as painful. They lack, therefore, the pleasing or self-inflating component, the delight usually found in sublime experience, when after initial intimidation the subject discovers something in himself more flattering than the power to reduce reason to madness. The Augustan satirists themselves nonetheless do indirectly reclaim a measure of power in their depictions of skepticism, and like the recuperations described in other accounts of sublime experience, this reclamation grants theirs its special character. Though they repeatedly mock and disown skeptical doubt, they also find ways of aligning themselves with its power. Most simply, they claim an insight into it that their satirical butts who fall into it lack. Often in the period's satire, skepticism's victims seem unaware, or only half aware, that it has befallen them, declaiming with hysterical optimism into the abysses produced by their misbegotten reasoning. While Pope, Swift, Dryden, and Rochester often chart the sublime reversal of rational confidence into skeptical despair as a narrative trajectory, they also present the intellects of those whom they satirize as always divided between dogmatic certainty and doubting alienation: as Pope says in the *Dunciad*, the "gloomy Clerk" and his associates are "Of nought so certain as our *Reason* still, / Of nought so doubtful as of *Soul* and *Will*" (IV, 481–2). Pope and others intimately connect themselves to skeptical doubt by understanding its threat better than those who foment and suffer by it.

But the most significant alignment of radical doubt and the power of the Augustan satirists lies in their use of it to punish their satiric victims, acknowledging it as an instrument of justice. The order of epistemology, in which reason begets doubt, and the demand for certainty a fearful skepticism, is thus indirectly affirmed. The indirectness of the satirists' endorsement of this structure must be stressed: they think reasoning along Cartesian, enthusiastic, or other dogmatic lines is not only wicked and foolish but also avoidable. Their alternatives include various modes of common sense, "the Brain, in its natural Position and State of Serenity" (171), in Swift's words, or "thinking right, and meaning well" (*Essay on Man*, IV, 32)—assertions usually emptied of positive content, often themselves ironized (especially in Swift), but almost always seen as viable alternatives to lubricous self-inflation. As Bolingbroke puts it in an essay addressed to Pope, "our knowledge on many subjects, and particularly on those which we intend here, must be superficial to be real" (vol. 3, 52)—and rarely do the Augustans doubt that such superficiality may be achieved.

Such formulas do, however, expose their shaky epistemological foundations: our assurance of the reality of human knowledge depends on our ability to conceive of it as superficial from the point of view of an absolute, godlike certainty that we must admit we can never assume. The Augustan satirists become free to explore the gulf they posit between these two perspectives only vicariously, through the disastrous flights, the imagined enormities they place in the minds of their satiric butts. This practice of disowned or alienated imagination more than anything makes a satirical register inevitable for the skeptical sublime: the satirist assumes the might of the order of epistemology itself, even as he disowns its temptations and excesses, to characterize the threat of skeptical tendencies to culture. An outcome of this ascription of vast powers to skepticism is the final *Dunciad*, in which Pope dramatizes his own poetic voice's incorporation in the doubt-inducing powers of Dulness. But even this is part of a strategy of satirical criticism, however self-confessedly doomed. As Weiskel puts it, "Only irony, not any alternative semiotic, separates bathos and the true sublime. Indeed, in the ironic notion of bathos the mock-heroic and the aesthetic of the sublime converge" (20). Even as the satirist distinguishes himself from the intellect sublimely overwhelmed by skepticism, he assumes its alienating power himself as the core of his satirical agenda. Skepticism grants the satirist the pleasing sense of achieved power regularly discovered in sublime experience, but only by being continuously, critically displaced or disowned. The instability of this position is obvious. If it is also untenable, as Weiskel perhaps implies, it is only because its very untenability serves ironically to express the sublime power the satirist seeks to accrue— a power to remain ironic, as it were, in the very insistence that the ironic distance between himself and the satirized butt has collapsed. At this limit of ironic reflection and differentiation, the satirist has brought the typical sublime blending of object into subject into its uniquely Augustan register.

II

The epistemological condition of late-seventeenth- and early-eighteenth-century British discourse encourages the displacements and disownings that mark skepticism's presence in the sublime tradition. Three species of skepticism were defined in the period by being assiduously compared to and differentiated from each other. The first one, "constructive or mitigated skepticism" (in Richard Popkin's phrase),[34] is the most common epistemological posture of the age, guiding mainstream Latitudinarian Anglican theology, the natural-scientific endeavors of the Royal Society, law, medicine, literature, and other disciplines. This view maintains that "infallible certainty" on most or all issues is impossible but that a reasonable degree of assuredness is obtainable on practical questions sufficient to guide our conduct. When Dryden says in the preface to *Religio Laici* (1682) that he is "naturally inclin'd to Scepticism in Philosophy,"[35] he means skepticism in this orthodox sense, marked by epistemological modesty in all intellectual matters; when Glanvill assaults overconfidence in philosophy in *Scepsis Scientifica* (1665), the revised version of *Vanity of Dogmatizing* (1661), he does so because he sees "Confest *Ignorance,* the way to *Science*," as the subtitle says, dedicating his work to the Royal Society's efforts at "*improving the minds of Men in* solid *and* useful notices *of things, helping them to such* Theories *as may be serviceable to* common life."[36] While admitting that most things—even, according to some, mathematical demonstration[37]—fall short of ideal certainty, British epistemology of the time stresses that our probable knowledge is grounded firmly enough to make unmitigated doubt utterly irrelevant and perverse in nearly all circumstances.

The second species of skepticism is the radical version, usually called Pyrrhonism or Academicism by the age, after its roots in ancient Greek philosophical schools, taken to argue that nothing may be known for certain and that we should withhold assent from all propositions. It is regularly accused of leading to intellectual and social chaos (as had been argued from antiquity), a product of insanity or insincerity. ("Pyrrhonism is not a sect of persons convinced of what they say, but a sect of liars," according to the *Port-Royal Logic* [1662].)[38] For these reasons English writers almost universally revile it. As Bolingbroke puts it in *Fragments or Minutes of Essays,* "The Pyrrhonian is against all sides: and all sides are against him. The Academician would pass, if he could, for a neuter, who is for no side, nor against any; or else for a trimmer, who changes sides often, and finds the probable sometimes on one, sometimes on the other" (vol. 4, 278). Radical skepticism is just what the constructive variety sets out to mitigate, and the latter always portrays the former as irresponsible intellectual extravagance or madness itself.

Following these negative connotations, a third sense of skepticism emerges, more a principle of application than a settled meaning: the term *sceptick* is often applied to people who would not accept it as a description of their views but who are, according to their opponents, really skeptics without knowing it. Metaphysical dogmatists, Cartesians, Dissenters, Catholics, deists, Epicureans, and even Royal Society members may all be called skeptics, usually because of radical tendencies or implications of their ideas that they would disown. These methods of ascription are often elaborate. The anonymous author of *Remarks Upon the Letter to a Lord Concerning Enthusiasm* (1708), an attack on Shaftesbury, concludes that "this Gentleman sets up for one of the greatest of all *Scepticks,* which he has not so little Wit as not to *know* he does (and *he* knows best whether he does so in *good earnest*)."[39] Catholics like Sergeant (quoted earlier) and Thomas White[40] tirelessly argue that the moderate skeptical postures of the Latitudinarians unwittingly lead to radical doubt. Anglican moderates in turn argue that Catholics' blind faith in the Church as the interpreter of tradition amounts to a skepticism of which they are unaware. This general reversing tendency resembles that of other terms like *atheism,* with which skepticism is increasingly associated:[41] though a professing atheist is almost nowhere to be found in contemporary writing, polemicists regularly fling the term at any of their opponents who do not seem orthodox. Beyond mere unfairness, the third sense or principle of skepticism signifies its reversing, slippery, divisive force in discourse, a tendency to be passed around—a lubricity that indicates that its meaning and applications in general are built on basic divisions. Skepticism, however much it may be mitigated to uphold a set of moderate, pacific intellectual practices, remains a potentially radical power never entirely under control—which again marks its affiliation with the sublime.

The many influential intellectual histories of the Restoration period and after do not tend to emphasize this instability and the often unwelcome fluidity with which various skepticisms define each other. Nearly all historians notice that a mitigated skeptical critique produces the major shift in thought commonly seen in the period, used to ward off various dogmatisms, arbitrary authorities, and tyrannies (Aristotelianism, Cartesian rationalism, French-style autocracy, the pope, Puritan enthusiasm), but usually these studies argue that this critique leads unproblematically to the institutional stability of philosophy, theology, poetry and drama, rhetoric, law, and so on. In his *Probability and Literary Form* (1984), Douglas Lane Patey links a new order of probability in literary theory to Academic-skeptical views of Carneades and Cicero's *Academica,* among other things.[42] Barbara J. Shapiro's *Probability and Certainty in Seventeenth-Century England* (1983) applies a similar view of probability's dominance over every department of institutionalized intellectual life.[43] While emphasizing neo-Epicurean strands in natural science and language theory, Richard Kroll, in *The Material Word: Literate Culture in the Restoration and the Early Eighteenth Century* (1991), "take[s] the emergence of probability (broadly defined) as a given," in light of previous intellectual histories.[44] Steven Shapin, in *A Social History of Truth: Civility and Science in Seventeenth-Century England* (1994), describes the social assumptions and conditions growing out of the style of truth claims of the Royal Society, typified by the character of Robert Boyle, also recognizing the probabilistic nature of the period's epistemology and adding that "in early modern culture the definition of gentility implied a conception of truth."[45] While disputing the exact historical moment of the turn's inception,[46] these studies (among many others) support the general idea that probabilism and other forms of socially acceptable uncertainty contribute, in Kroll's words, to "a remarkably coherent if plural cultural reorganization at the Restoration" (44), defining the dominant epistemological trends in all fields of cultural endeavor. They also accept—with the partial exception of Shapin[47]—that skeptical arguments motivate the move to probabilism.

The force of this consensus is irresistible. The richness of detail with which scholars have described the era's well-elaborated theories and practices of probability, the linkages discovered among historiography, theology, linguistic and literary theory, establish beyond doubt the remarkable dominance of the probable order. But by emphasizing the stability of procedures of inference and the "hierarchy of probable signs" (in Patey's phrase, 84) in the period's institutions, intellectual historians tend to neglect the ironies evolving from probabilism's roots in more radical skepticism, from the disproportion between the destructive power of its critique of dogmatism and the modest, constructive method it puts in dogmatism's place. The point is not that this disproportion makes probabilism unworkable or our picture of its dominance in the period wrong but that a constitutional instability is crucial to the period's epistemological functioning, seen not as part of any systematic theory but in moments of tension. While "on the *margins* of trusting systems" (19), in Shapin's phrase, a skeptical sense of these systems' contingency and vulnerability to global questioning remains vital to their motivation and operation.

This irony has been mentioned in the studies described here. Kroll recognizes that

> if neoclassical discourse fragmented the claims of dissent by appealing to sceptical modes, its own magisterial claims to authority were instantly threatened by an identical sceptical move, a strategy Catholic apologists were quick to exploit. When Anglicans attacked Catholics and inspirationalists for their dogmatic attitudes to knowledge, they were subtly but surely undermining a secure basis for their own need to ensure conformity to their position. (78)

Patey describes the power of probability to incorporate elements seemingly subversive of it, citing Hutcheson's ingenious argument that the very improbability of creation proves God's hand in it: Patey remarks, "our very failure to discover probable signs becomes itself a probable sign" (69). But foregrounding the coherence of the period's institutions has made a sustained focus on eruptions of disorder, contingency, and madness impossible and occasionally has produced some strained readings.[48] A literary-critical account like this one, learning much from the magisterial studies cited but more naturally drawn than they to anomaly and ambiguity, has its own historical contribution to make. The skeptical sublime, always a departure from the systematic and the procedural, appears at moments when upholders of the moderate epistemological order find themselves willing to recognize and articulate the ironies of its operation.

Such recognitions appear in different contexts and degrees of explicitness. Despite mitigated skepticism's sustained, self-defining efforts to differentiate itself from the radical type, influential thinkers occasionally proclaim their essential identity. Pierre Bayle, in his article "Pyrrho" in the *Historical and Critical Dictionary* (1697), argues that contemporary scientific procedures do not oppose ancient practices of radical doubt at all. Pyrrhonism, while seemingly a threat to (some) theology, hardly seems so with regard to the natural sciences or to the state. It does not matter much if one says that the mind of man is too limited to discover anything concerning natural truths, concerning the causes producing heat, cold, the tides, and the like. It is enough for us that we employ ourselves in looking for probable hypotheses and collecting data. I am quite sure that there are very few good scientists of this century who are not convinced that nature is an impenetrable abyss and that its springs are known only to Him who made and directs them. Thus, all these philosophers are Academics and Pyrrhonists in this regard. Society has no reason to be afraid of skepticism; for skeptics do not deny that one should conform to the customs of one's country, practice one's moral duties, and act upon matters on the basis of probabilities without waiting for certainty.[49]

Mainstream British scientists like Robert Boyle would concur "that nature is an impenetrable abyss and that its springs are known only to Him who made and directs them." Moreover, as Sextus Empiricus defines it in his *Outlines of Pyrrhonism*, widely available in England in Thomas Stanley's *History of Philosophy* (1662, which Pope owned in its third, 1701 edition), Pyrrhonism is itself a way of dealing productively with appearances, not a denial of them: "They who say, *the Scepticks take away* Phænomena's seem not to understand what we have said . . . when we raise questions concerning the *Phænomenon,* we endeavour not to subvert the *Phænomena's* (these we presuppose) but only to discover the Temerity of the Dogmatists."[50] This view finds a prestigious exemplar in Montaigne: his *Apology* is "the womb of modern thought" (in Popkin's words, *History of Scepticism,* 54) in part because it inspires the moderate scientific procedures of Marin Mersenne and Pierre Gassendi and their counterparts in England.[51] Despite scientific probabilism's often violent disavowals of Pyrrhonism, it remains open to Bayle and others to discover their logical and genealogical connections.

A further complication is that some scholars have proposed that specifically Academic skepticism represents a middle way between dogmatism and Pyrrhonistic doubt in the minds of many: its practical ranking of probabilities arguably helps model the moderate doubt dominating scientific and religious debate of the era.[52] Boyle's mouthpiece in *The Sceptical Chymist* (1661) is called Carneades, after all, after the prominent Academic.[53] But as the quote from Bolingbroke earlier indicates, it is not true that Academic skepticism is always embraced as a useful mitigation of radical doubt. Some readings present it as more extreme than Pyrrhonism itself. The opening paragraph of Sextus's *Outlines of Pyrrhonism* (in Stanley's translation) says that "they who think [truth] incomprehensible, are *Clitomachus, Carneades,* and other *Academicks;* they who still enquire, are the *Scepticks*" (475b). At the end of the final *Dunciad,* Pope condemns Shaftesburyan philosophy for "wander[ing] wild" in "Academic Groves" (IV, 490), and a footnote makes clear that he has Academic skepticism in mind. These instances do not prove that Academicism failed to influence scientific and other moderate epistemological doctrine but only that it, like Pyrrhonism, appears as an inconsistent energy in the period's thought, at times employed and at others disavowed.

Skepticism's duplicity most subtly appears in mainstream assertions of probabilistic epistemology, which sometimes rejects radical doubt strangely by insisting that it is possible and enumerating ways in which it could arise. As John Wilkins remarks in his work *Of the Principles and Duties of Natural Religion* (1675), "*Doubt* is a kind of *Fear,* and is commonly stiled *formido oppositi,* and 'tis the same kind of madness for a man to *doubt* of any thing, as to *hope for,* or *fear* it, upon a meer possibility."[54] A person gripped by this fear "must not stay within Doors, for fear the House should fall upon him, for that is possible: Nor must he go out, lest the next Man that meets him should kill him, for that also is possible," and this goes for "any other Action" (25) as well. Wilkins's mitigated skeptical strategy leads him to "*concede the correctness of almost everything the skeptic says*" (in Putnam's phrase, vii) as to the possibility of such things to argue the practical necessity to ignore it. The point is not that this ongoing possibility makes arguments for moral certainty inadequate. Rather it is only to note how skepticism survives in the thought of the time as an extravagantly possible reaction to the evidence, exposing in principle all of common life to the skeptic's insanity, inspiring an entire genre of wild thought experiments like Wilkins's here ("Is there any thing imaginable more wild and extravagant amongst those in *Bedlam,* than this would be?" [30]). As John Tillotson (editor and son-in-law of Wilkins) puts it in his influential sermon *The Wisdom of Being Religious (Preach'd at Saint Paul's, March 1663/4),*

> the greatest affairs of the world, and the most important commencements of this life are all conducted onely by *moral* demonstrations. Men every day venture their lives and estates onely upon *moral* assurance. For instance, men who never were at the *east* or *West-Indies,* or in *Turky* or *Spain,* yet do venture their whole estate in traffick thither, though they have no *Mathematical demonstration* but onely *moral assurance* that there are such places.[55]

Tillotson's insistence that moral certainty or assurance underwrites all our affairs is meant to emphasize the firmness of the similar basis of our beliefs in biblical history. But the irony of this strategy appears in how much of "this life" it discovers to be supported by "onely" such grounds. The possibility of demented "*fear*" that the reader is demanded to entertain and then disavow models the logic of the essentially unthreatening (though not merely fictional or factitious) terror of sublime aesthetics to be elaborated in the century to come.

For Tillotson, Wilkins, and other liberal Anglicans and men of science of the time, this ascription of madness to anyone who would question moral certainty functions to refute skepticism. (Wittgenstein also describes skepticism in terms "suggestive of madness," on Cavell's reading, but madness for Wittgenstein is as much a part of the natural human condition as a departure from it, part of it by virtue of its departures from it, and so ascribing it to someone does not exactly "refute" anything.)[56] Regardless of how such arguments are supposed to work, their volatility is obvious, especially in the minds of those besieged with illness, dread, and other pressing circumstances—sublime figures disposed to recognize the contingency of human experience. For instance, the Latitudinarian divine Gilbert Burnet (friend of Glanvill and Wilkins, enemy of Swift) tells the dying Rochester that doubting probable religious assurances is as unreasonable as it is "to tell a man that is abroad, and knows he is awake, that perhaps he is in a dream, and in his Bed"; but as Burnet relates, "All this [Rochester] said he did not understand, and that it was to assert or beg the thing in question, which he could not comprehend."[57] Probable argumentation often itself raises the possibility of uncertainty and so invites extravagant, atheistical, unsound, or otherwise unnatural responses.

But the disproportion of what constructive skepticism undermines to what it gives back appears not just in arguments with atheists or other doubters. It may animate pious Anglican expressions of intellectual submission as well. In *The Sceptical Muse: or, A Paradox on Humane Understanding* (1699), the utterly conventional John Pomfret asserts the order of probability by denigrating it:

But yet what's worse, we know not when we err
What mark does Truth, what bright distinction bear?
How do we know, that what we know is true?
How shall we falsehood fly, and truth persue?
Let none then here his certain knowledge boast,
'Tis all but probability at most.[58]

Later, Pomfret's "sceptic" musings lead him to a quasi-Cartesian faith that God cannot be a deceiver, but he ends the poem by linking faith to skepticism's less constructive power: "No more, Ye *Dogmatists,* your Wit shall harm / My liss'ning Soul, no more my Reason charm; / No more you shall my Faculties controul: / Suspicion guards, and Doubt defends my Soul" (244–8). Similar references to "mere Probability," "onely Probability," abound in the period, as in Thomas Heyrick's poem "The Skeptic, against Mechanism" (1691): "All here we know's but Probability, / The Utmost Bound, to which our Wit can fly, / And that which Terminates Philosophy"

(440–2).[59] These instances must be seen not as attacks on the probable epistemological order but as expressions of it, assertions of its insufficiency from one point of view to establish its sufficiency from another. Pope in this spirit describes his progress on his opus magnum to Swift: "my system is a short one, and my circle narrow. Imagination has no limits, and that is a sphere in which you may move on to eternity; but where one is confined to Truth (or to speak more like a human creature, to the appearances of Truth) we soon find the shortness of our Tether."[60] The meditative perspective seems "short," "narrow," "confined" to mere appearances yet is the only authoritative one to be adopted.

The articulators of the probable order themselves accept, even insist, that extremes of thought and enormities of reason frame their systems and consistently describe them as "sublime," as "sublimities." In Boyle's *Discourse of Things Above Reason* (1681), one interlocutor expresses timidity upon venturing on "so unusual and sublime a subject,"[61] while Walter Charleton, Royal Society member, accepts the Copernican hypothesis in his *Immortality of the Human Soul* (1657) "upon grounds of as much certainty and clearness, as the sublime and remote nature of the subject seems capable of."[62] The word refers to objects whose elevation above ordinary powers of thought or observation makes them treacherous to think about. For Boyle the most intractable of these are "unsociable truths," truths that fail to associate "harmoniously" with others, including "that grand absurdity which subverts the very foundation of our reasonings, *that contradictories may both be true*" (235). But even such sublimely subversive elements do not endanger the order that Boyle, Glanvill, and others articulate. Rather our intimations of their sublime force testify to our ability to arrange hierarchies with a modesty that accords, however blindly, with providence.

The writers treated principally in this study, Dryden, Rochester, Pope, Swift, and others, explore the ironies and instabilities of the probable order more fully than its official sponsors and are less confident than Boyle that we may assert our own incomprehension as a sublime providential mechanism. These satirical writers do not directly challenge the dominant epistemology. They are as committed as any to the rejection of dogmatism and the adoption of mitigated skeptical attitudes to stabilize civil society. But within this order, their sharper sense of skepticism's volatility helps them distinguish themselves from their Latitudinarian, Royal Society, Whig friends and enemies. Thus Swift's moderate skeptical strictures in his sermon "On the Trinity" mirror and energize the epistemologically destructive excursions of the Tale-Teller. The *"anxious Thoughts in endless Circles"* (36) that Dryden mollifies in *Religio Laici* are less happily concluded in Adam's confusions about human will and divine law in the *State of Innocence* (1677). Such a sense of irresolution appears not only in stated principles or arguments but less explicitly in tastes and sympathies as well. Pope can praise "Of the Inconstancy of Our Actions" in a marginal jotting in his copy of Montaigne's works as "An incomparable Essay"[63] despite the fact, as he notes to Spence, that it "concludes Pyrrhonically"[64]—and this qualified admiration for a radically skeptical position ambiguously affects those of Pope's poems that treat human inconstancy through the 1730s, as I will argue in chapters 5 and 6. It is true, as Barbara Shapiro has argued, that "the skepticism so often voiced in French intellectual circles rarely was heard in England" (22). This alone suggests that the consistently high admiration in which Montaigne, Charron, and Pascal were held by writers like Pope and Prior signals a slight but important intellectual distance between them and the British epistemological consensus. The satirical writers described here adopt the mitigated skeptical assumptions of their age, as concerned as any to question the dogmatic pretensions of political and religious figures, as well as dogmatisms in philosophy and science. Pope's own Catholicism— "the Religion of Erasmus,"[65] he says—is as irenic as the most Latitudinarian Anglicanism, always renouncing religious dispute among Christian sects concerning "things indifferent." But the Augustans constitute a countertradition when they refuse, question, or satirize the assurances that the mainstream discovers at the limits of probability, instead emphasizing the emptiness met at these limits, where the humiliation of our faculties is the only evidence we can get of anything absolute. As exceptional and brief as such sublime moments are in mitigated skeptical discourse, with all its reassuring procedures and degrees of certainty, they reveal important differences in the ways writers thought they could appeal to the absolute to justify the social order.

III

Ideology ultimately motivates and elaborates these differences. Mitigated skepticism in general, shared by writers of various political persuasions after the Revolution,[66] performs an ideological function, as has long been recognized. It appears, as Richard Kroll puts it, as "a reaction to the psychohistorical conditions of the Civil War and Interregnum, which came to be symbolized by all forms of epistemological dogmatism," and constructively works "to fix the stabilizing rules or boundaries of a newly reinstituted social fabric and to exclude all those perceived as a threat to its instability, most specifically in the form of Catholics and dissenters" (50). Probabilism vitally supports the post-1688 public sphere, in which disagreement may occur with civility because no group or individual may claim privileged access to transcendent truths and force an apprehension of them on others. In serving this vision of society, mitigated skepticism functions in the unreflective, automatic way commonly ascribed to ideology: its methodological and epistemological appeal seems distinct from any particular position that anyone of any party or religion would assume in debates of the moment; it informs widely disparate cultural endeavors, many remote from actual politics; and its challenge to all dogmatisms automatically performs the work of social cohesion, whether those who practice it know it or not. Experimental science, religious and political debate, law, medicine, commerce, and literature, among other pursuits, proceed in all their diversity and conflict without degenerating into social chaos because the dominant voices of society agree that truth is always to be sought and that seeking truth proceeds best when citizens of various convictions argue different sides of each case until the best possible, most probable answers emerge. Mitigated skepticism, in short, provides an epistemological justification of what has been called the ideology of eighteenth-century liberalism.

But this shared epistemology does not produce a culture of universal agreement during the long peace of civil society in Britain after 1688. It provides terms in which opposing groups within that order could explain their political differences. Among the most influential historians of ideological conflict in the period has been J. G. A. Pocock, who sees a dialectical opposition between two views of political and social life (often referred to as civil and civic humanism) shaping contemporary political discourse, "two modes of individualism,"[67] he says, "both . . . formulations of the late seventeenth century" (111), "an enduring conflict between two explicitly post-feudal ideals, one agrarian and the other commercial, one ancient and the other modern" (109). Pocock's work turns on "contrasting a conception of property which stresses possession and civic virtue with one which stresses exchange and the civilization of the passions, and thereby disclosing that the debate between the two is a major key to eighteenth-century social thought" (115)—including eighteenth-century aesthetic ideology.

Both sides accept, in the spirit of mitigated skepticism, that society's driving forces—increasingly seen to be public credit, the stock market, and "feminine" consumerism[68]—make the social world a world of uncertainty as much as the natural one is. Each, however, draws different political conclusions from this fact. The civic tradition, with roots in seventeenth-century republicanism but later associated with the Tory and "Country" opposition to Walpole, seeks to mitigate modern society's constitutive uncertainty by tying true citizenship to the relatively stable commodity of land, arguing "that the political individual need[s] a material anchor in the form of property no less than he need[s] a rational soul," in Pocock's words: land "guarantee[s] him leisure, rationality, and virtue" (111). The commercial, "Court" tradition, identified with the inventors and apologists of the stock market, the national debt, public credit, and the standing army, accepts irrationality, uncertainty, and speculative fantasy as the material from which society must be constructed—much as the uncertain appearances of the universe constructively motivate a Royal Society scientist to produce a system of probable hypotheses. This view also finds that "government and politics seem . . . to have been placed at the mercy of passion, fantasy and appetite" (112), but Court-Whig political theory sets about to effect "the conversion of the pure fantasies of speculation upon the future into the well-grounded opinions of continued experience in an on-going and dynamic political economy" (113). Court ideologues like Defoe seek to navigate through the irrationality of social forces by appealing to reasonable (but never certain) probabilities and their ultimate (but ungraspable) sponsor, providence[69]—while the Country ideologues' skeptical attitude encourages the citizen to distance himself from (though rarely to entirely reject) the irrationality of modern political economy. The skeptical insistence that reason cannot master the vagaries of social life,[70] made by those on both sides of the ideological divide, thus leads in drastically different directions: either to a retreat from or an embrace of the uncertainty of markets, credit, and the fluctuations of opinion in the public sphere.

The opposition, moreover, cannot be seen as a simple one between the Country gentleman's "leisure, rationality, and virtue" and the restless but enlightened irrationalism of the marketplace. The civic "rationality" of Country ideology differs critically from rationalistic Continental philosophy and all other metaphysical and religious dogmatisms: in the British context, as Pocock puts it, "the ideal city of the Enlightenment is populated not by illumined and contemplative philosopher kings, but by judiciously skeptical senators and magistrates."[71] But while these ideal figures sometimes appear in Tory rhetoric as Roman Stoic patriots, writers like Swift and Pope typically satirize even the Stoic Sage's pretensions of *apatheia* along with every other dogmatic posture. As I argue in chapters 5 and 6, Pope is fond of ironizing the supposedly rational personality by accepting the sway of those irrational, inconstant, often "feminine" forces—fits, vapors, passions, fantasies—that the Whig ideologues propose as the raw material of all socializing exchange. He does so not to surrender rationality but to assert its skeptical dimensions, which resonate with the ancient models of selfhood he finds in Montaigne: "the puff of every accident not only carries me a long with it, according to its own proclivity, but moreover I discompose and trouble my self, by the instability of my own posture; and whoever will look narrowly into his own Bosom, will hardly find himself twice in the same Condition" (vol. 2, 9)—another passage that Pope marked, which reverberates throughout his Horatian poetry. Though admitting, even embracing the inconstancy of social activity, a personality thus modeled is still superior to those of ignorant fantasists and speculators of market ideology—"all those who know not what they mean" (*Epistle I*, I, 144), Pope says. In this way, the skepticism of Pope and others of his political persuasion keeps them in close contact with the uncertain social world at the same time that it allows them to distance themselves from it: skeptical self-scrutiny is a point at which ideologies for and against modern political economy are articulated.

This mutual articulation takes place with particular subtlety and potency in debates that appeal, sooner or later, to the sublime. For both sides, sublime experience verges on areas outside, beyond, or destructive of the order of probable truths on which society depends, discovering "unsociable truths" that we nonetheless must admit are true—the point at which the skepticism implicit in moral certainty must be recognized, at which the ultimate contingency of otherwise secure systems appears. Confronting the limits of reasoning forces us to pull back and reoccupy our probabilistically ordered culture with renewed allegiance to it: sublime intimations of the abyss thus help discipline a society that relies on admissions of uncertainty for cohesion. In *The Ideology of the Aesthetic* (1990), Terry Eagleton warns, "it is now almost a commonplace of deconstructive thought to see the sublime as a point of fracture and fading, an abyssal undermining of metaphysical certitudes; but while there is much of value and interest in this view, it has served in effect to suppress just those modes in which the sublime also operates as a thoroughly ideological category."[72] In eighteenth-century mitigated skepticism, these alternatives are identical: the sublime moment that undermines metaphysical certitudes functions ideologically to establish order, presenting the subject with the abyss to reaffirm the probable limits within which civil society must operate.

But if the sublime's skeptical significance constitutes a common ground in the early eighteenth century, it also marks a point at which writers of different sides may be seen to diverge—strikingly apparent when Swift's *Tale of a Tub* (1704) is set alongside Shaftesbury's *Letter Concerning Enthusiasm* (1708). Both texts skeptically mock the pretensions of the enthusiastic character, the dogmatist who (in Swift's words) sets about "subduing Multitudes to his own *Power*, his *Reasons* or his *Visions*" (171). The *Tale* resembles the purposes and style of Shaftesbury so closely, in fact, that contemporary readers took the authors for the same person—which Swift in his "Author's Apology" (1710) *"directly affirms to be a thorough mistake"* (6). As my third chapter argues, it is above all their subtly different views of the role that sublime literature ought to play in post-1688 society, after sublimities of religion, politics, and reason have been skeptically exorcised, that distinguish the two texts and begin to articulate a principal ideological opposition of the eighteenth century. Of course the notion of the sublime is used in multiple ways by writers of both sides in the period, and very often a schematic distinction cannot be drawn. References to sublimity are, furthermore, frequently too remote from concrete political struggles to be read on strict party lines. Nonetheless, the differing ways that writers of opposing political camps read the skeptical implications of sublimity permit some general conclusions about typically conservative and liberal appeals to it (though the account hereafter differs substantially from some recent influential contrasts between a "Whig sublime" and "Tory sublime").[73]

A certain Whig perspective, discernible in Boyle, Dennis, Gilbert Burnet, Shaftesbury, Blackmore, Addison, Steele, and Burke himself, finds that our felt or intuited failures to grasp a sublime truth beyond the probable order themselves sublimely affirm that order. This view coincides with a general ideological effort to show that society benefits from the proper, probabilistically tempered embrace of essentially irrational feelings and fantasies. Within society, no particular position may be justified by its defender's supposed divine inspiration: only the order itself, and certain poets, critics, and philosophers (like Shaftesbury) receptive to disinterested intimations of it, carry a divine endorsement. The Whig aesthetic tradition typically describes an exceptional feeling, a nonrational intuition, a sensation that excess affords us—a medium through which a higher level of grounding or authority appears, incomprehensible yet finally reassuring and fundamentally constitutive of a particular, enforceable social order. Here the ultimate ideological feature of sublime experience in the thought of the time is exposed: it is the point of contradiction within an otherwise logically consistent and orderly social system, the point where probability breaks down and some other form of assurance is required. The sublime is the exceptional mode of experience that justifies the system of liberal probabilism in terms unavailable within the system itself.

From its inception, then, the sublime functions ideologically to affirm the probable order by drawing on metaprobable resources. Howard Caygill has argued in his *Art of Judgement* (1989) that in the eighteenth-century British discourse of taste, the je ne sais quoi, like the sublime, performs an ideological function "inseparable from the tendency of late seventeenth-century British scepticism to draw activist political conclusions from theoretical scepticism."[74] The "activism" appears in how "Shaftesbury justifie[s] the 'Revolution Principles' with a philosophy of taste" (45): "Shaftesbury argues . . . that the order of providence, with its expressions in virtue and beauty, is prior to any division of individual interests" (47) and that our universally shared, sensitive capacity to grasp this order is prior to our commitment to these interests, to any potentially divisive political, religious, or economic motive. The sublime and the je ne sais quoi are the magic means that reconcile universal order with the competing economic and political interests of individual citizens, general necessity with personal liberty, and absolute justification with probabilistic skepticism. From within our contingent, provisional, skeptically hedged perspective, our sublime passions tell us that society's civil order is and must be providentially right. It is important to stress that in such Whig theories of taste and civil society, the skeptical component necessarily complements the justificatory one. If access to sublime justification were complete and absolute, if the subject could claim to "personify" transcendent authority (in Knapp's sense), to become the embodiment of virtue, truth, providence, or reason, then civil society on everyone's terms would collapse: thus Shaftesbury devotes much of his work to ridiculing enthusiasts and fanatics. An essentially nonrational, sensitive response, "whatever [is] sublime in human passions," he says,[75] ideally serves to justify civil society and the governmental, economic, and cultural apparatuses that hold it up. The skeptical failure to grasp rational authority does more to establish the post-1688 social order than a successful arrogation of it ever could.

Shaftesbury's connection of the sublime to a nonrational, apolitical, but providential arrangement of exceptional feelings is reflected in an array of writers of broadly similar ideological agendas. These Whig ideologues all tend to describe the sublime as a special moment that organizes and stabilizes social relations, a feeling conveyed through poetry, through special dispensations of the senses, and through the treasured anomalies of individual subjectivity, often awakened by the form of the universe, especially when it exceeds our capacities. Such excess always turns out to signify the order of God. In Burke's *Philosophical Enquiry Into the Origin of Our Ideas of the Sublime and the Beautiful* (1757), at a climax of this sublime tradition,[76] order is secured most persuasively through our God-given senses, not our dubious rational faculty:

> whenever the wisdom of our Creator intended that we should be affected with any thing, he did not confide the execution of his design to the languid and precarious operation of our reason: but he endued it with powers and properties that prevent the understanding, and even the will, which seizing upon the senses and imagination, captivate the soul before the understanding is ready either to join with them or to oppose them.[77]

As it happens, God himself is not just the contriver of the imagination's nonrational power. He is also paradigmatically the most captivating object of it, the ultimate referent of all sublime experience, and as such he emphatically does not reveal himself "merely as an object of understanding":

"we are bound by the condition of our nature to ascend to these pure and intellectual ideas [of God], through the medium of sensible images, and to judge of these divine qualities by their evident acts and exertions" (68). The irrational operations of our affections and imagination thus fulfill their destiny as they approach the ultimate sublime object, God, beyond all reason. Burke's sublime subject follows "power through all its several gradations unto the highest of all, where our imagination is finally lost" (70), when providence affirms the imagination's operation by the subject's very loss of it.

Therefore the sublime does not merely tidy up the loose ends at the upper reaches of the moderate skeptical ethos that underwrites eighteenth-century British "liberal" ideology. It helps this ideology lay its foundations. Jonathan Lamb quotes such a foundational moment from the oratory of William Pitt: "I will not recur for precedents to the diabolic divans of the second Charles and James—I do not date my principles of the liberty of this country from the Revolution: they are eternal rights; and when God said, *let justice be justice,* he made it independent." As Lamb astutely notes, "This is the true Longinian inflection of the sublime, the unprecedented shedding of precedents in a pointless and utterly factitious instance of self-evidence"[78]—an echo, Lamb hears, of Longinus's citation of the divine fiat in section 9 of *On the Sublime.* But it is not quite pointless, nor merely factitious in isolation from a wider program of interested political theory: absolute authority is invoked ironically to enforce a principle of liberty, a conferral of godlike "eternal rights" on the liberal subject. The sublime moment hence amounts to the foundational move of what we would call universalist individualism, which "firmly secure[s]," in Shaftesbury's words, "our hitherto precarious liberties, and remove[s] from us the fear of civil commotions, wars, and violence, either on account of religion and worship, the property of the subject, or the contending titles of the Crown."[79] In the long Whig tradition of appeals to the sublime, the experience consistently conveys a special knowledge that assures the subject of his accord with universal providence while never violating the moderate skepticism demanding that the equal epistemological limitations of all citizens guarantee them equal liberties. Though Weiskel remarks that "What created an immediate and growing audience for Longinus was the dilemma or anxiety of modernism" (8), the sublime proves attractive to many writers in England because it provides a ready, satisfying resolution to the contradictions inherent in one of modernity's main political ideologies.

A sense of anxiety or dilemma in regard to the sublime nonetheless pervades the writings of Swift and Pope, foreshadowed in Dryden, Rochester, and others. It is true, of course, that the satirical attitude that I associate, in the chapters to come, with conservatism does not always appear, explicitly or implicitly, in endorsements of Tory agendas: for instance, Rochester, the ally of Buckingham and enemy of the Tory laureate Dryden, if politically classifiable, seems more associated with the Whig side, and the young Whig Swift dedicates *A Tale of a Tub* to Somers, the head of the Whig Junto. But while the ideology of Toryism undergoes radical, sometimes contradictory changes as it is elaborated at very different historical moments, from Dryden's writings during the Exclusion Crisis to Swift's *Examiner* papers during the last four years of Anne's reign to Pope's Opposition cries for liberty during the 1730s, these writers share a skeptical tendency to refuse the individual subject any access to absolute authority, to certainty, to irrefragable reason, to the ultimate truth, or to any other sublime object discovered either intellectually or sensitively. This epistemological posture must be seen as a staple of political conservatism even if it does not always translate into a doctrine of the political subject's subservience to royal, church, or state authority. Deeper than the politics of the moment, this skeptical fracturing of the individual subject from the sublime object performs ideologically to locate citizens in a social world in which they may never unambiguously claim absolute authority for themselves.

It has been easiest for many to view the Tory satirists, and Pope and Swift in particular, as simply hostile to or dismissive of sublimity. But this misses the complexity of their attitudes, apparent not only in Pope's approving remarks on Longinus in the *Essay on Criticism* and his notes to Homer, or his defense of the true sublime against its obverse in *Peri Bathous,* but in the way both Swift and Pope consistently invoke and elaborate on Longinus's logic of reversal in their satire and the way the vexed experience of absolute powers remains central to their imaginative worlds. Their depiction of the mind's failure to grasp the absolute object itself articulates a sublime mode and affirms authority. But this version of sublimity remains distinguishable from the Addisonian, Shaftesburyan tradition. Swift and Pope view such experience as inevitably strained and ironic, as a failure without a reassuring subjective recuperation. Their skepticism runs deeper than the Whig tradition they satirize, which insists on a skeptical dimension of sublime experience only to guard against the appropriation of transcendent authority by any putatively knowing subject or group. For the Tory satirists, the sublime enforces a skepticism that explicitly undermines the liberal assurance that our "natural" faculties, tastes, subjective depths, and freedoms accord with providence and ironizes or satirizes such attempts at self-confirmation. It is the gap alone between ourselves and providence, not our nonrational, subjective bridging of it, that conveys the authority of the sublime object, of God or of reason.

Nonetheless, the conservative satirists make this stand by accepting and even exaggerating the skeptical elements of the liberal vision, the nonrational, fantastic elements actually driving society. The civic-humanist ideology does not just nostalgically look back to some lost feudal ideal: it grows up in response to modern forces, defining itself in opposition to commercial ideology while sharing its epistemological terms. The career of Pope in particular testifies to these skeptically sustained interactions. The *Essay on Criticism* (1711) presents a view of the sublime that is virtually indistinguishable from the principles of Addison, Shaftesbury, and many others who describe taste in literature as a socially cohesive mechanism. At times, he admits that excellent literary works may violate the order of probable rules—with *"nameless Graces* which no Methods teach" (144), expressions that *"gloriously offend"* (152)—but such moments function only to reinforce the providential order of poetry that the rules normally express: in fact, in order to affirm the rules' probable operation, we must admit that they do not function dogmatically to rule out all anomalies. Taste thus proves a way to apprehend order even through *"brave Disorder"* (134) or sublime excess.

The *Essay on Man* (1734) itself has seemed an example par excellence of a Shaftesburyan gleaning of providential order in the universe from our sublime failure to grasp it. But as I argue in chapter 4, Pope avoids offering an account of how we may subjectively construe such order because he is too skeptical to do so: he posits no subjective mechanism that would turn failure into a special feeling by which providence may be recognized and confidently asserted by the poetic or philosophical genius. This skeptical refusal of the order of aesthetic subjectivity accounts for the poem's distinctive emptiness, its emphasis on merely verbal assurances denying any more substantial sensory means of connecting personal experience to providence. Pope's poems of the 1730s, discussed in chapters 5 and 6, accept the social uncertainties attending the triumph of commercial ideology: satirized figures find themselves motivated by passions, fantasies, and desires, and this motion, not their rational self-possession, directs society. He critiques this manner of sociability from the standpoint of ancient virtue. But instead of withdrawing behind a Stoic barricade, he mixes with the inconstant world, even admitting his share in its nature: he aligns himself with Montaigne's Hellenistic skepticism, which admits the inconstancy of the self only to attain an invisible self-mastery, superior not only to the unthinking, inconstant crowd who "know not what they mean" but also to the dogmatist who thinks escape from inconstancy is possible. Pope now redeems the uncertain, merely probable order ironically by his own skeptical bemusement with it. The final *Dunciad* dramatizes the collapse of such "ancient" skeptical detachment: while still self-definitively critical of the ideological order of commercial, modern society, Pope may express his disdain only by submitting his own voice and all culture to its dullness. The journey begun from Swift's ideological ascription of miserable uncertainty to seventeenth-century religious conflict in the *Tale* ends in Pope's recognition that a sociably skeptical commercial ideology finally replicates and worsens all such enthusiasms.

The ideological significance of the sublime in disputes of the period tends to appear, then, not just in the opposite positions that writers of different political and social views take but in the fact that all tend to see their own opinions on the sublime as beyond their control, as forced on them—ideologically, we would say—by the epistemological terms of the discursive world in which they operate. Shaftesbury's sublime dialogue *The Moralists* works itself into a rapture by discussing rapture, while Swift's *Tale* and Pope's *Dunciad* delight in dramatizing their incorporation into the debased sublimities they satirize. Early British writing on the sublime presents an "ideology of ideology," in Jerome Christensen's phrase,[80] an account, itself serving ideological purposes, of how our capacities unknowingly are enlisted under external powers and authorities. More than an abstract, politically suggestive aesthetic category, the sublime is seen by its promoters and theorists, then and now, as a force imposed on individual subjects—especially by themselves. In this sense Peter de Bolla has stressed that the "discourse on the sublime" in the eighteenth century swells into the "discourse of the sublime," as the theoretical definitions of sublime power become ideological enactments of it.[81] For the Whig tradition, ideology is a happy thing: feelings, the senses, the mechanisms of human psychology, our commercial appetites place us in a productive relation to otherwise ineffable ideals, to providence, and to our "eternal rights." The opponents of this tradition see the Shaftesburyan embrace of "whatever is sublime in human passions" as ideological because it deludes the subject with fantasies of his own authority—the authority of fantasy—and so promotes the entire social world of what Pocock calls "post-civic man."[82]

But this Tory countertradition, critical as it is, does not promise an escape from ideology as such, any more than it envisions an escape from the post-civic world of eighteenth-century British culture. The sublime object remains an instrument of ideological enforcement, however mysterious and ineffable: it assumes its own darker authority over the mind even if we turn away from it to embrace quotidian patterns of life, as conservative satire so often advises us to do. In the work of Swift and Pope, the sunny, commonsense world of "Children [at] their Bread and Butter" (*Tale*, 165), of "Nature's path," consistently finds itself beset, despite assurances that "All states can reach it, and all heads conceive" (*Essay*, IV, 32)—beset either from without, by an ever self-degrading social world, or from within, by abstruse philosophical defenses (like the *Essay on Man*'s) that common sense unfortunately seems at times to require. Here appears a signal instance of the dialectical instability at the heart of conservative ideology in the period, which, as Michael McKeon puts it, "involves a contradictory sort of belief whose stabilizing motive to conserve what is given is predicated on a desta-bilized attitude toward what is entailed in that very 'givenness' ":[83] their very articulation of the skeptical sublime as a threatening power to be shunned leads Pope, Swift, and others not only to accept it as the principal sign of the insurmountable fallenness of modern society but to employ it (or find themselves employed by it) as the disowned, divided logic of their irony.

At last it is the "gloom of the Tory satirists," to use Louis Bredvold's phrase,[84] that distinguishes their ideological vision, not just from their Whig opponents but also from their Whig allies, like Pope's friends in the 1730s Opposition who idealistically and patriotically salute Liberty, "Sub-lime of Port," as Thomson describes her (1735–6).[85] If this persistent gloom is the sign of conservatism, a longing for old authorities and unquestioned modes of action, it is a conservatism that often accepts defeat as its initial gesture. Pope secretly may endorse the establishment of some transcen-dentally just social order, personified by the figure of the divinely sanc-tioned king, but his convictions remain "emotional Jacobitism"[86] only—a phrase critics have used to indicate a gap between his longings and what he could consciously hope for or expect in the real world. Part of this gloom stems from the skepticism that Swift, Pope, and others see as constitutive of the probabilistic order of society: having accepted the rigors of episte-mology, with whatever measure of ambivalence, they tend to view any as-cent into certainty as a false solution, as bathous instead of hupsous. While their own version of sublimity expresses itself consistently in a withering, critical exposure of such reversals, their critique accepts the ideological en-forcement of unthought authority on the mind as the true expression of humanity's epistemological predicament. The recurrent sense in Augustan satire that thinking itself is a kind of trap reveals their commitment to viewing their own thought as ideology, as placed at an always mediated, dissatisfied, subjugated remove from the truth.

2

The Abyss of Reason

Rochester, Dryden, and the Skeptical Origins of Sublimity

Rochester's *Satyr* [Against Reason and Mankind] (before 23 March 1675–76)[1] and Dryden's opera *The State of Innocence, and Fall of Man* (written 1674[?], published with preface 1677)[2] both demonstrate how the ambiguous epistemological conditions in England in the 1670s are poised to receive the idea of the sublime appearing with Boileau's Longinus (1674) in that decade. Both Rochester and Dryden say, at least, that they are epistemological moderates: they distance themselves from rationalistic excesses, from overconfidence in the mind's ability to reach transcendent truths, which they think will lead only to excessive confusion, a miserable uncertainty, and intellectual darkness. When Dryden declares later in his career that he is "naturally inclin'd to Scepticism in philosophy,"[3] he means the mitigated skepticism, common in English intellectual society of the Restoration, that guards against more radical doubts inadvertently engendered by philosophers' and enthusiasts' dogmatic, self-exalting delusions.

But Rochester's and Dryden's works also expose the dependence of this defense on the epistemological excesses it denies. Vital to the motivation of moderate skepticism is its assumption that the immoderate power of radical doubt awaits anyone who transgresses our humble epistemological limits: in Rochester and Dryden, this disruptive power is not just assumed but imagined, rendered vividly absolute, unanswerable, all the more uncannily powerful for being fearfully shunned. Turning our backs to it, as their works reveal, is a gesture to it. Their ambiguous attitudes toward epistemological immoderation, disowned as it is, link radical doubt in their works with the incipient tradition of the sublime: the viewing of the stormy seas of uncertainty at a distance by the modest, empirical, probabilistic epistemology of the day constitutes an early instance where "aesthetic" experience marks a tension in British cultural ideology. The perception of doubt's ironic, persistent power in Rochester and Dryden, moreover, leads them to recognize and develop the satiric implications of sublime experience more extensively than other writers at the beginnings of the aesthetic tradition.[4] Their satire seems to reject sublimity, to turn from enormities of philosophical reason, perception, and imagination, but it accepts and even exaggerates their forbidden power, and their power to forbid.

I

It is symptomatic of the epistemological complex of his times that Rochester, so often called a skeptic himself,[5] should ascribe his most powerful and famous picture of doubt to the consciousness of a figure he has undertaken to violently disparage. "Stumbling from thought to thought," the "misguided follower" of reason in *A Satyr Against Reason and Mankind* "falls headlong down / Into doubts boundless sea, where like to drown."[6] The power of skeptical doubt in the period is typically both acknowledged as a source of terror and disowned or foisted onto the thought of others, and Rochester offers a particularly acute example of an intellect whose special insight into skepticism leads him to displace his own experience of it into a mind he despises. This displacement helps situate Rochester in the sublime poetic tradition, as Harold Bloom would characterize it: "I would venture one definition of the literary Sublime (which to me seems always a negative Sublime) as being that mode in which the poet, while expressing previously repressed thought, desire, or emotion, is able to continue to defend himself against his own created image by disowning it, a defense of *un-naming* it rather than *naming* it."[7] Rochester's poem explores the ambiguous satirical dimensions of such a sublime act of disowning. On its surface, it reflects the usual contemporary attitude toward intellectual extravagance: doubt violently overtakes the mind only when reason is trusted too uncritically, and Rochester goes on to reject radical doubt as a danger from which his happy, undogmatic "*Reason* that distinguishes by sense" (100) preserves him. But throughout the poem, his own imaginative and intellectual extravagances seem peculiarly linked to those of the despised rationalist, especially to his doubt: it is at once the object and the instrument of satire, as Rochester imaginatively assumes its absolute power to expose and punish dogmatic perversity. Far from a self-thwarting accident, this disowned reflection demonstrates Rochester's insight into the epistemological predicament he critiques and contributes to the sublime tradition more interestingly than his less reserved submissions to intellectual darkness in other poems.[8]

The poem's three successive encounters with conceptual enormity—by reason's "misguided follower" (12–45), by the optimistic "formal Band, and Beard" (46–71), and by Rochester himself (72–97)—together express this structure of identification and disavowal. The first explores the skeptical implications of intellectual elevation in terms resembling Longinus's discussion of the self-reversing tendency of the sublime: as John Hall puts it in his 1652 translation, "so *flaming* oftentimes above the measure of their *fewell* [our thoughts] *extinguish* and miserably *decay*" (42). Rochester's rationalist also ascends only to fall into intellectual misery:

Reason, an *Ignis fatuus,* in the *Mind,*
Which leaving light of *Nature,* sense behind;
Pathless and dang'rous wandring ways it takes,
Through errors, Fenny-*Boggs,* and Thorny *Brakes;*
Whilst the misguided follower, climbs with pain,
Mountains of Whimseys, heap'd in his own *Brain:*
Stumbling from thought to thought, falls headlong down,
Into doubts boundless Sea, where like to drown.
Books bear him up awhile, and makes him try,
To swim with Bladders of *Philosophy;*
In hopes still t'oertake th'escaping light,
The *Vapour* dances in his dazling sight,
Till spent, it leaves him to eternal Night. (12–24)

Similar spatializations appear in *On the Sublime,* as when Longinus says that "*Sublime,* by being high, becomes extremely slippery and dangerous."[9] Both Longinus's sublime and Rochester's reason are closely linked with what negates them: falling downward into risible bathos functions as an inverted sign of the boldness of the flight, as reason's light leads down to darkness. Longinian sublimity is likewise said to vitiate reason by enhancing it: when we follow a sublimely turned argument, we are "drawn from the *Argumentative* part to a *smiting phantasie,* whereby the other is both *hid* and *enlightened*" (Hall, 36). Here the "other"—reason, argument—both suffers and gains by sublime "*phantasie,*" at once more and less illuminating than the plain, purely rational "*Argumentative* part," "drawing" us astray like Rochester's ignis fatuus. The *Satyr*'s initial flight resembles sublime experience in its ironic, doubt-inducing aspects, which negate the Longinian celebration of the soul's potential grandeur.

Rochester's skeptical emphasis emerges through reason's involvement in its own downfall, not simply "*hid* and *enlightened*" by fantasy but productive of it, of treacherous "errors" and "*Mountains* of Whimseys." The near identification of reason and delusive imagination distinguishes Rochester's picture from Joseph Glanvill's similarly skeptical views in *The Vanity of Dogmatizing* (1661), which helps define the intellectual tenor of the Royal Society:[10]

Yea the highest and most improved parts of Rationality, are frequently caught in the entanglements of a tenacious *Imagination;* and submit to its obstinate, but delusory *Dictamens.* Thus we are involv'd in inextricable perplexities about the *Divine Nature,* and *Attributes;* and in our reasonings about those sublimities are puzled with contradictions, which are but the toyings of our *Phancies,* no absurdities to our more *defæcate* faculties. What work do our *Imaginations* make with *Eternity* and *Immensity?* and how are we gravell'd by their cutting *Dilemma's?*[11]

Though the "perplexities" that entangle reason here are "inextricable," it nonetheless is able to clear itself of "the toyings of our *Phancies,*" of "absurdities." Reason, a "*defæcate*" faculty, may ascend to "sublimities" like "the *Divine Nature,* and *Attributes,*" and "*Eternity* and *Immensity*" on its own—contrary to Rochester's view, who will deny (77–9) reason's power to sublimate itself as it attempts the absolute. Despite Rochester's mockery of doubt's victims, he recognizes that philosophical reason always perversely produces unreason, distinguishing him from the moderate skeptical tradition of the Restoration with which he has so much in common.[12] In fact, Harold Love has plausibly identified Glanvill as the author of what Rochester calls "a scurrillous answer" to the *Satyr* in his prose piece "To the Reader" (written to introduce a projected new edition of the poem), where Rochester scorns his attacker's "Cartesian" commitments.[13] *The Vanity of Dogmatizing*'s strong skeptical current never leads Glanvill to denigrate the "highest and most improved parts of rationality" as such. Though admitting that Cartesian certainty is nearly impossible, he, like others of his set, affirms the powers of "*defæcate* faculties." For the more skeptical Rochester, reason itself inevitably leads to perplexity, and "gravelling" mental dilemmas arise not from the abuse of reason but from its exercise.

Rochester figures the fantastic power of the rationalist's thoughts in the passage's ascending scale of images, "*Boggs,*" "*Brakes,*" "*Mountains,*" and "sea," resembling the typically vast natural forms that call forth the soul's grandeur in the sublime tradition, from Longinus's "fournaizes du mont Ætna" and "le Danube, le Nil, le Rhin, & l'Ocean sur tout" (Boileau, 73–4) to Burke's enumeration of sublimely terrifying natural objects[14] to Kant's "dynamical sublime," raised by "volcanoes with all their destructive power, hurricanes with all the devastation they leave behind, the boundless ocean heaved up,"[15] and so on. But while Rochester's imagery may look ahead in the sublime tradition to objects that inspire the beholder's own instinctive "Emulation of whatever seems to approach nearer to Divinity than himself" (as Smith's translation runs, 84–5), it also looks back to traditional views of natural turmoil, as a sign not of God's admirable power but of his absence, of nature's deviation from his scheme. As Rochester's confessor, converter, and biographer Gilbert Burnet puts it in a travel letter (1686), the Alps "cannot be the primary Productions of the Author of Nature: But are the vast Ruines of the first World, which at the Deluge broke here into many inequalities."[16] Before his conversion, Rochester's *Satyr* illustrates the desolation of the lost intellect with chaotic, natural powers lapsing into "eternal Night" (24). Unredeemed nature thus figures the doubting mind, which itself cannot be sublimely redeemed, cannot recover a pleasure in terror, as Burke shows, or, more grandly, a Kantian sense of our "super-sensible power" (106) in the face of what overwhelms us.

Nonetheless, the mind's assumption of a "boundless" natural object as a figure for its doubt attests to its own excessive if unredemptive power—a power destructive of and beyond the rationalist's fatuous delusions, his "*Mountains* of Whimsey," the "*Vapour,*" the frail, "escaping light" of reason, a power attaining a quasi-objective status alienated from all he thinks or could think, swallowing up consciousness from within. The sea of doubt itself is an absolute authority beyond appeal, its boundlessness linking it to "eternal Night" as the destiny of all, not just the misguided. Descartes, whose work Rochester seemed to know,[17] presents a similarly quasi-objective image of doubt as deep water[18] at the beginning of the second of the *Meditations* (1641): "By yesterdays Meditation I am cast into so great *Doubts,* that I shall never forget them, and yet I know not how to answer them, but being plunged on a suddain into a deep Gulf, I am so amazed that I can neither touch the bottome, nor swim at the top."[19] Doubt persists against Descartes's intentional power, part of what he finds astonishing about it. The poem's misguided follower similarly struggles "To swim with Bladders of *Philosophy*" against the currents of his own doubt. These internal depths differ critically from those Young would explore as the aesthetic tradition develops in the next century in "Conjectures on Original Composition" (1759), which happily finds that our inner "bounds are as unknown, as those of the creation":[20] boundless doubt in Rochester, essentially hostile to the emergent tendency to glorify creative, individual subjectivity, remains antiegotistical, impersonal, unfathomable by any exertion of proto-Romantic genius. Still, it is nothing if not a mental object, exerting authority over no one but the doubter, at once too big for the mind to grasp and therefore alien to it and wholly arising from the mind's failure and therefore a product of it. While such uncanniness impels Descartes in the second *Meditation* to rise to an absolutely certain system, Rochester abandons reason's follower to it.

But as this internal excess leaves its subject in a state of unredeemed confusion, it grants the satirist, who appreciates its power far better than the engulfed intellect, a peculiar authority. Without claiming absolute rational authority himself, and safe from the genuine pain and fear that such attempts at self-inflation entail, Rochester assumes the boundlessness of doubt as his own weapon, watching it engulf the mind of another. It is the satirist, then, who achieves a kind of sublime redemption: safe from the storm, he confirms his insight into its boundlessness and wields its force against those who cannot occupy his superior position—all while denying any skeptically questionable alignment of himself with some proto-Kantian supersensible reason or "law within." This authoritative satirical stance is itself ironic: it depends on invoking a power that no one, including the satirist, could ever master. Rochester acknowledges in subsequent metaphors that doubt is contagious, resulting from wit's "vain frivolous pretence" (35): "The pleasure past, a threatning doubt remains, / That frights th'enjoyer, with succeeding pains" (39–40). Here doubt, reduced from a "boundless sea" to a venereal disease, maintains its power by reversal, by controverting and persisting beyond the intentions of the "Witts" (37) who pass it around in pursuit of pleasure. In light of this figure, Rochester's claim later in the poem to avoid doubt by indulging "Appetites" (105) according to his own coarser, more robust type of reason—"Hunger call's out, my Reason bids me eat" (107)—seems comically questionable. Still, he will claim to inoculate himself against doubt: "This plain distinction Sir your doubt secures, / 'Tis not true Reason I despise but yours" (110–1). The point is not that the *Satyr* undercuts Rochester's security in "true Reason." It is that this security is established by a sublime, authoritative insight into what he despises, a power of vision that the self-exalted rationalist ironically cannot achieve.

This link between satirical rejection of and sublime identification with excessive doubt will find perhaps its sharpest expression at the heart of Hume's *Treatise of Human Nature* (1739). At the end of book I, he says, skepticism "reduces me almost to despair, and makes me resolve to perish on the barren rock, on which I am at present, rather than venture myself upon the boundless ocean, which runs out into immensity" (264), but later, he says, "I dine, I play a game of back-gammon, I converse, and am merry with my friends" and finds his foregoing doubts "so cold, and strain'd, and ridiculous, that I cannot find in my heart to enter into them any farther" (269). As in Rochester, the terrifying image of doubt as a boundless ocean ironically supports an attitude of satirical ridicule toward it. Hume's achievement of self-possession is especially poignant because it exacts an alienation from his own philosophical reflections, as if someone else, some fool, had thought them. Like Rochester, Hume really believes the doubter ridiculous: his own doubt has been utterly buried by a stabilized, ordinary life and has no claim on him whatever. And like Rochester, he compares it to a recurrent disease: "a malady, which can never be radically cur'd" (218). For Rochester it is someone else's disease, but its boundlessness does occasion the assertion of his own integrity in a way typical of sublime experience. Steven Knapp has argued in another context that "the goal of the sublime *is* a certain stabilization of the self, though not quite by means of a unifying identification"; the sublime instead employs a "structure of partial identification."[21] Rochester's identification is not partial but disowned, signified by rejection, grasping and wielding the power of doubt without actually doubting.

This linkage between Rochester's imagination and that of the despised rationalist is made clearer with the figure who next blusters into the poem, "some formal Band, and Beard" (46), himself a rationalist who pointedly lacks any forewarning of the pit of doubt awaiting him. A type of the Restoration enlightened clergyman, the formal Band first endorses Rochester's critique of human "Wit": *"any thing that's writ / Against this gibeing jingling knack call'd Wit, / Likes me abundantly"* (48–50). The character shares the age's distaste for intellectual arrogance, expressed in the foregoing satire, which he tries to assimilate to the assumptions of enlightened Anglicanism, even crudely affecting Rochester's pretense of keen insight into what he disparages: *"For I profess, I can be very smart / On Wit, which I abhor with all my heart"* (53–4). The satire again works not through rejection but through ironic identification. Abhorrence of wit does not disguise the Band's allegiance to sublimated reason, however, just as Glanvill's renunciation of dogmatizing does not prevent him from praising reason as a *"defæcate"* faculty:

Reason, *by whose aspiring influence,*
We take a flight beyond material sense.
Dive into Mysteries, then soaring pierce,
The flaming limits of the Universe.
Search Heav'n and Hell, find out what's acted there,
And give the World true grounds of hope and fear. (66–71)

This rhapsody forgets the pain of rational inflation imagined by Rochester moments earlier. Doubt seems even more threatening here by being even less an item of consciousness, even more like an "external" object about to be blundered into: the formal Band ominously *"Dive[s] into Mysteries"* but anticipates pulling himself out gloriously. His optimism resonates with Longinus's passage on humanity's great-souled efforts to surpass the universe's limits, as Boileau renders it: "Aussi voisons-nous que le monde entier ne suffit pas à la vaste estenduë de l'esprit humain. Nos pensées vont souvent plus loin que les Cieux, & penetrent au delà de ces bornes qui environnent & qui terminent toutes choses" (73–4). The formal Band's phrase *"The flaming limits of the Universe"* echoes the famous one of Lucretius, apparently associated in readers' minds with section 35 of *On the Sublime:*[22] Rochester satirizes the cosmopolitan philosophical tradition of aggrandizing the mind that would enthusiastically receive Longinus's treatise.[23] The irony of a "formal" clergyman invoking the Epicurean materialist poet again ominously hints that he is unleashing philosophical powers with implications that he imperfectly understands. Unlike various Longinian assertions, which insist on the godlike power of our "fancies" or our "boundless thoughts," the formal Band's vehicle here is specifically reason, which discovers its authority to order our beliefs, to dictate *"true grounds of Hope and Fear"* to the world below it, by surpassing the hard reality of *"material sense."* It is just this reality that Rochester himself is concerned to reassert: "Our *Sphere* of Action, is lifes happiness," he will say, "And he who thinks Beyond, thinks like an *Ass*" (96–7).

The authority of this rejection of reason nonetheless derives from Rochester's own apprehension of spheres beyond our own, evident in his reply to the sham transcendence of the "formal Band":

'tis this very reason I despise.
This supernatural gift, that makes a *Myte*,
Think he is the Image of the Infinite:
Comparing his short life, void of all rest,
To the *Eternal,* and the ever blest.
This busie, puzling, stirrer up of doubt,
That frames deep *Mysteries,* then finds 'em out;
Filling with Frantick Crowds of thinking *Fools,*
Those Reverend *Bedlams, Colledges,* and *Schools.*
Borne on whose Wings, each heavy *Sot* can pierce,
The limits of the boundless Universe. (75–85)

Rochester does not imagine the infinite, let alone consider himself an "Image" of it, any more than he claims to transcend the conditions of his own "short life" by anticipating "The *Eternal,* and the ever blest," yet he appeals to these absolutes negatively in his very assertion of their remoteness from our sphere. Here his strategy of satirical rejection through identification finds its paradoxical epistemological support. The acceptance of the absolute as such entails his rejection of it: it lies beyond appeal because it really is absolute. The formal Band's earlier claim to *"pierce, / The flaming limits of the Universe"* (68–9) is mockingly rephrased—"Borne on [reason's] Wings, each heavy *Sot* can pierce, / The limits of the boundless Universe"— referring to the idea, fashionable among contemporary natural scientists, that the universe really is limitless.[24] For Rochester, the bounds of material sense are reached not by arrogantly transcending matter but by exhausting the senses in a boundless material universe. Rochester's emendation, moreover, echoes the earlier reference to "doubts boundless Sea" (just as the

"*Eternal*" here echoes the "eternal Night" in the first passage)—again linking his own perception with the rationalist view he rejects.

This self-distancing from the destabilizing power that Rochester employs himself suggests why the poem's main crux has divided critical opinion.[25] Some critics accept his claim to have discovered equilibrium in instinct— "Thus I think Reason righted" (112), he affirms—and in his contemptuous distinguishing of himself from "the pretending part of the proud World" (175). Others suspect this equanimity, citing the poem's subsequent hints that "Savage *Man* alone" (130) by his nature must act perversely *against* self-sustaining instinct, raising doubts about the viability of Rochester's "righting" of reason and turn from disquieting skepticism. While the connection between his mockery and his use of doubt's power in the early sections does not resolve this dilemma, it does indicate its source: Rochester justifies his embrace of instinct by referring to an absolute, an "Infinite," that makes human life seem "short" and "void of all rest." As comfortable as Rochester's turn from the absolute is, the absolute still motivates the turn. The rationalist's pretensions, and the related pretensions of man's "boasted Honor, and his dear bought Fame" (144) and all other moral excellences, may ultimately never transcend their degraded nature—the philosopher's doubtful ignorance and the moralist's "Base fear, the source whence his best passion came" (143). But Rochester may secure himself in appetite, "material sense," "Our *Sphere* of Action," only by referring negatively to spheres that exceed reason—not only the reason of the pretentious but instinctual reason, his own "right reason," as well. This irony does not invalidate Rochester's method of satirical rejection through identification but it explains its violence and instability.

Enforcing limits on reason by referring to realms of experience above or beyond it is one of the Restoration's foundational epistemological gestures, but Rochester's ironic method offers something subtly different. Robert Boyle, whom Steven Shapin proposes in *A Social History of Truth* (1994) as "an embodied identity" of "the matter, form, and power of the new practice" of gentlemanly experimental science (126–7), presents a mainstream view in *A Discourse of Things Above Reason, Enquiring whether a Philosopher should Admit there are Any Such* (1681), aptly (given Shapin's stress on the sociability of inquiry in the period) presented as a philosophical dialogue. Pyrocles, one interlocutor, wonders how things above our reason can be apparent to it at all: "it is strange to me how you would have our reason comprehend and reach things that you yourself confess to be above reason, which is, methinks, as if we were told that we may see things with our eyes that are invisible."[26] Sophronius, the dialogue's leading voice, calls this the "weightiest" (216) objection that can be brought against his belief that such things exist and finally accepts this summary of his position stated by Eugenius:

we do not properly *perceive things above reason*, but only *perceive that they are above reason*, there being a dark and peculiar kind of impression made upon the understanding while it sets itself to contemplate such confounding objects; by which peculiarity of impression, as by a distinct and unwonted kind of internal sensation, the understanding is brought to distinguish this sort of things (namely transcendent or *privileged* ones) from others, and discern them to be disproportionate to the powers with which it uses thoroughly to penetrate subjects that are not impervious to it: as when the eye looks into a deep sea, though it may pierce a little way into it, yet when it would look deeper it discovers nothing but somewhat which is dark and indistinct, which affects the sensory so differingly from what other more genuine objects are wont to do, that by it we easily discern that our sight fails us in the way before it arrives at the bottom, and consequently that there may be many things concealed there that our sight is unable to reach. (226)

This resolution of "so unusual and sublime a subject" (210) appeals, in a manner to become typical of the sublime mode, to an economy between reason and sensation or imagination. Reason may not reason out its limitations but grasps them by "a dark and peculiar kind of impression," "a distinct and unwonted kind of internal sensation." Sensory imagination thus grants reason a knowledge of itself that it could not attain on its own—a transaction illustrated by mysterious imagery itself suggestive of sensation's own limits. What reason gains, however, is far from a mediated, Kantian grasp of its supersensible destiny: rather it receives a sense of its vocation within its sphere and an assurance of working in accordance with God's authority. As Sophronius puts it more confidently later, "the wise Author of nature has endued the understanding with such a quick, though internal, sensation (if I may so call it) that, when due attention is not wanting, it can feelingly discern between other objects and those that are disproportionate to its ability" (241). Reason, perceiving its limits by an "internal sensation," aligns itself with this authority to order discourse within the human sphere.

Boyle's "deep sea," in which reason sees nothing but "somewhat which is dark and indistinct," and Rochester's "boundless sea" of doubt both employ sublime imagery to address a central problem of discourse-legitimization. They insist on reason's limits, on its inability to "penetrate" or "pierce" (a word both use) transcendent orders of thought and experience, in order to secure human thought within an undogmatic milieu, to disallow Puritans, Papists, "Lucretian" Anglican divines, and other arrogant characters from assuming unwarranted authority. The difference is that Rochester lacks

Boyle's appeal to the mediating "distinct and unwonted kind of internal sensation" that performs the crucial function of allowing us to grasp, "when due attention is not wanting," our proper place in terms of what lies beyond us. This sensation, which for Boyle bridges what we can and cannot know, reconciles our discourse with the "transcendent," "*privileged*," or sublime order while keeping the two distinct: it functions in typical sublime fashion to divinely sanction the operations of the mind by articulating not its reflection of but its distinction from the absolute. Rochester lacks such a bridge. The two realms in the *Satyr* are defined in opposition to one another: reason either leads to eternal night or immediate appetite: as "Hunger cries out, my *Reason* bids me eat" (107). This polarizing tendency, often noted by critics in Rochester's works,[27] reflects his characteristic refusal to view reason as something that can be moderated or contained, despite his claims in the poem to embrace his instincts happily. As he writes in a letter to his mistress Elizabeth Barry, "madness, both in love and reason, bears a better character than a moderate state of either."[28] The point is not quite that Rochester demonstrably sympathizes with the madness of misguided follower of reason in the poem but that the human sphere cannot be embraced except through the satirical appreciation of the dangers of diving into what lies utterly above it: no Boylean compromise between the two in the form of a special mediating feeling appears.

It is thus Rochester's insistence on the authority of absolute doubt, not his own endorsement or experience of it, that separates him from others who seek to limit "flights beyond material sense." He thereby acknowledges a volatility within the dominant epistemology of the period that Boyle's discourse is designed to contain. Boyle includes among "things above reason" elements that would seem to skeptically threaten even the most basic, mundane truths. Sophronius says that the rational soul

finds (sometimes to her wonder as well as trouble) that she cannot avoid admitting some consequences as true and good which she is not able to reconcile to some other manifest truth or acknowledged proposition. And whereas other truths are so harmonious that there is no disagreement between any two of them, the heteroclite truths I speak of appear not symmetrical with the rest of the body of truths, and we see not how we can at once embrace these and the rest, without admitting that grand absurdity which subverts the very foundation of our reasonings, *that contradictions may both be true*: as in the controversy about the endless divisibility of a straight line . . . which seems repugnant to common sense, and to contradict one of those common notions in Euclid whereon geometry itself is built. (235)

But Boyle simply designates such heteroclite truths as *"unsociable"* because they fail to associate with things within reason's grasp.[29] Such moments amply bear out Steven Shapin's claim that in the intellectual culture that Boyle helped define, "Skepticism . . . was something that happened on the margins of a well-working, routinely trusting system" (291). It is remarkable that even presenting arguments for radical skepticism as Boyle does here turns out to reinforce the generally comforting "sociability" of (most of) truth. Rochester is Boyle's antitype, what Shapin calls an "unreliable gentleman,"[30] not just because of his passion for dissembling and disguise but because he recognizes the volatility induced by all denigrations of overvaunting authority, even those that seek to replace it with modest, earthbound reason—including his own. Boyle, "a master of credibility" (291) in Shapin's terms, instead seeks to demonstrate the stabilizing force even of radical doubt itself.

Despite Rochester's extravagance, he still seems worth redeeming to friends of Boyle like the probabilistically inclined Whig clergyman Gilbert Burnet, who converts him and writes his biography. Burnet seems capable of appreciating Rochester's extravagance precisely because of the emerging vocabulary of the sublime. As he writes in *Some Passages of the Life and Death of John Earl of Rochester* (1680), "He had a strange Vivacity of thought, and vigour of expression: his Wit had a subtility and sublimity both, that were scarce imitable."[31] Such emphases on Rochester's unique power of wit resonate with Longinian discourse, which (in Boileau's words) emphasizes an *"Elevation d'esprit naturelle,"* "une image de la grandeur d'ame" (18). Though the *Satyr* is probably written too early to bear marks of Boileau's Longinus, Rochester himself proves interested its power soon. His poem *An Epistolary Essay from M. G. to O. B. upon Their Mutual Poems,* dated "Shortly after 21 Nov. 1679" by Vieth, seems to refer concretely to Longinian sublimity:

In all I write, shou'd Sense, and Wit, and Rhyme,
Fail me at once, yet something so sublime,
Shall stamp my *Poem,* that the *World* may see,
It cou'd have been produc'd by none but me;
And that's my end, for *Man* can wish no more,
Than so to write, as none e're writ before. (44–9)

He puts the speech in the mouth of *"M. G."* to parody his enemy the earl of Mulgrave: as in the *Satyr's* presentation of the "formal Band," the claim here to transcend conventional thought and expression deflates itself. The sublime's appearance at a moment of intellectual and formal breakdown—when "Sense, and Wit, and Rhyme, / Fail me at once"—correlates it with the exceeding of common expression. While Rochester enters the sublime tradition early on, having the sublime character imputed to him by Burnet and others,[32] his participation thus is ambivalent, both employing and mocking its pretensions to power. Hazlitt's remark on Rochester in *Lectures on the English Poets* (1818) expresses the ambivalence of such characterizations: "His extravagant heedless levity has a sort of passionate enthusiasm in it; his contempt for everything that others respect, almost amounts to sublimity."[33] Extravagance sublimely distinguishes "la grandeur d'ame" of Rochester even as his contemptuous energy seems at odds with more exalted strains of sublimity concerning what "others respect."

Still, it is just Rochester's tendency to exaggerate extremes that places him within the epistemological tradition that Burnet will manipulate to convert him. As Burnet says, Rochester "was sure *Religion* was either a mere Contrivance, or the most important thing that could be" (77)—again, the odd conjunction of his denigration of absolutes and his elevation of their importance. Burnet's conversion narrative itself is something of an object lesson in the disinterested, unprejudiced inquiry characterizing the Royal Society intellectual temper, according to historians like Shapin:[34] Burnet insists, "I have been strict in the truth of what I have related" (87), including Rochester's impious arguments, to enjoin other libertines to examine themselves with Rochester's own "disengagement and impartiality" (88), traits that augur well for his capacity to see things Burnet's way.

Initially, Rochester rejects the "Mysteries in the *Christian Religion* . . . since it is not in a man's power to believe that which he cannot comprehend, and of which he can have no Notion" (72)—placing the transcendent and mysterious beyond our comprehension as a way at once to take them seriously and to ridicule those who claim such knowledge. Burnet answers along Boyle's lines that a special form of apprehension grants this knowledge to some: "For as God . . . opened in some a capacity of apprehending high and sublime things, of which other men seemed utterly incapable: So it was a weak assertion that God cannot awaken a power in some men's Minds, to apprehend and know some things, in such a manner that others are not capable of it" (68). The "high and sublime" for Burnet refer to objects "that agree not with our Common Notions" (74) and that are necessarily above our comprehension but that we nonetheless may believe. Rochester replies that a believer's forceful religious convictions "might be fancy":

But to this I [Burnet] answered, That as it were unreasonable to tell a man that is abroad, and knows he is awake, that perhaps he is in a dream, and in his Bed, and only thinks he is abroad, or that as some go about in their sleep, so he may be asleep still; So good and religious men know, though others might be abused, by their fancies, that they are under no such deception: and find they are neither hot nor *Enthusiastical,* but under the power of calm and clear Principles. All this he said he did not understand, and that it was to assert or beg the thing in question, which he could not comprehend. (68)

Burnet's slippery example from the first *Meditation* inexplicitly assumes a strand of Cartesian skepticism in appearing to reject it: he seems to dismiss Descartes's skeptical worry that our waking lives could be dreams but concludes that common-sense convictions (like knowing that we are awake) are grounded no better or worse than religious beliefs in "high and sublime things." Common sense itself thus leans on the sublime. Rochester resists by recognizing this as an egregious form of begging the question, but its reversal must have appealed to him: like his own habit of finding the low in the high, Burnet identifies the ordinary with the mysterious. He quite happily confesses this strategy, in a manner common in Anglican religious controversy of the day, arguing that "it is plain that there is in every thing somewhat that is unaccountable" (73). Burnet comes to concede everything the skeptic would say, emphasizing how little we know of anything, including gestation, the soul's relation to the body, and the senses, so that the mysteries of Christianity ultimately do "not appear much more incredible, than some of the common Objects of sense and perception" (74). To get Rochester to accept beliefs that he cannot comprehend, Burnet insists that even common sense entails mysteries. Like Boyle's acknowledgment of pesky "unsociable" truths, Burnet uses the same words to affirm a common-sense (and here, religious) conclusion that a skeptic would use to question it: he infuses the boundless sea of doubt that Rochester thinks must result from "high and sublime" reasoning into the most intimate details of ordinary life.

Rochester's previous extravagance in reason turns out to be the perfect training to get him to accept such a reversal. His account of his ultimate conversion while reading a scriptural passage (as Burnet reports it) stresses that mystery and reason, hand in hand, instill religious conviction in him:

> *he felt an inward force upon him, which did so enlighten his Mind and convince him, that he could resist it no longer: For the words had an authority which did shoot like Raies or Beams in his Mind; so that he was not only convinced by the Reasonings he had about it, which satisfied his Understanding, but by a power which did so effectually constrain him, that he did ever after as firmly believe in his Savior as if he had seen him in the Clouds.* (82)

The *"inward force"* works in concert with, but is different from, the power of *"Reasonings"* (left unspecified): Rochester remains of his historical moment by not wholly succumbing to an enthusiastic, self-confirming mysticism and experiences sublime power only *"as if"* it were a vision.

The *Satyr* resists such an "inward" reconciliation of limited reason and the absolute, but its sense of the gap between them prepares Rochester to bridge it at his conversion: such a bridge at least maintains the poem's insistence on a distance between the two, unlike his satirical butts' ridiculous claims to achieve full unity with the transcendent object. His correspondence with Charles Blount, the deist, may have tempted him to succumb to the other extreme, to intellectual darkness. Blount remarks that vague beliefs in a *"divinium aliquid,* as Hippocrates terms it . . . which does all things,"* are the "only such twilight conjectures as our human reason (whereof we so vainly boast) can furnish us with," concluding that "all philosophy excepting scepticism is little more than dotage."[35] Such terminal doubt in the *Satyr,* however, had seemed a ridiculous position. Rochester's contemporary attackers, like the Tory playwright John Crowne, closely link his satire against reason and the mitigated skepticism dominant among Latitudinarians. In *City Politiques* (1683, three years after Rochester's death), a rakish character named Florio, obviously modeled on Rochester, dissembling illness, pretends to convert to Whiggish Protestantism and uses speeches from the *Satyr* to express his new religious beliefs: "Man is a shallow Animal, can bear no excess, too much Wit makes him as mad as too much Wine, and a little over sets him: yet he thinks his silly Scull contains all things, rules all things, and Omnipotence it self is afraid of that pitiful Engine"[36]—echoing the *Satyr*'s early climax, "Hudled in dirt, the reas'ning *Engine* lyes / Who was so proud, so witty, and so wise" (29–30).

In Rochester's case, such contempt for reason helps place him within the moderate religious fold: his indirect experience of "doubts boundless Sea" does not lead him to shelter fideistically in the comforting, mystically authoritative power of Catholicism, as Dryden has been seen to do. Roman Catholic writers of the period try desperately to show that the moderate skeptical attitude of the Royal Society leads inevitably into "Pyrrhonistic" doubt, which could only be cured by accepting the pope's infallible authority. Answering Glanvill earlier in the period, Thomas White had insisted that philosophers accept the authority of Aristotle to stave off the skepticism engendered by their inquiries. Later, the English Catholic John Sergeant would argue (1697) that the mitigated skepticism of the likes of Glanvill and Wilkins introduces more radical, disconcerting doubts unawares, *"by insensible Degrees into even the most Learned Societies"*—he means the Royal Society—and operates, as if with its own intentions, to *"extinguish the Natural Light of Men's Understandings, and drown their best Faculty in a Deluge of Profound Ignorance."*[37] Rochester's sea of doubt in the *Satyr* does not prepare him to submit to external authority: only a rationally opaque yet rationally convincing "inward force" can perform the delicate work of mediation.

The *Satyr*'s practice of stabilizing its authority by ironically identifying with what it satirically disowns, however, resists this sublime solution. The resistance appears most openly at the poem's conclusion:

But a meek humble Man, of modest sense,
Who Preaching peace, does practice continence;
Whose pious life's a proof he does believe,
Misterious truths, which no *Man* can conceive.
If upon *Earth* there dwell such *God-like Men*,
I'le here recant my *Paradox* to them. (215–20)

Such a figure can be read as a ludicrous exaggeration only if his positive characteristics are accepted as ideals beyond our powers of realization. The failure of Rochester's contemporaries to show themselves to be "such *God-like Men*" satirically reinforces his own confident assumption of the absent absolute's power to expose pretension. His conversion will demonstrate just how readily this absence can be transformed into a "pious life," an acceptance of positive *"authority which did shoot like Raies or Beams in his Mind."* Burnet's success will pivot on getting Rochester to accept the "Misterious truths, which no *Man* can conceive" that here can only seem self-refuting. In the *Satyr*, Rochester finds a satirical balance in negativity: its invocation of inconceivable truths to authorize its satirical position— "doubts boundless Sea," "the boundless universe," and "the *Eternal*, and the ever blest"—derives its potency from its being an essentially unrealizable gesture. Rochester more sharply poses the problem of the absolute with this "meek humble Man" because he represents an attractive hypothesis, whose humility and "modest sense" contrast with the traits of reason's "misguided follower" and the "formal Band, and Beard." This last ironic appropriation of the absolute may anticipate his unreserved acceptance of Burnet's high and sublime Christian mysteries known by good and religious men, but on its own it employs the competing powers of absolute and human to undercut each other.

II

As in Rochester's work, skepticism not only helps define Dryden's positions on literary wit, religion, and politics: its unsettling energy enables him to hold competing positions uneasily together or make transitions in his career from one to another.[38] The early poem "To My Honor'd Friend,

Dr Charleton . . . " (1663) expresses the moderate skeptical attitude of the Royal Society (to which Charleton would soon help elect him), decrying Aristotle's dogmatic "Tyranny" (1) over Englishmen's "free-born *Reason*" (2) and celebrating Royal Society members as "th'*Assertors* of free Reason's claim" (21)—a correlation of intellectual and political liberty complicated by the poem's concluding description of kings as "our Earthly Gods" (48) and Charles II's "Sacred Head."[39] The less moderate antidogmatism of a later poem, *Religio Laici* (1682), was seen by Bredvold in *The Intellectual Milieu of John Dryden* (1934) as sympathetically reflecting the "Pyrrhonism" of Roman Catholic controversialists, who expose reason's untrustworthiness to urge our need for the authority of the Church, and so as foreshadowing Dryden's conversion to Catholicism in 1685.[40] In the "Preface" of that poem, where Dryden owns his skeptical inclinations, he presents views similar to those expressed by Burnet in his narrative of Rochester's conversion published two years before:

> And indeed 'tis very improbable, that we, who by the strength of our faculties cannot enter into the knowledg of any *Beeing,* not so much as of our *own,* should find out by them, that Supream Nature, which we cannot otherwise define, than by saying it is Infinite; as if Infinite were definable, or Infinity a Subject for our narrow understanding.[41]

Dryden reverses Burnet's terms here, accepting their premises: Burnet had insisted on the mysteriousness of even ordinary items to put Christian mysteries on a level with common sense, but Dryden's suggestion that we cannot even know ourselves emphasizes the unfathomable remoteness of the infinite. While Phillip Harth and others justly note very similar sentiments among Latitudinarians like Tillotson (in part to refute Bredvold),[42] Dryden's diffidence and repeated expressions of reason's insufficiency (e.g., "So pale grows *Reason* at *Religions* sight; / So *dyes,* and so *dissolves* in *Supernatural Light,*" 10–1) occupy the skeptically unsettled territory where Anglican and Catholic polemics meet and part, encouraging if not demanding adjustments in his attitudes toward intellectual freedom and authority.

This skeptical unsettledness is strikingly linked to the sublime in his unperformed opera, *The State of Innocence and Fall of Man* (1677; written 1674?), based on *Paradise Lost,* and its preface, "The Authors Apology for Heroique Poetry; and Poetique License," which raise the problem of individual liberty and its relation to authority as it pertains both to poetic practice and to religion (and so to politics). No easy critical or ideological answer emerges, and Dryden limits himself to exploring and maintaining the epistemological tensions that had set the discourse in motion—tensions that the notion of the sublime seems to Dryden particularly suited to engage. The two texts immediately establish precedents that will give the sublime its character in English in the centuries to come. The *State of Innocence* represents a very early celebration of *Paradise Lost* (1667; 1674, twelve-book edition), which the "Apology" calls "undoubtedly, one of the greatest, most noble, and most sublime POEMS, which either this Age or Nation has produc'd"[43]—initiating the practice of eighteenth-century theorists to cite Milton's epic as (in Monk's words) "the supreme illustration of whatever particular type of the sublime they advocated" (20). The "Apology" also invokes Longinus, just three years after Boileau's translation, to celebrate Milton's sublimity and claim Dryden's own. Most significant, both opera and preface explore the problem of transcendence in terms of a competitive disproportion among human faculties, derived from Cartesian epistemology, and, as in Rochester, the puzzles introduced by Descartes linger beyond any putative resolution of them. This derivation of an understanding of sublimity from Cartesianism suggests why the sublime, a supposedly antirational, Romantic impulse in poetry, found its first champions among poets like Dryden, "the favourite exercise" of whose mind, as Johnson says, "was ratiocination:"[44] the very fascination with reason uncovers the irrational ironies of its operation. Dryden's engagement with the sublime raises ideological complications as well, appearing at a transitional moment in his career: as James Winn points out,[45] Dryden the (then) Anglican laureate adapts the masterwork of the Puritan Milton and dedicates it to the Catholic princess Mary Beatrice d'Este of Modena, recently wedded to James duke of York, Dryden's patron. The sublime helps him pose the problems of freedom and authority plaguing his variously constituted culture and suggests how nascent "aesthetic" theory may function to negotiate, or forestall, competing ideological claims.[46]

The reference to Descartes's cogito in Adam's first speech, when he appears on stage *"as newly created"* (act 2, scene 1), condenses a number of remarkable insights, all pertaining to Adam's use of reason to grasp the "Creator's Law" (2.1.26.) and act its unfathomable mysteries before the audience. The speech verges on a parody of Cartesianism, exposing the connection between rational purity and bathos that characterizes the skeptical sublime:

What am I? or from whence? For that I am [*Rising.*]
I know, because I think; but whence I came,
Or how this Frame of mine began to be,
What other Being can disclose to me?
I move, I see; I speak, discourse, and know,
Though now I am, I was not always so.
Then that from which I was, must be before:

Whom, as my Spring of Being, I adore.
How full of Ornament is all I view
In all its parts! and seems as beautiful as new:
O goodly order'd Work! O Pow'r Divine,
Of thee I am; and what I am is thine! (2.1.1–12)

Beyond just quoting the cogito, Adam briskly follows the entire course of the *Meditations,* using his own self-evident existence as the fundamental first fact from which the existence of God ultimately follows. Descartes does not appear much as an influence in Dryden's work—and some see the inane effect of the speech as Dryden's deliberate satirization of him.[47] But while Dryden must have known that a twelve-line condensation of the *Meditations* risks seeming ludicrous, it comes from an irreproachable figure, and Raphael immediately endorses it ("Well hast thou reasoned," 15) when he arrives on the scene.

This mixed attitude toward Descartes, moreover, matches the back-handed compliments that other British writers of the period pay to him, for instance Glanvill:

> I think the *method* of the most excellent *Des-Cartes* not unworthy its Author; and . . . a *Scepticism,* that's the only way to *Science.* But yet this is so difficult in the impartial and exact performance, that it may be well reckon'd among the bare *Possibilities,* which never commence into a *Futurity:* It requiring such a free, sedate, and intent minde, as it may be is no where found but among the *Platonical Idea's.*[48]

Adam's performance similarly seems dubious only because of its elevation. By placing the cogito in the soliloquy of an exalted being like Adam, Dryden can, like his fellow Royal Society members, praise Descartes's method even while hinting that his rationalism exceeds our own postlapsarian powers. As in Rochester, reason seems satirically vulnerable because its objects really are (from our perspective) unattainably raised, not because they do not exist: refusing the absolutizing tendencies of Cartesianism means accepting their ideal status.

Another remarkable aspect of Dryden's scene lies in its suggestion of an imperfect analogy between God's creation of Adam and Adam's assurance of himself of his own existence. This hints at problems inherent even in Adam's own ideal use of reason, which become painfully apparent later. There is something almost perversely gratuitous about the impulse to rationally assure yourself of your own existence the very moment you have appeared in the world *"as newly created"* by God. Adam's own quest for such assurance seems nervously supplementary to the physical, God-caused fact of the matter *"Rising"* on the stage before us. Adam does not, of course, claim to create himself with the cogito, any more than Descartes does. Thinking may indubitably prove that thinking exists, and it may be that (as Descartes claims) we must think in order to exist, but this does not prove that thinking creates the being who is thinking—does not, as Satan insists in *Paradise Lost,* prove us "self-begot, self-rais'd / By our own quickening power."[49] In fact, the very need to reason out their own existences indicates to both Adam and Descartes that they are *not* self-sufficient beings, not God, and need to postulate some "other Being" to account for them-selves—as does Adam in his condensed inference, "Then that from which I was, must be before."[50] This requirement demonstrates both Adam's dependence on and his remoteness from God: while he first asks that an "other Being . . . disclose" his origins, it is his own proof of that other Being, not the Being himself, that answers the question.

The comparison between Cartesian philosophy and the creative power of God will be strikingly made a few years later in the preface to the first English translation of the *Meditations* (1680) by William Molyneux, with a similar sense of reason's power to lift the reasoner to quasi-divine status, though without the irony that will evolve from Dryden's treatment:

> such is the Excellence of these six Meditations, that I cannot resemble his Perfor-
> mance herein better than to the Six Days Work of the Supream Architect; and cer-
> tainly next to the Creation of All things out of Nothing, the Restauration of
> Truth out of Errors is the most Divine Work; so that (with Reverence be it spo-
> ken) the Incomparable Des-Cartes does hereby deserve as it were the name of a
> Creatour. In the first Meditation we are Presented with a Rude and Indigested
> Choas [sic] of Errours and Doubts, till the Divine spirit of the Noble Des-Cartes
> (pardon the Boldness of the Expression) moves upon the confused face of
> these Waters, and thereout produces some clear and distinct Light; by which
> Sun-shine he proceeds to bring forth and cherish other Branches of Truth; Till
> at last by six Days Labour he Establishes this Fair Fabrick (as I may call it) of the
> Intellectual World on foundations that shall never be shaken. Then sitting
> down with rest and satisfaction he looks upon this his Off-spring, and pronounces
> it Good.[51]

Molyneux's comparison emphasizes the absolute scale of Descartes's pro-duction of certainty from doubt, beginning "out of Nothing" in the "clear *and* distinct Light" of the cogito after which literally everything follows. Descartes's act may suggest only an absolute analogue, God alone bring-ing forth something out of nothing with the fiat cited by Longinus in sec-tion 9 of *On the Sublime* as a paradigm of sublime self-expression. Such sub-limity, the philosopher-creator solitary in his work yet thereby reflecting the creative solitude of God, carries forward into Molyneux's own discourse, whose "*Boldness of . . . Expression*" itself seems inspired by the boldness of the work that he has translated. The typical sublime procedure of reflection in differentiation appears at the beginnings of Descartes's influence on the English imagination.

The cogito thus does much to emphasize Adam's solitude, as the absolute precursor of Descartes in his isolation beginning modern philosophy, as the *Discourse on the Method* remembers it, "shut up alone in a stove-heated room," with "complete leisure to occupy [him]self with [his] own thoughts," as "one individual alone:"[52] Dryden ascribes an air of Bloomian belatedness to Descartes's project. For Adam, however, this solitude is imposed, not chosen. He compulsively repeats the word *I* (fifteen times in the short passage), centering all creation, its fullness of "Ornament," around his "view" of it: the observation that everything "seems as beautiful as new" indexes creation's beauty and its newness to the way they subjectively seem so to him. This reasoning solitude in Dryden's scene contrasts sharply with *Paradise Lost:* Milton's Adam recounts his early thoughts of a creator to Raphael in book VIII as occurring to him after he puts the question to the "fair Creatures" he has just named—"Tell, if ye saw, how came I thus, how here? / Not of myself; by some great Maker then" (277–8).[53] Dryden's first man puts his first questions only to himself. Adam's reason combines a sense of its own lofty, self-intimating, and self-confirming power with a recognition of its source in an adored but absent "Spring of Being," and Adam's tragedy will emerge from this tension.

A final extraordinary aspect of Dryden's cogito derives from the fact that he imagines it performed on a stage before an audience. Some philosophers have seen the cogito as itself a kind of performative utterance, one that in a sense accomplishes what it claims (it is perhaps thus significant that both Glanvill and Molyneux call Descartes's work a performance). Dryden recognizes the theatrical potential of Adam's discovery that his first moments of consciousness affirm their existence in his utterance of them.[54] Again, he claims not to create himself by doing so but only to affirm his status as created, as it were recapitulating God's act of creation, maintaining it in lieu of God's active, discernible presence in him—a devout imitation or reprise of the initial almighty performative fiat. The audience who (Dryden imagines) will watch this adds an ironic dimension to the notion of the cogito as performed. Adam thinks in order to establish his existence, but for the audience, and God, this order is reversed: Adam is physically on stage before saying anything, and the (perhaps smiling) audience sees a being, probably barely clothed, whose existence hardly needs to be proved. The scene thus reveals the satirical potential of the cogito missing from Descartes's unwitnessed musings. Still, the ontological distance between stage and audience preserves or even intensifies the solitude of the cogito's subject. Dryden offers us an image of a self perhaps amusingly isolated with his reason who nonetheless needs to be watched at a distance, by God and by us, to make his performance good. Dryden presents a peculiarly literal anticipation of what Stanley Cavell will call the self's theatricalization: "the cogito can be seen as an interpretation of the advent of melodrama—of the moment (private and public) at which the theatricalization of the self becomes the sole proof of its freedom and its existence."[55] For this, some absolute spectator, at once present and absent, seems required. Moreover, the position of the audience in respect to the performance resembles God's: our viewing of Adam's actions proceeds on the condition of our detachment, and God's, from him, without interference. This distance from those to whom his actions are addressed helps to constitute Adam's irresolvable predicament in the play.[56]

Such dimensions of Adam's initial Cartesian performance represent reason's power as well as its weakness, its centering and alienation of the self in the created world. This mixed effect appears next as a topic of the conversation when Raphael arrives, after praising Adam's cogitations. Adam, "who but begin[s] to think and know" (24), loses his remarkable early self-confidence, immediately doubting his capacity to attain certain knowledge: "What hopes have I, from Heav'n remote so far, / To keep those Laws, unknowing when I err?" Raphael answers: "Right Reason's Law to every humane heart / Th'Eternal, as his Image, will impart" (2.1.26–30). Cartesian reason immediately presents a lofty but duplicitous aspect, or one whose loftiness entails duplicity: its demonstrative directness and purity seem exaggerated from the audience's fallen perspective, while its very capacity to bring an "Image" of "Heav'n remote" into Adam's heart makes him worry (with good reason, it turns out) that it is too remote from him to be appealed to effectively. Dryden will consider this imperative to produce an "Image" of "Th'Eternal" as a central problem of the sublime in his preface to the opera. The very loftiness of Adam's powers introduces an epistemological tension in *The State of Innocence* that is more profound than Dryden's religious or scientific expressions of skepticism elsewhere.[57]

The strain that this absolute, all-or-nothing view of reason exerts in the play appears most clearly in act 4, scene 1, when Adam, very unlike Milton's meek, accepting pupil, vigorously debates the question of free will with the angels. The debate does more than simply lay out doctrine and justify the play's outcome. Adam's absorption in rationalist conundrums itself could be seen as a distinctive mode of theatricality in *The State of Innocence,* different from the bombast typical of heroic drama, in a sense perhaps anticipating the absorbed postures of human figures that Michael

Fried has found at the heart of the anti-Rococo movement in eighteenth-century French painting.[58] Dryden dramatizes Adam's inward employment of reason, on which humanity's fate turns: as Gabriel warns to begin the scene, "Ills from within, thy reason must prevent" (18). He raises the thorny issue of free will unasked, as if to lure Adam into controversy:

Praise him alone who, God-like, form'd thee free,
With will unbounded, as a Deity;
Who gave thee reason, as thy Aid, to chuse
Apparent good, and evil to refuse. (23–6)

The passage associates "will unbounded" with reason, an "Aid" to help Adam deal with it, and Raphael stresses that our freedom somehow deifies us. ("God-like" initially seems to refer tautologically to "him alone"—God—but the passage's sense transfers the attribute onto "thee," or at least shows it reflected between God and Adam.) This notion matches Descartes's claim in the fourth *Meditation* that the will, of all faculties, is "*Circumscribed by no Bounds*" (61): "there is therefore only my *Will* or *Freedome of* Choice, which I find to be *so Great,* that I cannot frame to my self an *Idea* of *One Greater,* so that 'tis by this *chiefly* by which I Understand my self to *Bear* the *likeness* and *Image* of *God* . . . being taken *Formally* and *Precisely Gods Will* seems *no greater* than *Mine*" (62).

Adam accepts the idea that a truly free will is "*so Great*" that it is a god-like attribute but, in the spirit of Rochester's *Satyr,* denies that he could possess it on just these grounds:

Adam. Freedome of will, of all good things is best;
But can it be by finite man possest?
I know not how Heav'n can communicate
What equals man to his Creators state. (33–6)

True "Freedome of will" here is an infinite or "unbounded" quality because it frees us from the world of cause and effect, what Adam will call "the chain which limits men / To act what is unchangeably forecast" (53–4), and hence transcends the physical universe, demonstrating the human spirit's absolute distinction from matter. Some have found that Adam's insistence on man's confinement to material nature aligns him with Hobbes in contemporary debates concerning free will.[59] But his immediate admission that free will elevates or equals man to God is most significant, especially since he will soon come to admit that he has it. More than pure reason itself, the angels portray rational will, the power "to chuse / Apparent good, and evil to refuse," as the sublime element within us, the thing (as John

Hall puts it in the dedication of his Longinus) "somewhat Ethereal, some-what above man, much of a soul separate"[60] that raises us above mere materiality.

But this sublime element has its price—and for Dryden its meaning is its price. Mere free will does not "equal" man to God, as Raphael insists: "Heav'n cannot give his boundless pow'r away; / But boundless libertie of choice he may" (37–8). According to the angels, Adam's initial (mistaken) deterministic insistence that heaven must be the cause of any human sin itself is a sign of the limitations of his intellectual power:

> *Gabriel.* Such impious fancies, where they entrance gain,
> Make Heav'n, all pure, thy crimes to preordain.
>
> *Adam.* Far, far from me be banish'd such a thought:
> I argue only to be better taught. (75–8)

In Gabriel's view, Adam's reasoning is susceptible to "fancies" when thinking on such lofty subjects, much as Glanvill in the *Vanity of Dogmatizing* fears that rational thoughts concerning the divine may be "but the toyings of our *Phancies*." The specific problem of free will and God's foreknowledge is commonly cited in the period as an instance of a "thing above reason," and Boyle numbers it among his "unsociable truths."[61] But for Dryden delusive fancy supplants rather than supplements reason, marking the fall away from divine authority and our failure to reflect his will in our own—a fall perhaps less bathetic than that of Rochester's "misguided follower" of reason but even more disastrous.

The debate itself, moreover, puts Adam's reason in an absurd position, its form undercutting its content. As the angels insist that Adam has free will, Adam rejects their arguments: "I can but chuse what he has first design'd, / For he before that choice, my will confin'd" (73–4). In arguing for determinism here, Adam perversely demonstrates his independence from heavenly decree: the insistence on his lack of freedom bizarrely asserts it better than his acceptance of the doctrine of free will ever could, and acknowledging God's full authority over his actions is a form of resistance to it. He tries to recant the deterministic view—"Far, far from me be banish'd such a thought"—but this does not alleviate his predicament. The insincere effect of this rejection derives less from his unwillingness to obey than from his dutiful commitment to his own reason: if he cannot understand the doctrine, he cannot submit to it. His need to "argue to be better taught" demonstrates both this commitment and its insufficiency, asserting his deviation from the divine agenda even as he uses reason to follow it. Man thus finds himself torn between his "boundless," godlike will and his bounded "pow'r."

Adam recognizes, after the angels *"fly up in the Cloud"* (4.1.112), that the radical asymmetry within him of infinite and finite elements, an exaggeration of the dualistic disjunction between spirit and matter, builds a danger into the very structure of his subjectivity:

Hard state of life! since Heav'n fore-knows my will,
Why am I not ty'd up from doing ill?
Why am I trusted with myself at large,
When he's more able to sustain the charge?
Since Angels fell, whose strength was more than mine,
'Twould show more grace my frailty to confine.
Fore-knowing the success, to leave me free,
Excuses him, and yet supports not me. (113–20)

With this Adam finally rejects physical necessity and accepts the angels' Cartesian picture of the will as unbounded, but he remains consistent in his forlorn wish not to have it: forgetting his earlier view that freedom "of all good things is best," he sees it as an alien element within him, the source of an unmanageable self-division, leading him to repine at being "trusted with [him]self," and seems here to recognize in it the inevitability of his fall.

Adam consistently defines the "pow'r" or "strength" to control his god-like freedom as his capacity to use reason properly, as he says to Eve: "Such is our state, as not exempt from fall; / Yet firm, if reason to our ayd we call: / And that, in both, is stronger than in one" (4.1.173–5). But later in the scene, reason seems less pure and powerful a faculty, more susceptible to Adam's physical desires, when Eve convinces him to allow her to take her fateful trip alone, and "Reason it self turns folly when she speaks" (202). Freedom at this crucial moment shows itself to be greater than whatever power reason could secure, and this disproportion causes the fall. Descartes similarly locates the origins of sin in the disproportion between the will and understanding:[62]

> From *Whence* therefore proceed all my *Errors?* To which, I answer, that they proceed from *hence* only, that seeing the *Will* expatiates it self *farther* then the *Understanding*, I keep it not within the *same bounds* with my *Understanding*, but often extend it to those things which I *Understand not*, to which things it being *Indifferent*, it easily Declines from what is *True* and *Good;* and consequently I am *Deceived* and *Commit Sin.* (64)

The will's extension beyond the compass of understanding depicts sublime excess in terms of subjectivity's disproportionate powers, as reason "is both *hid* and *enlightened*" by the "folly" and "fancy" (antithetical to itself) that it produces, as in the Longinian account. Dryden elsewhere evokes similar rational strain, as in the preface to *Religio Laici:* "Reason is always striving, and always at a loss, and of necessity it must so come to pass, while 'tis exercis'd about that which is not its proper object" (*Works*, vol. 2, 101). But in the opera the improper object that puts reason at a loss is the will itself. An earlier piece, the dedication to *The Rival Ladies* (1664), portrays poetic elevation similarly as an overextension of the faculties: "The Fancy, Memory, and Judgment, are then extended (like so many Limbs) upon a Rack; all of them Reaching with their utmost stress at Nature; a thing so almost Infinite, and Boundless, as can never fully be Comprehended, but where the Images of all things are always present."[63] But the range of Adam's will itself is boundless and therefore productive of "impious fancies": the subject's very power exposes his weakness. He will fall not because he deviates from God but because he too much resembles him, or resembles him in deviating from him.

The ambivalence of the scene and the *State of Innocence* as a whole prevents any easy resolution of Dryden's philosophical, religious, and political attitudes on the matter of freedom: he seems to sympathize with Adam's desire to be ruled by an absolute authority even as he insists that God's remoteness leaves us to our flawed wills. In *Dryden and the Problem of Freedom* (1997), David B. Haley has taken this scene as a key to Dryden's entire worldview: referring to act 4, scene 1, he writes, "In [Dryden's] writings, he relates the problem variously to criticism, to politics, and to religion, but nowhere does he formulate it more succinctly than in the non-Miltonic lines he added to *The State of Innocence*."[64] When Adam asks, "why am I trusted with myself at large," he could be seen to dread the dangers of republicanism that Dryden saw gnawing at English politics—but he also here recognizes authority's failure to assert itself infallibly as part of the very order of creation. As close as this scene is to heart of Dryden's thinking, it remains curiously dissatisfied with itself, tentative, and uncertain in its attitudes toward authority, willing to elaborate the difficulties in the subject's relation to God (and, by extension, sovereignty in general) but unable to resolve them in either an obedient or insurgent direction. Later, in his prologue to John Banks's *Unhappy Favourite* in 1681, Dryden would more decisively determine the issue of freedom and authority, claiming no tension between them. "Must *England* still the Scene of Changes be?"[65] he asks; "All that our Monarch would for us Ordain, / Is but t'Injoy the Blessings of his Reign. / Our Land's an *Eden,* and the Main's our Fence, / While we Preserve our State of Innocence" (25–8). But in the *State of Innocence* itself, "*Eden*" is a much less secure place, and the ambiguous relations between freedom and authority make it so.

As in Adam's initial performance of the cogito, his "boundless libertie of choice" seems in a peculiar tension with the medium of theatrical representation. The confined area of the stage is anything but a limitless arena for the will, especially given the known outcome already scripted by Dryden, Milton, and Scripture itself. Adam's theatrical body is both more "bounded" and more fully present than the boundless will he is supposed to have, which is visible perhaps in his actions but tenuous, elusive, and immaterial enough for him to doubt it throughout. The opera in general, with its opening scenes in Hell, strains to evoke realms beyond material sense and so amounts to a sustained departure from ordinarily presentable, probabilistically determinable experience—as Johnson said of its Miltonic model, "the probable therefore is marvellous, and the marvellous is probable."[66] Such sublimity is most apparent in the stage directions:

> The first Scene represents a Chaos, or a confus'd Mass of Matter; the Stage is almost wholly dark; A symphony of Warlike Music is heard for some time; then from the Heavens, (which are opened) fall the rebellious Angels wheeling in the Air, and seeming transfix'd with Thunderbolts: The bottom of the Stage being opened, receives the Angels, who fall out of sight. (1.1)

The extravagant detail called for has been taken variously as evidence either that Dryden had no expectations of actually mounting the opera or that he did have specific plans (including the King's Company's available stage machinery) in mind.[67] But by the time of publication (1677), Dryden seems resigned to the idea that it would never be acted, and some have taken this fact as signifying a turn from theatricality as such. As Robert D. Hume remarks concerning the "Apology" prefaced to the published work, "Dryden is finally turning to specifically verbal means of rousing his audience instead of relying on representation. Though the 'Apology' is prefixed to a play, it was an unperformed play, perhaps not altogether a coincidence . . . in emphasizing language he tends to move out of drama altogether—hence his discussion here of heroic *poetry*."[68] Yet the inappropriateness that so many critics have found in the effort to theatricalize Milton's purely verbal presentation of "what surmounts / The reach of human sense" (V, 571–2) is in a sense just where the *State of Innocence*'s profundity lies. Reason, as Dryden's Raphael says, does present us with an image of the absolute: "Right Reason's Law to every humane heart / Th'Eternal, as his Image, will impart" (2.1.29–30). But such an "Image" can never picture any object or stage any action. Rather the power of imaging that Raphael describes exceeds the bounded world of the visible. The paradoxical status of this

"Image" as a representation of what cannot be represented performs the alienating function of the sublime in the opera.

Dryden discusses such supersensible "Imaging" in the "Author's Apology"—the piece's main use of Longinus's *On the Sublime*—and discovers in poetic terms the same irony that troubles Adam concerning his own license and its imperative to reflect the authority of Heaven. Like most of his prefaces, the "Apology" is written in an occasional, casual mode. But it is consistent and forceful in its defense of "boldness of expression" and "poetic license" as appropriate to heroic poetry, approved by the best critics through the ages, well suited to elevate our passions, and thereby "natural" in a sense not appreciated by those who consider it "bombast, unnatural, and meer madness" (90). "Imaging" provides Dryden the best example of such elevated poetic tendencies: "Imaging is, in it self, the very height and life of Poetry. 'Tis, as *Longinus* describes it, a Discourse, which, by a kind of Enthusiasm, or extraordinary motion of the Soul, makes it seem to us, that we behold the things which the Poet paints, so as to be pleas'd with them, and to admire them" (94). This account tends against defining Longinian "Imaging" as a method of straightforward representation. It cannot apply to theater, insofar as it functions to make it seem that we behold, and so cannot be realized in our actual beholding of anything,[69] even the elaborate proposed sets of the *State of Innocence*. Further, this mock beholding is achieved not by mere accuracy or vividness but rather "by a kind of Enthusiasm, or extraordinary motion of the Soul." Such excess emphasizes more the incredibility of imaging than its appeal to ordinary credibility. So too for Longinus: "les *Images* dans la Poesie sont pleines ordinairement d'accidens fabuleux, & qui passent toute forte de créance" (39). Most significant, it is unclear in the "Apology" just where or in whom this enthusiasm or extraordinary motion inheres: it sounds at first as if "the Soul" in motion is in the "Discourse"—it is the "life of Poetry," after all—then as if it must be raised by the discourse in "us," and then as if its source could just as well be the "Poet" himself. This blurring of objective, textual power into subjective effect, definitive of sublimity throughout the aesthetic tradition, seems precisely what Dryden and Longinus find extraordinary about this "Imaging," what makes it surpass ordinary representation and particularly suits it to "sublime subjects": as Adam and God share in "boundless libertie of choice," here poet, text, and reader all partake of the soul's extraordinary motion.

This power becomes especially extraordinary, Dryden continues, when the epic poet leaves behind the natural world to venture into "Poetical Fictions": "how are Hippocentaures and Chymæras, or how are Angels and immaterial Substances to be Imag'd; which some of them are things quite out of Nature; others, such whereof we can have no notion?" (94). His solution to the problem of compound creatures is "easie" and familiar: we simply mix known elements. But representing immaterial substances, the very problem raised by *Paradise Lost* and *The State of Innocence* in their depictions of angels, presents a greater difficulty, and Dryden's answer exhibits the blend of license and limitation that marks his attitude toward the sublime. First, he proposes a technique inspired by something like Milton's doctrine of accommodation articulated by Raphael in book V (and more fully in *The Christian Doctrine,* chapter 2), who describes the war in Heaven "By lik'ning spiritual to corporal forms, / As may express them best" (573–4). Dryden looks to Scripture to authorize similar descriptions of immaterial substances, citing moments when "the Text accommodates it self to vulgar apprehension, in giving Angels the likeness of beautiful young men" (95)—doctrine to influence the casting of an opera. But the "Apology" turns from such theatrical, embodied "Imaging" toward representations of more extraordinary dimensions:

> I wish I could produce any one example of excellent imaging in all this Poem: perhaps I cannot: but that which comes nearest it, is in these four lines, which have been sufficiently canvas'd by my well-natur'd Censors.

> Seraph *and* Cherub, *careless of their charge,*
> *And wanton, in full ease now live at large:*
> *Unguarded leave the passes of the Sky;*
> *And all dissolv'd in Hallelujahs lye.* (95)

This "image" of angels does not accommodate them to our vulgar apprehension "by describing them like other beings more within our knowledge" (95) but rather strains to evoke the very aspect of angels most alien to it: their incorporeality, that which makes them unrepresentable, not likening spiritual to corporal forms at all but depicting them at their most insubstantial, dissolving away from even immaterial embodiment—melting, furthermore, into their sublime song, *"Hallelujahs,"* with which Dryden's own sublime, "excellent imaging" itself poetically seeks to blend.

This dissolution, moreover, results from their "wanton" liberty and "full ease," leaving the "passes of the sky" "Unguarded," living "at large"—a state inviting to the extent that it seems almost to encourage Satanic transgression. The extreme freedom of the poet to offer sublime representations melts into a representation of extreme freedom. Within the opera, Adam anxiously uses the phrase "at large" to characterize the peril in which his transcendent liberty places him: "Why am I trusted with myself at large?" (4.1.115). In an earlier poem, *To My Honored Friend, Sir Robert Howard,* Dryden had used similar wording to attack excessive license in poetry:

Of Morall Knowledge Poesie was Queen,
And still she might, had wanton wits not been;
Who like ill Guardians liv'd themselves at large,
And not content with that, debauch'd their charge. (vol. 1, 45–8)

The "Apology" itself is concerned with how such "Imaging" can similarly fail, and Dryden ruefully cites a coffee house censurer's "Witty-cism" about the passage: "I have heard (sayes one of them) of Anchove's dissolv'd in Sauce; but never of an Angel in Hallelujahs" (95). The antisublime critic implies that a poetic escape from material substance or common sense is impossible—anticipating the satire of Swift's *Tale of a Tub* and Pope's *Peri Bathous,* in which a straining toward transcendence offers no more than degraded or perverted pictures of common materiality. Dryden cites his opponent's witticism to acknowledge the risks of flights beyond material sense, even to enjoy the potential absurdity of his own successful flight—analogous to the absurdity that hovers around a theatrically physical Adam cleverly proving his existence by thinking. Like Rochester's satire of reason's misguided follower, Dryden acknowledges the satirical possibilities of an escape from sensory grounding. Representing immaterial substance for Dryden is at once the height of poetic endeavor and hopelessly alien to common sense, never entirely safe. This awareness reflects the interconnection between high and low in other satirists' minds and chimes with Dryden's divided attitude in other works—his assertion of the comic unchastity and the dignity of David in *Absalom and Achitophel,* or the entwined heroic and comic plots of *Marriage à la Mode.* Here, the epistemological conundrum faced by the poet who produces images of "such whereof we can have no notion" at once elevates and diminishes his effort, drawing out his strength by exposing him to failure and ridicule.

Thus while Dryden describes such extreme images as a prerogative of *"Poetique Licence"*—that is, "the Liberty, which Poets have assum'd to themselves in all ages, of speaking things in Verse, which are beyond the severity of Prose" (96)—he also maintains a lively sense of freedom's peril, stressing Longinus's idea that sublime always must be artfully regulated and managed. As Boileau translates it, "Et à dire vray, quoi que la Nature ne se montre jamais plus libre que dans les Discours Sublimes & Pathetiques, il est pourtant aisé de reconnoistre qu'elle n'est pas absolument ennemie de l'Art & des regeles" (6). Dryden similarly concludes that the freedom of sublime language demands "a propriety of Thoughts and Words . . . elegantly adapted to the Subject" (97).[70] At the same time, like Longinus, Dryden insists that language is never more free ("jamais plus libre") than when infused with sublimity: language "elegantly adapted to the Subject" when that subject is sublime simply means language employed with great freedom. At such moments the regular is the unconfined and the unconfined is regular. Poetry like Milton's or his own employed on "a supernatural Argument" (97) must obey such paradoxical propriety: "all reasonable men conclude it necessary, that sublime Subjects ought to be adorn'd with the sublimest, and (consequently often) with the most figurative expressions" (97). When the subject surpasses our knowledge, reason itself dictates that expression must depart most extremely from common usage: in the sublime mode, mimesis and the figurative, decorum and poetic risk, must be identical. The caution he urges in handling sublime images hints that caution may be insufficient. His affirmation of wanton poetic liberties maintains a deeper doubt, shared with Descartes and Adam, concerning our power to limit our own inescapable license.

As in the opera itself, then, the sublime in the "Apology" appears when our unconfined freedom meets our necessarily limited knowledge of how to apply it, especially in imagining the unimaginable. Like Adam's "boundless libertie of choice," the extensive "Liberties" of the sublime poet do not imply that they cannot be abused. Rather their very boundlessness makes "sin and error" seem unavoidable. The sublime in the "Apology" is hence expressed as the disproportionate relation between the poet's freedom, his godlike, bold, "creative" will, and the inherently limited nature of his capacities. Bowing to authority proves as problematic as asserting personal freedom, for reasons derived from a single epistemological complex. While Dryden will proceed in his career to a complete submission to the Catholic Church, here, in his encounter with the English language's great sublime text and antiquity's theorist of sublimity, at a historical moment of violent polarization between republican and royalist political claims, he introduces the sublime to British culture to present the relation between freedom and authority, license and propriety, as necessarily unresolved.

Rochester and Dryden both show that putatively absolute elements within the mind—reason, the will—must destabilize our discourses because their very loftiness makes them unmanageable. The skeptical sublime emphasizes the troubled, not the providentially comforting, dimensions of such traffic in absolutes. Rochester's poem anticipates the Longinian reversal of intellectual glory into miserable decay (very soon if not already available in Boileau's translation), while Dryden immediately seizes on Longinus to help him explain the problematic relations between boundlessly powerful license and bathetic failure, in poetry and in the rational operations of the mind in general, with powerful religious and political overtones as well. Their distrust of our overweening faculties makes them very much of their time. Burnet must assure Rochester before his conversion that the convictions of "good and religious men" are "neither hot nor *Enthusiastical*," and the sublime for Dryden, "a kind of Enthusm, or extraordinary motion of the Soul," must on that account be approached warily. Both also refer to Cartesian rationalism as a perilous elevation of the intellect. Nonetheless, both accept, reluctantly or indirectly, the power of the soul's extraordinary motions and infuse it into their work. Their commitment to recognizing the trouble that this acceptance must cause, to the individual and to society, defines them intellectually and distinguishes them from other voices that find ways of accommodating elevated truths within systems based on intellectual modesty, through Boyle's "distinct and unwonted kind of internal sensation," through the mysterious yet nonenthusiastical knowledge of Burnet's good and religious men.

The skeptical refusal of this sublime self-assurance expresses an epistemological conservatism often obviously aligned to a religious and political desire for undoubted, external authority, leading the subject to accept his utter blindness facing what Dryden calls "th'abyss of light" in *The Hind and the Panther*. Still, strict correlations between ideology and attitudes toward the sublime are easily overstated, not least because the politics and religious views of various figures, including Dryden, Swift, Gay, and Pope, evolve over time. Matthew Prior's long philosophical poem *Solomon On the Vanity of the World*—published in 1718 after he negotiated the Tory Treaty of Utrecht in the last years of Anne but written in 1708 or before, when he was actively working with the Whig Junto—presents a mixture of conservative denigration and protoaesthetic celebration of our faculties' experiences of their limits. Solomon expresses a Montaignean and Pascalian distrust of reason and the senses[71] and concludes, "How mean the Order and Perfection sought / In the best Product of the human Thought, / Compar'd to the great Harmony that reigns / In what the Spirit of the World ordains!"[72] But our very skeptical incapacity to know the universe in absolute terms permits our discovery of providence: "these fair Stars, these Objects of Delight, / And Terror, to our searching dazl'd sight, / Are Worlds immense, unnumber'd, infinite" (book I, 546–8). The sublime combination of delightful terror itself is the conduit through which God communicates his authority to our otherwise frustrated capacities—a commonplace among the Whiggish Cambridge Platonists like Cudworth.[73] While Dryden and Rochester both seem to deny the subject any established commerce with the absolute, this similarity cannot indicate a shared politics. Rochester, in his associations with Buckingham, was seen as aligned to the Whig cause: for instance, Crowne's *City Politiques* links Rochester's libertinism and a love of republican liberty.[74] If an emphasis on the ironic fissure between our need and our failure to have commerce with transcendent authority has a political meaning, rarely does it appear to be a simple one. Still, most significant early theoretical assimilations of Longinus in English tend to forego the vexations and ironies of Rochester's and Dryden's skeptical views of elevation, instead presenting the sublime as a mode of indirect providential address, more modest than the enthusiastical Puritan fit or the papal bull yet still subtly claiming divine authority for a vision of order. John Dennis and Joseph Addison (both of whom happen to be Whigs) approach the sublime by noting the disproportion among the faculties caused by our confrontation with objects of vast size or power, but they resolve this imbalance to the subject's benefit.

Dennis's major critical works, *The Advancement and Reformation of Modern Poetry* (1701) and the *Grounds of Criticism in Poetry* (1704), frequently address the tension between reason and imagination, a tension that reflects and bridges the gulf between the mind and God's power and authority as seen in his works. Both treatises prize passion above all in poetry and argue that religious topics raise it best. The language of passion, strongly associated with imagination, has a tendency to challenge or even override the dictates of reason. Like Dryden's section on images in the "Apology," chapter VI of Dennis's *Advancement* owes much to Longinus (though he does not name him at this point).[75] Characteristically Dennis stresses the degree to which passion is essential for an image to be successful:

> But these Passions that attend upon our Thoughts, are seldom so strong, as they are in those kind of Thought, which we call Images. For they being the very lively Pictures of the Things which they represent, set them, as it were, before our very Eyes . . . the warmer the Imagination is, the more present the Things are to us of which we draw the Images; and therefore, when once the Imagination is so inflam'd, as to get the better of the Understanding, there is no Difference between the Images, and the Things themselves; as we see, for Example, in Fevers and Madmen.[76]

This raising of images to the status of present things through warm passion follows Longinus's own account in section 15 (*chapitre XIII* in Boileau): the name of image is given " 'When the Imagination is so warm'd and affected, that you seem to behold yourself the very things you are describing, and to display them to the life before the Eyes of an Audience' " (Smith, 40). Dennis exaggerates imagination's triumph more than Longinus does, finding "no Difference" between its creatures and the things presented to understanding. His comparison of sublime images to the deceptions produced "in Fevers and Madmen" remembers Longinus's example from Euripides, when "the Image had seiz'd [Orestes's] fancy, because the mad Fit was upon him, and he was actually raving" (Smith, 44). Imagination proves its special power by posing as and thereby negating understanding.

But though Dennis emphasizes this alarming collapse, he completes his theory by discovering the mysterious harmony of reason and imagination: as he puts it in the *Grounds of Criticism,*

> At the same time 'tis a little odd to consider, that Passion, which disturbs the Soul, should occasion it to produce Harmony, which seems to imply the Order and Composure of it. Whether this proceeds from the secret Effort that the Soul makes to compose it self, or whatever the Cause is, the Effect is certain. But as Passion, which is the Disorder of the Soul, produces Harmony, which is Agreement; so Harmony, which is Concord, augments and propagates Passion, which is Discord. (364–5)

The "secret Effort [of] the Soul" recalls Boyle's "distinct and unwonted kind of internal sensation" that informs us of supersensible realms that otherwise could not be perceived: in Dennis, poetic passion does not leave the mind in disorder, as other enthusiasms would, but articulates its disordering power as harmony. Dennis furthermore analogizes poetry to religion: "the Design of the Christian Religion is the very same with that of Poetry, which can be said of no other Religion; that the business of both is to delight and reform Mankind, by exciting the Passions in such a manner, as to reconcile them to Reason, and restore the Harmony of the human Faculties" (365–6). For Dennis, religious poetry best expresses this dynamic, filling the mind with "Divine Ideas, or Ideas which shew the Attributes of God, or relate to his Worship, [and which] are worthiest to move the greatest and wisest Men; because such Ideas belong to Objects which are only truly above them" (340). The wise man's "Ideas" both show him God's attributes and indicate that they are "truly above," inconceivable. These apparently incompatible impulses are mediated by a providentially installed, harmonizing passion.

Poetry shares this harmony of knowledge and the inconceivable not just with religion but also with science:

> Natural Philosophy is absolutely necessary to a Poet, not only that he may adorn his Poem with the useful Knowledge it affords, but because the more he knows the immense Phænomena of the Universe, the more he will be sure to admire them. For the more we know of Things that are never to be comprehended by us, the more that Knowledge must make them appear wonderful. (350)

Again, as in Boyle, a feeling or passion—wonder, admiration—redeems our otherwise frustrating encounter with "Things that are never to be comprehended by us," and the limits of scientific inquiry turn out to be as "useful" as what lies within them. Reason's failure assures us both as the negative basis of our pious intellectual modesty and as the positive, providential wonder at the universe's order. Religion, science, and poetry together position the subject in a productive, affirmative relation to things never to be comprehended.

Similarly, Addison's "Pleasures of the Imagination" numbers of the *Spectator* (1712–14) resolve the epistemological tension inherent in our relation to God's incomprehensible authority with the language of the sublime— what he calls "the great"—by positing a mysterious economy among the faculties. In number 412, he argues that "great" objects, "a vast uncultivated Desart . . . huge Heaps of Mountains, high Rocks and Precipices, or a wide Expanse of Waters,"[77] please because the "Imagination loves to be filled with an Object, or to graspe at any thing that is too big for its Capacity" (vol. 3, 540). This exercise of the imagination reflects a similar one of reason: "Such wide and undetermined Prospects are as pleasing to the Fancy, as the Speculations of Eternity or Infinitude are to the Understanding"(541). The next paper, number 413, also links the perception of grandeur with the contemplation of it, explaining that we take pleasure in God's vast works because they reflect his nature:

> Because, therefore, a great Part of our Happiness must arise from the Contemplation of his Being, that he might give our Souls a just Relish of such a Contemplation, he has made them naturally delight in the Apprehension of what is Great or Unlimited. Our Admiration, which is a very pleasing Motion of the Mind, immediately rises at the Consideration of any Object that takes up a great deal of room in the Fancy, and, by consequence, will improve into the highest pitch of Astonishment and Devotion when we contemplate his Nature, that is neither circumscribed by Time nor Place, nor to be comprehended by the largest Capacity of a Created Being. (545)

Thus Addison easily solves what will prove to be the thorny question of how otherwise terrifying, humiliating, obscure sublime objects cause pleasure: they appeal to our innate instincts of religious devotion, which themselves raise a fearful yet rapturous sense of subjection and our relative insignificance. Natural powers like storms, waterfalls, and deserts, seemingly devoid of religious content, nonetheless "by consequence" lead us to more abstract considerations of God's incomprehensible boundlessness. The imagination and reason work in tandem toward the same providential end.

Later, however, in number 420, considering the pleasures of the imagination offered by "the Authors of the new Philosophy" (574)—natural scientists—Addison discovers an asymmetry between our capacity to visualize nature and our capacity to understand it. The imagination cannot present us with a true picture of the infinitesimal gradations of experience as the understanding knows they must be:

> The Understanding, indeed, opens an infinite Space on every side of us, but the Imagination, after a few faint efforts, is immediately at a stand, and finds her self swallowed up in the Immensity of the Void that surrounds it: Our Reason can pursue a Particle of Matter through an infinite variety of Divisions, but the Fancy soon loses sight of it, and feels in it self a kind of Chasm, that wants to be filled with Matter of a more sensible Bulk. We can neither widen nor contract the Faculty to the Dimensions of either Extreme: The Object is too big for our Capacity, when we would comprehend the Circumference of a World, and dwindles into nothing, when we endeavour after the Idea of an Atome. (576–7)

While Dryden found will stronger than understanding, and Dennis argued that imagination can "get the better" of it, here Addison contends that imagination or fancy cannot keep pace with it. Addison's point is familiar enough: we cannot see distinctions and proportions that reason (with the aid of mathematics) measures easily—for instance, Descartes's *cliliagon*, mentioned in this connection by Boyle in *A Discourse of Things Above Reason* (223) and Locke's *Essay* (1689).[78] But instead of being simply benumbed or made to feel incompetent by extreme size or minuteness, the imagination "finds her self swallowed up," as if our incapacity to imagine such objects created its own negative "immensity." Earlier, Addison had emphasized the easy pleasure of the slide from the lower to the higher faculty: "nothing is more pleasant to the Fancy, than to enlarge it self, by Degrees, in its Contemplation of the various Proportions which its several Objects bear to each other"(575). But now he seems alarmed at their unequal precision. The problem is especially acute because the religious analogy between the grandeur of visible nature and God in number 413 depended on the cooperation of "Fancy" and "Understanding," the former leading "by consequence" to understanding's "Speculations of Eternity or Infinitude," seeming to underwrite understanding's power. The imagination's pleasure in big objects seemed to require a direct and clear connection to speculations about God to be understood as enjoyable, or understood at all. If vastness or minuteness hopelessly severs imagination from reason, Addison's account of sublime pleasure risks incoherence.

But Addison enlists himself in the sublime tradition that raises such disturbing asymmetries only to blithely resolve them. At the end of number

420, he anticipates a redress of the disproportion: "it is probable the Soul of Man will be infinitely more perfect hereafter in this Faculty, as well as in all the rest" (577). This resolution echoes his earlier application of Lockean psychology in number 413, noting the distinction between the secondary qualities projected by imagination onto reality and the colorless primary qualities of the material world itself. There he says that "our Souls are at present delightfully lost and bewildered in a pleasing Delusion, and we walk about like the Enchanted Hero of a Romance, who sees beautiful Castles, Woods and Meadows" (546). He then speculates that all the "fantastick Scene" (547) will break up when our souls depart our bodies. As much as Addison's description of sublunary life as a "Delusion" in number 413 may betray epistemological anxiety, he is confident enough in the complementary (if deceptive) nature of relations between primary and secondary qualities to find the delusion pleasing—a confidence seconded by reference to "Mr. *Lock*," whose doctrine of qualities is "a Truth which has been proved incontestably by many Modern Philosophers" (547). As Howard Caygill's *Art of Judgement* describes the Lockean view in the *Essay Concerning Human Understanding*, "The very limitation of our understanding is part of [God's] providence, for we have been given the ability to make certain discriminations without knowing their grounds" (40). Though Addison admits the epistemological gap between ourselves and providence and finds it reflected in gaps between our faculties exposed by sublime experience, these gaps themselves prove to be the source of an affirmative pleasure.

The epistemological tensions in these texts from the early history of the sublime in English are thus deftly turned to account to confirm the providential workings of individual subjectivity. Sublime discourse develops from the widespread skeptical view that our capacities discover their limitations in the face of the absolute, as presented in religion, natural science, or politics. Writing on poetry and taste in general in the period redeems this failure and so encourages not just our religious beliefs but also our social practices—particularly those that exclude dogmatic, enthusiastical, and overconfident pronouncements from public discourse. The sublime in the hands of its early theorists mediates between a moderately skeptical society and its continuing need to authorize its practices by claiming divine authority for them. In the work of Dryden and Rochester, a countertradition focuses attention on the sometimes laughable gulf between human pretension and the absolute authority it attempts to arrogate. This countertradition must still be seen as supporting the general turn away from dogmatism that so many historians of ideas have chronicled. It furthermore cannot always be cleanly separated from the larger movement toward a providentially constituted liberal society: Rochester's ironic separation of absolute from human prepares him to accept Burnet's clever arguments for a nonenthusiastic Christian mysticism, and Dryden himself always accedes to providence, even within the epistemologically nervous atmosphere of *The State of Innocence*. Still, skepticism also affords opportunities for irresolution and satire and presents views of the gap between culture and its absolute justifications more critical than the mainstream of sublime theory could tolerate.

3

✿

Civil Enthusiasm in
A Tale of a Tub

Swift uses sublime discourse skeptically in *A Tale of a Tub* (1704) to characterize the failure of human subjects to arrogate transcendent authority in many contexts: *"The Establishment of New Empires by Conquest: The Advance and Progress of New Schemes in Philosophy; and the contriving, as well as the propagating of New Religions."*[1] Under these headings fall Dissenting enthusiasm and Roman Catholic authoritarianism, tyrannies of monarchs and the crowd, literary criticism blinded by archaic philological minutiae or the taste of the moment, and dogmatic philosophy ancient and modern. The sublime works in the *Tale* as a rubric under which to put a diversity of pretensions—thus its first French translator calls it *Le Conte de Tonneau Contenant tout ce que les Arts, & les Sciences Ont de plus Sublime, Et de plus Mysterieux* (1720). The range of targets at which *Tale* directs its antidogmatic humor indicates its participation in what Richard Kroll has called "a remarkably coherent if plural cultural reorganization"[2] in the period, in which "neoclassical discourse fragmented the claims of dissent by appealing to sceptical modes" (78). Swift, like others of various political persuasions, questions dogma to move the culture beyond the violent ideological battles of the seventeenth century.

But the *Tale's* use of sublime language to parody the inflated convictions of ideologues tends to exaggerate his skepticism so much that it makes the recuperation of any authority, however mediated or cautious, seem impossible. While the spokesmen of post-1688 "cultural reorganization" commonly employ protoaesthetic modes of experience like the sublime to recover a mysterious but reassuring sense of harmony among diverse subjects and a blind but felt accord with providence, Swift's sublime discovers the irony inherent even in such mediated appeals. The *Tale's* very participation in its culture's hegemonic movement against enthusiasm thus produces a countermovement questioning the evolving terms of civil society. Recent studies offer a bewildering array of views concerning the political commitments of Swift's early career: Daniel Eilon has discussed elements of "Lockean radicalism" in Swift's politics and Robert Phiddian the similarities between Swift's and Shaftesbury's liberal uses of ridicule; while Ian Higgins describes his thought as always consonant with Jacobite-Tory discourse, and Warren Montag as trapped in the ideological contradictions of fading church-state authoritarianism.[3] Swift's participation in the paradoxical cultural functions of skepticism and their expression in the idea of the sublime suggests a deep epistemological basis of this diversity of impressions. The *Tale*'s antienthusiastic rhetoric derives from the moderate skepticism of emerging civil society and so resembles (and was mistaken for) that of Whigs like Shaftesbury and Addison. But it also presses a conservative suspicion of the general operations of "the mind of Man," a reaction especially apparent in the understanding of taste offered in the "Author's Apology" prefixed to the *Tale* in 1710. Swift's ironic appropriations of a Longinian notion of rhetoric and literary taste, his elaboration of the equivocal form of skepticism that the sublime inspires, help him occupy this ideologically divided position.

I

Studies of Swift's intellectual background, recent and classic, have usually located him squarely within a current of moderate Anglican fideism or mitigated skepticism, widely shared by the bland and the orthodox by 1704.[4] But it has also been common among critics in a different vein to note more radically skeptical tendencies in his work, ones that tend to dislocate his satire or set him apart from other writers of his (or any) time: Claude Rawson, for instance, describes Swift's "strategy of the undermining doubt,"[5] a strategy that seems to discredit all tenable doctrines in part IV of *Gulliver's Travels*, while Phiddian argues that "*A Tale* exemplifies the ironic scepticism and centrifugal textual playfulness to which the discoveries of post-structuralist criticism apply most vividly" (4). It has been less common to stress the connections and dependencies between Swift's moderate and radical skepticisms, unless to resolve the relationship by finding one to be definitive and predominant. (Often the first group would see mitigated skepticism as Swift's true stance behind the radical play of his various "personae," while the second would argue that his epistemological unsettledness makes such a distinction impossible.) The *Tale* testifies to the fact that a culturally crucial line existed in post-Revolutionary society between moderate and immoderate doubt as well as to the permeability of this line. Neither would exist without the other in Swift's thought. But this doubleness itself cannot appear in his work as an explicit position because it entails an oscillation between two that were seen to be incompatible.

Intellectual historians often turn to Swift's sermon "On the Trinity"[6] for an expression of mainstream, mitigated skepticism in his work. The sermon makes the "old and true Distinction, that Things may be above our Reason without being contrary to it" (164). Nothing much marks this view as uniquely Swift's own: it strongly resembles the rhetoric that his ideological foe, the Latitudinarian Gilbert Burnet, used to convert Rochester into his kind of Anglican. Swift's sermon continues: "The Growth of an Animal, of a Plant, or of the smallest Seed, is a Mystery to the wisest among Men" (164). This descent from the lofty mystery of the Trinity to mysteries of low, common things is a familiar move by no means limited to the period's religious debates. The "Essay Upon the Ancient and Modern Learning" (1690) by Swift's patron and mentor, the Whig statesman William Temple, cautions moderns against too readily assuming that they surpass the ancients in the arts and sciences:

> We are born to grovel upon the Earth, and we would fain soar up to the Skies. We cannot comprehend the growth of a Kernel or Seed, the Frame of an *Ant* or *Bee*; we are amazed at the Wisdom of the one and Industry of the other, and yet we will know the Substance, the Figure, the Courses, the Influences of all those Glorious Cœlestial Bodies, and the end for which they were made. . . . Nay, we do not so much as know what Motion is, nor how a stone moves from our hands when we throw it cross the Street.[7]

Rising to contemplate celestial mysteries in order to discover the incomprehensibility of the motion of stones serves common sense by relieving it of the imperative to explain everything rationally or theoretically. The *Tale* occasionally glances at this skeptical security, as when it mocks "the great Introducers of new Schemes of Philosophy," who "advance new Systems with such an eager Zeal, in things agreed on all hands impossible to be known" (166). Social agreement is reached by revelations of our shared ignorance, which Swift, like Temple, often emphasizes by showing how the false ascents of dogmatists call to mind our ignorance even of ordinary things.

But the *Tale* also radically transfigures these very turns into more violent reversals, calculated not to reassure but to outrage common sense—and while parodying the language of the sublime in the *Tale* may not be the only way it performs this operation, it is one of the leading ones. Throughout the *Tale* links elevation and degradation in terms of the sublime, establishing principles in the "Preface" whereupon his readers "should descend to the very *bottom* of all the *Sublime* throughout this Treatise" (44), asserting his confidence in "*A Digression in the Modern Kind*" that he has "included and exhausted all that Human Imagination can *Rise* or *Fall* to" (129). Longinus's own remarks already hint at the uncanny relation between height and depth taken up by the *Tale*: as Longinus says, "its very Height and Grandeur exposes the Sublime to sudden Falls" (Smith, 79). The opening of section 2 of *On the Sublime* ambiguously makes the connection of the sublime to its opposite underlying so much Scriblerian satire, when Longinus raises the question of "whether there be an art of the hupsous or bathous." Scrupulous translators have variously rendered the phrase "of sublimity or of its opposite,"[8] or "of elevation or profundity."[9] But Boileau obviated the problem by asking simply "s'il y a un Art particulier du Sublime"(6), and most early English translators after Boileau, including Smith (1739), similarly simplify the matter by lopping off the reference to bathos. But Pope (perhaps with Swift's or Arbuthnot's help) seizes on the word, probably from the Greek text of Longinus,[10] for the Scriblerian work *Peri Bathous* (1728), and for Swift the association between height and depth, rising and sinking, in all its satirical implications, already lies at the heart of the *Tale*'s irony.

The concept of sublimity is so closely identified in Swift's mind with radical reversal that it seems in part to motivate the *Tale*'s relentless ironies—right down to the orthographic level. The word *sublime* is usually printed in italics in the text, like many of the cant terms it obsessively repeats. It hence is addressed by the command in the "Preface" that "whatever Word or Sentence is printed in a different Character, shall be judged to contain something extraordinary either of *Wit* or *Sublime*" (47). This reflexivity or self-referentiality—"*Sublime*" itself containing something sublime—is a dominant movement in the *Tale,* with its "*Digression in Praise of Digressions,*" its dedication "to the sublimest Genius of the Age" (23) recognized by every "Wit" as himself, and so on. The word *sublime* betokens the mysteries that the Tale-Teller uses it to describe. The joke, of course, is that this extreme self-identification or involution empties the term of meaning rather than indicates its contents, debasing rather than heightening or intensifying it. Even as it is "printed in a different Character" to refer especially to itself, the word *sublime* in the *Tale* is used by Swift to refer to its opposite, to foolish, empty pretension—a definitive example of one of the *Tale*'s favorite ironies, the discovery of the difference generated by asserting a thing's self-identity.

One orthodoxy of "On the Trinity" exaggerated into seeming heterodoxy with the help of this sublime logic of reversal concerns the relation of soul and body. The *Tale*'s bewildering combinations of spiritual impulses and physical grossness find an analogue in the sermon's commonplace notion (its locus classicus in Augustine)[11] that "the Manner whereby the Soul and the Body are united, and how they are distinguished, is wholly unaccountable to us. We see but one Part, and yet we know we consist of two; and this is a Mystery we cannot comprehend, any more than that of the Trinity" (164). This insight helps Swift parody the impossible efforts of Dissenting preachers, represented in the *Tale* by the Æolists, to demonstrate their own spirituality: trying to transcend the body only entraps them more fully in the materiality of their own belches and flatulence.[12] Here Swift ventures beyond even quite extreme, earlier satires on enthusiasm like Henry More's *Enthusiasmus Triumphatus* (1662), which tended to demonstrate that "sundry *material* things" inside and outside the body interfere with our more refined, spiritual faculties.[13] Swift also describes movement in something like the opposite direction: the effort to display one's spiritual nature will in the end only magnify the body's power, so much as to seem implicitly to support a materialist stance. Yet through this very heterodoxy, the *Tale* uncannily rearticulates the sermon's pious platitude. If we know that we consist of two but may see only one, then a descent into the body's crude, despiritualized textures demonstrates the orthodox view of the spirit's unknowable nature better than any spiritual claim ever could. The *Tale*, in its fruitless probings of the body for "Things Invisible" (169), presents the only available examination of the soul's mode of existence.[14]

This dual meaning of the body in the *Tale*—at once the destiny of deluded enthusiasts and the vehicle of an otherwise inexpressible spiritual insight—functions to make it impossible to characterize Swift's position as anything, as ultimately either materialism or dualism. The text's meaning is rather a skeptical movement or oscillation between the two, each revealing the dogmatically empty pretensions of the other.[15] Lofty reason descends into the material, "with Tools for cutting, and opening, and mangling, and piercing, offering to demonstrate, that [bodies] are not of the same consistence quite thro' " (173), coming to subvert its own "pretended Philosophy which enters into the Depth of Things" (173). The famous passage seems to resolve this disappointing encounter between reason and the body by praising the person who "can with *Epicurus* content his Ideas with the *Films* and *Images* that fly off upon his Senses from the *Superficies* of Things" and finds this "the sublime and refined Point of Felicity, called *the Possession of being well deceived*" (174). Sublimity finally lies on the surface, and the depths plumbed by reason prove merely material, degraded, and worthless. While some have taken the seeming endorsement here of Epicurean materialism as definitive of Swift's view,[16] it is hard not to hear mockery in the momentary projection of sublimity onto deceptive surfaces—and a similar suspicion adheres to any philosophical resolution found in the *Tale*. Even the modest intellectual positives occasionally invoked through the text—"the Senses, and common Sense, as well as common Understanding" (171)—here prove no match for the imagination, which finally soars so high as to assert the sublimity of "the *Superficies* of Things," vitiating the senses and common sense by philosophically endorsing them. Again, the sublime in Swift tends to signal not the discovery of some truth, material or spiritual, but a skeptical movement that undercuts each truth with its opposite.

These dialectical reversals of spirit and matter do not serve merely to parody all sublime discourse, or any attempt to get at the absolute truth: even that is too secure a position for Swift to occupy. Rather they express a particular vision of sublimity, which may perhaps best appear in light of Slavoj Žižek's comments in *The Sublime Object of Ideology* (1989) on Hegel's paradoxical statement, "the Spirit is a bone." For Žižek, "the Sublime is an object whose positive body is just an embodiment of Nothing"[17]—not some unrepresentable, transcendent object that we permit ourselves to infer in our very failure to conceive it, as in Kant, but a gross, physical object inviting no spiritual hypotheses, a flayed woman, a dead surface of no depth: "we overcome phenomenality not by reaching beyond it," Žižek says, "but [in] the experience of how there is nothing beyond it" (206). Swift's spirituality always lies in this absolute denial that we may reach beyond our immediate, bodily experiences, beyond "the *Superficies* of Things," to find some satisfying subjective mediation between them and the absolute. As Žižek says, "this proposition appears, of course, as an extreme variation of vulgar materialism; reducing the spirit, the subject, pure negativity, the most mobile and subtle element, an ever-escaping 'fox,' to a rigid, fixed, dead object, to total inertia" (207). But as in Swift, it is only through the apparent embrace of vulgar materialism that the spirit is duly regarded.[18] For Žižek, this movement approaches the essence of Hegelian (and Lacanian) thought, "the 'last secret' of dialectical speculation": "that this very negativity," the spirit, "to attain its 'being-for-itself,' must embody itself again in some miserable radically contingent corporeal leftover" (207). In Swift, the spirit's ironic, dialectical reversion into the corporeal finally conveys a sublime insight, but at the expense of the possibility of even a negative representation of it.[19]

The *Tale* carries sublime reversal beyond these exchanges between spirit and matter into the constitution and operations of "the mind of Man" itself, which finds itself internally divided in its attempts to act according to reason. Again, Swift's placid, mitigated skepticism models the radical ironies incompatible with it in the *Tale*: as "On the Trinity" declares, "*Reason* itself is true and just, but the *Reason* of every particular Man is weak and wavering, perpetually swayed and turned by his Interests, his Passions, and his Vices" (166). This promotes a moderate, defensive doubt, which presumes that collectively we may attain a tolerable degree of rationality, combating the irrationality of "every particular Man." But putting the problem this way installs a fissure within the subject, with ironic consequences that the *Tale* relentlessly exploits. Reason at once directs and eludes every particular mind: the problem stems not just from reason's lofty remoteness but also from its intimacy, setting the terms of individual understanding as it renders understanding inescapably problematic. Another expression of this bind appears in Swift's posthumously published "Thoughts on Religion": "I am not answerable to God for the doubts that arise in my own breast, since they are the consequence of that reason which he hath planted in me."[20] Swift's skepticism does not deny the influence of reason, of the higher term. Such a denial would not be skepticism: it would amount to the materialistic or instinctual dogmatism that he loves to ridicule. Like matter that houses a spiritual essence we can never see, our rational nature refers to the absolute without our ever being able to grasp it with confidence.

The mind is thus constituted as a subject by its alienation from authority, not its freedom from nor its embodiment of it. The theoretical disquisitions that fill the *Tale,* ironic as they are, define the "natural" state of the mind by its divided relation to authoritative absolutes:

> AND, whereas the mind of Man, when he gives the Spur and Bridle to his Thoughts, doth never stop, but naturally sallies out into both extreams of High and Low, of Good and Evil; His first Flight of Fancy, commonly transports Him to Idea's of what is most Perfect, finished, and exalted; till having soared out of his own Reach and Sight, not well perceiving how near the Frontiers of Height and Depth, border upon each other; With the same Course and Wing, he falls down plum into the lowest Bottom of Things; like one who travels the *East* into the *West;* or like a strait Line drawn by its own Length into a Circle. Whether a Tincture of Malice in our Natures, makes us fond of furnishing every bright Idea with its Reverse; Or, whether Reason reflecting upon the Sum of Things, can, like the Sun, serve only to enlighten one half of the Globe, leaving the other half, by Necessity, under Shade and Darkness: Or, whether Fancy, flying up to the imagination of what is Highest and Best, becomes over-short, and spent, and weary, and suddenly falls like a dead Bird of Paradise, to the Ground. (157–8)

The passage's description of the descent resulting from intellectual elevation resonates with the passages from Longinus cited earlier, for instance, "so *flaming* oftentimes above the measure of their *fewell* [our thoughts] *extinguish* and miserably *decay*" (Hall, 42). But Swift's passage most significantly develops the sublime tradition by its presentation of the mind's essentially, "naturally," "commonly" divided relation to the absolute as a split within the mind itself, opened when it "soar[s] out of [its] own Reach and Sight."[21] The raising of the mind's powers divides it in two, just as the insistence on the sublimity of the word *sublime* doubles (and reverses) its meaning. The mind encounters a duplicity in itself, but like the difference between height and depth in absolute space, or east and west on a globe, the mind's self-differentiation is undelineable. This dividedness pertains to the mind's agency as well, at once free and forced to invent its authorities, "fond of furnishing every bright Idea with its Reverse" from one point of view yet "by Necessity" constrained to do so from another: after having "some way or other, climbed up into a Conception of a *God,* or Supream Power," he says next, the inspired "seldom forgot to provide their Fears with certain ghastly Notions," according to "the usual Method of Mankind" (158). Psychological liberty and necessity conjoin to define our predicament, subjected to the very authorities we freely invent.

Even the parody of philosophical tone and style of this and other passages in the *Tale* executes such doubleness—a fact that obviates the problem of whether Swift is offering a straight-faced account of the "mind of Man" or travestying philosophical attempts to do so. The passage's stammering—"Whether," "Or, whether," "Or, whether"—undercuts the theory the Tale-Teller enunciates, revising again and again its idea of the ultimate source of the mind's dividedness ("Malice," "Reason," "Fancy") and so discrediting his own philosophical reach. But in such failure the passage illustrates and validates the very vision of sublime trajectory that it describes, that is, the fall implicit in each attempt at intellectual elevation, here his proposals of theory after theory. So the passage succeeds in enunciating its theory by failing to do so, and vice versa. We are used to ascribing this kind of paradoxical brilliance to the radical, uniquely restless nature of Swift's writing. But it is equally important to see its source in the ambivalence toward rational authority fundamental to his age's official epistemology. Swift offers a theoretical picture of subjectivity that cannot work without failing in its effort at depiction.

The subject's constitution by his alienated dictation of absolutes to himself in this passage presents what I have been calling the skeptical sublime in a paradigmatic form. Again, as Hilary Putnam puts it, skepticism "is a perpetual dissatisfaction with the human position, a demand for a God's Eye View or Nothing, that degrades the only perspective that is actually available to us."[22] In Swift's sublime scenario, the demand for godlike transcendence is a kind of disguised demand for an absolute degradation of subjectivity. To a degree it resembles Thomas Weiskel's Kantian model in *The Romantic Sublime:* "this ambiguity of participation in an ideal which is greater than the psyche—*beyond* it and at the same time *within*—may be met on every page of Kant's account."[23] But in Swift the subject is unable to reach what Weiskel sees as the typical Kantian resolution, "psychologically an identification with the superior power" (93), to his own satisfaction. The mind "doth never stop," constitutionally unable to flatter itself with its ascendancy for long. Nonetheless, the passage also contrasts with what Paul de Man proposes, in the essay "Hegel on the Sublime," as a counter to Weiskel's view.[24] De Man praises Hegel's sense of "the definitive loss of the absolute experienced in the sublime," refusing the self the comfort of discovering "how an absolute lack can be turned into an absolute surplus" (115). In a sense the *Tale*'s passage performs what de Man calls "the critical undoing of belief" in absolutes, or in Swift's words, in "what is most Perfect, finished, and exalted." But the experience in the *Tale* is portrayed as requiring the mind's credulity in absolutes in order to critically discover its incapacity to attain them. Again, skepticism functions, in both its moderate and radical forms, by acknowledging the authority of absolutes, of sublime epistemological objects, only to insist that an adequate identification with them is impossible.[25]

A third reversal in the *Tale* elaborates on this tendency of the rational mind to operate against its own intentions—which directly produces an inherently dubious social world of fantasy, alienation, and delusion. Again, this movement appears among the commonplaces of "On the Trinity." Those who foment controversy about the Trinity because it is "not agreeable to their own corrupted Reason" (159) do not know what they are doing: "raising Difficulties concerning the Mysteries in Religion. . . . whatever they pretend, will destroy their inward Peace of Mind, by perpetual Doubts and Fears arising in their Breasts" (166–7). The reversal is more striking when orthodox divines use reason to combat anti-Trinitarians:[26] the doctrine of the Trinity "hath suffered very much," he writes, "by the Weakness and Indiscretion of busy (or at best, of well-meaning) People, as well as by the Malice of those who are Enemies to all Revealed Religion" (159). Any "farther Explanations . . . by Rules of Philosophy" will "multipl[y] Controversies to such a Degree, as to beget Scruples that have perplexed the Minds of many sober Christians, who otherwise could never have entertained them" (160). The theme of rational controversy getting the better of its participants' intentions is common enough, and is taken up (for instance) by Swift's friend Francis Gastrell, whose *Principles of Deism Truly Represented and Set in a Clear Light, in Two Dialogues Between a Sceptick and a Deist* of 1708 (containing one of the few approving printed references to the *Tale* before the "Author's Apology") argues that deism and skepticism, despite apparent oppositions, ultimately generate the same confounding doubts.

In the *Tale,* the connection between a loss of one's own intentional power and the infection of others with a similar loss appears in the "Digression on Madness," where persuasive power is shown to be a special kind of weakness:

> when a Man's Fancy gets *astride* on his Reason, when Imagination is at Cuffs with the Senses, and common Understanding, as well as common Sense, is Kickt out of Doors; the first Proselyte he makes, is Himself, and when that is once compass'd, the Difficulty is not so great in bringing over others; A strong Delusion always operating from *without,* as vigorously as from *within.* (171)

Here subjecting the rational self to "Fancy" and "Imagination" is necessary for "bringing over others," and social power is seen to live off the power of self-delusion. Dustin Griffin has argued, in his essay "Interpretation and Power: Swift's *Tale of a Tub*" (1993), that "Swift commonly thinks of the writer as a *political* animal, always contending to control his own faculties, or other writers, or readers, and in that sense constantly driven, like Hobbesian man, by a 'perpetual desire of power after power.' "[27] But contending to control your own faculties is political only in a very odd sense, and losing the battle oddly appears to be a condition prior to nearly all the relationships between subjects in the *Tale.*

One group constituted by its shared lack of self-control comprises religious fanatics seeking to be filled with sublime inspiration, "the Sectaries in all Nations, who did, and do, and ever will, daily Gasp and Pant after it" (155)—represented, as a 1720 footnote tells us, by "Our Dissenters in England." Swift proposes the "Antient Oracles" as primary models for this kind of relinquishment of intention, "whose Inspirations were owing to certain subterraneous *Effluviums* of *Wind,*" managed by "*Female* Officers, whose Organs were understood to be better disposed for the Admission of those Oracular *Gusts*" (157)—resembling Longinus's description of sublime "Imitators . . . ravished and transported by a Spirit not their own," like "the *Pythian* Priestess" straddling "a Chasm in the Earth, *from whence exhale divine Evaporations,* which impregnate her on a sudden with the Inspiration of her God" (Smith, 36-7). "Sectaries" are activated not by a canny desire for religious authority but by the identification of the power of inspiration with weakness and submission, freedom with brute physical necessity, that occurs in sublime experience.

Such linkages between power and psychological weakness dominate the *Tale*'s account of politics in general, usually figured in oratorical situations that reduce rhetorical eminence to purely physical terms, as the "Introduction" puts it: "WHOEVER hath an Ambition to be heard in a Crowd, must press, and squeeze, and thrust, and climb with indefatigable Pains, till he has exalted himself to a certain Degree of Altitude above them" (55). Such power depends on various "Oratorical Machines," which function, the Tale-Teller theorizes, according to mechanical laws:

> Air being a heavy Body, and therefore (according to the System of *Epicurus*) continually descending, must needs be more so, when loaden and press'd down by Words; which are also Bodies of much Weight and Gravity, as it is manifest from those deep *Impressions* they make and leave upon us; and therefore must be delivered from a due Altitude, or else they will neither carry a good Aim, nor fall down with a sufficient Force. (60)

The parody of rhetorical "Altitude" again vitiates the orator's mastery by describing the thoughtless, mechanical forces that control his performance.

But Swift's parody of the rhetorical sublime extends instead of rejects its implicit character, here its power to bypass intentional modes like reason, judgment, and assent: as Boileau's translation puts it, "il ne persuade pas proprement, mais il ravit, il transporte" (5). Swift's description of this motion contrasts with what Jonathan Lamb, in "Longinus, the Dialectic, and the Practice of Mastery" (1993), finds characteristic of post-Boileauvian Whig theorists: according to Lamb, these define oratory as an "oral performativity" (552), "a sheer, win-or-lose competition for mastery unlimited by conditions, truths or nostalgias" (551). Lamb associates this sublime with a notion of performative, practical persuasion, "which shifts power around [n]o matter how highly troped it may be" (558). Swift's vision of sublime oratory mocks the supposedly radical freedom of the Whig tradition as Lamb portrays it. In the *Tale,* rhetoric is not a simple stratagem to gain "an Auditory" but a move in a game in which the only way to usurp power is to be usurped by it, "by Force of certain *Vapours* issuing up from the lower Faculties" (171), elaborating on the mechanical terms in which Longinus describes inspiration: "So from the sublime Spirit of the Ancients there arise [sic] some fine Effluvia, like Vapours from the sacred Vents, which work themselves insensibly into the Breasts of Imitators" (Smith, 37). As often as the *Tale* offers accounts of the transfer of power from orator to "Imitator," it insists on the insensibility and emptiness of both parties that make this transfer possible.

In short, what the *Tale* offers is an account of the subject in society not as a *"political* animal," in Griffin's phrase, but as something like an ideological one. Our social being is determined not by what we choose to think about it but by psychological powers that necessitate particular thoughts and actions and involve us in sects, crowds, and unthinking discipleship.[28] On the face of them, the Æolists' delusions could seem too idiosyncratic and violent to constitute an ideology, which is usually seen as subtly investing its claims in common sense, the natural, and the universal to mask a view of the world that serves a particular class or group—fostering, as Žižek puts it, "a kind of basic, constitutive *naïveté*: the misrecognition of its own presuppositions, of its own effective conditions, a distance, a divergence between so-called reality and our distorted representations, our false consciousness of it" (28). Swift portrays the egomaniacal French autocrat, the mad Cartesian philosopher, the Dissenting preacher, bent on "subduing Multitudes to his own *Power*, his *Reasons* or his *Visions*" (171), as violent disrupters of common sense and naïveté, not subtle ideologues shaping them into false consciousness. These figures belong in the last age or at least not in England, in some other country where civil society fails to harmonize the people's basic presuppositions and permits eruptions of political and religious violence.

But for Swift such harmony had by no means been achieved by 1704, and in fact it proves difficult to distinguish the unthinking sublime reversals he imputes to insane, isolated revolutionaries, enthusiasts, and Cartesians from those ascribed to his Whig political opponents. The Whigs are out of power when Swift's *Examiner* starts in 1710 (the year of the *Tale*'s fifth edition, with its "Apology"), but many historians have seen the recently defeated Whig Junto as a preview of the consolidation of Whig power under Walpole, anticipating the principles of stability of British civil society in the eighteenth century.[29] Mockingly defending the irreligion of Whig Latitudinarians, for instance, the Examiner remarks that as "ST. *Paul* tells us, *There must be Heresies in the Church, that the Truth may be made manifest;* and therefore by due Course of reasoning, the more Heresies there are, the more *manifest* will the Truth be made" (vol. 3, 54); and the Examiner lists the backward methods by which the Whigs supported religion when in power. This strategy implies that the only possible religious tendencies of the Goldophin ministry must work in opposition to their professed doctrines: the only way that Whigs can reveal the truth is in reverse of their intentions. As Swift's political career develops after the *Tale*'s initial publication, he consistently portrays the tendencies of normal Whig politics as evolving according to an unintentional logic.

As unofficial spokesman for Anne's Tory ministry, Swift refuses to see his political enemies as united by any coherent principles or rational goals. But their very lack of political beliefs constitutes them as a potent group. As he argues in *Examiner* number 43,

the Bulk of the *Whigs* appeareth rather to be linked to a certain Sett of *Persons,* than any certain Sett of *Principles* . . . those who were Partisans of the late Men in Power, and privy to their Designs; or such who joined with them, from Hatred of our Monarchy and Church; as Unbelievers and *Dissenters* of all Sizes: Or Men in Office, who had been guilty of much Corruption, and dreaded a Change . . . Or lastly, the *Money-Traders*, who could never hope to make their Markets so well of *Præmiums* and Exorbitant Interests, and high Remittances, by any other Administration. (vol. 3, 165)

Swift cannily portrays the linkages among the seemingly unrelated impulses of the corrupt and the unorthodox, the monied interest and the Dissenters, the prowar Marlborough group and the promoters of the national debt, throughout the *Examiner,* at once emphasizing their unity and their lack of principle—the way a passionate, greedy, restless, irrational lack of principle unifies them in a single interest group. Pocock has described Swift's role, among others,[30] in identifying this new basis of social being in irrational interest divorced from rational self-possession:

> new and dynamic forces, of government, commerce, and war, presented a universe which was effectively superseding the old but condemned the individual to inhabit a realm of fantasy, passion, and *amour-propre* . . . he could identify and pursue the goals proposed to him by his passions and fantasies; but he could not explain himself by locating himself as a real and rational being within it. The worlds of history and value therefore extruded one another, and what would later be described as the alienation of man from his history had begun to be felt.[31]

One name for this alienation has been ideology—the idea that subjects' passions and fantasies, even delusions, constitute their social, corporate being rather than the independent exercise of their reasons and their rational relation to their own property. Swift, apart from expressing what could loosely be called a "Country ideology" in opposition to the "Court ideology" propounded by (e.g.) Defoe, offers a vision in the *Examiner* of ideology itself. He portrays "the mind of Man" as constitutionally disposed to submit to ideas that are somehow at once its own and beyond its control, and the society resulting from this disposition.

The reversing logic of the sublime in the *Tale,* with its basis in material inspiration, in subjectivity divided against itself by reason, and in oratory induced by and inducing irrational transport, helps prepare the way for Swift's later, more politically motivated descriptions of his opponents during the Harley ministry. Of course his own political commitments at the time of the *Tale*'s publication are nothing if not intricate: it is, after all, dedicated to Somers, a leader of the Whig Junto, which he would later attack.[32] But the *Tale*'s tendency to explore the extreme implications of moderate Anglican skepticism, not its reassuring if irrational subjective links to providence, leads in a conservative direction: the skeptical view that the "mind of Man" cannot lay claim to "Idea's of what is most Perfect, finished, and exalted" in justifying its opinions, political, religious, or otherwise. Such skepticism could seem to put a confident controversialist like Swift in an awkward position. But his power as a satirist derives from the acceptance of his own limitations as a form of authority. Nowhere does this contradictory but potent position appear more clearly, as I argue in the next section, than in the "Author's Apology," added to the fifth edition of the *Tale* in 1710, at a much evolved point in his political development. There the notion of taste, reprising the reversing logic of the sublime expounded in the *Tale*, helps him speak the language of authority without exceeding the limits he imposes on human powers of conception—a position that differs from the appeals to taste of his Whig friends and opponents as much as it crucially resembles them. The protoaesthetic concepts of taste and the sublime thus prove to be signal points of differentiation between the "liberal" ideology of civil society and its conservative critique.

II

Sublimity in the *Tale* fills not just the Dissenting preacher claiming to personify supernatural authority but the poet asking for inspiration, and the sensitive reader seeking the special, distinguishing "spirit" of the great text. Such literary maneuvers persist in eighteenth-century polite society long after the promoters of more socially disruptive enthusiasms have been shown outside. The placement of rarefied, "spiritual" effects among the pleasures of the imagination helps mark the transformation of a politically and religiously combustible society into a polite one, as taste directs the subject's passions and pleasures, essentially opaque to reason, into sociable channels. For a historian of aesthetic theory in the eighteenth century like Terry Eagleton, this operation eventually seems "the very paradigm of the ideological":[33]

> What is at stake here is nothing less than the production of an entirely new kind of human subject—one which, like the work of art itself, discovers the law in the depths of its own free identity, rather than in some oppressive external power. . . . The new subject, which bestows upon itself self-referentially a law at one with its immediate experience, finding its freedom in its necessity, is modeled on the aesthetic artifact. (19–20)

The dividedness of Swift's "mind of Man," soaring and falling, "fond of furnishing" itself with sublime ideas that "by Necessity" dominate it, critiques this "new kind of human subject" as it rejects the old kind of enthusiastic one, undermining incipient "aesthetic discourse," understood as "a means for the individual's valuation of self as both a subject of discernment and ultimate valued object," in Tony Bennett's words.[34] Swift's view of the embarrassing force of the new subjective economy of the aesthetic leads him, however, to promote an ironic version of it, not to reject it entirely—as the "Author's Apology" for the *Tale* employs taste to ideologically support an anti-Whiggish conservatism.

Writers about taste early in the period often employ a skeptical rhetoric at once to promote a judicious attitude toward literature and to cast a disdainful glance at the enthusiastic temperament. In his essay "Of Poetry" (1690), Swift's mentor William Temple denies the supposed supernatural component of inspiration associated with Longinus.

> I can easily admire Poetry and yet without adoring it: I can allow it to arise from the greatest Excellency of natural Temper or the greatest Race of Native Genius, without exceeding the reach of what is Human, or giving it any Approaches of Divinity, which is I doubt, debased or dishonoured by ascribing to it any thing that is in the compass of our Action or even Comprehension, unless it be raised by an immediate influence from it self.[35]

But for Temple, poetry finally provides a way to reconcile our hunger for supernatural force with an even, skeptical sense of control:

> Without the Forces of Wit all Poetry is flat and languishing; without the succors of Judgment 'tis wild and extravagant. The true wonder of Poesy is, That such contraries must meet to compose it: a Genius both Penetrating and Solid; in Expression both Delicacy and Force; and the Frame and Fabrick of a true Poem must have something both Sublime and Just, Amazing and Agreeable. (81)

The call for "a Genius both Penetrating and Solid" alludes to the distinction of spirit and matter that informs his discussion: Epicurean materialism holds that the world consists of impenetrably solid atoms, while the penetration of the true genius seems to transcend a material world so constituted. In Temple, as in so many other Whig theorists, the aesthetic object is seen as a site of reconciliation of freedom with force, unruliness with justice, and so offers an escape from the incivility that necessarily attends religious, political, and philosophical dogma.

For Swift, however, the problem of taste turns not on harmonizing opposing terms but on ironic reversals of them into each other. In the "Digression Concerning Critics," the *Tale* offers a definition of taste pointed particularly at the sublime, in perhaps the only moment when the *Tale* unironically upholds sublimity as a literary value: "by this Term [*Critick*] was understood such Persons as invented or drew up Rules for themselves and the World, by observing which, a careful Reader might be able to pronounce upon the productions of the *Learned,* form his Taste to a true Relish of the *Sublime* and the *Admirable,* and divide every Beauty of Matter or of Style from the Corruption that Apes it" (92). The Tale-Teller calls this type of critic "utterly extinct" and ironically praises the "TRUE CRITICK" (93), a category comprising Swift's literary enemies—"*B-tly,* and *Rym-r,* and *W-tton,* and *Perrault,* and *Dennis*" (94). Taste specifically functions here to master the difficult connections and distinctions among high and low manipulated throughout the *Tale:* it does not just distinguish beautiful from corrupt style but defines the nature of corruption by its unsuccessful aping of beauty, recognizing resemblance in difference and difference in resemblance.

Taste in the "Apology," written "June 3, 1709" (20) and published with the fifth edition of 1710, is similarly attuned. As engaged as the *Tale* is in what we would call aesthetic issues, in its references to poetry and poets (called "Wits" and ranked with the enthusiasts, systematizers, and projectors) and usages of the term *sublime,* it is the "Apology" that determines its status as a literary work, to be understood and enjoyed in a special way. There Swift repeatedly invokes the idea of taste to defend it, as he says immediately: "*those who approve it, are a great Majority, among the Men of Tast*" (3). Though offering no precise definitions, the "Apology" nonetheless uses taste as his last word against his detractors, "*the Sour, the Envious, the Stupid, and the Tastless*" (4). Part of this emphasis could come from Swift's friendly appreciation of Addison and his circle as "*Men of Tast*" around the time of the "Apology" 's composition, in contrast to "*the* weightiest *Men in the* weightiest *Stations*" (6) who were denying him preferment in the church.[36] A classic account of taste inaugurates Addison's papers on "the Pleasures of the Imagination," appearing two years after the publication of the "Apology." After stressing that it is "very difficult to lay down Rules for the Acquirement of such a Taste,"[37] Addison gestures toward describing the role of the "true Critic" who manages to impart it:

> I could wish there were Authors of this Kind, who, beside the Mechanical Rules which a Man of very little Taste may discourse upon, would enter into the very Spirit and Soul of fine Writing, and shew us the several Sources of that Pleasure which rises in the Mind upon the Perusal of a noble Work. Thus altho' in Poetry it be absolutely necessary that the Unities of Time, Place and Action, with other Points of the same Nature should be thoroughly explained and understood; there is still something more essential, to the Art, something that elevates and astonishes the Fancy, and gives a Greatness of Mind to the Reader, which few of the Criticks besides *Longinus* have consider'd. (vol. 3, 530)

This linkage between the Longinian sublime and the "essential something," the je ne sais quoi discerned by good taste, targets taste's defining object in a way that would influence critical theory in the century to come. Addison at once mystifies taste, suggesting it lies beyond mere rule, and recovers it as teachable or conveyable, provided a critic can use it to enter into fine writing's very soul and spirit and pass it on to us. Swift's "Apology" presents taste as similarly shared by a particular group ("*Men of Tast*") who exercise it upon objects only they may recognize.

But just here Swift's emphasis hints at a difference between him and Addison—not just one of temperament but a contrast in their views of taste's socializing (hence ideological) function. The "Apology" is fond of stressing how the "fine taste" required for appreciating the *Tale* does not extend to everyone, while Addison, though admitting that "this Faculty must in some measure be born with us" (529), offers "several Methods for Cultivating and Improving it," including "Conversation with Men of a Polite Genius" (529). Of course in defending the *Tale,* Swift must dismiss the taste of Wotton and others who do not grasp its ironies. But his characteristic view of human limitation leads him, unlike Addison, to cast out boors and false wits as irredeemable. (Even his essay "Hints towards an Essay on Conversation," roughly contemporaneous with the "Apology," concentrates more on most people's natural limitations as conversationalists than on their potential.)[38] As Ehrenpreis points out, such contrasts between Addison and Swift, however intimate they were at this period, indicate a profound intellectual difference between them: he concludes, "Addison inclines to dwell on the natural dignity of rational man, as against Swift's obsession with the stumbling passions of crippled humanity . . . Swift yearned for boundaries and Addison for expanses."[39] While Addison elaborates the psychological and social mechanisms whereby taste operates, Swift flatly implies that the *Tale* has a self-evident quality discernible by "*Men of Tast*" alone—"an inescapable circularity of thought," as one commentator on the "Apology" puts it, that "ultimately undermines itself," inasmuch as no rule or principle emerges to distinguish the tasteful from the tasteless.[40] As for Addison, taste for Swift operates by passing "the very Spirit and Soul of fine Writing" from a critic to others, generally functioning as nearly all subsequent British eighteenth-century discussions of taste would do, presenting value as objective enough to be sociably shared, but recognizable only "subjectively"—a "Spirit and a Soul," a "Something" irreducible to mere rule.[41] For Swift, however, its circulation is notably limited and draws exclusive rather than inclusive boundaries.

As determined as the "Apology" is to proclaim the *Tale*'s literary and moral virtue, it is the text's peculiar, inaccessible circularities that mobilize the discourse of taste in its defense. After noting the anomaly of its initial reception—the fact that though *"a great Majority among the Men of Tast"* (3) approve it, most of the printed comment on it has been negative—Swift boldly predicts its lasting acclaim: *"since the Book seems calculated to live at least as long as our Language, and our Tast admit no great Alterations, I am content to convey some Apology along with it"* (4). The similarity of this to the extravagant claims of the teller of the *Tale*, "Written for the Universal Improvement of Mankind," has often been noted, as has the general way in which the apparently "straight" "Apology" plays the same ironic games it pretends to elucidate.[42] But ironic or not, Swift's defense invokes a standard of taste as durable as language itself—not unquestionable by any means, inasmuch as many, including Dryden and Swift himself, expressed anxiety over possible alterations in English.[43] Stability it does suggest, however, and this seems to contradict the claims to novelty that Swift next makes: *"He resolved to proceed in a manner, that should be altogether new, the World having been already too long nauseated with endless Repetitions upon every Subject"* (4). The tension between the *Tale*'s *"altogether new"* manner and its capacity to satisfy lasting standards and uphold them into an indefinite future does not cripple the authority of Swift's appeal to taste but rather expresses it: the utter novelty shows that the standards of *"our Tast"* are perhaps best satisfied by a sort of brilliance that always anticipates any sharable articulation of them.

This doubleness carries into the next paragraph, which uses taste at once to excuse certain inessential indiscretions of the *Tale* and to guarantee its essential quality: when he wrote it, *"He was then a young Gentleman much in the World, and wrote to the Tast of those who were like himself; therefore in order to allure them, he gave a Liberty to his Pen, which might not suit with maturer Years"* (4). The *Tale*'s taste here seems particularized and ephemeral enough to suit young worldly wits and leads young Swift away from correctness and universality, from standards that would appeal to all, or at least to maturer men of taste. Perhaps the young author relinquished control of himself, submitting to the influence of others by giving a liberty to his pen—a genteel version of the mind of man whose "first flight of Fancy" unites freedom with constraint. Yet he immediately retracts the use of taste as an excuse and reasserts it as his defense: *"Not that he would have governed his Judgment by the ill-placed Cavils of the Sour, the Envious, the Stupid, and the Tastless, which he mentions with disdain"* (4). Taste functions not so much as the anomaly that makes objective judgment impossible as the anomaly that solicits accurate subjective judgment, investing its masters with an ironic authority not to be communicated or widely circulated.

One group excluded from taste's authority is the clergy, whose prerogatives the *Tale* aims to protect—*"those who have neither Candor to suppose good Meanings, nor Palate to distinguish true Ones"* (4–5). In fact the *Tale* *"was not intended for their perusal*" (5). While truth and virtue separate Swift from those whom the *Tale* attacks, taste separates him from those he sees himself as defending. Moreover, the tastelessness of the clergy leads them astray from more than just the *Tale*'s meanings: "*And I wish,*" Swift says next, "*there were no other Instance of what I have too frequently observed, that many of that Reverend Body are not always very nice in distinguishing between their Enemies and their Friends*" (5). Here niceness of taste seems as important to the survival of Anglican purity as virtue itself. The "Apology" 's concept of taste does not merely distinguish Swift the aspiring clergyman from Swift the wit, the conversationalist, and the man of letters. It advances a principle whereby not just wit but virtue and sound doctrine can be distinguished and promoted. Swift in fact credits the *Tale* for his success with Harley in securing first fruits for the Church of Ireland. As he writes to Esther Johnson in the *Journal to Stella* (7 October 1710): "They may talk of the *you know what* [i.e., the *Tale,* the authorship of which he had not publicly avowed]; but, gad, if it had not been for that, I should never have been able to get the access I have had; and if that helps me to succeed, then the *same thing* will be serviceable to the church."[44] The Church receives sorely needed aid from a text that its members are not very nice in appreciating. Unlike virtue, which is properly elevated in itself above all corruption, taste mediates and distinguishes between the Church's friends and enemies, its strengths and corruptions, valuable precisely because it moves between high and low as they inevitably are confounded and grasps their reversals without becoming inoperative.

The practical political consequences of good taste appeared vividly to Swift around the time of the "Apology" as the new powers soon to assume control of the government demonstrated their own discrimination by recognizing Swift's value to them through the *Tale.* As Ehrenpreis notes, "a confidential agent of Robert Harley's, writing in the summer of 1708, referred to Swift not by name but simply as 'the author of the *Tale of the Tub*' " (vol. 2, 330). Swift comes to think of the members of the Harley ministry, especially Harley himself and St. John, as distinguished by their good taste, qualifying them to govern a corrupt England, and contrasts them with the merely appetitive, greedy, carnal ministry of Goldophin in *Examiner* number 26. Harley is praised as "of great Learning, and as great a Favourer and Protector of it"—presumably demonstrated to Swift by his own employment; Dartmouth as "a Man of Letters, full of good Sense"; and St. John is ironically praised as having "clearly mistaken the true Use of *Books,* which he has thumbed and spoiled with Reading, when he ought to have multiplied them on his Shelves: Not like a great Man of my Acquaintance, who knew a Book by the Back, better than a Friend by the Face, although he had never conversed with the former, and often with the latter" (*Prose Works,* vol. 3, 79–80)—an index of taste to be familiarly formulated in Pope's attack on Timon in the *Epistle to Burlington* ("In Books, not Authors, curious is my Lord," 134). Swift's portrayal of the Tory ministry as a literate elite thus qualified to manage England's affairs is of a piece with the "Apology" 's defense of the *Tale* as a text intended for the perusal of the tasteful.[45]

But while confined in the "Apology" to an elite coterie, taste is exercised by expanding linguistic possibilities, subsisting on language's potential for irony always revealed in the *Tale*—another point of contrast with Addison. In the *Spectator* number on taste, he describes his aversion to "forced Conceits" (530) and endeavors "to banish this *Gothic* Taste" (530), referring the reader to *Spectator* number 62's attack on false wit, primarily puns. Swift's own "Modest Defense of Punning" (1716) affirms what is apparent in the *Tale*'s references to spirit, wind, and related terms, that his love of wordplay surpasses anything Addison could find acceptable.[46] As the "Apology" insists, the *Tale* engages the taste of the reader not so much through its beauties as its duplicities: "*There is one Thing which the judicious Reader cannot but have observed, that some of those Passages in this Discourse, which appear most liable to Objection are what they call Parodies, where the Author personates the Style and Manner of other Writers, whom he has a mind to expose*" (7). The moral objections of clergymen stem from their failure to read judiciously, to notice how a moral meaning lies embedded in an immoral expression. The text's duplicity extends beyond its parodies of immorality: "*Another Thing to be observed is, that there generally runs an Irony through the Thread of the whole Book, which the Men of Tast will observe and distinguish, and which will render some Objections that have been made, very weak and insignificant*" (8). He leaves the discovery of these ironies to the discernment of the men of taste for whom the *Tale* is written, pointedly not giving examples or "shew[ing] us the several Sources of that Pleasure which rises in the Mind upon the Perusal" of it, as Addison would.

Irony offers the leading opportunity for taste to "divide every Beauty of Matter or of Style from the Corruption that Apes it," a problem that the *Tale* amply poses, through in reverse, as the "Apology" insists, presenting overtly ill meanings, styles, and manners that Swift "*has a mind to expose.*" Taste grasps the ironic and parodic principle whereby good lies within overtly bad matter, dividing one from the other by recognizing their identity "*through the Thread of the whole Book.*" It is the faculty whereby we distinguish not the high from the low but the high in the low, thus performing the crucial mediation between the spirit of the text and its overt expressions, paralleling the mysterious, connecting distinction between spirit and body that dominates the *Tale* thematically, allowing us to move from the "one Part" we can see to its implicit opposite united to it. While such reversals victimize the fool who brashly pronounces on the text's ill meaning and so harms religion while trying to aid it, they enable the men of wit and taste to distinguish themselves.

The ideological significance of taste in the "Apology," and of Swift's general insistence on the mind's confinement to ironic, sublime reversals, appears in contrast to Shaftesbury's *Letter Concerning Enthusiasm,* which the *Tale* in many ways strongly resembles. (Like the *Tale,* the *Letter* is dedicated to the grand Whig, Somers.) The "Apology" acknowledges this similarity while denying any connection between them: several readers, Swift says, have *"pronounced another Book to have been the Work of the same Hand with this* [as his note informs us, the *Letter Concerning Enthusiasm*]; *which the Author directly affirms to be a thorough mistake; he having yet never so much as read that Discourse, a plain Instance how little Truth, there often is in general Surmises, or in Conjectures drawn from a Similitude of Style, or way of Thinking"* (6). Swift's letter to Ambrose Philips of September 1708 proves his denial of having read Shaftesbury's *Letter* to be a fib: "Here has been an Essay of Enthusiasm lately publisht that has run mightily, and is very well writt, All my Friends will have me to be the Author, *sed ego non credulus illis.* By the free Whiggish thinking I should rather take it to be yours; But mine it is not; For thô I am every day writing my Speculations in my Chamber, they are quite of anothr sort."[47] Such misattributions are themselves failed acts of taste, mistakenly recognizing *"a Similitude of Style, or way of thinking"*— classic objects to which taste is attuned, as Addison's essay points to them, "the several Ways of thinking and expressing himself, which diversify him from all other Authors" (528). Swift's praise of and distancing of himself from the *Letter,* both to Philips and in the "Apology," hint at the political stakes of decoding such resemblances and distinctions between his *"way of thinking"* and the "free Whiggish thinking" of Shaftesbury, when he was still close enough to Philips and Addison and the Whigs in general to exchange intimate letters with them yet began increasingly to differentiate his thinking from anything that could be called "Whiggish" in his drift toward outright support of the Tory Harley in 1710. This complexity extends beyond the immediate political occasion into the heart of the *Tale*'s use of the sublime in its similarities to and differences from Shaftesbury's text.

The obvious connection between the *Tale* and the *Letter* lies in their attack on enthusiasm, on enthusiasts' false conviction that they are worked upon by transcendent forces. Swift and Shaftesbury also share a confidence that a certain style of ridicule can expose such impostures—better, apparently, than mere reason and argument.[48] Shaftesbury uses the same kind of physicalist vocabulary as Swift does to describe the operations of enthusiasm: "There are certain humours in mankind which of necessity must have vent. The human mind and body are both of them naturally subject to commotions: and as there are strange ferments in the blood, which in many bodies occasion an extraordinary discharge; so in reason, too, there are heterogeneous particles which must be thrown off by fermentation."[49] Elsewhere he speaks of how "vapours naturally rise" (13) in a manner that recalls the Tale's account of the Æolists: Shaftesbury declares, "I find by present experience, as well as by all histories, sacred and profane, that the operation of this spirit is everywhere the same as to the bodily organs" (32). Like Swift, he seems to leave very little room for discernibly nonmechanical operations of the spirit.

The two also resemble each other in their insistence that ridicule benefits society, though this point marks the great divergence of Swift's procedure from that of the Letter. Shaftesbury declares that he has "often wondered to see men of sense so mightily alarmed at the approach of anything like ridicule on certain subjects; as if they mistrusted their own judgment" (10). Swift similarly expresses irritation at "*the weighiest Men in the weightiest Stations* [who] *are pleased to think it a more dangerous Point to laugh at those Corruptions in Religion, which they themselves must disapprove, than to endeavour pulling up those very Foundations, wherein all Christians have agreed*" (6). However, the "free Whiggish thinking" from which Swift distances himself lies in the Letter's assumption that an undiscriminating, free indulgence of ridicule will necessarily produce social harmony.

Something of this contrast appears in the overtly similar introductions of the arguments of both pieces. Section II of the Letter begins, "If the knowing well how to expose any infirmity or vice were a sufficient security for the virtue which is contrary, how excellent an age might we be presumed to live in!" (9) Swift's "Apology" starts with similarly conditional statement: "*IF good and ill Nature equally operated upon Mankind, I might have saved my self the Trouble of this Apology*" (3). As ironic about its own conditional as the Letter's sentence sounds, it turns out that Shaftesbury believes that virtue depends on the liberty of criticism in society:

> And one might hope, at least from this good symptom, that our age was in no declining state. . . . There can be no impartial and free censure of manners where any peculiar custom or national opinion is set apart. . . . 'Tis only in a free nation, such as ours, that imposture has no privilege; and that neither the credit of a court, the power of a nobility, nor the awfulness of a Church can give her protection, or hinder her from being arraigned in every shape and appearance. 'Tis true, this liberty may seem to run too far. . . . But who shall be judge of what may be freely examined and what may not? (9)

Swift, ever the advocate of censorship,[50] could not approve of this indulgence of freedom of expression as a good in itself, especially if weighed against the awfulness of the Church. The "Apology" 's first sentence unironically insists that good and ill nature do not operate equally upon mankind and implies that indulging human nature to express itself freely would not introduce a self-correcting principle of rational judgment into the public sphere as Shaftesbury says (10–11) but rather would increase the preponderance of vice. For Swift, "the Men of Wit and Tast" know who they are and must provide support to church and state to correct the mistakes made in the public sphere's free functioning. The superior judgment of men like Swift, Harley, and St. John does not improve by being circulated through the misunderstandings of discarded factions, Whig bishops, and party hacks.

The deep incompatibility between Swift and Shaftesbury lies, therefore, in their views of taste or judgment. Here as elsewhere, Shaftesbury insists that the collective operation of our judgments must produce a rational, harmonious society but that individually we can never be sure whether our individual judgments are correct. His skepticism about the latter is the prime motivation for his promotion of the freedom of the former. "Who shall be judge?" he asks. Only our skepticism about our own judgments makes the free operation of everyone's judgment, no matter how opposed to our own, seem desirable. Individual self-doubt produces collective security. In the *Letter,* Shaftesbury does recommend ways of optimizing the accuracy of our judgments—by trying to remain calm and in good humor—but his recommendations remain carefully circular: " 'Tis not in every disposition that we are capacitated to judge of things. We must beforehand judge of our temper, and accordingly of other things which fall under our judgment. But we must never more pretend to judge of things, or of our own temper in judging them, when we have given up our preliminary right of judgment"—that is, by being too "grave" and positive about our untried positions. Apart from the need for this radically open-minded temperament, Shaftesbury offers no first principles. This temperament itself must be judged, moreover—we must step back to discern whether we are being levelheaded enough to offer disinterested opinions—so he puts us in the circular position of using judgments as principles of judgment. This circularity points to a more serious problem: how can we, from our necessarily partial, provisional, individual perspectives, know that general freedom of opinion must result in general harmony? To anxious advocates of the Church of England like Swift, the all-too-recent chaos of the previous century must seem a more likely outcome.

At the *Letter*'s conclusion, Shaftesbury makes the final move to answer such objections and thereby complete his position, appealing to sublime experience to provide the justification that his otherwise skeptical view of competing opinions requires—an appeal that sharply distinguishes him from Swift's own ironic sublimity and the alternative social vision it supports.

Shaftesbury admits that there is a true enthusiasm, particularly sensitive to universal harmony, to be distinguished from the false, and asks how we can ever tell the difference: "inspiration is a real feeling of the Divine Presence, and enthusiasm a false one. But the passion they raise is much alike" (38). As ironic as the subsequent passage sounds—an irony enhanced by his footnotes to Plato's own skeptical comments concerning inspiration—it does not seem clear that Shaftesbury means to dismiss all sublime experience:

> Something there will be of extravagance and fury, when the ideas or images received are too big for the narrow human vessel to contain. So that inspiration may be justly called divine enthusiasm; for the word itself signifies divine presence, and was made use of by the philosopher whom the earliest Christian Fathers called divine [Plato], to express whatever was sublime in human passions. This was the spirit he allotted to heroes, statesmen, poets, orators, musicians, and even philosophers themselves. Nor can we, of our own accord, forbear ascribing to a noble enthusiasm whatever is greatly performed by any of these. So that almost all of us know something of this principle. But to know it as we should do, and discern it in its several kinds, both in ourselves and others; this is the great work, and by this means alone we can hope to avoid delusion. (38–9)

His list of respectable citizens qualified to receive divine inspiration— "heroes, statesmen, poets, orators, musicians, and even philosophers themselves"—quietly but pointedly omits religious figures, effecting the transformation of violent enthusiasm into the peaceable variety that will infuse the fine and liberal arts through the eighteenth century. He proceeds with a version of his tutor Locke's argument from the *Essay Concerning Human Understanding* that "God when he makes the Prophet does not unmake the Man" (704). But as his footnote to his other essays in the *Characteristics* indicates (especially to the sublime flights of his character Philocles in *The Moralists*), he does not mean to pour scorn on the idea of true, "noble enthusiasm," and his wry conclusion that "even philosophers themselves" may receive it must refer to his own insights in the text at hand, discovering a rational harmony in a society where criticism is free. His notion of an ideal, providentially guided social and natural order, itself "too big for the narrow human vessel to contain," seems to require that we may receive disinterested intimations of it somehow. Though the false and true sublimes, delusion and inspiration, of necessity resemble one another, he repeats his faith in his "antidote against enthusiasm," that is, "keeping to good humour"—which will still allow us to discern true, "noble enthusiasm" without letting it overwhelm our fundamentally sociable skepticism. Shaftesbury must both skeptically ask "Who shall judge" and sublimely affirm that he shall: both are essential to his justification of the free indulgence of ridicule. The paradox of the *Letter*'s conclusion, its "having, after all, in some measure justified enthusiasm, and owned the word" (39), resolves itself on this curiously double view of judgment, at once skeptically tentative and sublimely confident in its ability to intimate the noble harmony that its skepticism ultimately upholds.

The significance of Swift's "Apology" and the *Tale* at large appears in part in his skeptical refusal to admit our capacity to make Shaftesbury's easy distinction between false and "noble" enthusiasms—a refusal of Shaftesbury's solution to the ideological contradiction of his text. Swift's virtual identification of high and low, transcending and sinking, spirit and matter is demanded by his belief that "noble," truly inspired enthusiasm is something we cannot "justify," "own," or safely distinguish from its opposite. His skepticism dictates that our encounters with notions "too big for the narrow human vessel to contain," as Shaftesbury puts it, set in motion a process in which our own delusions subject us, embroiling us in the low in our efforts to ascend. Taste in the "Apology" functions as the capacity to decode these ironies, to profit from the madness or delusions of others— to use their madness, or perhaps even our own, as an expression of our sanity. For this reason Swift's own orthodoxy comes to find expression parodically in the most unorthodox insistences on materialism, on the material body that exhaustively defines all that we can know. Power in his system does not circulate by the "free Whiggish" principles of Shaftesbury, who believes that all will be well and that virtue will out, if only opinions, enthusiasms, bodies, and minds are allowed maximum circulation.[51] For Swift, the power of matter determines the spirit, and accepting this determination accords not just with the Epicureanism that he disparages but with his view of our unknowing Christian state.

He furthermore presents a decidedly critical view of ideology by recognizing the power our own ideals have over us and the cognitive failure built into our experience of them. Shaftesbury represses the recognition of this compulsion and failure and instead presents a spectacular picture of society's functioning, perfected by the combination of our imperfect individual perspectives. His faith that we may finally, philosophically escape the degradation to which the *Tale* always returns us accounts for his violent distaste for Swift's work, belying his own easy tolerance of free expression: "that detestable writing of that most detestable author of the *Tale of a Tub*, whose manners, life and prostitute pen and tongue are indeed exactly answerable to the irregularity, obscenity, profaneness, and fulsomeness of his false wit and scurrilous style and humour," as he says in a letter to Pierre Coste[52]—a resolute refusal to read the high in the low, expressing his desire ultimately to keep the two apart.

For Swift, such an effort can only fail. As the "Apology" implies, taste functions like critical thinking, the possession of a few who recognize the irony fostered by our ideals without hoping self-deludedly for a theoretical escape from it—for a Shaftesburyan overview that transforms irony into harmony. But it would be a mistake to argue that Swift's critique proposes an escape from ideological determination and that taste allows him a freedom of movement among reflections of high in low so as to seize confidently the "Idea's of what is Perfect, finished, and exalted" that no one else may reach. The point of taste in the "Apology" is to deny such freedom, to accept the mind's immersion in the corruption that apes objects of sublime transcendence in order to be ironic about it. Only by following the risings and sinkings of the mind of man presented by the *Tale*, without recourse to some external standard or sublime intimation, can the reader of taste appreciate the book's point. Far from liberating him, the irony of this perspective must embroil him utterly in the dead degraded matter, the "miserable radically contingent corporeal leftover," of the *Tale*'s world.

4

The Public Universe
An Essay on Man *and the Limits of the Sublime Tradition*

The philosophical contradiction most often seen in *An Essay On Man* is the principal one that theories of the sublime typically seek to resolve, and the *Essay's* failure to satisfy its readers on the point accounts to some degree for their sense of its deficiencies both philosophical and poetic.[1] The *Essay* insists on its confinement to the sphere of "Man"— "His knowledge measur'd to his state and place, / His time a moment, and a point his space" (Epistle I, 71–2)—yet adopts a perspective transcending this sphere to make our limitation to it seem providentially "RIGHT" (I, 294). From its early readers[2] to today, critics have seized on this as the *Essay's* main philosophical outrage, stated incisively by A. D. Nuttall: "If we maintain that man is unable to conceive anything beyond his own sphere, and make that limitation of *conception* a principal element in our low estimate of man, the view in question can consistently be put only by a being with supernatural powers of insight. Man, so limited, would never know that he is limited."[3] The *Essay* at once renounces and arrogates supernatural, godlike authority to justify the universe's order, and its doing one seems strangely identical to its doing the other.

Yet on this contradiction rests the logic of not just the *Essay* but also what must be seen as a dominant current of eighteenth-century British epistemology. It is hard to see how a version of it is not implied by Hume's call in the *Enquiry Concerning Human Understanding* (1748) for "the limitation of our inquiries as are best adapted to the narrow capacity of human understanding"[4] or Locke's effort in the *Essay Concerning Human Understanding* (1689) to "*see, what Objects our understanding were, and were not fitted to deal with.*"[5] Such attempts to limit our knowledge—called "middle-state skepticism" by one commentator on the period's philosophy[6] after the *Essay's* vision of humanity "Plac'd on this isthmus of a middle State"—ask us to intuit what lies beyond our limitations to recognize them as such.

This demand raises the question, still haunting (some) philosophy,[7] of how we may refer meaningfully to orders of thought that lie beyond what we can know. It may be, as Pope's protégé Walter Harte puts it in *An Essay on Reason* (1734), that " 'Tis Reason finds th'Horizon's glimm'ring line / Where realms of Truth, and realms of Error join" (156–7). But such could seem to demand a rational perspective somehow above our earthbound one, our truths and our errors, to see the "glimm'ring line" at all. The problem is not just philosophically urgent. It faces any attempt to claim a providential justification for the antidogmatic basis of what has come to be called eighteenth-century British liberalism.

The *Essay*'s odd contribution to this ideological context lies in its refusal or incapacity to imagine a resolution to the contradiction while keeping it in more or less full sight. Pope does not invent any subjective mediation between the absolute and the limited perspectives, like Boyle's account of how the mind "can feelingly discern between other objects and those that are disproportionate to its ability,"[8] discussed in chapter 2. The *Essay* avoids, in short, presenting a Whig theory of the sublime, which would employ (in Boyle's words) "a domestic monitor, or a kind of an internal *criterium,* always at hand to help us" (241) to recognize inaccessible orders of thought when we brush up against them, or Dennis's "secret Effort [of] the Soul"[9] that takes unknowing delight in "Things that are never to be comprehended by us" (350). Nor does Pope's *Essay*, like Locke's, firmly turn our attention away from the absolute[10] to fill out a system of modest empirical procedures and criteria within our limits. The *Essay* thus reveals more strikingly than other less openly contradictory texts the main breach within the mitigated skepticism that dominates the epistemology of the period and its corresponding political milieu.[11]

Accounts of the *Essay*'s ideological significance tend to underrate not just the ubiquity of the contradiction in mainstream, politically moderate thought but its tenacity. The absolute perspective and the limited perspective are at once incompatible and inseparable: incompatible because the limited perspective may never adequately conceive of the absolute and must turn away from it but inseparable because the limited perspective must meaningfully refer to the absolute to define itself as limited. Critics often just focus on the former and either condemn the poem for purveying insights that it on its own terms cannot have or seek some logical or rhetorical resolution to render the two perspectives compatible.[12] Their inseparability has been less often stressed. The critics of the 1980s and thereafter who understand contradiction as an ideological matter tend, like the philosophical analyses, to see Pope's blend of modesty and authority as contradictory only in a weak sense: the poem pretends to an unassuming, middle-class ethos of sympathy and toleration only to mask an opposite, distinct ideological investment in aristocratic privilege or an absolutist, crypto-Jacobite agenda, appearing subtly in the poem's authority, its gentlemanly address, the smug, proprietary posture it adopts toward the natural world, its imperialistic remarks about "the poor Indian" and his "untutor'd mind" (I, 99), its imagery of cosmic order and hierarchy,[13] and even its exploitative, patronizing attitude toward animals.[14]

But seeing the *Essay* as contradictory in a strong sense—its "liberal" tentativeness not belied by but paradoxically entailing its authoritative vision—reveals its share in a more central cultural dilemma. In the poem's immediate political context, ideologues of all political persuasions deny absolute authority to particular religious groups, parties, and constituencies to motivate the free exchange of probable or partial beliefs in public and claim that this denial reflects God's will, seen in the constitution of our minds, the nation, and the universe. They thus posit the relation of society's ordering energies to the absolute in their very denial of our ability to perceive such a relation. As his work on the *Essay* begins in earnest in 1730, Pope feels relatively well disposed toward Walpole and the Whigs,[15] and his rhetoric in the poem and correspondence is arguably at its most inclusive. He writes to Swift, "I have personal obligations which I will ever preserve, to men of different sides, and I wish nothing so much as publick quiet, except it be my own quiet" (vol. 3, 276). Such unassuming tolerance of a diversity of opinion, like liberal universalism itself, comports instead of conflicts with Pope's authoritative insights: he is "Slave to no sect, who takes no private road / But looks thro' Nature up to Nature's God" (IV, 331–2). But the poem's insistence on our limited perspective also tends to expose the failure of such authoritative visions, the emptiness of our invocations of providence. Pope's refusal to resolve this contradiction with an account of sublime experience expresses a conservative skepticism but one that emerges only through his best efforts to be liberal. This irresolution indicates fissures within what Habermas calls the "bourgeois public sphere" better than its unambiguous defenders, with their more elaborate theories of the sublime, ever could.

I

At many points in Pope's writing, the sublime arises to mark an attitude toward authoritative public utterance more equivocal than those of other important British thinkers. Shaftesbury, for instance, confidently claims that "heroes, statesmen, poets, orators, musicians, and even philosophers themselves" must on occasion find themselves sublimely inspired, when "the ideas or images received are too big for the narrow human vessel to contain."[16] With equal confidence, David Hume rejects such sublime influence on the public sphere as at best delusory, at worst manipulative:

> The *imagination* of man is naturally sublime, delighted with whatever is remote and extraordinary, and running, without control, into the most distant parts of space and time in order to avoid the objects which custom has rendered too familiar to it. A correct *judgment* observes a contrary method . . . leaving more sublime topics to the embellishment of poets and orators or to the arts of priests and politicians. (*Enquiry,* 170)

While at opposite extremes, Shaftesbury's and Hume's views mirror each other inasmuch as both use the sublime to put constraints on civil discourse: Shaftesbury's sublime appears as a special exception to the usually false enthusiasms he skeptically mocks through his *Letter,* while Hume's very skepticism gestures negatively to sublime regions, "the most distant parts of space and time," to expose wily political and religious manipulators here at home. Pope's *Essay* hovers somewhere between these views, both rejecting the notion that sublime experience may be used to justify social action and using intimations of the absolute to order and discipline the public sphere's operation. In this he resembles Swift's "Man of Tast," discussed in the last chapter, who neither succumbs to the occasional impositions of Shaftesbury's "true sublime" nor, like Hume, confidently asserts that "a correct judgment" will adequately guard against imaginative excess: for Swift, taste ironically plays imagination and judgment off each other, refusing to settle authority on either. Although the *Essay's* even-handedness contrasts with the *Tale's* addiction to violent reversals, Pope similarly expresses his view of authority in society by leaving the status of the sublime object unresolved.

Beyond the famous lines in the *Essay on Criticism* (1711) on Longinus—"Whose *own Example* strengthens all his Laws, / And *Is himself* that great *Sublime* he draws" (679–80)—Pope sustains an interest in the Longinian mode through his early career, referring to him as a prime authority on epic in the preface of the *Iliad* (1715–20), the postscript of the *Odyssey* (1725–6), the notes to both, and *Peri Bathous* (1728). The notes in the epic translations that refer to Longinus often concern Homer's representation of the gods, significant for Pope in its identification of problems of poetic and religious (and so, indirectly, political) propriety. He endorses Longinus's attitude toward the divine or transcendent but tends to attenuate it: sublime, absolute authority for Pope must somehow be at once perceptible and imperceptible, there to be invoked and beyond all invocation. Such remarks anticipate the *Essay's* reading "thro' Nature up to Nature's God," as in his comment on the lines on Neptune from the *Iliad's* thirteenth book:

At *Jove* incens'd, with grief and fury stung,
Prone down the rocky steep, he rush'd along;
Fierce as he past, the lofty mountains nod,
The forests shake! earth trembled as he trod,
And felt the footsteps of th'immortal God.[17]

Pope approvingly notes that "*Longinus* confesses himself wonderfully struck by the sublimity of this passage," which portrays "a God such as he is, in all his majesty and grandeur, and without any mixture of mean and terrestrial images" (628). The interesting thing about Pope's assessment is that the passage portrays Neptune with nothing but "terrestrial images"— the rushing mountain stream, the trembling of "earth . . . as he trod." He endorses the decorous way in which terrestrial images both represent and veil the god's image, or represent it by veiling it: we see no trident, no furious bearded figure, and none of the notorious "defects with which *Homer* draws the manners of his Gods" (628). Neptune manifests himself indexically, by the terrestrial effects of his presence, not otherwise accommodated to human perception.

Longinus links this Homeric example in section 9 of *On the Sublime* to his crucial, famous praise of Genesis 1:3, which immediately follows: "So likewise the *Jewish* Legislator, no ordinary Person, having conceiv'd a just Idea of the Power of God, has nobly express'd it, in the beginning of his Law. '*And God said*—What?—*Let there be Light, and there was Light. Let the Earth be, and the Earth was*'" (Smith, 22–3). Pope no doubt remembers this, Longinus's only reference to the Bible, when his own note furnishes what seems a more apposite scriptural comparison to Homer's Neptune passage, "a description of the like sublime manner of imagery": "*O God, when thou wentest forth before thy people, when thou didst march through the wilderness, the earth shook, the heavens dropped at the presence of God, even Sinai itself was moved at the presence of God, the God of* Israel" (*Iliad*, 628). Pope's choice of Psalm 68 in fact could be read as a gentle correction of the Longinian reading of Genesis 1:3 (—a passage that theorists have seen as paradigmatic of his theory of sublime expression).[18] Most important, Pope does not share Longinus's stress on how "the Jewish legislator, no ordinary person . . . in the beginning of his Law" takes God's utterance upon himself: God's expression becomes Moses' "noble expression," God's beginning of the world Moses' beginning of his text, God's fiat Moses' law. As legislator, Moses is able to assume God's authority even as it is portrayed as an unfathomably powerful, wholly other creative force.

The tenor of Pope's note works against such typically Longinian mixtures of human and divine. His scriptural quote is more veiled: God says nothing and shows his divine presence again indirectly, and no human being steps forward to interpret or address his acts. (In the next verse of Psalm 68, not quoted by Pope, God "did send a plentiful rain," again acting divinely through nature.) Yet the psalm also stresses that God *"wentest forth before thy people,"* becoming somehow publicly manifest without direct self-representation. This insistence that God at once presents himself in nature and avoids "mean and terrestrial" public self-displays resembles the tension that will dominate the *Essay's* own attempts to articulate the relation of absolute authority to the perceptible world. It furthermore reflects the skeptical attitude toward the sublime apparent in Dryden and Swift: the absolute is only truly so, truly authoritative, if it lies beyond our capacities of representation. Knowing this, we may not credit any human perceptions and expressions of it, not even Moses', with divine authority.

This skeptical attitude toward the sublime, as it pertains to Genesis 1:3 and representations of God in general, is expressed powerfully by the famous French skeptic and bishop of Avranches, Pierre-Daniel Huet, in his debate (with his ally Jean Le Clerc) against Boileau about the sublime, published in English by Curll in *The Posthumous Works of Monsieur Boileau* (1713).[19] Often taken to argue simply that the sublime cannot be expressed in the plain style,[20] Huet presents a much more subtle and interesting view. Its core is Huet's denial of the equivalency asserted by Longinus between God's fiat and Moses' sublime utterance in Genesis 1:3, the "mixture" of divine and terrestrial expression. For Huet, the action of God is indeed sublime, but Moses' description of it is not. The latter derives all its grandeur from what it describes, not from anything with which Moses' own verbal expression could be credited: *"Moses* was very sensible, that his Subject carry'd its own Recommendation along with it, and its Sublime too; that barely to relate, was raising it high enough; and that the less of his own there was in it, 'twould be so much the better."[21] Just as Pope implies that the divine ought never to be expressed, represented, or embodied in mean and terrestrial images, Huet insists that God lies beyond all human representation, even by Moses. As he relates, "The Philosopher Aristobulus, tho' a Jew . . . yet did not forbear to distinguish the Speech which God made use of to create the World, from the Speech which *Moses* made use of to recount that Creation to us" (36). We may recognize the sublimity of Genesis 1:3 only by seeing through it to the act it represents and denying the expression itself any share of grandeur.

The implications of this view go to the heart of sublime theory and resonate strongly with Pope's convictions expressed in the notes to the *Iliad* and beyond. Of particular interest is Huet's insistence that, in the final analysis, "Things" are the sublime's only true sources and that any contribution to the object's sublimity by the human subject, through words, rhetorical figures, or thought, is superfluous and deceptively self-aggrandizing: "this

Sublime of Things is the true Sublime; the rest are only so by Imitation and Art. The Sublime of Things has its own Sublimity in it self, the others but borrow it from without. The first does not impose upon the Mind; what it represents as great really is so. On the contrary, the Sublime of Art lays Snares for the Mind, as is only made use of to give an Appearance to what has no being, or to make it appear bigger than it is" (44). Huet thus seeks to deny the subject any artful recuperation or legitimate borrowing of the power he confronts and describes: what is truly sublime lies beyond all sub-jective reflection and may be represented only by a gulf, not a bridge, be-tween the sublime thing and the human mind. But inasmuch as aggran-dized human speech can do no more than "impose upon the Mind" falsely, Moses' simple utterance is paradoxically the more truly sublime for its re-fusal to be so, the more grandly revealing of the gap between God and himself. Early on, Huet complains of the violations of boundaries between object and subject, sacred and human, Christian and pagan, ancient and modern, all going on willy-nilly in Longinus's account of Genesis and Boileau's defense of it: "Neither did I any more believe that all *Longinus* says is Gospel, and may not be contradicted without incurring the Guilt of Presumption; or that we were oblig'd to believe, as if it were an Article of Faith, that these Words of *Moses* are Sublime, and that not consenting to it was as good as questioning whether the Books of *Moses* were inspir'd by the Holy Ghost" (25).

Huet's motivation for pressing this attack is ultimately religious, the par-ticularly skeptical-fideist religious position characteristic of his thought:[22]

in endeavouring to raise the Beauty of that Expression, [Longinus] de-bases the Grandeur of God, and has evinced that neither the lowness of human Wit, nor the Elevation of the Divine Majesty, were sufficiently known to him. He was ignorant that our Conceptions, and our Words, were too short to reach the Infinite Heighth of the Wisdom of God, whose Riches never enter'd into the Heart of Man, and which are incom-prehensible to it. (44–5)

Moses' simplicity keeps the divine and human separate and thus demon-strates the more insight into grandeur, more sublimity, and hence the more true authority by skeptically renouncing them. Huet's forthright assertion of what has throughout this book been called the skeptical sublime does not deny that true sublimity exists or even that language may indicate it: rather he elevates the sublime object by a strict denial of our capacity to conceive of it or infuse its power into our own expressions and satirically mocks those who discover in themselves powers to produce such concep-tions and representations. Against this view, Boileau continues to insist that

Moses' expression *"has something Divine in it"* (*Posthumous Works*, 52), as do our own elevated responses to the text: sublimity for him works by crossing boundaries, by mixing divine and human, and with this he proves himself a true Longinian.

An elaboration of Pope's similar stricture against such mixtures appears several years after the *Iliad* translation in another work concerning the sublime, *Peri Bathous*. In its involved parody of Longinus's *Peri Hupsous*, Pope describes "how the most Sublime of all Beings is represented"[23] in several depictions of God in *The Paraphrase on the Book of Job* by Richard Blackmore, the Whig physician to William III. Like Huet, Pope ridicules all implied equivalencies between the sublime object and the human subject, laughing at Blackmore's decision to describe a storm by imagining God as "Th'Almighty Chymist":

Th'Almighty Chymist does his work prepare,
Pours down his waters on the thirsty plain,
Digests his lightning, and distils his rain. (194)

Pope notes other instances in Blackmore's *Job* when God appears as "a Recruiting Officer," "a Painter," "a Guarantee," "a Mercer, or Packer," "an Attorney," "a Butler," "a Baker" (194–5), and so on. These images seem anti-sublime not just because they portray God's actions as too explicable, too bound by humanly discovered laws of the natural sciences, but also because they project him into distinctly human occupations, too familiarly reflecting (as some complain of the gods of Homer) our own "manners." Huet decries similar failures of writers about divinity:

> Not being able to raise themselves up to Him, they bring him down to them, and speak of Him as a Man. They give him a Face, a Mouth, Eyes, Ears, Feet and Hands. They make Him sit, walk, speak, they ascribe human Passions to him, Joys, Desire, Repentance, Wrath . . . dare we give the Name of Sublime to a Discourse, which infinitely depreciates and dishonors its Subject? (45)

Far from rejecting the sublime, *Peri Bathous* defends a version of it along these lines, a "Sublime of Things," immanent in creation yet never representable in concrete anthropomorphic terms. This Huetian strand of thought about the sublime reaches a culminating point in Kant's famous remark in the third *Critique* (1790): "the most sublime passage in the Jewish Law is the commandment: Thou shalt not make unto thee any graven image, or any likeness of any thing that is in heaven or on earth, or under the earth" (135). The false elevation of ourselves by appropriating God's authority in our own imagination or concepts is identical to the impious shrinkage of God to human shapes or scales of being: subjective inflation and objective reduction meet in bathos. Pope's attack on Blackmore anticipates the *Essay on Man*'s dual warnings to "presume not God to scan" (II, 1), to forbear reducing him to an image, and to recognize our incapacity to "See worlds on worlds compose one universe" (I, 24) or identify our intellectual powers with his.

The ideological significance of Pope's distaste for Blackmore has been explored by Jonathan Lamb, who remarkably defends the representational overkill of Blackmore's *Paraphrase*, its compiling of what he calls "the compelling vulgarity of little circumstances."[24] Lamb claims that the poem ideologically offends Pope not because of its excessive representations of God but because of its elaboration of Job's suffering. (The 1700 edition comprises forty-two chapters, like Job itself, but in Blackmore each is between 100 and 150 lines.) In mocking the *Paraphrase*'s representation of God's actions like distilling rain, *Peri Bathous* "tirelessly identifies those images which are particularized as spillage, discharge, expenditure, and regurgitation" (207), which signify Pope's displaced anxiety about Job's oozing wounds. For Lamb, then, the human subject Job is the sublime figure, and the poem's divine and natural imagery indirectly reflects the power of Job's own representations of his pain—a regard for the individual citizen suggestive of Blackmore's Williamite-Whig politics: "the Whig refusal of arbitrary authority makes way for a singular and possibly extravagant account of private injury" (211). Pope's mockery of the representation of suffering in the poem indicates what Lamb takes to be his opposite ideological investments in Catholic absolutism, Stuart autocracy, and Jacobitism,[25] comporting with his putative aesthetic of order, universality, and generality.

This view would thus recognize the sublime in the most "mean and terrestrial" image imaginable, Job's afflicted body,[26] traversing the boundaries drawn by Huet, and Lamb rightly argues that Pope cannot grant this kind of authority to the human subject. But Blackmore's humanization of the sublime—and Pope's mockery of it—seem open to a political reading very different from Lamb's. The idea that Job's amplified complaints represent radical liberty does not quite square with his equally copious acknowledgment of God's authority when he gets his property back at the end of Blackmore's poem. A Whig allegory it may be, but not one of rebellion: the *Paraphrase* suggests how the citizen's freedom to elaborate his passions ironically must confirm the centralizations of power, the "fiscal-military state," of William III's ministry, fighting the Nine Years' War against the French on high taxes.[27] "After 1694," in J. H. Plumb's words, "the Whig aristocracy is concerned not to limit but strengthen monarchy and authority."[28] In the more abstract terms of political theory, as Pocock puts it, "the commercial, which the Marxists call the bourgeois, order was from its first appearance in theory geared to the stabilisation of authority."[29] Job, the wealthy citizen arbitrarily dispossessed of health and property, learns first this authority's terror and then its ultimately reassuring necessity: the co-operative expressions of his passions and God's power allegorically reflect the political interdependence of a strong Whig executive and the "free," commercial individual.

Pope distrusts this sublime mixture as it is bodied forth in Blackmore's imagery not because it grants too much range to the individual's radical freedoms but because it too readily invests the divine in social and political visions. For Pope, the description of Job's suffering as *"Fresh troops of Pains, and regimented Woes"* (219) recruits subjective feelings into a politi-cally suspect public display, a standing army all too supportive of the Whig oligarchic order—an image that neatly cooperates with Blackmore's rep-resentation of God during a rainstorm as "a Recruiting Officer" raising the army for the Whig ministry: *"For clouds, the sun-beams levy fresh supplies, / And raise recruits of vapours, which arise / Drawn from the seas, to muster in the skies"* (194). Pope's mockery in this resembles the Kantian insistence on the sublime object's potential to be politically abused: "governments have gladly permitted religion to be amply furnished with such accessories: they were trying to relieve every subject of the trouble, yet also of the ability, to expand his soul's forces beyond the barriers that one can choose to set for him so as to reduce him to mere passivity and so make him more pliable" (135). As Steven Knapp remarks, "For Kant, it is the presence, not the absence, of im-ages that serves repression" (80). In promoting a similar line, Pope is curi-ously more chary of representing authority than the Whiggish Blackmore himself: his skepticism demands that no human may represent God's au-thority poetically, personally, or politically, and Blackmore's use of the sub-lime to make such representations seem less authoritarian, more an expres-sion of our natural, personal passions, only disguises their political nature.

Such rhetoric reaches more impressive levels when Addison, a few years after Blackmore's poem, celebrates Marlborough's lucrative European vic-tories during the War of Spanish Succession in "The Campaign" (1704), which identifies the great general with Job's mysterious God in the whirl-wind: "Calm and serene [Marlborough] drives the furious blast; / And pleas'd th'Almighty's orders to perform, / Rides in the whirl-wind, and di-rects the storm"[30] (a passage parodied in the *Dunciad*).[31] As in the *Para-phrase*, the infliction of suffering and the suffering itself naturally work to-gether, as the serene Marlborough, "Amidst confusion, horror, and despair, / Examin'd all the dreadful scene of war" (281–2): what renders this "the True Sublime" for Richard Steele (in *Tatler* number 43) is Marlborough's calm in the face of "an Uproar of Nature, a Confusion of Elements, and a

Scene of Divine Vengeance."[32] Steele's taste for this "Sublime Image," which he finds "as great as ever enter'd into the Thought of Man" (310), indirectly supports the land war in Europe that was so bound up in generating wealth for its participants. As Shaftesbury suggests, on great public occasions, the sublime unites the sensibilities of "heroes" and "statesmen" with those of the literati, providentially contributing to England's glory, here specifically publicized by an image of Marlborough's serene inflictions on the French, and Steele's own sublime appreciation of Marlborough's divine vocation, transferred through Addison's "Sublime Image." *Peri Bathous* mocks Blackmore's *Paraphrase* as a cruder version of just this suggestion that God descends to manifest himself in terrestrial images and invests his own sublime power in the subjective powers of citizens and participants in the public sphere.

A renunciation of these mixtures of divine and human inspires the *Essay on Man*'s divided attitude toward authority. The poem's inoffensive philosophical generalities seek to avoid concrete religious and philosophical debates because certainty in such matters belongs to God alone. While readers have noted that the *Essay* manages to take controversial positions anyway (whether inadvertently or to express Pope's secret opinions)[33] and so contradicts his professed anticontroversialism, a more profound contradiction lies on the poem's surface. Like Huet's sublime, the *Essay*'s very denial of authority asserts it, as its discursive modesty assumes a providential mandate. When the *Essay* appeared in pieces anonymously, Pope gleefully reported that its author was mistaken for respectable persons of different parties,[34] and when the secret was out he told Swift that the poem's authority depended on its effacement of links to any identifiably interested position: "The design of concealing myself was good, and had its full effect; I was thought a divine, a philosopher, and what not? and my doctrine had a sanction I could not have given to it" (*Correspondence*, vol. 3, 433). Most gratifying was the letter from government writer Leonard Welsted to the then unknown author of Epistle I, praising it as "a performance deserving the name of a poet," in contrast to the "vilest and most immoral ribaldry" (vol. 3, 355–6), by which Welsted apparently meant some of Pope's own works.

Pope attains the authoritative philosophical scope of the *Essay* by refusing to express any position that would betray his identity, any concrete religious, political, social, or even philosophical alignments. The *Essay*'s generalizing tendency is an effort not so much to claim godlike authority for himself as to imply that nobody in the universe may arrogate it. In this, the *Essay*'s universe seems designed to undergird what Jürgen Habermas calls "the public sphere" mobilized "against the public authorities themselves, to engage them in a debate over the general rules governing relations in the basically privatized but publicly relevant sphere of commodity exchange and social labor."[35] Following Habermas, scholars have identified various genres of bourgeois expression and interaction (including politeness, the sentimental, the "feminization" of culture, the novel) suited to this emerging sense of the public.[36] Beneath such activities, the *Essay* offers a supportive, general, philosophical framework, regulatory of public life without looking too much like any particular public authority. This is why contemporary Whigs like Welsted found the poem so congenial and why generations of critics have seen in it the Whiggish principles of Shaftesbury and other writers.[37]

The introductory material of the *Essay* is devoted to explaining its anti-controversial aims and seeks to neutralize its arguments' potential to create disagreement as much as possible. The note "To the Reader" published with the earliest editions of the first epistle seeks not to enter but to remove itself from the fray: *"As he imitates no Man, so he would be thought to vye with no Man in these Epistles, particularly with the noted Author of* Two lately published*" (TE,* vol. 3:1, 6)—that is, himself—so insuring his own good faith in neutrality. He laughs, that is, that Epistle I could as well be taken as an argument against himself as against anybody. As he tells Caryll with satisfaction, "I find there is a sort of faction to set up the author [of the *Essay*] and his piece in opposition to me and my little things" (*Correspondence,* vol. 3, 354), as if to travesty the very idea of factionalism. "To the Reader" continues, *"But this he may most surely say, that the Matter of them is such, as is of* Importance *to* all in general, *and of* Offense *to* none in particular" (6)— echoing another model public text, the *Spectator's* dedication to Henry Boyle: "the profest Design of this Work is to Entertain its Readers in general, without giving Offense to any particular Person."[38] The correlation of the public interest with generality and offense with particularity defines the public sphere at its inception in both Whig and Tory versions. Such gestures may be unconvincing: Swift begins his *Examiner* papers by asserting the value of "convers[ing] in equal Freedom with the deserving Men of both Parties,"[39] but his Tory partisanship immediately becomes unambiguous. Nonetheless, their prevalence at least as a pretense indicates their foundational importance in framing the terms of British public dispute. Pope deploys the generalities of the *Essay* not to assert his own superior perspective so much as to provide, like Shaftesbury and Addison, an anti-dogmatic frame to comprehend debate among particular voices.

This correlation between party discourse and the rejection of party discourse appears sharply in a text roughly contemporaneous with the *Essay,* Bolingbroke's *A Dissertation upon Parties,* appearing in 1733–34 in the Country party journal, the *Craftsman*—with which (along with the *Gentleman's Magazine*), Habermas remarks, "the press was for the first time established as a genuinely critical organ of a public engaged in critical political debate" (60). Bolingbroke writes:

The nation is not only brought into an uniformity of opinion concerning the present administration, by the length and the righteous conduct of it; but we are grown into a unanimity about principles of government, which the most sanguine could scarce have expected, without extravagance . . . [and] experience and the evidence of facts . . . [have] destroy[ed] all our notions of party, and substitute[d] new ones in their place. (5)

Like the *Essay*'s view of "Discord" as "Harmony, not understood" (I, 291), Bolingbroke's argument assumes that a vast agreement underlies the merely epiphenomenal divisions in British society, that the Country party has overridden the now antiquated division between Whig and Tory and unites them in opposition to the Court clique of Walpole's ministry—an effort to impose an "ideological consensus" on the 1730s Opposition that was, as one historian argues, perhaps too heterogeneous to accept it.[40] The *Essay*'s appeal to the structure of the universe may be seen as a version of Bolingbroke's party-neutral appeals (e.g. to the ancient, Gothic constitution) but one even more remote from any actual or potential political struggle. Pope's refusal even to mention Christianity in the poem—which has led critics to discover a range of different religious sympathies in it, including deistic or Roman Catholic authoritarian ones—reflects the *Craftsman*'s efforts to set aside all potentially divisive religious disputes to build a coalition between High Church Tories and Opposition Whigs of differing convictions: as Christine Gerrard puts it, "the conciliatory 'Country' platform of the *Craftsman* remained singularly silent on religious issues."[41] It is a similarly conciliatory imperative, not a heartfelt, covert dedication to natural religion, that makes the *Essay*'s neutral rationalism occasionally sound deistic.[42]

The basis of this harmony in the *Essay* turns out to be its unknowability, its being "not Understood" in the final analysis. The short introduction added to the whole poem in 1734, "The Design," introduces this skeptical thread. It begins by sounding the authoritative note on which so many critics have seized: Pope dedicates himself to "considering *Man* in the abstract, his *Nature* and his *State*: since, to prove any moral duty, to enforce any moral precept, or to examine the perfection or imperfection of any creature whatsoever, it is necessary first to know what *condition* and *relation* it is placed in, and what is the proper *end* and *purpose* of its *being*" (7). But next he hedges such apparently dogmatic pronouncements with skeptical doubts about our capacities: "The science of Human Nature is, like all other sciences, reduced to a *few clear points*: There are not *many certain truths* in this world" (7). This dictum sets a course diametrically opposed to the one promised by dogmatic philosophy, in which the paucity of the clear points implies not the scarcity of truths but their plenitude: as Hume puts it in his essay "Of Commerce" (1752), this is the aim of "universal propositions, which comprehend under them an infinite number of individuals, and include a whole science in a single theorem."[43] Pope's *"few clear points"* by contrast appear against the wide background of our uncertainty concerning the majority of particular instances "in this world" that our truths cannot adequately illuminate.

Pope's severing of general from particular aims to realize his vision of a pacified public sphere: "It is therefore in the Anatomy of the Mind as in that of the Body; more good will accrue to mankind by attending to the large, open, and perceptible parts, that by studying too much such finer nerves and vessels, the conformations and uses of which will for ever escape our observation" (7). Pope is not claiming that particularity ought to suppressed or obviated by authoritative truth, theorized and explained away with "science," moral or natural. Rather he claims that "good will accrue to mankind" by skeptically insisting that particularities remain inviolable: "The *disputes* are all upon these last, and, I will venture to say, they have less sharpened the *wits* than the *hearts* of men against each other, and have diminished the practice, more than advanced the theory, of Morality" (7). Public intercourse becomes contentious and violent when we lose a healthily skeptical awareness of our limitations.

The complementary but estranged relation of general and particular in the *Essay* does not quite match the picture of eighteenth-century ideology of which the poem is taken as paradigmatic by some of the main theoretical histories. Terry Eagleton's *Ideology of the Aesthetic* (1990) claims that in the eighteenth century "philosophy suddenly wakes up to the fact that there is a dense, swarming territory beyond its own mental enclave which threatens to fall utterly outside its sway" (13): aesthetics, among other things, is invented to lay claim to this territory but finds particulars recalcitrant to rational authority. Even as "bourgeois reason" rediscovers the body's anomalies, it represses their otherness and pretends to bring them within reason's general scope. But in Pope, the otherness of the particular is explicit, not repressed: the whole point of his *"few clear points"* is to preserve the "finer nerves and vessels" from ever being assimilated. In this he oddly anticipates the postmodern theories of Eagleton and others like Peter Stallybrass and Allon White, which tend to posit "particularity," "heterogeneity," and the "low" as unknowable absolutes, an always receding horizon of discourse, not as general terms themselves to be filled in by the way some general theory (like their own) happens to "wake up" to them.[44] (This resemblance, of course, does not attest to a hidden radicalism in Pope but rather to a consonance between bourgeois and some contemporary radical views of particularity.)[45]

In Pope's case, if not in that of postmodernism, the interdependent opposition is especially empty on one end because it is entirely blind on the other, the generalities "few" and "clear," the particulars "forever escap[ing] our observation." Some have seen a conflict between Pope's authoritative stance and this skeptical sense of the paradoxical, contradictory status of human knowledge. For instance, in the famous opening section of Epistle II, which portrays man as a "Chaos of Thought and Passion, all confus'd" (13), he fails, in Jonathan Lamb's words, to "betray . . . any sense of the clash between the rival functions of tautologies and paradoxes."[46] But it is difficult to see how Pope's skeptical recognition that most of knowledge remains forever beyond our discernment could better complement his commitment to purveying inoffensive generalities and tautologies ("Happiness is Happiness," IV, 28; "Whatever is, is RIGHT," I, 294). Religiously—privately—we learn the full extent of our chaotic, unknowing condition, in order to motivate the public acceptance of orderly, general frames of debate. The "Design" 's paradoxical linkage of general assertions and particularities (a key opposition for Lamb as well) has a similar effect: "the finer nerves and vessels" *must* always escape theoretical observation for our theories to have any validity at all.[47] And it is through this position that the *Essay* seeks to accomplish its tempering of public debate: "If I could flatter myself that this Essay has any merit, it is in steering betwixt the extremes of doctrines seemingly opposite, in passing over terms utterly unintelligible, and in forming a *temperate* yet not *inconsistent*, and a *short* yet not *imperfect* system of Ethics" (7). The poem's authority rests on its "steering betwixt" and "passing over" the irreconcilable or mysterious more than on its explanation of it.

But despite the inseparability of the *Essay*'s authoritative generality and its deference to the unknowable particular, of tautology and paradox, the poem also testifies to the two attitudes' incompatibility. The *"few clear points"* become more powerful and necessary through their very lack of theoretical reach, deriving their authority from what cannot be explained, an authority at once enhanced and limited by the details that escape it. This amounts to an ideological contradiction, a flaw in the justification that the poem and the public sphere at large offer themselves, ultimately signifying their incoherence: in this case, the clash in early capitalism between the skepticism directed against any invocation of authority that would restrict free public exchange and the unskeptical assurance that providence, and ministerial policy, must guarantee a system so constituted. The *Essay* corroborates John Barrell's and Harriet Guest's argument concerning the frequent appearance of contradictions in eighteenth-century literature, which "trained the readers of poetry to admire most the poems which, by their very nature, were most liable to contradict themselves, and so enabled those readers to make use of contradictory meanings in the formation of their beliefs and in the conduct of their lives."[48] But while Barrell and Guest emphasize how a hodgepodge of justifications is found to be convenient in a mixed society—how poems embrace quasi-aristocratic virtue at one moment only to tout the providential benefits of unthinking commercial passions at another, "knotting together . . . disparate discourses" (123)—the *Essay*'s main philosophical contradiction is all of a piece. It expresses its limits in order to providentially found a tolerant, inclusive public discourse. Like Huet's idea that the law of Moses is only truly authoritative because it knows enough not to presume to scan God, the *Essay*'s authority rests on its failure to resolve the contradiction, its refusal to convert doubt into a mysterious feeling of sublime assurance.

II

Pope's very refusal to subjectively consummate his own transcendent terms, however, ironically constitutes his unique contribution to the sublime tradition and an interpretation of its inherent logic (much as Moses' unsublime utterance succeeds for Huet as a sublime expression par excellence). Beyond the questions of subjective mediation at stake in early-eighteenth-century British aesthetic ideology, the *Essay* participates in a wider, longer exploration of sublime subjectivity, echoing Pascal and influencing Kant with crucial passages that still articulate what is distinctive about Pope's strain of sublimity. One such passage appears early in Epistle I, which Warburton calls "a sublime description of the Omniscience of God and the miserable Blindness and Presumption of Man":[49]

He, who thro' vast immensity can pierce,
See worlds on worlds compose one universe,
Observe how system into system runs,
What other planets circle other suns,
What vary'd being peoples ev'ry star,
May tell why Heav'n has made us as we are.
But of this frame the bearings, and the ties,
The strong connections, nice dependencies,
Gradations just, has thy pervading soul
Look'd thro'? or can a part contain the whole? (I, 22–32)

Such passages in the *Essay* pointedly fail to perform the subtle confirmations of subjective power found in similar ones in Pascal and Kant. But in this incapacity to play any very productive role in the sublime tradition lies the power the poem has to reflect critically on it.

At this early moment in Epistle I, the reader is immediately admonished that transcendental vision is a kind of mistake. Pope leads us to see that "He" here refers not to the perceptive, Lucretian philosopher but to God alone, the only being capable of fathoming "the whole" of the universe. This withdrawing of the comprehensive perspective in the very act of appearing to offer it stages the contradiction that Pope wants us to entertain: we are simultaneously to perceive that the universe is a "whole" comprising "Gradations just" and to recognize that we cannot see them at all adequately. The stricture in *Peri Bathous* against representing "the most sublime of all Beings" here becomes one against our viewing the "whole" as "He" views it: the *Essay* as frequently denies us a godlike subjectivity (or offers it to deny it) as it forbids us the capacity to scan God as an object. But the passage acknowledges that we must assume such a perspective and illegitimately identify with the "He" so as to recognize our inability to do so. Just as "the lowness of human Wit" is our only means to grasp "the Elevation of the Divine Majesty" in Huet, the *Essay*'s discourse operates by balancing mutually defining opposites.

Pope here closely follows Pascal, at least verbally, whose *Thoughts* he apparently read in the 1727 edition of Kennet's popular translation: "If a Man did but begin with the Study of himself, he would soon find how incapable he was of proceeding farther. For what Possibility is there, that the Part should contain the whole?"[50] Pascal proceeds to move like Pope to the "nice dependencies," the minute constituents of experience, denying us knowledge of parts as well: "It seems, however, more reasonable that we should at least aspire to the Knowledge of the other Parts; to which we bear some Proportion and Resemblance. But then the parts of the World are so nicely interwoven, so exquisitely link'd and encased one within the other, that I look upon it as impossible to understand one without another, or even, without All" (348). Conceptually if not affectively, Pope's passage conveys the Pascalian notion that our partial perspective on "other Parts" offers only a radically decentered and unsettled apprehension of our position in the universe.

This disturbed epistemological radicalism fits the poem's placid surface in a way that has been difficult to explain. Seeking to harmonize the two, Harry M. Solomon, in *The Rape of the Text: Reading and Misreading Pope's "Essay on Man"* (1993), claims that the poem's embrace of contradictions expresses a moderate skepticism and allows us to place Pope in a more or less stable tradition of "Academic discourse" between dogmatism and radical Pyrrhonism—answering critics of the *Essay* "from Crousaz to 'Crousazian' Nuttall" (185) who find the poem's contradictions to be merely unfortunate blunders. For Solomon, the *Essay*'s Academicism establishes it in a genre, the "philosophical poem," with its own appropriate mode of nondogmatic assertion. But this seems questionable because the poem does not really demonstrate such stability, generic, philosophical, or otherwise. (The genre itself seems contrived to give the *Essay* something to succeed at.)[51] Instead of striking a modest but steady course between doubt and knowledge, Pope seems strangely given to making extremely confident assertions right alongside radical, Pascalian worries about our intellectual instability. The result is more jarring than an Academic middle way guided by probable appearances.

The famous assertion of human contradiction at the beginning of Epistle II demonstrates this extremism, again in terms borrowed from Pascal. As Pascal argues that "to study *Man* . . . [is] the proper Employment and Exercise of Mankind" (308) (echoed by the epistle's opening couplet), he views humanity as a "Subject of Contradiction" (206) to suggest unsettledness, not stability. "Man" is, as Pope says, "a being darkly wise, and rudely great":

With too much knowledge for the Sceptic side,
With too much weakness for the Stoic's pride,
He hangs between: in doubt to act, or rest,
In doubt to deem himself a God, or Beast;
In doubt his Mind or Body to prefer,
Born but to die, and reas'ning but to err . . . (II, 5–10)

As confidently declamatory as this is, it is in a sense more radically skeptical, more "Pyrrhonistic," than even those critics who have emphasized skepticism in Pope have found it. We cannot even confidently assert that we know nothing and exist "in doubt," hanging between knowledge and the acceptance of uncertainty. Many, including Solomon, have taken this as an argument for moderation.[52] But here, at least, the middle place seems the most dubious of all: Pope's depiction of our betweenness does not refer to our inherent ability to moderate between untenable extremes or urge us to do so but sees our uncertain oscillations as naturally, definitively human. As Pascal puts it, "We have an Idea of Truth, not to be effaced by all the Wiles of the Sceptick: we have an Incapacity of Argument, not to be rectified by all the Power of the Dogmatist" (204). Other statements in the *Pensées* similarly portray the volatility of this betweenness: for example, "we discern some faint Image of Truth, while we possess nothing but Lies, being alike incapable of absolute Ignorance and of accomplished Knowledge" (78); it is "alike impossible for [Man] to avoid both these Sects ['*Pyrrhonism*' and '*Dogmatism*'], and to repose himself in either!" (200) Pope's passage aims likewise to demonstrate our fundamental lack of intellectual repose. The "weakness" that humbles our "Stoic's pride" is as least as much intellectual as physical, because pride usually refers in the *Essay* to the pride of rationality: for instance, "From pride, from pride, our very reasoning springs" (I, 161), "In Pride, in reas'ning Pride, our error lies" (I, 123).

Pope's anti-Pascalian irony, however, is that extreme admissions of doubt produce the demonstrable security of the *Essay*—as the "few clear points" mentioned in the "Design" ironically increase in potency by their very failure to explain much of anything: the deeper the insecurity, the deeper the security. The *Essay* endorses Pascal's arguments that human subjectivity comprises incompatible extremes but only to consistently withhold the intensification of self-consciousness that must accompany such arguments, we would think, for them to be thought at all. The distinctiveness of the *Essay*'s economy emerges in comparison and contrast to Paul de Man's description of Pascal's Longinian sublimity:

> The convergence of discourse and the sacred . . . occurs by way of phenomenal cognition. No matter how strongly the autonomy of language is denied, as long as the language can declare and know its own weakness and call itself mute, we remain in a Longinian mode. Pascal's paradox applies: "In a word, man knows that he is miserable. Thus, he is miserable since that is what he is. But he is very great inasmuch as he knows it." A dialectized sublime is still, as in Longinus, an intimation of poetic grandeur and immortality.[53]

To some degree, this also applies to the *Essay*. No matter how strongly Pope's language denies its autonomy, no matter how skeptically it renounces its claim to judge the universe and to reason with authority, it nonetheless also affirms the reason that makes its self-questioning possible. Though he insists that "To reason right is to submit" (I, 164), he still recuperates a paradoxical authority by contending that to denigrate reason submissively is "to reason right." In fact, the more reason is denigrated, the more authoritatively right the *Essay*'s reasoning is.

But in de Man's terms, there is a sense in which the *Essay*'s perspective is even more "dialectized" than that of the *Pensées,* at least insofar as the poem refuses to mediate rationally incompatible extremes with tragic self-consciousness. Pope's Pascalian borrowings do not rise to the "intimation of poetic grandeur and immortality," the proto-Romantic, egotistical sublime that de Man finds in Pascal, that displays the depth, richness, and potential of his subjectivity even as he confronts its insignificance. The subject in the *Essay* is interested less in acquiring personal grandeur than in stabilizing the social context in which all may interact on an equal—equally unknowable—footing. As often as critics see the *Essay* as defending a symbolically commercial or imperialistic mentality, it does not quite match typical descriptions of the acquisitive, Romantic ego, like Weiskel's of the Wordsworthian, egotistical sublime: "Sublimation melts the formal otherness of things and reduces them to material or to substance. The formal properties of the perceived particular are canceled and replaced by their 'significance'. . . . In Wordsworth, the imagination is the faculty which transforms everything into the money of the mind."[54]

Many readers would be tempted to see such an account as applicable to Pope's attitude toward the degrees of nature laid out before him. But his rejection of our purchase on the universe's meanings is an overt, defining component of the *Essay*'s perspective:

Ask for what end the heav'nly bodies shine,
Earth for whose use? Pride answers, " 'Tis for mine:
"For me kind Nature wakes her genial pow'r,
"Suckles each herb, and spreads out ev'ry flow'r;
"Annual for me, the grape, the rose renew
"The juice nectareous, and the balmy dew;
"For me, the mine a thousand treasures brings;
"For me, health gushes from a thousand springs;
"Seas roll to waft me, suns to light me rise;
"My foot-stool earth, my canopy the skies." (I, 131–40)

Though some critics have found this ironic mouthing of anthropocentrism to state what they take, after all, to be Pope's own position,[55] it is clear that he is playing a more complicated game, explicitly determined by the imperative both to reject and to assert his authority. In what Mack calls "a highly elliptical passage" (*TE*, vol. 3:1, 145–8n), the poem rebukes Pride, emphasizing the sometimes apocalyptic powers of nature indifferent to humanity ("burning suns," "earthquakes," nation-destroying "tempests"). Pride retorts that " 'the first Almighty Cause / 'Acts not by partial, but by gen'ral laws,' " incorporating even such faith-shaking anomalies in his own self-flattering account of general order, which he adds to the list of roses, grapes, and health that Nature provides him. For Pride, then, "our very failure to discover probable signs becomes itself a probable sign," to reapply Douglas Lane Patey's formula.[56] It is true that this resembles Pope's own general explanations of the universe. In fact Epistle IV embarrassingly quotes Pride's overconfident sentiments with apparent approval: "Remember, Man, 'the Universal Cause / 'Acts not by partial, but by gen'ral laws' " (35–6). But it is a mistake to see this later moment as a revelation of Pope's true position. Again, he believes both the skeptical and dogmatic views, in their incompatibility and inseparability: in this case the former literally enables his articulation of the latter. What is sacrificed in this paradoxical exchange, as egotistical bombast metamorphoses into a quoted, sociable bromide, is our ability to locate the requisite perception of universal order in a specific, creditable consciousness, whether Pride's, the poet's, or anyone else's.

The *Essay*'s assault on Pride hence reflects the French antidogmatic tradition while specifically avoiding the sense of subjective recuperation it sometimes affords. As Montaigne puts in the *Apology for Raimond de Sebonde,*

> Who has made [man] believe, that this admirable Motion of the Celestial Arch, the Eternal Light of those Tapers that roll over his Head, the wonderful Motions of that infinite Ocean, should be established and continue so many Ages, for his Service and Convenience? Can any thing be imagined so ridiculous, that this miserable and wretched Creature, who is not so much a Master of himself, should call himself Master and Emperour of the World, of which, he has not the power to know the least part, much less to command the whole?[57]

Pope marks the passage in his copy of the *Essays,* and his jotting "De Vanitate Humana" in the margin apparently endorses the view.[58] But even as the *Essay* follows the canonical skeptical strategy to denigrate human reason in order to establish the right relation to God's sublime authority, Pope brushes the tragedy of this consciousness of limitation aside:

> If plagues or earthquakes break not Heav'n's design,
> Why then a Borgia, or a Cataline?
> Who knows but he, whose hand the light'ning forms,
> Who heaves old Ocean, and who wings the storms,
> Pours fierce Ambition in a Cæsar's mind,
> Or turns young Ammon loose to scourge mankind?
> From pride, from pride, our very reas'ning springs;
> Account for moral as for nat'ral things:
> Why charge we Heav'n in those, and these acquit?
> In both, to reason right is to submit. (I, 155–64)

This comports with de Man's assessment of Pascal's sublime, its glorification of reason through reason's embarrassment. But what is missing, again, is Pascal's sense of the individual subject's dignity, secured by that subject's pathetic assertion of his own weakness, his capacity to value himself through the very tragedy of consciousness. The potentially tragic characters here, "Cataline, Borgia," and "Cæsar," perform not as vexed subjectivities but as leavening in an objectively mysterious system, unconscious of their own function in it: God "Pours fierce Ambition in a Cæsar's mind," making a marionette of him, without self-awareness. Pope does here as he does throughout, muting the individual ego to facilitate the complacent acceptance of our shared inability to grasp the universal order. He thus stands outside the development of the Romantic ego defined by its own glorious self-risk and instead presents uncertainty as a universally shared, community-defining force that does not distinguish poetic, imperialist, or capitalist geniuses from the ordinary gentlemanly participants in the public sphere. Pope's *Essay,* always "OF Man *in the abstract,"* deploys the sublime not egotistically but always in reference to the harmony of social relations. Even the individual subject comprises various counterbalancing social forces that drain his uncertainties of pathos.

This is not to say that Pope's unknowing attitude toward the universe, shared with Montaigne and Pascal, constitutes an opposition in the *Essay* to its vision of the "great Chain of Being." It is Pope's very belief in the chain that makes belief in it impossible. Here again Pope's partial model is Pascal, who, in A. O. Lovejoy's words, "better than any writer makes evident a certain ironic aspect of the history of the principle of plenitude":[59] Pascal demonstrates how a belief in an infinitely great chain can finally "make reality essentially alien to man's reason, permeated throughout with paradoxes and contradictions" and turn out to be "destructive of the assumption from which it had been derived" (130). But again, the difference between Pope and Pascal is equally significant. The *Essay* does not explicitly consume its own arguments in order to convert its reader into "such a *pyrrhonien accompli* as made, in Pascal's eyes, the most hopeful material for a *chrétien soumis,"* as Lovejoy puts it (130). While Pascal says that everyone, Christian, heathen, and infidel alike, may recognize that "nothing in this World is productive of true Contentment" (49), he insists that only Christians may find peace: "all they who seek God without JESUS CHRIST can never meet with such Light in their Enquiries as may afford them true Satisfaction, or solid Use."[60] Grace is indispensable and consists in our acceptance of the Christian miracles, the fulfillment of the Old Testament prophecies, and the fact that "in *JESUS CHRIST* all the various Dissonancies are reduced to perfect Harmony" (140).

Pope, in contrast, is so committed to maintaining discursive oppositions that he permits neither Christian revelation nor deistic rationalism to emerge decisively as relief for the subject's uncertainty. Commentators have pointed out that the *Essay's* persistent denigration of reason makes it seem implausible that Pope actively sought to reject Christianity and embrace deistic principles,[61] which affirm (as Leslie Stephen summarizes them) that "reason must be the only foundation of certitude," that "assent should follow demonstration alone," and that "all faith now in the world . . . is 'entirely built upon ratiocination.'"[62] The poem everywhere attacks such rational assurance. But it also refuses to mention Christian revelation, the typical remedy for reason's insufficiency. As Pope writes to Caryll (before owning the *Essay*), the author demonstrates his Christianity by mentioning charity and love of God and man, but "More *particular* than this he could not be with any regard to the subject, or manner in which he treated it" (vol. 3, 400)—as if he felt obliged, in disagreeing with their positions, to adopt the deists' "subject," the visible universe, and their "manner" of reasoning from general principles. This puts the poem in an impossible position, a discursive no man's land, because the imperative to reason from universally apparent general principles itself preordains it in a deistic direction—whence the charges of deism to the *Essay* in the first place. Pope withholds both reason and revelation from the subject as compensations for its essentially dubious position, as well as a compensatory, Pascalian sense of this position's pathetic dignity.

British philosophical poetry in the period often omits or delays direct reference to Christian revelation, but it frequently sets itself in Old Testament contexts to imply a strong analogy between the limited perspective of humanity in the universe and the situation of Hebrew prophets and rabbis awaiting the Messiah. In *Solomon on the Vanity of the World* (1718), Matthew Prior also consciously echoes Pascal, here toward the end of his third and final book, *Power*: "What shall amend, or what absolve our Fate? / Anxious We hover in a mediate State, / Betwixt Infinity and Nothing; Bounds, / Or boundless Terms, whose doubtful Sense confounds / Unequal Thought."[63] Solomon next prays to God for relief, and an angel descends to prophesy upcoming Hebrew history for some one hundred lines, culminating with the assurance of the coming of Christ: "ONE shall spring, / Greater in Act than Victor, more than King / In Dignity and Pow'r, sent down from Heav'n, / To succour Earth" (III, 859–62). A lesser known but also pertinent poem is John Pomfret's *Sceptical Muse* (1699), which refers to Genesis 1:3 to establish the context of our limitations—"To make a World, and stretch the bulky Frame / Beyond where Thought or Fancy ever came: / The great Creator's Fiat did suffice / Mov'd by one Word the Massy Sphere did rise" (1–4)—and concludes by affirming that "Suspicion guards, and Doubt defends my Soul" (248). Harte's *Essay on Reason,* contemporary with the *Essay on Man*, similarly begins with a discussion of Adam and Eve and finds resolution when "a Saviour speaks! lo darkness low'rs no more" (272).

The *Essay* does often echo the Old Testament, especially, as many have noted, the sublime Book of Job. But the most significant aspect of such echoes is their submersion in the range of second-person addresses used by the poem, as in the Pascalian passage quoted earlier, concluding, "Is the great chain, that draws all to agree, / And drawn supports, upheld by God, or thee?" (I, 33–4). Such questions resemble the voice of God addressing Job out of the whirlwind: "Hast thou perceived the breadth of the earth? declare if thou knowest it all" (38:18), "Knowest thou the ordinances of heaven? canst thou set the dominion thereof in the earth?" (38:33). But Pope modulates his stern tone by implying that the impulse to ask questions originates not from an inscrutable, intimidating God but from a "Presumptuous," theodicean inquirer: "the reason wouldst thou find, / Why form'd so weak, so little, and so blind! / First, if thou canst, the harder reason guess, / Why form'd no weaker, blinder, and no less!" (I, 35–8) Pope has comfortably descended to a sociable level, where hard reasons are hard for everybody. This relinquishing of authority soon intensified: "Of Systems possible, if 'tis confest / That Wisdom infinite must form the best"(43–4)—not at all a confession, inasmuch as the proposition's self-evidence (to Pope's mind, at least) is designed so as not to trouble us for an inner act of assent to it. Another admission of ignorance nudges the inquirer to accept that "There must be, somewhere, such a rank as Man" (48) and that any further questioning is nothing more or less than socially unpleasant: "And all the question (wrangle e'er so long) / Is only this, if God has plac'd him wrong?" (49–50) This transformation of the questioning mode from God out of the whirlwind to a genial, unimposing exchange that ideally falls short of actual parlor-room wrangling demonstrates the poem's unification of the uncertain and the secure: cosmic uncertainty does not frustrate or belie genial sociability but vitally underwrites it. Pope next displays his reluctance to be assertive even about tautologies: "Respecting Man, whatever wrong we call, / May, must be right as relative to all" (51–2)—hesitating from "May" to "must" if only to show just how hesitant he can be. The exchange concludes by revising the Joban and Pascalian challenge ("or can a part contain the whole?" [I, 32]) having accomplished this tonal modification: " 'Tis but a part we see, and not a whole" (60). The aim of the poem at large is to show how the security of the second can be neatly superimposed on the first's skeptical interrogations, even while the second represents a correction of the first's too authoritative tone.

This mollification of the uncertainty raised by God's authority contrasts with other more explicit usages of the interrogative passages of Job in the period. Young's *Paraphrase on Part of the Book of Job* (2d ed., 1719) notes that "*Longinus* has a Chapter on Interrogations, which shews that they contribute much to the Sublime. This Speech of the Almighty is made up of them. Interrogation seems indeed the proper Style of Majesty incensed."[64] The *"Part"* of Job that Young paraphrases is largely God's questioning: when God in the poem asks "can thy Span of Knowledge grasp the Ball?" (61), Young's poetic voice assumes an authority that Pope anxiously displaces. Similarly, Blackmore's earlier *Paraphrase on the Book of Job* (2d ed., 1716) amplifies God's authoritative questions (as everything else), which finally force Job to accept divine authority:

Convinc'd by thy Reproofs, I freely own
That I have rash, audacious Folly shown;

Vent'ring with Reason's short and treach'rous Line,
To sound the Depths of Providence Divine . . .
My stupid Arrogance I now condemn,
That made me speak on so sublime a Theme.
Such Wonders all Created Wit exceed,
And should our silent Admiration feed. (XLII, 13–6, 21–4)

Unlike these, Pope brings the divine interrogatives into a discursive milieu
even as they point to knowledge that must always surpass us. Divine questioning does not silence discussion in the *Essay* but rather leads it to a more
sociable register, incorporating a Pascalian uncertainty to enforce a liberty
of discourse in which no dogmatic authority may silence speech. By placing the dogmatic voice at the sublime, outer reaches of the public sphere,
decorum incorporates its negativity as a line of discipline.

But ironically Pope's manner of cherishing the liberalized public sphere
tends to turn it into a kind of never-never land in which an unknowing,
skeptically uncommitted toleration looks beyond the deeply held individual beliefs and actual disagreements that motivate the embrace of toleration in the first place.[65] The incompatible labels remain only as steps to a
more copious, emptier sense of agreement. As he writes to Swift in 1729,

> you know I am no enemy to the present constitution; I believe, as sincere
> a well-wisher to it, nay even to the church establish'd, as any minister in,
> or out of employment, whatever; or any Bishop of England or Ireland. Yet
> I am of the Religion of Erasmus, a Catholick; so I live; so I shall die; and
> hope one day to meet you, Bishop Atterbury, poor Craggs, Dr. Garth,
> Dean Berkely, and Mr. Hutchenson, in that place, To which God of his in-
> finite mercy bring us, and every body! (vol. 3, 81)

While Pope finds his Catholicism compatible with his support for the Constitution and the Anglican establishment, he implies that this compatibility,
extending to all his friends of various political and religious convictions,
will be fully satisfied only in Heaven and hence subsists in a tension with
actual social conditions. Strikingly, however, in 1733, when most of the
Essay has appeared, Pope writes to Swift: "The day is come, which I have
often wished, but never thought to see; when *every mortal that I esteem is of
the same sentiment in Politics and in Religion*" (vol. 3, 384). "An inexplicable remark!" is all Sherburn makes of it in his footnote to the letter, inasmuch as
Pope's friends included Catholics, Anglicans, Opposition Whigs, and even
Court Whigs like Fortescue.[66] The *Essay* does not claim that differences
among such groups have disappeared: as he insists in Epistle III, "In Faith

and Hope the world will disagree, / But all Mankind's Concern is Charity" (307–8). The very necessity of disagreement motivates our recognition of charity as the fundamental point of agreement. As he says in an earlier letter approving of a remark by Edward Blount, "the Variety of opinion in Politics or Religion is often rather a Gratification, than Objection, to people who have Sense enough to consider the beautiful order of Nature in her Variations" (I, 331). The public sphere as the poem imagines it is something like a heaven on earth but one that can be recognized and supported only through the necessary differences of opinion that compose it.

This ideal, however, is fundamentally resistant to explicable definition. Any too specific or defined set of principles would suppress differences among people and violate the principle of inclusion that establishes sociability in the first place. The public sphere thus must be perceived, ultimately, to be as mysterious as God's unfathomable providence, the ordinance of his higher authority that we can invoke only by urging that we cannot ever invoke it. Pope's unification of sociability and the relinquishing of theoretical reasoning manifests itself in an intense nominalism, an identification of our moral-social condition with the discourses we may agree upon to use to discuss it: "Cease then, nor ORDER Imperfection name: / Our proper bliss depends on what we blame" (I, 281–2). This injunction comes after the great vision of the universe as "one stupendous whole" (267), suggesting that we indeed perceive an "ORDER" that should forestall our caviling at the universe's apparent imperfections. But here and elsewhere Pope seems to ironize his own sublime vision, at least from a social standpoint: "Our proper bliss depends" not on our sharing an account of order—a religion or philosophy—but on our willingness to "name" whatever exists "ORDER."

Pope's refusal to reconcile vision with blindness, to theorize a serious, specifiable function for the sublime in our encounters with greatness and elaborate a nontautological economy between limit and unlimited, sets the *Essay* forever at the margins of the sublime tradition. But this marginal status itself proves potent as a challenge to theories that too readily perform their subjective mediations. It is the *Essay*'s discouragement of sublime vision, not any accomplishment of it, that influences Kant's *Universal Natural History and Theory of the Heavens* (1755),[67] published when he was twenty-one—an influence that reaches into the *Critique of Judgment* (1790) itself. The *Universal Natural History* quotes Pope throughout, and the *Essay* figures particularly importantly in the third and last part, "which contains an essay on a comparison, based on the analogies of nature, between the inhabitants of the various planets."[68] The part's epigraph, like Kant's other quotes from the *Essay*, comes from a bad German translation, which he doctored without apparently referring to the English original:

He who knows the relation of all worlds from one part to the other,
He who knows the quantity of all suns and each planetary orb,
He who recognizes the various inhabitants from each and every star,
To him alone is possible to grasp and to explain to us,
Why things are as they are. (182)[69]

—a version, of course, of Epistle I, lines 23 to 28, themselves derived from
Pascal, which offer a prospect of "What vary'd being peoples ev'ry star"
(27) only to deny it to us.

The most important element that Kant inherits from the *Essay* is its dual
dynamic of withholding and offering sublime vision, offering it by withholding it. This oscillation allows Kant to redraw Pope's ambivalent line between what we can and cannot know, seeking to limit the *Universal Natural
History*'s cosmological musings to "science" yet finding an invitation at such
limits to reach beyond them. More literally than Pope, Kant transforms this
dividedness into a definition of our limited, middle state: "the earth and
Mars . . . are the middle members of the planetary system, and perhaps not
without probability an intermediate physical as well as moral constitution
between the two extremes may be assumed about their inhabitants" (195).
Such "probable" speculations permit Kant to theorize about what the inhabitants of the other planets must be like: "*The stuff, out of which the inhabitants of different planets as well as the animals and plants on them, are built,
should in general be all the lighter and of finer kind, and the elasticity of the fibers
together with the principal disposition of their build should be all the more perfect,
the farther they stand from the sun*" (189). But all along Kant undercuts such
lofty speculations by referring to our own mental incapacity: "The sluggish-
ness of [humanity's] ability to think, which is a consequence of its dependence on gross and rigid matter, is the source not only of depravity but also
of error" (188). As in Pope, however, such recognitions seem to raise rather
than dampen his philosophical confidence. After citing the passage from the
Essay's Epistle I about "distances which the eye can never / Reach or view!"
Kant whimsically asks, "Should we permit ourselves one more escapade
from these [scientific] tracks into the field of phantasy? Who shows us the
limits where the well-founded probability ends and arbitrary fictions begin?"
(195) The line between science and phantasy is in one gesture drawn and vi-
olated: Kant distinguishes between "Arbitrary fictions" and "well-founded
probability" even as the difference provokes him to indulge in speculation.

But what emerges from such a clash of mutually implicating perspectives is not quite Pope's tautological emptiness. Kant's book reaches its
conclusion by rejecting its falsely "scientific" fantasies in favor of an essentially contentless apprehension of truth, which nonetheless reflects the
"secret motions of the soul" coursing through the sublime tradition:

It is permitted, it is pleasing to entertain oneself with such speculations; but nobody shall base the hope of future life on such uncertain pictures of the force of imagination. . . . In fact, when man his filled his soul with such considerations and with the foregoing ones, then the spectacle of a starry heaven in a clear night gives a kind of pleasure which only noble souls can absorb. In the universal quiet of nature and in the tranquillity of mind there speaks the hidden capacity for knowledge of the immortal soul in unspecifiable language and offers undeveloped concepts that can be grasped but not described. (196)

Thus Kant's extravagant musings, much like Pope's, prepare the mind for an apprehension of the truth even as this truth surpasses such musings, as well as any adequate expression: the universe speaks to us but in "unspecifiable language" and "undeveloped concepts." Kant finally recasts the *Essay*'s forbidding and encouragement of our adoption of God's perspective that he takes for his epigraph: it is the failure to be scientific, not the failure to be God, that throws us back on the sublimely indescribable. Pope's ironic theodicy, at once established and invalidated by the impossible survey of "distances which the eye can never reach," is thus taken up by Kant's cosmology, or his articulation of the line at which cosmology and our imaginative powers meet: "a kind of pleasure which only noble souls can absorb" helps Kant draw this line, not very different from the "strange and unwonted kind of internal sensation" of Boyle that allows us to intuit truths above reason. But Pope's *Essay* shies from positing such powers, insisting that our attunement to nature may appear only insofar as "All states can reach it, and all heads conceive" (IV, 30), noble or not: "Obvious her goods, in no extreme they dwell, / There needs but thinking right, and meaning well" (31–2). The subject, any subject, easily enough reads nature's objective, obvious goodness correctly by being emptily, tautologically disposed to be good.

Beyond theodicy and cosmology, the similarities and differences between Pope and Kant point to the "aesthetic" domain as the sublime helps to define it. The concluding passage of the *Universal Nature History* closely anticipates one in the "Analytic of the Sublime" in the *Critique of Judgment*. There, Kant defines the aesthetic judgment as apprehending a "purposiveness without purpose" in nature, a dim echo of the problematic demand in Pope's *Essay* for us to intuit creation's telos without positing it. As in the *Universal Natural History,* the third *Critique* forbids us to extend our terrestrial knowledge outward:

We must in all this be mindful of the injunction given above, namely, that the transcendental aesthetic of judgment must be concerned solely with pure aesthetic judgments. Hence we must not take for our examples such beautiful or sublime objects of nature that presuppose the concept of a purpose. . . . Therefore, when we call the sight of the starry sky *sublime,* we must not base our judgment upon any concept of worlds that are inhabited by rational beings, and then [conceive of] the bright dots that we see occupying the space above us as being these worlds' suns, moved in orbits prescribed for them with great purposiveness; but we must base our judgment regarding it merely on how we see it, as a vast vault encompassing everything, and merely under this presentation may we posit the sublimity that a pure aesthetic judgment attributes to this object . . . we must be able to view the ocean as poets do, merely in terms of what manifests itself to the eye. (130)

This only appears to reject his own earlier position. The line now serves to distinguish not the domains of science and "phantasy" but those of reason and aesthetics. Kant does not say that we can never view the universe as a purposive order: he says only that the aesthetic judgment does not do so. This stricture resembles others by Kant addressing the sublime, specifically the one quoted earlier concerning "the most sublime passage in the Jewish Law," that is, "the commandment: Thou shalt not make unto thee any graven image." Here, instead of forbidding the representation of God in what Pope called "mean and terrestrial images," sublime experience forbids projecting images of "rational beings" onto the "bright dots" that we see in the sky, finding a validating reflection of our own rationality in the heavens by populating them with beings like us—and so elevating the "mean and terrestrial" to sublime heights. Kant, at this late date, again faintly echoes Pope's stricture against speculating about "What vary'd being peoples ev'ry star." The key here, as in the *Universal Natural History* and the *Essay* itself, is to keep us from adopting God's perspective on the universe, from making the universe over in our image, even though this must tempt us. But despite Kant's sense of the limits of the aesthetic attitude, sublime experience calls forth a "pure aesthetic judgment" that indirectly confirms our "supersensible vocation" and higher destiny. The indirectness of this transcendental self-discovery, presented "merely in terms of what manifests itself to the eye," only enhances the subtlety and power of our union with the absolute, the mixture of human and divine.

But in Pope the sight-lines always seem to extend in the wrong direction. The end of the *Essay*'s Epistle IV presents a sublime vision of universal benevolence that connects the earthbound individual to Heaven:

God loves from Whole to Parts: but human soul
Must rise from Individual to the Whole.
Self-love but serves the virtuous mind to wake,

As the small pebble stirs the peaceful lake;
The centre mov'd, a circle strait succeeds,
Another still, and still another spreads,
Friend, parent, neighbor, first it will embrace,
His country next, and next all human race,
Wide and more wide, th'o'erflowings of the mind
Take ev'ry creature in, of ev'ry kind;
Earth smiles around, with boundless bounty blest,
And Heav'n beholds its image in his breast. (361–72)

As the "virtuous mind" expands, taking in more and more, Pope seems on his way toward affording it a sublime glimpse of "Heav'n," but he concludes, utterly characteristically, by reversing direction, so gently and reassuringly that it is easily missed: the spreading of human consciousness culminates not in the subject's transcendentally achieved perception of vast order, but in a vision of "Heav'n" beheld only by "Heav'n" itself, miniaturized to fit a human breast. A truly sociable citizen would have no need to behold any such image, either within or above himself, anyway. "To reason right" in the *Essay* does anticipate the Kantian aesthetic demand "to submit" our conceptual grasp of order in the universe to our negative awareness of God's absolute grasp of purposes we can never know. But it elaborates no subjective mechanism whereby our conformity to these purposes may be felt or beheld.

Kant's mediated, subjective appeal to authority performs, among other things, a quasi-political function (as commentators have argued).[70] His description of the aesthetic realm as essentially disinterested, a universal yet free exercise of subjective judgment, institutes a sphere in which individuals may and must disagree that itself demands the possibility of universal participation: "nothing is postulated in a judgment of taste except such a *universal voice* about a liking unmediated by concepts. Hence all that is postulated is the *possibility* of a judgment that is aesthetic and yet can be valid for everyone. The judgment of taste itself does not *postulate* everyone's agreement" (60). An emblem of such a society, again, appears in the universe, which invites and forbids our view of it as populated by "rational beings"—our desire, always open to failure, to find our judgments reflected back to us, from the stars, or from each other. Though perceivable as a rational community that includes us, the universe seen as sublime removes this possibility behind a veil of the purely visible. It thus models liberal society in its law against imposing an external vision of order on subjects already associated through their free exercise of subjectivity within it.

The *Essay*'s political significance lies in presenting a similar problem without offering a satisfying solution to it. Pope knows that subjects' disagreement in the world must be seen as "Harmony not understood" but refuses us access to the transcendental perspective that would allow us to recognize it as such. He cannot complete the system of the *Essay* as a sublimely satisfying depiction of liberally organized society because he cannot overcome the antidogmatism inherent in liberalism itself. Instead of positing nondogmatic, nonrational intuitions of harmony, as in the Whig sublime tradition, or a specially cohesive structure of "subjectively universal" judgments, as in Kant, Pope offers either tautological generalities or skeptical constraints on the ambitions of the universe's "parts" to comprehend the whole. As he accepts liberalism's problem, his conservatism traps him in it.

This divided skeptical view in the *Essay* bears out the attitude toward the sublime that appears in the notes to the *Iliad* and in *Peri Bathous*. There Pope suggests that divine authority may be recognized only in its disappearance behind the veil of the world, neither reducing itself to mean terrestrial images nor allowing the human sensibilities subject to it to identify sublimely with its fiats. Pope's sublime thus resembles Huet's, which mocks such elevations and reductions: "Not being able to raise themselves up to Him, they bring Him down to them." Skepticism, far from abolishing a sense of the sublime, elevates it out of sight, itself a paradoxical movement that generates a commanding but peculiarly empty authority. This sublime emptiness has convinced generations of readers of the *Essay's* sterility, as well as Pope himself, partially, who looks forward in "The Design" to further epistles that "will be less dry, and more susceptible of poetical ornament" (8)—an anxiety taken up in a slightly later letter to Swift, where he complains, "what I gain on the side of philosophy, I lose on the side of poetry" (vol. 4, 5). His Horatian poems in the 1730s do involve Pope more with the particularities of social and political life, yet he retains and even intensifies his desire to disappear into a state of skeptical beliefessness, a radical detachment from and disinterestedness in the social world that defines him. He furthermore will expressly associate this impersonality with what "poets do." Thus the embrace and rejection of the public sphere motivated by the logic of human limits in the *Essay* do prepare a kind of aesthetic attitude for Pope, though one still too deeply enmeshed in a Montaignean skepticism to realize any true anticipation of a "transcendental aesthetic of judgment."

5

Pope's *Imitations of Horace* and the Authority of Inconsistency

A skeptical current runs through Pope's *Imitations of Horace* (published from 1733 to 1738) that determines their most complicated ideological functions, especially his presentation of himself as a poet at once aloof from and mixing in the bewildering cultural forces driving 1730s Robinocracy. Pope's skepticism in the Horatian poems, equivocal as it is, elaborates on the desire expressed in *An Essay on Man* for his authority to disappear, no longer by losing himself in the neutral, unknowable structure of the universe but now by presenting a specific poetic voice that detaches him from his own beliefs and feelings through the very candor with which he expresses them. This detachment resembles skeptical attitudes discussed in earlier chapters, a modest rejection of the self-confidence and positivity of rationalist dogmatism, as Pope expresses it in his *Thoughts on Various Subjects* (1727): "Since 'tis reasonable to doubt most things, we should most of all doubt that Reason of ours which wou'd demonstrate all things."[1] But though resembling the Anglo-Catholic fideism of Dryden, or Swift's embrace of commonplaces of Anglican intellectual modesty, or the Pascalian humility modified by the *Essay*, Pope's Horatian discursive world is shaped not so much by religious controversy as by the explorations of virtue modeled in the Hellenistic philosophical schools, among them Pyrrhonistic and Academic skepticism.

In the 1730s, Pope confronts a society in which a kind of irrationality has prevailed, determined by uncertain fluctuations of opinions, party alignments, property, commerce, credit and debt, and even gender roles. As Pocock characterizes it, "the Walpolean writers proclaimed a world of kinetic history, without principles or virtue, in which men were governed through the interests and passions that made them what they were at the moment."[2] But instead of retreating from these modern threats behind a mask of Stoic sagacity, Pope engages them with his own gentlemanly skeptical attitudes, drawn especially from his beloved Montaigne, who teaches him to embrace inconstancy, contradiction, and doubt in order to master them, transforming contemporary chaos into a Hellenistic-Renaissance ideal of the self-possessed, worldly, undogmatic intellect. He thereby may remain actively bemused by the inconstancy of women, uncertain fluctuations of public opinion and party alliances, and the vagaries and vulgarities of the market, even admitting his share in their nature, without ultimately sullying himself with them—like investing in South Sea stock without assuming the moral nature of the stockjobbers. The ancient skeptical model furnishes him a powerful means of practicing what Maynard Mack has called "the pursuit of politics from the vantage of retirement."[3]

Apart from contributing to Pope's well-known ambivalence toward his satirical targets, this Montaignean posture offers a striking instance of aesthetic ideology, immersing the self in systems of modern subject-formation in its very claim to remain aloof from them. The aesthetic gains of such self-divisions particularly pertain to accounts of the sublime: the self finds itself split in its capacity to enjoy the powers that threaten it, ironically affirming its integrity in its subjection to chaos, disorder, and confusion. Unlike the self-division described by Swift in the *Tale* when the "mind of Man" soars "out of its own Reach and Sight," Pope deploys the self-divisions in the *Imitations of Horace* to stabilize himself and affirm his superiority to the forces to which he seems to succumb. What emerges is something like the theory of the sublime that the *Essay on Man* lacks, a discovery of how the self's loss of power can be turned into a source of power. Pope nonetheless preserves a distinctly skeptical sublime, refusing to posit the experience of some special feeling that rescues the self from its dissolution. Rather the dissolution itself is the rescue—an ideologically potent maneuver that elements of ancient skepticism suggest to him.

I

Criticism of Pope has long noted his intensely self-divided attitudes and considered them to be part of what makes his poetry compelling. Early in the 1970s, S. L. Goldberg stressed the "thoroughly dialectical" cast of Pope's imagination, and before that Thomas R. Edwards's *This Dark Estate* (1963) insisted on his ambivalence about his own "Augustan" values.[4] Others have given this portrait various political inflections: Laura Brown argues that his work reveals the contradictions inherent in the ideology he espoused, focusing on (e.g.) "the implicit ambivalence of Pope's imperialist poems" (27). In the introduction to *Critical Essays on Alexander Pope* (1993), Wallace Jackson summarizes the trend to view Pope's equivocations ideologically: "the poems articulate a political unconscious by involuntarily revealing obsessive associations that they cannot otherwise (that is, consciously) disclose. Note that it is often the poems and not Pope who does [sic] this, but the point is that Pope cannot do it, which is what is meant by 'self-divided.' "[5] Earlier critics had found unconscious forces at work in Pope that were less ideologically charged and had sometimes gropingly described them as his necessarily unaware anticipations of Romanticism—even "existentialism."[6] Despite these differences, both recent critics and their precursors have portrayed Pope's self-dividedness as not entirely intentional and instead presented it as coming from his rich imagination or his centrality in an ideologically constructed (hence self-contradicting) canon.[7]

But recognizing Pope's engagement with skepticism suggests how he chooses instead of represses equivocation, in support of an ideological position no less conservative but much more subtle and unstable than the one regularly ascribed to him. The ancient skeptic recognizes radical discontinuities among the various beliefs passing through him but only in order to secure the virtuous, becalmed integrity (*ataraxia*) sought by the philosophical schools of antiquity. Pope comes upon such a model of virtue in the Pyrrhonism of his favorite author, Montaigne—through whom he finds that the term can mean something more positive and edifying than mere intellectual extravagance or madness. He marks the following passage from the *Apology for Raimond de Sebonde* with hooks in the margins of his copy of Montaigne's *Essays:* "Whoever shall imagine a perpetual Confession of Ignorance, a Judgment without Bias, Propension or Inclination, upon any Occasion whatever, conceives a true *Idea of Pyrrhonisme*" (vol. 2, 297). Pope's Horatian poems often assert the moral and intellectual value of such a detachment from his beliefs and circumstances.

This sympathy cannot lead him to profess Pyrrhonism explicitly. There is no reason to suppose that he did not endorse Bolingbroke's condemnatory assessment, expressed in *Fragments or Minutes of Essays,* that "the Pyrrhonian is against all sides: and all sides are against him"[8] or Atterbury's complaint to Pope that skepticism "endeavours only to put us into a way of distrusting our own faculties, and doubting whether the marks of truth and falsehood can in any case be distinguish'd from each other."[9] It is perhaps skepticism's intellectually illicit nature that grants it special power in his work, something he enjoys entertaining but does not profess. Academic skepticism, though seen by some commentators as a more moderate strand, also smacks of intellectual danger and illegitimacy in Pope's immediate intellectual circle. Bolingbroke attacks it in terms even angrier than those flung at Pyrrhonism: "the Academician would pass, if he could, for a neuter, who is for no side, nor against any; or else for a trimmer, who changes sides often, and finds the probable sometimes on one, sometimes on the other" (vol. 4, 278). The idea, proposed by Harry Solomon in *The Rape of the Text*, that Academic doubt is something that Pope could comfortably profess because it was recognized as respectably moderate, seems belied by the commonness of such extreme characterizations. But negative and extreme as it is, Bolingbroke's depiction of the Academic's protean nature resonates with many of the postures adopted by Pope in the *Imitations*, sometimes in direct, playful opposition to his "Guide, Philosopher, and Friend." It is skepticism's very extremism, in both its Pyrrhonistic and Academic forms, that appeals to Pope: it appears in his work across a finely shaded continuum, from his most explicit admirations for Montaigne and other challengers of reason to his less conscious attractions to intellectual extravagance and disorder.

The power of doubt, at once dangerous and stimulating, encourages Pope to adopt an authorial persona rife with ironies, admitting his various contradictory beliefs and desires without fixing himself in any of them. In ideological terms, ancient skepticism allows him to express his sympathy for Roman Republican, anticommercial, "civic" conceptions of virtue while accepting the speculative, unstable, epistemologically unraveling forces that he saw rampant in his culture—in essence a method of having things both ways. Skepticism in this sense responds to Pope's own equivocal position in eighteenth-century politics. For those with whom Pope was politically associated, as Pocock argues, property in land remained the best way for the virtuous personality to ward off the inevitably corrupting influence of "relationships governed by the media of exchange" in a ceaselessly active marketplace always destabilized by the fluidity of public credit.[10] Of all the models of virtue that Horace presents from the ancient schools, the skeptical version helps Pope best negotiate the irony of his achieving virtuous independence through the marketing of his translations of Homer and of guarding this integrity in rural retirement on a leased estate.[11] Since skeptical philosophy always advises extreme conservatism, finding the status quo to be the safest bet in a radically dubious world, the ascription of it to Pope complements the prevalent views of him from Brown and others. But the skeptic's undermining of all justification makes him at best an ambiguous ally of the civic order, and the doubt Pope uses to enunciate his allegiance to conservative cultural ideals also at times exposes their unjustifiability.

The identification of a sense of selfhood with virtue distinguishes Pope's discourse in the *Imitations* from more purely epistemological, modern debates about personal identity begun by Locke, in the *Essay Concerning Human Understanding* (2d ed., 1694, when the section "Of Identity and Diversity" was added as chapter 27 of book II), who found the language of personhood (especially in its forensic function) to be incommensurable with the language of substance.[12] Locke's position itself has been seen to render personal identity dubious in a new way but must be differentiated from the issues of ethical identity raised in Hellenistic philosophy and the role that ancient skepticism plays in securing the virtuous self. The commentator Christopher Fox seeks to determine the influence of the Lockean debate on Pope and Swift, specifically whether they accepted Locke's depiction of the "self-in-consciousness" or the position, forcefully argued by Bishop Butler,[13] that the self must be an unchanging substance: a soul. Fox tentatively concludes that Pope's sympathies lay with what we would see as Butler's position—largely from his reading of the following passage from *To Cobham*:

Oft in the Passions' wild rotation tost,
Our spring of action to ourselves is lost:
Tir'd, not determin'd, to the last we yield,
And what comes then is master of the field.
As the last image of that troubled heap,
When Sense subsides, and Fancy sports in sleep,
(Tho' past the recollection of the thought)
Becomes the stuff of which our dream is wrought:
Something as dim to our internal view,
Is thus, perhaps, the cause of most we do. (41–50)

Fox argues that "Something" could refer to the substantial soul, suggesting that Pope is "positing that our personality does inhere in 'something' simple and individual."[14] While denying us adequate knowledge of this substance that grounds our identities, Pope betrays his faith that it must exist. Locke's notion of "consciousness" as the sole factor determining identity seems to be rejected because Pope specifically derives the motives definitive of the self from elements of which it is unconscious or semiconscious.

However, if "Something" is meant to refer to the self's substantial grounding, the soul, it would not be the cause of "most we do" but of all we do, insofar as it is seen as the factor causally constitutive of identity. The contrast between "most we do" and the rest of it—the former caused unconsciously, the latter consciously—instead extends from the ancient contrast of passion and reason. We lose or are unconscious of "our spring of action" because it lies in our unreflective or opaque passions, which evade rational scrutiny. Our deeds are "not determin'd" by reason or judgment but instead are motivated nonrationally, by feelings (or, as here, exhaustion of feeling). Similarly "Fancy" predominates over good rational sense. If "Something" refers to such nonrational forces, as seems plausible, then it may indeed cause just "most we do," not all. (Pope here does not care to deny that reason causes a few actions now and then.) But on this reading "Something" cannot refer to our dim intimations of the substantial soul because it is absurd in the world of Pope's discourse to see passion as more affiliated with spiritual substance (or any source of personal stability) than reason. "Something" means "some passion or other," unstable in itself and constantly giving way to new passions, hence particularly ill-suited to provide the ground for identity. The phrase "internal view" is a peculiarly Lockean way to characterize reason's perspective on the passions. But as is often the case, Pope inlays a vocabulary that sounds modern somewhat inexactly into argumentative patterns familiar from antiquity.

Locke's view at the time was considered a kind of skepticism, so designated because he asserted "that *self* is not determined by Identity or Diversity of substance, which it cannot be sure of, but only by Identity of consciousness."[15] But Locke, far from denying in the spirit of ancient skepticism that the problem of personal identity (qua philosophical problem) could ever be solved, proposes his solution with confidence. His assertion that "we cannot be sure of" our substantial souls reflects a "skeptical" attitude toward a religious tenet. But by saying that our sense of self arises out of "identity of consciousness," Locke thinks he is explaining personal identity to us, not rendering the question insoluble. While Lockean epistemology prepares the way for Hume's radically skeptical and "modern" notion that "the identity, which we ascribe to the mind of man, is only a fictitious one,"[16] for Locke it was real enough.

The "Pyrrhonian" strand that Pope finds in Montaigne, arguing that human beings "are nothing but shifting, and inconstancy" (vol. 2, 4), belongs to an older, less purely epistemological tradition. In *Pope and Horace* (1985), Frank Stack rightly stresses the connection between the *Imitations'* explorations of selfhood and the eudaemonistic, self-disciplinary motives of the ancient schools. As Stack notes, the phrase Horace uses to refer to the consistent self is *æquus animus*, which Pope translates in the following lines on Bethel from his imitation of *Satire II, 2* (1734): "His equal mind I copy what I can, / And as I love, would imitate the Man" (131–2). For Pope, having an equal mind is equivalent to locating one's "true inner self"[17] (in Stack's phrase) because it assures one of personal coherence or identity through time regardless of changing circumstances: according to the ancient schools, personal coherence is the necessary condition for a virtuous life. Conversely, disequilibrium in our moral being threatens our sense of identity, as in Pope's imitation of *Epistle I, 6:* "Thus good, or bad, to one extreme betray / Th'unbalanc'd Mind, and snatch the Man away" (24–5). One cogent expression of this linkage of virtue and identity appears in Seneca's *Epistles to Lucilius,* in which he comments with a Stoic's disapproval on an inconstant person depicted in Horace's *Satire I, 3* (11–17):

The men I speak of are of this stamp: they are like the man whom Horatius Flaccus describes—a man who is never even like himself; to such an extent does he wander off into opposites. . . . That is how a foolish mind is most clearly demonstrated: it shows first in this shape and then in that, and is never like itself—which is, in my opinion, the most shameful of qualities. Believe me, it is a great role, to play the role of one man. But nobody can be one person except the wise man; the rest of us often shift our masks.[18]

Seneca here celebrates the moral consistency of "the wise man," the Stoic sage who attains stability through his apprehension of the world's true nature. Pope and Bolingbroke quote this epistle in a jointly written letter to Swift, in which they name "Perfect Tranquillity" as the wise man's proper goal: "Reflection and Habit have rendred the World so indifferent to me, that I am neither afflicted nor rejoiced, angry nor pleased at what happens in it" (*Correspondence*, vol. 2, 187–8). This attained detachment is the only philosophical route to constancy and provides the only basis for the personal identity that Pope seeks.

One of the most thorough cases in the *Imitations* for the virtues of an "equal mind" is made in one of the last of them, the *Nil admirari, Epistle I, 6,* published in 1738, which begins: " 'NOT to Admire, is all the Art I know, / 'To make men happy, and to keep them so.' " The importance of this tag to Pope's thinking is suggested by the fact that the motto "Nil admirari" appears on a scroll in the headpiece of Epistle I of the *Essay on Man* (1734 edition),[19] his "system of Ethics in the Horatian way" (*Correspondence*, vol. 3, 81). He explains the phrase's relevance in a letter to Swift about the *Essay* in progress, affirming that he seeks to "make mankind less Admirers, and greater Reasoners" (vol. 3, 250). Stack says of Horace's original that the "neat phrase 'Nil admirari' suggests the *ataraxia* of the Epicureans or the *apatheia* of the Stoics, a calm equanimity of mind, an absence of intense emotion" (207). Even as the poem recommends us to the good life, however, it seems to cast doubt on our capacity to attain it, both renouncing the sources of apparent happiness—wealth, popularity, power, sensory indulgence—and pointedly declining to represent good living otherwise than negatively as the lack of admiration for such things. Pope even shies from presenting an exemplary picture of a Stoic sage or Christian saint adhering to a rigidly virtuous code, because "For Vertue's self may too much Zeal be had; / The worst of Madmen is a Saint run mad" (26–7). Nor does he unequivocally come to celebrate moderate Epicurean pleasures. Rather he confines himself to enumerating false goods and describing their inescapable power. Stack notes this irony at the poem's heart in his appraisal of the critical reception of Horace's original: "It is very striking . . . that while modern critics discover sustained scepticism in this epistle, eighteenth-century interpreters saw it as an expression of high moral idealism" (203).

A short solution to the dilemma is that ancient skepticism itself is an expression of a kind of high moral idealism. Ataraxia is a key term not just for the Epicureans (as Stack notes) but also for the Pyrrhonian skeptics, who use it to designate the imperturbable calm, the equal mind essential to the virtuous life, that follows their procedures of total doubt—the payoff that dignifies Pyrrhonism as a eudaemonistic philosophy. Again, it could not be claimed that Pope or Horace explicitly sought to state Pyrrhonist principles. Niall Rudd, in his *Satires of Horace* (1966), shows that "by the time when Horace was writing his *Satires* . . . the distinctions between the main philosophical schools had become blurred on a number of points,"[20] and Horace's poetry bears traces of Academic skepticism, Stoicism, Epicureanism, and Cyrenaicism in an eclectic jumble. While commentators notice "skeptical" tendencies in Horace's poems, they do not speculate much about whether he adhered to the skeptical principles of the Academy. Many candidates for Horace's philosophical models have been put forward. In the preface of *Sylvæ* (1685), Dryden's collection of Latin translations, including several Horatian ones, he affirms, *"His Morals are uniform, and run through all of them; For let his* Dutch *Commentatours say what they will, his Philosophy was Epicurean."*[21] The "eighteenth-century interpreters" who identify the "high moral idealism" of the nil admirari mentioned by Stack (203–7), moreover, do not have skeptical ataraxia in mind: Dacier sees the poem as consonant with Stoicism and the Christian disdain for the world, and Shaftesbury draws parallels between the poem and Epictetus.

Nonetheless the view that Horace's poem represents a skeptical perspective is something of a commonplace in the French authors Pope names as his leading influences. This view would have been familiar to him from the *Apology for Raimond de Sebonde,* where Montaigne remarks:

> Some say that our well being lies in Vertue, others in Pleasure, others in our submitting to *Nature:* One in Knowledge, another in being exempt from Pain, another in not suffering ourselves to be carried away by Appearances: and this fancy seems to have some relation to that of the Ancient *Pythagoras:*
>
>> *Nil admirari prope res est una Numaci,*
>> *Solaque quae possit facere, & servare beatum.*
>> Nothing t'admire's the only thing I know
>> Can make us happy, and can keep us so.
>
> Which is the drift of the *Pyrrhonian Sect.* (vol. 2, 407)

Montaigne continues to suggest that for him the Horatian tag expresses the beliefs of "the *Pyrrhonians* . . . [who] say that the Ataraxy, which is the

Immobility of Judgment, is the sovereign Good" (vol. 2, 410). In his *Of Wisdome*, Pierre Charron (whom Pope calls "more sage Charron" in the *Epistle to Cobham*, 146) recasts this passage from Montaigne in arguing for his own ideal of skeptical detachment:

> This Temper is in some sense like that of *Ataraxie*, which *Pyrrho's* sceptical Followers called the supreme Happiness of Man: But if that Resemblance be a little over-strain'd, yet it may very well bear being compared to the Neutrality and Indifference which the Sect of the Academicks professed. And the natural Effect of such a Temper is, to be discomposed or astonished at nothing; which *Pythagoras* thought the Sovereign Good, and *Aristotle* called the true Greatness of Soul. So *Horace* . . . [22]

And he concludes by citing the Horatian nil admirari. Pascal also offers a version of this discussion in the *Pensées* (in a passage that Pope is unlikely to have known), though without endorsing Horace's solution to human happiness as his predecessors do: one school finds happiness "in happy ignorance, another in doing nothing, yet more in not being taken in by appearances, another in admiring nothing—*Nihil mirari prope res una quae possit facere et servare beatum*—and these fine Pyrrhonists with their Stoical ataraxia, doubt, and perpetual suspension of judgement."[23] There is evidence, furthermore, that Pope understood the skeptical possibilities of Horace's phrase as noted by Montaigne, Charron, and Pascal. He marks Montaigne's *Apology* in several places that associate a lack of admiration with Sextus's skepticism, like the passage quoted earlier that associates "a Judgment without Bias, Propension or Inclination, upon any Occasion" with "*Pyrrhonisme*," or another, emphasized with Pope's double hooks, asserting that "A Soul clear from Prejudice, has a marvailous Advance towards Tranquillity and Repose" (vol. 2, 299).

Beyond its opening, the poem's coupling throughout of an idealistic promotion of the good with its ironic tendency to keep the "Soul clear" of any philosophical alternatives to admiration replicates the Pyrrhonist program fairly exactly. In the ancient skeptic's view, any such alternative, any positive definition or depiction of the good, would be just another emptily admirable (and hence dubious) version of the truth. He must instead find the good by maintaining his doubt. As Sextus Empiricus writes in the *Outlines of Pyrrhonism* (which Pope owned in its entirety in his edition of Thomas Stanley's *History of Philosophy*, 1701):

> We say that the End of the *Sceptick* is *ataraxia, Indisturbance*, in whatsoever belongs to Opinion, and Moderation, in whatsoever belongs to Compulsion. For beginning to study Philosophy, that he may descern and comprehend which Phantasies are True, which false, and by that means not to

be disquieted, he lights upon an equivalent Contrariety, of which not being able to judge, he suspends; and whilst he is accidentally in this Suspence, there follows it an Indisturbance as to things Opinionative.[24]

Sextus's conception of opinion applies beyond matters of mere factual truth and falsity, extending to any sort of gratification that we (mistakenly) think equals true happiness. For Sextus, such faith in our desires amounts to the opinion that "there is something Good or Bad in its own nature":

> when those things which seem to him good, are not present, he imagineth himself tormented with things Ill in their own nature, and pursueth that he conceives to be Good; which having obtained, he falleth into more Troubles. For being unreasonably and immoderately transported, and fearing a change, he useth all endeavour that he may not lose those things which he conceives Good. Whereas he who defines nothing concerning Things naturally Good or Bad, neither flyeth nor pursueth any thing eagerly, so that he remains undisturbed. (477a)

Pope's imitation develops just this theme. Any attained pleasure betrays us to personal inconsistency and "Troubles" because unsettling fears of being deprived of it attend it by definition: "If weak the pleasure that from these [illusory goods] can spring, / The fear to want them is as weak a thing; / Whether we dread, or whether we desire, / In either case, believe me, we admire" (18–21). Throughout Pope emphasizes the "immoderate" tendencies of admiration, for instance, of wealth: "If Wealth alone then make and keep us blest, / Still, still be getting, never, never rest" (95–6). While admiration is strong enough to carry us to any extreme, it is also "weak" because it is unsteady and unsteadying.

It is true that for both Pope and Horace, virtue emerges as the unquestionable center of value: "Would ye be blest? despise low Joys, low Gains; / Disdain whatever CORNBURY disdains; / Be Virtuous, and be happy for your pains" (60–2); "Vis recte vivere? quis non? / Si Virtus hoc una potest dare, / fortis omissis/Hoc age deliciis" (29–31).[25] The commentator M. J. McGann argues that this moment in Horace is specifically Stoic: "As the austerity of fortis omissis deliciis suggests, Horace is speaking of the Stoic pursuit of virtue."[26] But both Horace and Pope are here and elsewhere content to define virtue negatively as the rejection of trifles, of "low Joys" (and all the schools would advise ridding oneself of "low" things), not by proposing a markedly Stoic definition of high ones. Pope's departure from the Horatian original, the addition of the compliment to Cornbury, again avoids defining virtue positively, holding it up as "whatever" the virtuous example "disdains," not what he affirms philosophically, or politically, in his association (though a Tory) with the Cobhamite Whig Opposition. Pope's avoidance of positive characterizations of virtue correlates with his aloof Horatian persona in the 1730s, reluctant to embrace any expressed political extreme,[27] which comports with the poem's sense of skeptical detachment.

But the poem most significantly reflects Sextus's procedure by uniting the disinclination to state any possible alternative to admiration with an attempt to free us from it: such freedom arises (if at all) like the skeptic's ataraxia, not by philosophical design or precept but "accidentally," after we are confronted with various powerful but ultimately empty and unstable desires. The poem's guiding double irony exacts this paradoxical dynamic. At line 17, Horace has *"I nunc, argentum & marmor vetus, æraque & artes / Suspice"* (17–8), which Pope renders as "Go then, and if you can, admire the state / Of beaming diamonds, and reflected plate" (28–9). The irony of such advice, composing the body of the poem, lies not just in its being so obviously bad—to heed it will pointedly not "make men happy"—but also in the fact that to advise anyone to admire something is a kind of category mistake. Part of the joke is that Pope and Horace prescribe various self-absorbing feelings as if the addressee could rationally will to have or not to have them. Pope's addition of the phrase "and if you can" underscores this suggestion, acknowledging that rational will, that is, the faculty that "philosophical" advice engages, cannot direct our admirations. One simply is or is not the type of person who gets excited by fine material objects. The same irony subsequently appears in oblique references to our passivity before our passions, for example, when Pope tells us to "Be struck by bright Brocade" (32) or admits that "If not so pleas'd"(34) we will turn to something else. No doubt these carry the subsidiary meaning that admirations can be acquired and cultivated. But the oddness of being told to "Be struck" by something comes from our knowing that we cannot really choose what is or is not striking to us. In a backhanded way, then, the ironic recommendations play on admiration's power. Though they implicitly advise us to do the opposite of what they say (do not admire diamonds), they also hint that no amount of sound advice can free us completely from admiration.

Similarly, the skeptic concedes admiration's ubiquitous "force," in fact requires it to attain ataraxia: because admiration is too powerful to be actively dispelled, the skeptic must use its power against itself to escape it. He allows destabilizing desires to operate, as it were, within him, that they may cancel each other out, purging him of them and landing him "accidentally" in the state of ataraxia he wanted from the beginning. Pope also uses desire against itself in a pattern taken up through a large part of the advice to come. He first asks a general question about the addressee's proclivities and then recommends that these be exacerbated to hideous extremes: "But art thou one, whom new opinions sway . . . ? Fly then, on all the wings of wild desire! / Admire whate'er the maddest can admire" (63–8); "Is Wealth thy passion? Hence! from Pole to Pole . . . Advance thy golden Mountain to the skies" (69–73); "But if to Pow'r and Place your Passion lye . . . Then hire a Slave, (or if you will, a Lord)" (97–99). The questions emphasize admiration's power by assuming that it already dominates us in one form or another. But they also clarify the moral purpose of Pope's irony: after identifying one of our possible propensities toward vice, he caricatures it to uncover its emptiness—as a reductio ad absurdum asks us to exaggerate a false principle we believe in to get us to stop believing it. In this sense his advice is sincere: he wants us to view as vividly as possible the grotesque extremities of lust, greed, and the rest so as to purge our own less exaggerated lusts and greediness.

Thus though the advice at one level suggests admiration's power over rationality,[28] the poem's irony seeks an aloof mastery over the admirations it depicts. Pope asks us to pursue false goods hypothetically as a kind of thought experiment in order to impart an especially skeptical wisdom to us, which consists in being tranquilly detached from them without substituting any stated good in their place. The Academic skeptic Carneades spectacularly illustrated this technique in a famous episode from antiquity, as Stanley describes it: "The Eloquence of *Carneades* was violent and rapid. . . . [he] one day disputed copiously concerning Justice before *Galba* and *Cato*, the greatest orators of that time. The next day he subverted all he had said before by contrary Arguments, and took away that Justice which he had so much commended" (*History of Philosophy*, 223b). This exemplifies the technique of arguing *in utrumque partem*, in Cicero's phrase in *Academica*:[29] Carneades' arguing both sides of the case demonstrates his lack of admiration for either without affirming any third position of his own,[30] confirming Bolingbroke's characterization of the Academic as a "neuter," as one "who changes sides often." Like Pope, Carneades obviously does not believe in what he recommends. He practices epochē, the withholding of assent, an ironic bracketing of each side even as he presents it. But nonetheless the propensity of our minds to be swayed by passions and opinions is essential for us to make our chance discovery of ataraxia: we need to be in some sense convinced of one version of the truth and then equally convinced of another. Our argumentative personae can cancel each other out only if we hold each with a measure of candor. Like Pope's irony in this epistle, the skeptical procedure functions through a dual assumption of the power and instability of admiration.

While skepticism offers us an "equal mind," a steadied identity, it does so by forcing us to acknowledge and indeed cultivate a special kind of self-division. When Carneades switches from justice to injustice, he presents us with an especially exaggerated, even formalized picture of the inconstant person deplored by Stoics like Seneca and satirized by Pope in the *Epistles to Cobham* and *To a Lady*. Pope displays his own inconstancy throughout the *Imitations*—"each Opinion with the next at strife, / One ebb and flow of follies all my Life" (*Epistle I, 1, 167–8*). But such admissions come to express, like Carneades' tactic, a sophisticated self-control separate from any and all opinions, which constitutes his superiority not only over his inconstant satirical targets but also over any proud "sage" who thinks escape from inconstancy is possible. This procedure depends on what may well be an impracticable self-fragmentation: the ancient skeptic in effect says (in philosopher Myles Burnyeat's words), "It is thought within me that *p*, but *I* do not believe it."[31] The *I* who hovers apart from his own opinions, his beliefs and desires, attains a ghostly equanimity at the expense of being expressible or even representable, occluded by the various admirations constituting "him."

It may be objected that the recommendations in *Epistle I, 6* are too obviously ironic to generate the tension required for skeptical ataraxia to arise. Rather they announce a lot of obvious vices that Pope himself could never begin to admire and thus by their very crudeness establish an unskeptical, Stoic possibility of a complete, rationally achieved escape from them. Whether or not Pope himself felt their pull, his poem turns toward an ambiguous acceptance of them at the end:

If, after all, we must with Wilmot own,
The Cordial Drop of Life is Love alone,
And Swift cry wisely, "Vive la Bagatelle!"
The Man that loves and laughs, must sure do well.
Adieu—if this advice appear the worst,
E'en take the Counsel which I gave you first:
Or better Precepts if you can impart,
Why do, I'll follow them with all my heart. (126–33)

The irony of Pope's attitude to the body of advice given in the poem floats off in a number of bewildering directions. These lines immediately follow the sarcastic advice that we "ev'ry Decency confound, / Thro' Taverns, Stews, and Bagnio's take our round" (119–20): we hardly expect a way out of such gross sensuality from Rochester ("Wilmot"), who "was of a very bad turn of mind, as well as debauched," as Pope told Spence.[32] But he seems to be approved, insofar as the line arguing that "The Man that loves and laughs, must sure do well" puts Rochester's advice on a par with Swift's. The passage blurs the distinction between ironic and unironic advice, placing the former on a continuum with the latter.

Pope finally seems to throw up his hands, refusing to privilege any advice thus far given. But the conclusion does balance candor and irony in a way that suggests the poem's affiliation with the skeptical procedure. Ambiguities of reference again make it difficult to distinguish the serious from the ironic advice: when Pope asks "if this advice appear the worst," we cannot tell whether "this advice" refers to that immediately preceding—"The Man that loves and laughs, must sure do well" (129)—or to all the heavily sarcastic recommendations through the body of the poem. Similarly, "the Counsel which I gave you first" (not present in Horace) could mean again the poem's sarcasm or its sincere first injunction, to admire nothing. The latter, perhaps predominant possibility mitigates Pope's commitment even to the notion of nil admirari itself, now set against the advice to love and laugh as if our deciding between them were a mere matter of taste. And in the same vein, his parting promise to follow "better Precepts if you can impart . . . with all my heart" (again, not present in the original) opposes the sense that nil admirari is the last word, both because he admits that some better advice may come along and because following any advice with all one's heart smacks strongly of admiration. The final reference to the heart reasserts the sincerity shadowing Pope's irony that resonates with the skeptical procedure: here and in other of the *Imitations of Horace* that offer wisdom and advice, Pope fosters an ironic detachment by keeping the possibility of candid, admiring engagement in belief alive.

II

The idea that unknowable elements of experience recommend a detachment from the passions and opinions passing through us helps Pope produce not just a general model of virtue but also a sense of his own vocation as a poet. To some, skepticism has seemed out of place among his poetry's dominant values: Thomas Edwards suggests that he cannot fully accept his own poetic "Augustan synthesis" because he is "the ungrateful heir of two hundred years of skepticism";[33] while Fredric Bogel treats the "skeptical imagination" as something that Pope must confront and overcome in his drive toward "Augustan knowledge."[34] Still, the idea of the unknowable consistently helps define the exemplary neoclassical poetic effect, from the emergence of the je ne sais quoi in France in the late seventeenth century onward. Pope articulates versions of it at various points in his career, from the *"nameless Graces"* of the *Essay on Criticism* to the *Epistle to Burlington*'s celebration of gardening elements that "pleasingly confound" and offer "artful wildness to perplex the scene," revealing a link between epistemological frustration and aesthetic pleasure. The idea that beauty's charms depend on its formal unknowability is commonplace. Shenstone's poem *"Je Ne Sçais Quoi"* (1737) strongly links the "The Poet's fancy'd Muse" (24) to skeptical uncertainty: "The Sceptick strove thy [the je ne sais quoi's] gen'ral claim to shew, / Disown'd by Moderns, yet from thee we know / Their wild Debates arose, to thee at last must flow."[35] The ideological force of this connection between taste and skepticism appears in Shaftesburyan and Addisonian critical discourse, as Howard Caygill argues, in order to align the mysterious design of providence with the practice of sociable virtue. Attuned to nonrational feelings, taste insures a harmony of social relations by suppressing inquiry into the actual, political "violence" of their production, which Mandeville points out as the hidden element of Shaftesbury's system.[36] In this the je ne sais quoi functions in much the same way as the sublime in various accounts, from Dennis to Shaftesbury and Addison, who appeal to it to square invocations of providential order with civil society's imperative to avoid dogmatic assumptions of authority.

Pope's Horatian postures of the 1730s participate in this tradition but add an intentional skeptical irony. Instead of succumbing to feeling blindly, in the conviction that it will discover a harmony among otherwise differing subjects in society, he cannily allows various admirations to overcome him in order to separate himself from them, standing aloof from the "world of kinetic history" even as he allows its chaotic forces to express themselves in his own fluid personality. The engaged detachment of Pope's skeptical attitude hence blends Shaftesbury's faith in the ordering power of the refined passions with Mandeville's critical awareness of their ultimately politically interested nature. Critics often note the combination of these opposite programs in his poems of the 1730s and usually see it as an inadvertent but ideologically potent kind of muddle: for instance, *To Bathurst* vacillates between accepting the greed of "Old Cotta" as a providentially beneficial social force and virtuously rejecting such admirations because they serve capitalistic delusions.[37] But Pope's deployment of the nil admirari suggests just how usefully and elaborately connected to a conscious pattern of poetic self-division these mixed attitudes are: he at once embraces and distances himself from admirations, and doing one allows him to do the other, participating in civil society's providential order through a critique of it.

The Longinian sublime offers a primary model for this poetics of self-fragmentation. In "A Reading of Longinus," Neil Hertz defines "the sublime turn" as "the movement of disintegration and figurative reconstitution" of the self, whether in Sappho's experience of self-dissolving admiration for her lover reconstituted in the lyric poem that Longinus's text preserves for us or in Longinus's critical use of fragments of other authors to compose his own sublime discourse.[38] Pope similarly seeks, at important moments of the *Imitations*, to admit that his poetic self is fragmentary and inconstant only to reassert its invisible coherence at a higher level. In "The Subject of the Subject and the Sublimities of Self-Reference" (1993), Jonathan Lamb attributes this dynamic to the sublime oratory of Pitt:

"It gave him great advantages to serve a turn," Shelburne pointed out, "by enabling him to change like lightning from one set of principles to another." The fact that he can do this and still keep command of his audience suggests that Pitt's choice of choices has led him to the exposure precisely of the negativity that lies behind the managed gesture of self-exposure, and that neither the gesture nor the negativity spoil the stunning effect of the performance they constitute as well as point to.[39]

Pope's poetic persona also performs "the managed gesture of self-exposure," not to win any immediate rhetorical goal so much as to assume the power of negativity in general. This power, again, can best be understood as a display of the ancient ideal of the equal mind, and its negativity is insured by its skeptical reluctance to identify with any single cause, agenda, or named, programmatic virtue. For Pope, this reluctance helps constitute the self in its role as the disinterested (hence protoaesthetic) poet.

This connection of the ancient skeptic's detached bemusement with the neoclassical poetic attitude obliquely contrasts with the emphases of Stanley Cavell, the most important writer on skepticism and literature—especially Romantic aesthetics, which he reads back into a Romanticized, epistemologized Shakespeare. Cavell consistently interprets texts in terms of the modern tradition of Descartes (reflected also in the sublime doubts attending Cartesian philosophy satirized by Rochester, Dryden, and Swift). In *Disowning Knowledge in Six Plays of Shakespeare* (1987), Cavell downplays the considerable (and documentable) influence on Shakespeare of Montaigne, who retains ties to the ancient mode, especially through Sextus Empiricus, in favor of comparing Shakespearean tragedy to the modern, Cartesian predicament:

> However strong the presence of Montaigne and Montaigne's skepticism is in various of Shakespeare's plays, the skeptical problematic I have in mind is given its philosophical refinement in Descartes' way of raising the questions of God's existence and of the immortality of the soul. . . . The issue posed is no longer, or not alone, as with earlier skepticism, how to conduct oneself best in an uncertain world; the issue suggested is how to live at all in a groundless world. Our skepticism is a function of our now illimitable desire.[40]

Cavell finds a brand of skepticism at work in Shakespearean tragedies that is compatible with their wrenching aesthetic effect and that points ahead to his own reading of Romanticism. His dismissal of "earlier skepticism" could be taken to imply that the ancient mode ("how to conduct oneself best in an uncertain world") is simply less severe than modernity's confrontation with absolute groundlessness, a merely expedient pose assumed toward a variety of uncertainties, always leaving some undoubted ground under our feet upon which we may conduct our lives. This contrast perhaps suggests that ancient skepticism fails to engage questions concerning intentionality, selfhood, and reason radically enough to energize poetry in a way comparable to the one that has interested Cavell in his literary criticism.

But Pyrrhonistic skepticism is no less *epistemologically* radical than Cartesian fantasies about the *malin genie* that Cavell takes to represent the modern type. Sextus seeks to show that we should suspend judgment on everything, from God and immortality to the most basic sensory appearances, including the way things look and feel. Ancient skepticism's extremity, moreover, has been recognized from its inception, as Stoics and others have criticized Pyrrhonism precisely because its doubts are too radical to sustain, charging that the very stability of the skeptics' lives (their tendency not to walk off precipices) confutes their position. Cavell's turn from it has ties to this tradition of criticism: central to his project is the idea that modern skepticism is inherently incompatible with ordinary life,[41] and he may find the ancient mode's promise to unite the two shallow or somehow false, at least since Descartes. This tradition of attack on the ancient mode has been considered by Myles Burnyeat in his seminal essay "Can the Skeptic Live His Skepticism?" He comes to answer this question in the negative, arguing that Sextus's program requires the skeptic to do something impossible: detach himself from the person (himself) who finds an argument convincing, "treating his own thought as if it were the thought of someone else . . . saying, in effect, [as I quoted earlier] 'It is thought within me that *p*, but *I* do not believe it'" (140). This operation is particularly difficult to perform when the arguments found provisionally (but not ultimately) convincing are the very skeptical ones that motivate it in the first place. Burnyeat concludes that while such an attitude may be struck fitfully, it cannot extend through a person's whole life—and therefore that ancient skepticism is deeply incoherent. In this his position resonates with characteristically modern depictions (including Descartes's and Hume's)[42] of skepticism as intolerable or otherwise unlivable.[43]

Insofar as a neoclassical poet offers ironic epochē as specially definitive of moments of poetic clarity in retirement, however, and not as a sustained attitude toward the world, the charge of skepticism's unlivability is less relevant. Some of the most famous moments in the *Imitations* reveal the specifically literary applications of Pope's epochē-like attempts to detach himself from any potentially stable self-portrayals, and their opposition to the world of political label-making of the 1730s. To paraphrase Burnyeat: Pope's Horatian attitude indicates that while a number of contradictory notions *are thought* within the poet, he himself never necessarily believes (or disbelieves) them. The burden falls on skepticism to produce not an unflappable wisdom but rather moments of pleasure, which arise from the poet's simultaneous engagement in and freedom from various beliefs and desires operating within him.

One of the most complex of Pope's remarks on himself as a writer comes in his first effort at imitating Horace, *Satire II, 1* (1733), which explicitly reveals the negativity that Lamb noted behind Pitt's "managed gesture of self-exposure." As is common in the *Imitations,* the poem presents justifications for Pope's satirical poetry with bewilderingly various degrees of irony. Central to them is his claim that poetic self-expression is his peculiar "Pleasure" (45):

I love to pour out all myself, as plain
As downright *Shippen,* or as old *Montagne.*
In them, as certain to be lov'd as seen,
The Soul stood forth, nor kept a Thought within;
In me what Spots (for Spots I have) appear,
Will prove at least the Medium must be clear.
In this impartial Glass, my Muse intends
Fair to expose myself, my Foes, my Friends . . . (51–8)

The difficulty of visualizing the self depicted here suggests the complexity of Pope's notions of poetic self-expression. (Horace's version is nowhere near as elaborate, figuring the exposure of the self as on a votive tablet.) Pope "pours out" himself, perhaps like fluid from a bottle. But the fluid itself is an impersonal, invisible medium, "clear" of just the distinguishing marks that make the self a self. His "Spots" (his moral blemishes) distinguish him as a particular person, but these are crucially different from or inessential to the poetic part of the self poured out. It may seem that in addition to the "spots" and the medium, Pope asks us to visualize a third item, a picture of his personal soul, his substantial, virtuous character, "standing forth" like the souls of Shippen and Montaigne. But Pope mentions only the medium and the infelicitous spots that set off its transparency—and it is only the spots that prove the clarity of the fluid, not Pope's full self-portrait, spots and all. The clear medium seems a figure not only for Pope's poetic language, in all its impersonal, unprejudiced accuracy, nor merely the purity of his style, but for a specially poetic, cleansed, fluid version of himself, apparent only in contrast with the ordinary self represented as the "spots" or personal flaws that appear in it, along with (as we find next) the vices of the factional "present Age" (59). Like the ancient skeptic, this self is the bearer of distinguishing attitudes, opinions, beliefs, and vices yet discovers a capacity to detach itself radically from them. Even so, a self so cleansed is a nothing, empty if not for what it bears, virtuous only in invisibility. A literary identity is secured by its negativity in relation to the inconstant cultural and political world of which Pope admits he is a part.

And poetic writing itself is specifically the medium through which this detaching happens: Pope says that his "Muse intends" the exposures appearing in his work. His relinquishment of intention is another way of insisting on the clarity of the poetic medium: his own personal agenda cannot color his work because his poetry succeeds only when the muse takes over and thereby transcends (while including) his personality. He thus associates himself with the tradition (familiar from Socrates' remarks on the poets in the *Apology* onward) that defines poetry as antiintellectual, here to the point of denying the personal intentionality of the poet. Such a denial more specifically resonates with the skeptical model. Cavell has argued throughout his career that the modern skeptic does not really "mean what he says." Skeptical doubt removes us from the ordinary uses of language into a bizarre, hyperbolized realm where our words insist on something we cannot want: an absolute certainty that negates the finite conditions of our humanity.[44] Skepticism as it were speaks through those who are caught up in it, forcing them to detach their words from ordinary usages and contexts. Similarly, the poetic process in Pope entails his detachment from the ordinary conditions of selfhood—from his "spots." These can appear with proper literary accuracy only if against a hyperbolically pure, "impartial" part of him—a detachment so extreme as to be impracticable, according to Burnyeat. Like Cavell's skeptic, Pope pays for this purification by sacrificing nothing less than his intentional powers. But instead of viewing this loss as a terrible alienation from his ordinary self, Pope sees it as a kind of inspiration: the muse allows him to register his spots happily without "meaning them" self-definitively. Ancient skepticism claims an affective result that is simply different from the anxiety and alienation cited by Cavell as characteristic of the modern kind. While a loss of intention for Cavell ("not meaning what we say") is the disturbing outcome of modern skepticism, it is just the state prized by the ancient skeptic, and just the state to which Pope as a neoclassical poet aspires.

As the passage develops, it becomes clear that Pope somehow identifies his literary self with the transparently impersonal fluid, particularly in contrast with various political and religious labels that may be affixed to him:

My Head and Heart thus flowing thro' my Quill,
Verse-man or Prose-man, term me which you will,
Papist or Protestant, or both between,
Like good *Erasmus* in an honest Mean,
In Moderation placing all my Glory,
While Tories call me Whig, and Whigs a Tory. (63–8)

The fluidity of the "Head and Heart" again distinguishes him from the nonfluid spots carried with them. Pope remarks in his *Thoughts on Various Subjects* that "the best way to prove the clearness of our mind, is by shewing its faults; as when a stream discovers the Dirt at the bottom, it convinces us of the transparency and purity of the Water."[45] In this image as well, the fluidity and clarity of the "mind" contrast with the opacity and stasis of the dirt: Pope's literary self indicates his faults by being distinct from them. While he would aver that candidly revealing his spots is at least as important in his writing as proving his mental transparency, the two must work together to appear at all: while mental transparency is good for revealing a writer's flaws, the flaws are paradoxically "good" insofar as they "prove the clearness of our mind."

It may seem that Pope's moderation, his "honest Mean" between various pairs of extremes, amounts to a positive characterization of his attitude as a writer. But the proliferation of labels in the passage and his profession of indifference about what we "term" him ("Papist or Protestant, or both between") declare not an effort to compromise between religions but rather the inessentiality to his literary self of any and all identifying labels. The glory of "Moderation" seems particularly ironic following the praise of William Shippen, who himself years before wrote a Tory poem called *Moderation Display'd* against the "Moderation" movement in 1704–8, which Pope specifically associated with him.[46] Pope invokes the political meanings of these terms as a way to set himself ironically apart from them, not so much to disavow all politics as to valorize his own political positions by reference to a purity that displays even as it distinguishes itself from them. The reference to Erasmus is telling: his "honest Mean," as Pope well knew, did not express itself as a compromise doctrine between Catholicism and Lutheranism, for he, like Pope, always acknowledges (in Erasmus's words) "a Church to which at all times I willingly submit my own views, whether I attain what she prescribes or not."[47] Rather moderation defines Erasmus's famously tolerant temperament, his eschewal of passionate, angry debate, and his reluctance to dogmatize, as he says: "so great is my dislike of assertions that I prefer the views of the sceptics wherever the inviolable authority of Scripture and the decision of the Church permit"(6). Erasmus's attitude is a Christianized version of ancient skepticism, which dictates that the skeptic will adopt the traditions and practices of his country on the basis not of internal conviction but of external authority. Pope here unlike Erasmus refuses to identify exclusively with any religion, or any political party for that matter. While variously identifiable political and religious attitudes find expression in the poetic medium, the "Glass," the fluid, reflecting literary self, remains "impartial."

This duality of Pope's self as it appears in his writing recalls the characteristic literary attitude of the other great Renaissance skeptic mentioned in the passage, Montaigne. Throughout the *Essays,* Montaigne pours himself out, famously declaring his book consubstantial with its author. Like Pope, Montaigne exhibits a bewildering variety of shifting attitudes, often admitting his radical inconstancy, as he does in "Of Vanity": "I now, and I anon, are two several Persons." Nonetheless, he does not intend this to negate the principle announced moments earlier in the same essay: "My Book is always the same" (vol. 3, 302–3). Like Pope, Montaigne claims to achieve a purity and tranquillity of self through writing that exposes the self's impurities, disunity, and divagations. This emphasis on purity and clarity appears especially in Montaigne's most programmatically skeptical essay, the *Apology:* the skeptic for him is "naked and empty, confessing his natural Weakness, fit to receive some foreign Force from above." Next he compares the skeptical self to "a blank Paper, prepared to receive such Forms from the finger of God, as he shall please to write upon it" (vol. 2, 300). Pope emphasizes both passages with marginal hooks. As in Pope's Horatian poems, Montaigne's characteristically candid admission of his spots proves the "clarity" and integrity of the medium of the work. Jean Starobinski comments in his *Montaigne in Motion* (1982):

> Division [in Montaigne's self] cannot be overcome. . . . The only recourse remaining to anyone still enamoured of unity is to establish it in the discourse that gives voice to change, in the judgment that describes and condemns (or excuses) variability. The project of that discourse is no longer to achieve moral stability but to explain "how" and "why" stability has vanished, to indicate what obstacles have prevented the desired repose from being attained and caused the mirage of a transparent, univocal, and simple wisdom to recede into the distance. The book is a unitary receptacle capable of encompassing diversity. Writing, though it spins itself out in one continuous thread, is not incompatible with the mutability of humors, the clash of contradictory ideas, "passage," movement, travel.[48]

Both Pope and Montaigne seek an elusive unity of self that can only appear behind a foreground of disunity: writing for both "encompasses diversity" in a way that subscribing to a univocal philosophical position cannot. And in this search they find their ideal in the skeptic, who cultivates any number of contradictory beliefs and personal variations to "prove" his own animus æquus, the "blank Paper" of his mind "clear from Prejudice." Unlike the tranquil self composed by the Stoic sage, who renders himself consistent by embracing virtue and shunning vicious discontinuity, the skeptic's tranquil self is produced by a sustained interaction between his vices of the moment and a transcendent vicelessness. As Pope demonstrates in his handling of the nil admirari, we require the ever-recurring, ever-shifting dictations of admiring passions in order to separate ourselves decisively from them.

It is true that later in *Satire II, 1* (and throughout the *Imitations* generally) Pope chooses moments to fix his role as a satirist, a heroic and vatic voice distinguished amid the degradation of his times: "arm'd for *Virtue* when I point the Pen, / Brand the bold Front of shameless, guilty Men, / Dash the proud Gamester in his gilded Car, / Bare the mean Heart that lurks beneath a Star" (105–8). But even then he tends to define his virtue by his essential separation from certain identifying labels—he is "Un-plac'd, un-pension'd, no Man's Heir, or Slave" (115). Perhaps more significant are the ambiguities into which he glides at the end of the poem: like the ironies concluding *Epistle I, 6*, Pope's remarks here preserve a sense of moral purpose even as they render it impossible to define exactly. He denies that he will write morally suspect "*Libels* and *Satires*," instead promising "grave *Epistles*, bringing Vice to light . . . Such as Sir *Robert* would approve" (150–3). Pope means us to see that linking the moral efficacy of his poems to their power to inspire Walpole's approval implies a contradiction: the vices to be brought to light are those of Walpole himself and the "shameless, guilty men" he leads. We are left wondering whether Pope means to retain or undercut his previous rejection of libel, especially since his joke here somewhat libelously presupposes the absurdity of enlisting Sir Robert in the cause of morality.[49] This equivocation destabilizes Pope's very claim to occupy his morally secure position as a writer of "grave *Epistles*." Nonetheless, he does not intend us to wonder seriously if he is perhaps just as bad as Walpole (the humor after all is predicated on an assumption of Walpole's moral inferiority). Pope's irony withdraws the possibility of fixing his moral center without compromising his superior moral status: the poetic medium itself expresses a kind of aloof purity, exposing both his inclination to libel and his moralistic pretensions, without strictly defining him in either mode. Herein lies the ideologically efficacy of his promotion of poetry as an impartial glass: far from renouncing its political motivations, it authorizes them by the very distinction Pope manages to create between them and the poetic self.

His denials that he associates this free-floating state of mind particularly with the writing of verse do not sever the connection between ataraxia and his notion of the literary attitude in the larger sense. Though he claims to be impartial about whether we identify him as a "Verse-man" or a "Prose-man" (or anything else), he has also declared that his "Muse intends" this sort of impartiality. Nonetheless, this tension between writing poetically (according to the Muse's dictates) and his indifference to (being perceived as) writing poetically is not insignificant. The skeptical operation that determines his practice guarantees that Pope can never securely characterize his poetry as the instantiation or achieved expression of wisdom—again, what differentiates him from his Whig Opposition friends in their patriotic agendas for the good of the nation. Skepticism itself makes him reluctant to represent his personal virtue as dogmatically secured, and "verse" can no more ground identity than can a dogmatic philosophical position.

This skeptical dynamic of refusal goes some way toward accounting for Pope's repeated turns throughout the 1730s away from poetry toward some vaguely hoped-for philosophy that will stabilize his identity (e.g., in *Satire II, 1, 1733, The Epistle to Dr. Arbuthnot, 1734*, especially 271–4, *Epistle II, 2, 1737*, especially 198–211, and *Epistle I, 1, 1738*). Pope's repudiation of verse comes to be a frozen gesture—as if writing poetry of self-questioning entails questioning the point of doing it at all. Nonetheless, he also subtly and not so subtly mocks the Bolingbrokean, philosophical promised land—"What right, what true, what fit, we justly call" (*Epistle I, 1, 19*)—to be found beyond the verge of the self-repudiating poem. This double attitude toward poetry and the philosophical recalls Montaigne's oscillation between rejections of and insistences on his own foolish inconsistency.

The most striking illustration of this doubleness occurs in the late imitation of *Epistle I, 1* (1738). Horace's repudiation of poetry, introducing the original, makes more plain sense as a defining moment in his career than it does in Pope's: Horace is bidding farewell specifically to lyric poetry, the writing of odes, and is undertaking verse epistles because he hopes they will be more philosophically edifying. But Pope has been writing verse epistles all through the 1730s. This turns out to be his last imitation of Horace, and so the sense of farewell here means something very different from that in the original: "Farewell then Verse, and Love, and ev'ry Toy, / The rhymes and rattles of the Man or Boy" (17–8). Unlike Horace, Pope here is apparently rejecting poetry of the very same generic type (epistolary-satirical) he is now beginning, again, to write. Not surprisingly, the philosophical attitude he imagines as the alternative to poetry matches the one longed for in earlier poems. He has asked for peace and retirement in the poem's opening lines, to fade into "Life's cool evening satiate of applause" (9), but the philosopher's life he expects to lead contrasts sharply with any fantasy of retired, disengaged self-containment:

But ask not, to what Doctors I apply?
Sworn to no Master, of no Sect am I:
As drives the storm, at any door I knock,
And house with Montagne now, or now with Lock.
Sometimes a Patriot, active in debate,
Mix with the World, and battle for the State,
Free as young Lyttleton, her cause pursue,
Still true to Virtue, and as warm as true:
Sometimes, with Aristippus, or St. Paul,

Indulge my Candor, and grow all to all,
Back to my native Moderation slide,
And win my way by yielding to the tyde. (23–34)

Here he describes his characteristic patchwork of intellectual and political sympathies, and if we find Locke and Montaigne or Aristippus and Saint Paul starkly contradictory, Pope can seem again to be invoking the model of the skeptical self's relation to beliefs: any self that can in the same breath claim (potential) sympathy with both Aristippus (the Cyrenaic hedonist) and Saint Paul cannot strictly speaking believe in them because the doctrine of each excludes the other.[50] Instead of pledging allegiance to either or both, Pope is predicting that these doctrines will be believed in him (to vary Burnyeat's formula) in a way that skeptically withholds wholehearted belief, unwilling to bind himself to either consistently as an expression of his identity. His allegiance to the cause of Patriot Lyttleton in the Whig Opposition is similarly qualified: while as free, warm, and true as more active public debaters, he simultaneously expresses an aloofness from them.

More telling is the bizarre kind of agency disclosed in the passage. Pope writes, "As drives the storm, at any door I knock," but what is the storm a metaphor for? Presumably his own stormy inclinations: he will read whatever he feels like reading at any given moment. But this way of putting it puts a division in himself—one part of him, his whims, buffeting the *I* about. The storm cannot stand for forces other than the self, or the outside world in general, for the passage is elaborating on Pope's intellectual independence, on the idea that he is "Sworn to no Master." Furthermore he finds himself driven by the storm sometimes to "Mix with the World" and sometimes to withdraw. If the storm driving him *were* the world, he would always be mixing with it. So his attempts to gain wisdom will not necessarily lead either outward into the world of politics or into disengaged repose but will rather expose his personality to its own stormy discontinuities. This division of self is even clearer in the line concluding the passage, when Pope predicts he will "win (his) way by yielding to the tyde." Again, we wonder what the metaphorical outside force stands for, and again, since the passage is all about his independent pursuits, the answer is simply his own inclinations. Translated then, the sense would be, "I'll attain my goal by surrendering to my whims." Pope is not merely saying "I'll read what I like" in an oblique way but rather noting a division in himself that produces a kind of self-defining (hence self-stabilizing) tension. He recognizes that his intellectual whims are and will be inconsistent and sometimes starkly contradictory, but instead of trying to stifle them he yields to them, winning a wisdom higher than any representable as a single, fixed position. Again, this attitude appears copiously in the passages in Montaigne's *Apol-*

ogy that Pope emphasizes with marginal marks. "I have a thousand sence-less and casual Actions within myself," Montaigne says, quoting Catullus: "I do nothing but go and come: my Judgment does not always advance, it floates and romes . . . Like a small Bark upon the swelling Main / When Winds does [*sic*] ruffle up the liquid Plain" (vol. 2, 405). The skeptical acknowledgment of deep divisions in the self results not in panic but in a recognizably Popean self-confidence.

This mood permeates the poem's conclusion, when he again stresses his contradictory nature. He reproves Bolingbroke for being more critical of his inconsistent dress than his inconsistent personality:

when no Prelate's Lawn with Hair-shirt lin'd,
Is half so incoherent as my Mind,
When (each Opinion with the next at strife,
One ebb and flow of follies all my Life)
I plant, root up, I build, and then confound,
Turn round to square, and square again to round;
You never change one muscle of your face,
You think this Madness but a common case . . . (165–72)

Pope himself has in fact just pointed out that protean madness is a common case, affecting both rich and poor (153–4), so his complaint about himself to Bolingbroke rings with irony. But it is this irony itself that marks Pope's difference from the preceding satirical portraits of inconstants. The inconstancy of others is driven by "some whimzy, or that Dev'l within / Which guides all those who know not what they mean" (143–4). Similarly, Pope yields at one level to forces beyond his own more sober intentions: as in the earlier images of fluidity (the "tyde" and the image of his poured-out self in *Satire II, 1*), his personality here is moved by "One ebb and flow of follies all [his] life." Again the sentiment appears in a passage he marks in Montaigne, in "Of the Inconstancy of Our Actions," which Pope says "concludes Pyrrhonically": "We do not go we are driven; like things that float, now leisurely, then with violence, according to the gentleness, or rapidity of the Current" (vol. 2, 4). But again, his awareness of this coercion amounts to a self-mastery that others lack. Insofar as he cannot escape the ebb and flow of his follies, Pope is like the herd, but his confession of incoherence reflects a special wisdom, ironic because it requires that he yield to inconstancy in order to master it.

The poem's final satirical stroke falls not upon unreflective people "who know not what they mean" but upon the sage, "That Man divine whom Wisdom calls her own" (180), the person who thinks he can escape personal instability: "In short, that reas'ning, high, immortal Thing, / Just less than Jove, and much above a King, / Nay half in Heav'n—except (what's mighty odd) / A fit of vapours clouds this Demi-god" (185–8). Pope demonstrates the inevitability of inconstancy by satirizing the so-called constant philosopher as well, converting his reproof of Bolingbroke's philosophical indifference concerning the "common case" of Pope's inconstancy to a mockery of Bolingbroke's own pretensions to philosophical poise. Pope, on the contrary, achieves a kind of purity of self by skeptically admitting his own lack of it. In *Resemblance and Disgrace: Alexander Pope and the Deformation of Culture* (1996), Helen Deutsch similarly views such moments in the *Imitations* as producing a complementary tension within the self between its pure and impure elements:

> Although both the Latin and English versions end with an ironic twist that puts each poet at the mercy of his body—Horace concludes with, "except when he has a cold" (108), Pope, "except (what's mighty odd) / A Fit of Vapours clouds this Demi-God" (188), aptly feminizing the malady—both poets create an aesthetic that reifies the self by redefining it as static and disembodied.[51]

Here, as elsewhere, Deutsch identifies the body as the impure element that sets off the self's purity: the concept of "deformity" guiding her study proves an elastic one, including Pope's own uniquely deformed body, the unsettling influence of the passions, various feminizing impulses, physical "Vapours," and other terms opposable to the true, pure self.

But attributing such mind-body dualism to Pope does not acknowledge his effort to include even his own mind's discontinuous activity among those elements of himself against which his æquus animus is proved: he in fact insists that his bodily appearance is not "half so incoherent as my Mind." The power of such admissions lies in how completely they include all elements of his character (beyond any notion of his "deformity," no matter how far expanded) among those to be opposed to his otherwise invisible, pure (though never "static") poetic self—a power derived not from an assertion of dualism but from a skeptical distance from all beliefs and self-definitions, which comes to be poetry's special province. Though he began the epistle by rejecting poetry because it seemed to permit or encourage instability, he finally mocks philosophy because it falsely promises that such a rejection is possible. But even poetry itself may emerge only as an implicit positive because the skeptical attitude prohibits his assertion of final allegiance to it.

Such an assertion, moreover, would go too far in placing unwarranted faith in poetry as the ground of his identity: the whole point of associating his writing with the skeptical model of selfhood is to derive the pleasure of self-control ironically by admitting his lack of it. As he suggests earlier in the poem, poetry may quell the fits endemic to human life no better than philosophy: "Know, there are Words, and spells, which can controll / (Between the Fits) this Fever of the soul: / Know, there are Rhymes, which (fresh and fresh apply'd) / Will cure the arrant'st Puppy of his Pride" (57–60). The grim joke here lies in the parenthetical deflations of rhyme: fits will always puncture our self-control regardless of our attempts to keep it, attempts that we must constantly repeat to secure what little poise we may gain. Like the sage discomfited by "A Fit a Vapours," the rhymer cannot maintain his peace by an act of will: poetry cannot be chosen as the path to the æquus animus any more than philosophy can. Literary expression can produce calm only if it chooses its subject, as it were, and not the other way around.

This dynamic places Pope within the long tradition, especially important in the modern period, that stresses the impersonality of the poet, and Pope's example presents a particularly concrete and explicit picture of this tradition's ideological function, by revealing the interests his disinterestedness serves. Other poets have adopted such impersonal postures to deny their relation to the concrete, historical, political world and replace it with more universal relations: the poet becomes "the mind of Europe," for instance, revealing, if anything, larger historical movements divorced from all that makes himself a self. Pope's Horatian poems, on the contrary, generate their impersonality by stressing his personal relationships and political alliances: he yields to a variety of moods and inclinations that define his self in all its disarray in order to assert the invisible mastery that poetry requires. For Pope, the ideological benefits of such a posture are obvious: he mingles with a political world increasingly identified with corruption, seconding the efforts of the Patriot Opposition, without ever quite identifying with it, with the sage voice of Bolingbroke's *Craftsman*. His attraction to Montaignean skepticism discourages him from too readily associating authority with the poet's voice. Modernity's theorists of the successful writer's impersonality—as diverse as Keats, T. S. Eliot, and Paul de Man[52]— tend to treat such detachment as its own form of authority, even as their skepticism renders it impossible to define positively. Like them, Pope attains his authority by rendering himself transparent, though his writing expresses more openly than they the concrete ideological commitments, and the personal and cultural ones, that his "impartial Glass" is intended to display. This division of his voice between its personal, provisional weakness and its invisible investment of authority places Pope's poetry of the 1730s in the sublime tradition.

The ideological potency of Pope's Horatian attitudes furthermore derives from their unambiguous affiliation to the virtue of the ancient schools, which sets him apart from what he perceives as the passions and interests driving contemporary commercial culture and their inevitable tendency toward corruption. Pope no more than Horace limits himself to any single ancient philosophical version of virtue, and models of selfhood other than the skeptical one appear often in the *Imitations* in striking, unambiguous forms—notably Stoic ones, as when he exhorts, "Let Us be fix'd, and our own Masters still" in *Satire II, 2* (180). Views from Montaigne, Charron, and Pascal of the philosophical tenor of Horace's epistolary and satirical musings similarly notice and exploit his wide intellectual range. But to these writers the skeptical thread in Horace seems the summation of the different potential senses of the nil admirari—in Montaigne's case the strong, blank, eudaemonistic current of the Horatian flux, in Pascal its useless emptiness. It is tempting to see the skeptical voice as similarly dominant in Pope precisely because of its capacity to express a variety of philosophical tenets, including moments of Stoicism, Epicureanism, Cyrenaicism, and others, to the point of self-contradiction, in order to express its own detachment from all beliefs—a fluidity incompatible with the rigidity of the Stoic sage. Without such avowals of personal inconstancy, Pope would risk utterly alienating himself from the corrupt society that he seeks satirically to address and render him as suspect as those who trumpet Sir Robert's virtue in government newspapers. His ironic power sets him apart from those "who know not what they mean" in his very resemblance to them. The degree to which it is possible consistently to hold this pose of detached engagement amid a wider cultural fragmentation, and keep one's skepticism ancient while confronting an irremediably modern world, will be determined in the final chapter's analysis of Pope's darker attitudes in the *Dunciad*.

6

♾

Knowing Ridicule and Skeptical Reflection in the *Moral Essays*

Pope's attitude toward inconsistency is inconsistent. He displays his own in the Horatian poems as a potent, candid pose that establishes his moral and satirical authority, the clearness of his poetic "Medium," but this seems at odds with the numerous passages of poems of the 1730s that satirically attack the inconsistency of others. In a generalizing, philosophical register, he accepts and often savors the idea that all human lives are baffling jumbles, but he also views inconsistency as the essence of what is distasteful or even horrifying in human behavior, of immorality or perversion—and so uses it as his main charge against the vicious and ridiculous. Even excellent critics of Pope resolve the issue unconvincingly. David Morris says that Pope distinguishes between inconstancy, a moral fault only wicked or insane people exhibit, and inconsistency, shared by all.[1] While this view is commonsensical enough, Pope never clearly articulates it, and nothing suggests he held such a firm distinction in mind from poem to poem. He furthermore seems aware that using inconsistency as a moral index is a fraught problem: since all deviations from the good are disruptive of one's æquus animus or moral center, it is an interesting fact that they are not all morally equal. Indecisiveness about landscape design is not as bad as treason, corruption, or rage: still, Papillia's cry in the *Epistle to a Lady* of "odious, odious Trees!" after having them planted in her park links her fault to Atossa's "warfare upon earth."

Exploring this linkage allows Pope to express his ideological position more subtly than denying it ever could. He certainly does not accept the "paradoxes" of Stoic ethics, frequently mentioned in early modern applications of Hellenistic philosophy, including the idea that any deviation from the good, however slight, is as bad as any other.[2] Still, Pope wants to think the paradoxes through—as does Montaigne, who cites them to begin "Of Drunkenness": "The World is nothing but Variety and Disproportion,

Vices are all alike, as they are Vices, and peradventure the *Stoicks* understand them so, but although they are equally Vices, yet they are not equal Vices" (vol. 2, 13). Montaigne then offers a Horatian illustration of the absurdity of Stoic doctrine from *Satire I, 3:* "Nor seems it reason, he as much should Sin, / Steals but a Cabbadge Plant, as he who, in / The dead of night, a Temple breaks, and brings / Away from thence the Consecrated things."[3] Like Montaigne, Pope enters this tangle, seeking a way to condemn especially vicious behavior while maintaining that all vices consist of inconsistency and that inconsistency is ubiquitous. The two *Moral Essays* on human character, *To Cobham* (1734) and *To a Lady* (1735), both adopt that basic structure: they begin by skeptically claiming that the characters of men and women both are "nothing but Variety and Disproportion" and proceed to single out individuals for blame, praise, or special comment.

Far from inhibiting Pope from satirically aiming social criticism at the vicious, this logical tension enables him to adopt a new attitude toward the self and how the self can be depicted in moral and quasi-aesthetic terms suited to the contradictory demands of civil society in his time. The previous chapter argued that Pope skeptically admits his own inconsistency to engage the social instabilities of 1730s England without being sullied by them. His satire on the inconstancy and contradictions of others in the *Moral Essays* realizes this strategy, with degrees of success. He discovers a sympathy for his satirical targets in these poems because their moral failings can be seen as expressing a universal human inconstancy in which he admits his share. Pope's version of Horace's *Satire II, 1,* which appears in February 1733, announces that he will "expose" everyone in society, "myself, my Foes, my Friends," revealing his own inconstancy along with that of everyone else. In the next two years, the two epistles *To Cobham* and *To a Lady* demonstrate how Pope's ambiguous attitudes toward inconstancy as a moral condition allow him to socialize virtuously in an essentially fluid world, full of shifting passions and interests. Whether a Jacobite traitor or a woman, each satirized figure is rendered sympathetic to the degree to which he or she is disapproved of: condemnable individuals thus ironically illustrate our shared human predicament. Pope's very act of mocking and disowning the reflection asserts that the figure reflects humanity.

This unity of contradictory attitudes bears on debates about the ideological significance of Pope's poetry, especially the critical divide generated by the *Epistle to a Lady*. Some critics have seen it as rising above the misogynistic norm by exhibiting a complex attitude toward women, a mingling of criticism and genuine sympathy, while Ellen Pollak sees only "an illusion of complexity"[4] because inconsistency remains a largely negative trait and women remain its strongest examples. But in Pope the illusion of complexity turns out to be more complex than complexity itself. Attention to

Pope's skeptically split attitudes shows *To a Lady* to be just as misogynistic, and just as sympathetic toward women, as each side of the dispute has always maintained, and furthermore that these opposed attitudes in fact entail each other, having a single source in Pope's Montaignean understanding of the inconsistent self. Their interdependence makes it wrong to see Pope's sympathy for women as mitigating his disapproval of them—each attitude inspires the other, after all—but it also makes it wrong to view misogyny as the underlying, univocal truth of Pope's attitude, inasmuch as it derives from its opposite. His view of women (and his satirical targets in general) is not complex or mixed but double. The portraiture motif of *To a Lady* reinforces the connection between such double vision and taste, particularly pertaining to sublime effects in painting (as theorized, for instance, by Pope's friend, the painter Jonathan Richardson). Beyond such critical debates, then, the significance of Pope's training an essentially divided perspective on the figures presented in his poems lies in its creation of a sophisticated field of judgment in which ethical standards and standards of taste merge. His identification of ethical disapproval with aesthetic fascination depends on a third term, the skeptical insistence on human inconsistency, and only through this assumption may his satire perform the delicate ideological work that conflates disavowal with acceptance and inconstancy with social discipline.

I

The most fully developed chain of skeptical reasoning in Pope's work, the first two-thirds of the *Epistle to Cobham*, derives its ideological usefulness in part from its connection to ancient discourses of virtue that Pope invokes to signal his aloofness from the corruption of his times. The skeptical notion that men are impossible to know explored in *To Cobham*, despite appearances, means something other than what has become for modern epistemology the traditional "problem of other minds," which emerges from the Lockean or Cartesian psychology of ideas.[5] This modern problem arises when the epistemologist notices that he has "privileged access" to his own mental states, his pains and other sensations, and all the other "ideas" before his mind, in such a way as to prevent the possibility of his ever being wrong about whether he has them or not. Concomitant upon this is a realization that he lacks anything like such assurance in respect to the ideas in other minds: even if he trusts a person to the last degree, the epistemologist can never be really sure that his friend is not faking it or otherwise deceiving him when he cries in pain. Pope only rarely appears to find this particular dilemma compelling. Perhaps it is part of what motivates him to declare in a letter to Jervas, "The old project of a Window in the bosom, to render the Soul of Man visible, is what every honest friend has manifold reason to wish for."[6] Another letter, to Lady Mary Wortley Montagu (vol. 1, 353), more elaborately treats the window image (which is commonplace throughout the eighteenth century, appearing at a famous moment of *Tristram Shandy*). Pope generally indulges a fantasy of perfect self-revelation throughout the *Correspondence* (though not without some duplicitous self-editing)—and notably in his effort to "pour out all" himself plainly in his imitation of Horace's *Satire II, 1*.

Still, such a desire for full disclosure differs from the anxiety arising from Descartes's more isolated position: "And yet what do I see from the window but hats and coats which may cover automatic machines?"[7] Pope does not wonder so much whether others are conscious, feel pain, or even dissemble or disguise their thoughts so consistently as to raise general fears about human trustworthiness. For him, human beings' various mental states are all too apparent, plainly indicative of their ever-shifting motivations. The *Moral Essays* concern our inability to interpret people, to view their various actions and motives and infer the principle that unites them so as to make their personalities coherent and therefore knowable: while this lets us wonder about how we can ever know what a person is thinking at a given moment, it originates in the desire to grasp the meaningful (hence knowable) organization of an individual life over time. Just as the æquus animus addresses the problem of the incoherent self, not the problem of personal identity arising from Lockean epistemology, Pope's meditations in *To Cobham* and *To a Lady* address the problem of discerning coherence in others, not the modern problem of other minds: in fact the self and the other in ancient discourse raise essentially the same problem of knowledge, the former from the inside, the latter from without.

To Cobham's skepticism has long been seen to be derived from Montaigne's essay "Of the Inconstancy of Our Actions," which argues that human behavior is "nothing but shifting, and inconstancy":[8] "We are all in form lumps, and of so various a contexture, that every piece every moment plays its own game, and there is as much difference betwixt us and our selves, as betwixt us and others" (vol. 2, 12). The poem elaborates on this same theme: "That each from other differs, first confess; / Next, that he varies from himself no less" (19–20). In a conversation recorded in Spence's *Table Talk* the week that *To Cobham* went to press, Pope said that Montaigne's essay "concludes Pyrrhonically, that nothing can be known of the Workings of men's minds."[9] Pope means this ascription of the most extreme ancient skepticism to Montaigne to be a kind of adverse criticism, it seems. As Bolingbroke's remark on it quoted in the previous chapter indicates, Pyrrhonism definitely had a bad name among Pope's circle, however attractive a genteel, mildly doubtful attitude was—and there is evidence that he deferred to Bolingbroke's opinion of it: in *To Cobham*, Pope refers to "Montagne, or more sage Charron!" (146), and Warburton says that this is because of Charron's "moderating every-where the extravagant Pyrrhonism of his friend"; but Bateson, commenting on this note, suggests that Pope is just blindly following "Bolingbroke's often expressed preference for Charron to Montaigne" (146n). Charron did not in fact moderate Montaigne's Pyrrhonism much: Popkin characterizes *De la Sagesse* as "little more than Montaigne's *Apologie* in organized form."[10] Pope's poem, in any case, pointedly does not "conclude Pyrrhonically." After its extended skeptical opening, he tells us to "Search then the Ruling Passion: There, alone, / The Wild are constant, and the Cunning known" (174–5). Despite these repudiations of Pyrrhonism, however, Pope still reveals mixed feelings about it, inasmuch as he calls Montaigne's essay "The best in his whole book" in the same conversation with Spence. At the beginning of it in his copy of Montaigne, Pope writes "An incomparable Essay" in the margin, emphasized with an *x*.

Pope's mixed feelings about "Pyrrhonism" further appear in the fact that he gives it even fuller treatment in his poem than it gets in this essay, which was written (1572–74) before Montaigne embraced the Pyrrhonism of Sextus Empiricus in the *Apology for Raimond de Sebonde* (1575–76, 1578–80).[11] *To Cobham* enhances the essay's general skeptical tenor, as some have noted,[12] leading it into more strictly Pyrrhonistic territory:

Yet more; the diff'rence is as great between
The optics seeing, as the objects seen.
All Manners take a tincture from our own,
Or come discolour'd thro' our Passions shown.
Or Fancy's beam enlarges, multiplies,
Contracts, inverts, and gives ten thousand dyes. (23–8)

Ancient Pyrrhonism does not single human beings out as especially unknowable objects as "Of the Inconstancy" does, but rather, as here, characteristically insists on the untrustworthiness of human observation, on the way "the optics seeing" always contribute to (and therefore possibly distort) our apprehension of objects before us (though Sextus Empiricus tends to view inconsistencies of the mind and of the world as mutually generated, as when he insists on our inability to "obtain Indisturbance by judging of the Unsetledness in *Phænomena's* and Intelligibles [thoughts]").[13] A similar line of thought appears in Pierre-Daniel Huet's work *De Imbecillitate mentis humanae*, which Pope had evidently discussed with Atterbury back in 1721. Huet writes that we "have a great deal of Reason to doubt of the

Agreement of these Forms or Image of the external Object, with the Object it self; of the Fidelity of the Medium, through which these Forms do pass from the Object to the Organ of Sense; of the Fidelity of Sense and of the Brain, and of the Perception of the Soul."[14] In a letter to Pope, Atterbury ridicules Huet's "doubting whether the marks of truth and falsehood can in any case be distinguish'd from each other" and rejects this extreme skepticism with revulsion: "Could that blessed point be made out (as it is a contradiction in terms to say it can,) we should then be in the most uncomfortable and wretched state in the world; and I would in that case be glad to exchange my reason with a dog for his instinct, tomorrow." Though the original letter is lost, Pope evidently felt sympathetic enough to these antiskeptical sentiments to append them to the 1721 Atterbury letter that appeared in the 1737 edition of his correspondence.[15] Still, Huet's views are nearly identical to those articulated with glee in *Cobham.* This ambivalence, and the poem's enhancement of the very "Pyrrhonism" of Montaigne's argument from "Of the Inconstancy" that Pope denigrates in Spence's *Table Talk,* suggest that he finds radical doubt at once attractive and repulsive, stimulating by its power to disconcert. But it is important to see this willingness to elaborate on what he appears to reject not as an embarrassing emergence of something otherwise repressed but as a literarily and morally useful contradiction.

What skepticism concretely grants Pope, in short, is the assurance that he is avoiding simplistic assessments of others' motives and characters, especially historical figures, and correspondingly, that his poetic portraits surpass earlier models that characterize literary figures by type: moral sensitivity and literary sophistication thus inspire each other. In adopting the typical skeptic's position against the Stoic Sage, Pope offers a more mature method of historical analysis: "In vain the Sage, with retrospective eye, / Would from th'apparent What conclude the Why" (51–2). After several explanations for Cæsar's behavior, Pope concludes, "But, sage historians! 'tis your task to prove / One action Conduct; one, heroic Love" (85–6). However, even as a skeptical attitude toward historical and other explanations of behavior opens up a wealth of possible motives and causes necessarily excluded from dogmatic accounts, it also renders the possibility of understanding and judging others impossible—something that Pope as a satirist continues to want to do. The apparent contradiction stimulates rather than stymies Pope's satirical exertions, here and especially in the *Epistle to a Lady:* it allows him at once to sympathize with and criticize the figures in his sights.

Pope deflates literary tendencies to characterize by type (exemplified by Roman New Comedy, with its bragging soldiers, impatient lovers, and old misers), and it is here that the ideological force of his skeptical attitude, in its relation to the cultural and religious politics of his time, begins to appear. He continuously insinuates that contemporary behavior belies the static attributes of stock characters, without explicitly stating that character in the 1730s is any more protean or deceptive than in the past. Pope ironically espouses clichés to make this point clear:

'Tis from high Life high Characters are drawn;
A Saint in Crape is twice a Saint in Lawn;
A Judge is just, a Chanc'lor juster still;
A Gownman learn'd; a Bishop, what you will;
Wise, if a Minister; but, if a King,
More wise, more learn'd, more just, more ev'rything. (87–92)

The irony is obvious: contemporary deviations from these figures' appropriate attributes prove the general point that mankind is more changeable, less predictable than any theory of types would allow. At a period when Pope was increasingly involved with Opposition politics, the wisdom definitive of a "Minister," and the learning and justice of a king, seem so sufficiently falsified by Walpole and George II as not to require explicit mentioning. While avoiding the claim that his own age is any more inscrutable or contradictory than its predecessors, Pope implies that current politics are particularly dubious. He assumes the double role so crucial in the *Imitations of Horace:* he is the detached skeptical observer recognizing the general, transhistorical tendency of people to deviate "from themselves," even as he hunts down certain striking contemporary examples to clinch this skepticism. Uncertain elements of contemporary society— "salaried office, reliance on private or political patronage, on public credit," as Pocock puts it, "the rise of forms of property seeming to rest on fantasy and false consciousness"[16]—at once bear out his general skeptical claim and stand forth to be denounced as degraded aspects of 1730s Britain. Skepticism performs an intentionally contradictory ideological function. On the one hand it signifies the timeless philosophic detachment so important to Pope's "civic" personality, but on the other it seems characteristic of the fluid, modern personality emerging from the intersubjective, fantastical flow of a corrupt society. Pope the Montaignean moralist sees mankind as "nothing but shifting, and inconstancy," but Pope the contemporary critic sees shifting and inconstancy besetting 1730s Britain in more threatening, less generalizable ways.

This contradiction determines the satirical irresolution of the rest of the poem. He begins by mocking a set of flat characterizations: "Boastful and rough, your first son is a 'Squire; / The next a Tradesman, meek, and much a lyar; / Tom struts a Soldier, open, bold, and brave; / Will sneaks a

Scriv'ner, an exceeding knave" (103–6). The effect grows confusing because Pope seems to be denouncing such persons even as he denounces typing them according to their professions or roles. Some of them represent the dubious practices that seemed to people of Pope's ideological bent particularly "shifting" about contemporary society: "Scriv'ners," for instance, "received money to place out at interest."[17] He concludes the passage with more ironically proposed, flat types, which confuse his skeptical argument further because they give it a kind of support: "Is he a Churchman? then he's fond of pow'r: / A Quaker? sly: A Presbyterian? sow'r: / A smart Free-thinker? all things in a hour" (107–9). He must mean to dispense with such clichés, but he also seems to endorse them: the final reference to the "Free-thinker" finally collapses skeptical and typed characterizations, inasmuch as the figure's typed attribute, extreme inconstancy, is the same one Pope has used to cast doubt on the interpretation of character by type. It is hard to imagine that Pope is sticking up for "smart Free-thinkers" as a richly diversified group of unclassifiable individuals—and the very means of classifying them unites them to mankind, each of whom "differs from himself." Beyond simple incoherence, Pope's skepticism leads him to a fertile confusion: religious factions provide us with instances of human deceptiveness (corruption, slyness, hypocritically sour religiosity, flightiness) so typical that they seem to support the very skepticism that would appear to undermine our understanding of them according to type.

Beyond such tail-chasing ironies, the poem finds more substantial ways in which the inconstancy of contemporary figures can generate at once satirical anger and a sympathetic sense of their complexity. The effect appears with special vigor in the portrait of Philip, duke of Wharton, the poem's longest, "the scorn and wonder of our days" (180), introduced for just this tendency to elicit both satirical animus and puzzlement. Wharton also illustrates the notion of the ruling passion, putatively to resolve the "extravagant Pyrrhonism" of Montaigne. It is clear that Pope thought that ascribing "the Lust of Praise" (181) to Wharton imparts enough coherence to his personality to dispel the notion that he is "nothing but shifting, and inconstancy," that he always "differs from himself." But most readers have denied that Wharton's character grants much philosophical stability to the poem,[18] and several elements of the portrait retain the poem's atmosphere of uncertainty. Pope emphasizes the ruling passion's elusiveness, calling it the object of "Search" (174), concluding the portrait with a warning: "Yet, in this search, the wisest may mistake, / If second qualities for first they take" (210–1). He (or his editor Jonathan Richardson the younger)[19] underscores this problem in the "Argument": these lines offer "*A caution against mistaking* second qualities *for* first, *which will destroy all possibility of the knowledge of mankind*" (vol. 3:2, 14). The insistence on the threat's extremity here ("*all possibility*") preserves much of the poem's skepticism even while solving it.

Most important, the ruling passion remains a dubious element because of its failure, in its very unification of Wharton's personality, to provide him a sense of his æquus animus, the repeated philosophical goal of the ancient discourse of selfhood that Pope takes up through his Horatian poems. Far from allowing him to achieve the "perfect Tranquillity" to which the wise man aspires, Wharton's ruling passion is just what prevents him from doing so. In Wharton's case, the ruling passion appears to have the unbreakable power to prevent its subject from ever recognizing that he has it—reflecting the *Essay on Man*'s rather different emphasis on the ruling passion not as explanatory but as essentially deceptive: "The ruling Passion, be it what it will, / The ruling Passion conquers Reason still."[20] Similarly, in *Cobham*'s illustration of it, Wharton "turns repentant, and his God adores / With the same spirit that he drinks and whores" (188–9): to do each contradictory activity "with the same spirit," he must fail to recognize he is doing so. There seems something necessarily self-thwarting about the ruling passion, rendering it more uncanny than self-stabilizing in the eudaemonistic sense: "His Passion still, to covet gen'ral praise, / His life, to forfeit it a thousand ways" (196–7). While discovering Wharton's ruling passion shows that the problem of interpreting others may be solved, it does not address the ancient dilemma of locating and mastering one's true inner self: rather it intensifies Pope's skepticism about this possibility. Nor does the idea of the ruling passion solve the "modern," Lockean problem of personal identity, of identifying the self as a constant item in a person's consciousness, "something simple and continu'd, which he calls *himself*," in Hume's words.[21] The "lust of praise" is not this item but only that which renders Wharton coherent (that is, we would not say that anyone whose ruling passion was "lust of praise" was the same person as Wharton).

But beyond merely maintaining the poem's epistemological instability, the elusiveness of even Wharton's example enhances Pope's power to imply a range of contradictory but useful political meanings. Some are of the crude order already noted: the oscillation between generalizing skepticism and concrete contemporary applications that seem both to support and belie it. Pope says that discovery of the ruling passion makes "The Fool consistent, and the False sincere; / Priests, Princes, Women, no dissemblers here" (176–7). The list here implies that dissembling and the ruling passions that allow us to decode it are universal, even as it singles out types for satirical attack. The inclusion of the dissembling of "Women" along with figures from the religious and political worlds suggests an expanded range of human inconstancy particularly appropriate to the shifting, inconstant nature of eighteenth-century society, with its intermingling of masculine and feminine realms, of private and public spheres.

Wharton himself is an especially apposite figure for contemporary instability. He stands in a line of self-contradicting figures in post-Restoration literature, including Dryden's Achitophel, "Sagacious, bold, and turbulent of wit, / Restless, unfix'd in principles and place" (153–4). Wharton, similarly, is "A Fool, with more of Wit than half mankind, / Too quick for Thought, for Action too refin'd" (200–1). Beyond this, Wharton's own father, Thomas, Marquis of Wharton, the Whig politician, was satirized in similar terms in several poems by William Shippen ("downright Shippen" of Pope's *Satire II, 1*), including *Faction Display'd* (1704): "To gain a Rake he'll Drink, and Whore, and Rant, / T'engage a Puritan will Pray and Cant. / So Satan can in diff'ring Forms appear, / Or Radiant Light, or gloomy Darkness wear" (180–3).[22] Following that poem, *To Cobham* had called the younger Wharton after the Roman name that Shippen gave his father ("Clodio"), though this was changed to Wharton's own name in the final editions. Another poem (probably) by Shippen about Wharton the elder, "The Character of a Certain Whigg," exemplifies the family tendency toward self-contradiction: "He doats on Mischief for dear Mischief's Sake; / Joins Contradictions in his wond'rous Make; / A flattering BULLY, and a stingy RAKE" (3–5).[23] The younger Wharton's family resemblance produces an irony that could not have escaped Pope's readers, inasmuch as he carries on the tradition of inconstancy of his father, the member of the Whig Junto, by becoming a Jacobite and converting to Roman Catholicism. Even as this transgenerational inconstancy illustrates the general contradictory quality of humanity, it also points to the volatilities of the political scene since the Revolution. Pope's stepping back from such figures to analyze them according to a theory of human nature does not diminish their capacity to represent a signally contemporary instability.

The reflections of Pope's own personality and history in Wharton's portrait reveal his most subtle ideological purposes. A number of the labels that Wharton takes on were affixed to Pope, correctly or incorrectly, by contemporaries. Wharton embraces Roman Catholicism and becomes a Jacobite in 1726.[24] Like Pope, he was a supporter of Atterbury, notably defending him during the trial in the House of Lords in 1723. Even the phrasing used to describe his inconstancy recalls that used by Pope to describe his own. At the height of his corruption, Wharton has "Grown all to all, from no one vice exempt" (194), ironically echoing Paul's text in I Corinthians 9:19–22: "I am made all things to all *men*, that I might by all means save some"—a text in which Paul admits to assuming a variety of postures (e.g., to Jews and Gentiles) to serve everyone and thereby affirms the piety of a certain kind of inconstancy. In the more explicit, also ironic reference to this Pauline topos in *Epistle I, 1*, Pope himself will promise to "Sometimes, with Aristippus, or St. Paul, / Indulge my Candor, and grow all to all" (31–2)—an echo lacking the sarcasm of that in Wharton's portrait but still jarring in its comparison of Saint Paul to the Cyrenaic hedonist Aristippus.

The phrase is for Pope a little emblem of inconstancy with ironic possibilities that can be slanted in various ways. These reflections are not suggestions that he is anything at all like Wharton. (For one thing, Pope always presents himself as immune to the "Lust of Praise" that bedevils Wharton: "What's *Fame?* the fancy'd Life in others breath!" [*Essay on Man*, IV, 237].) On the contrary, they function ironically to distinguish Pope from Wharton, or rather to indicate that the characteristics that they share—Catholic, supporter of Atterbury, (possible) Jacobite—are not definitive of their characters. Pope at once shares in and stands apart from the political volatilities of the time as Wharton represents them. Wharton's inconstancy allows Pope to distinguish vice from any single set of identifying labels: the portrait locates his vice not in any one political or personal lapse but the way his several contradictory lapses, mistakes, and outrages unite to indicate his ever self-defeating inconstancy:

A Tyrant to the wife his heart approves;
A Rebel to the very king he loves;
He dies, sad out-cast of each church and state,
And (harder still) flagitious, yet not great! (202–5)

While an air of outrage clings to Wharton's particular, treasonous political choices, Pope implies that the real enormity of his character lies in his ironic inconstancy and incoherence, his rebelling against his loved king, and the fact that neither England and the Anglican Church nor France and Roman Catholicism will have him (not true, in fact—he died in a Franciscan convent). Pope blackens Wharton as a way of clearing himself, whose own quiet, private Catholicism, the implication is, would never lead to treasonable Jacobitism: it takes a lunatic like Wharton, utterly beset by inconstancy, to career into such self-defeating political extremes.

Our shared inconstancy allows us to recognize in Wharton reflections of ourselves, and, as in Pope's case, even of his specific political and religious labels and sympathies. Wharton, after all, is the scorn and wonder of *our* days, and his display of shifting loyalties (including his family background) anthologizes the political options of the times. But this very sharing in social, political, and cultural inconstancy allows Pope to relieve himself of the damning force of any negative labels he has acquired. Wharton's character is damnable not because he has joined this or that party or religion but because he finds himself in all and therefore in none of them. This is wonderfully similar to Pope's own preferred attitude, the friend of virtuous Whigs or Tories, "Papist or Protestant, or both between," "yielding to the tyde" of his own inconstant inclinations. For Pope, such a similarity (as well as more concrete similarities) allows him sympathetically to wonder at Wharton, and to direct his readers to wonder at him too, even as it grants him, and his readers, an invisible position of comfort from which to scorn Wharton's extravagant inconsistencies. Similarity thus provides the most secure ground for both scorn and wonder.

After the poem finally rejects Montaigne's "Pyrrhonical" conclusion, much else goes with it: the attendant literary insistence on the mysterious complexity of character evaporates immediately after Wharton's portrait. The "solution" encourages Pope to view people again as types distinguished by certain defining traits, like lust for praise, foregoing the emphasis on the unknowable individuality of "men's minds." The poem closes with a series of flat figures, the sexually promiscuous "rev'rend sire" (228), Helluo the glutton (234), the "frugal Crone" (238), and so on, offering no histories similar to Wharton's extravagant career that would render their ruling passions anything beyond caricatures of selfhood. The ruling passion comes to defeat itself as an insight into the mysterious complexity of individuals. The final apostrophe to the poem's addressee, Viscount Cobham, again expresses a conventional sentiment:

And you! brave COBHAM, to the latest breath
Shall feel your ruling passion strong in death:
Such in those moments as in all past,
"Oh, save my Country, Heav'n!" shall be your last. (262–5)

The failure of this as a principium individuationis is demonstrated by the fact that Pope used a similar thought for his friend Atterbury's epitaph: "Is there on Earth one care, one wish beside? / Yes—SAVE MY COUNTRY, HEAV'N,—He said, and dy'd."[25] The same patriotic sentiment can be used to define the characters of an exiled Jacobite and a Whig peer. One identity may reflect another apparently incompatible one, and labels like "Whig" and "Jacobite" fail to describe the essence of people. But Pope suppresses the Atterbury epitaph in the 1735 edition of the works, and the easy resolution afforded by Cobham's patriotism to the poem addressed to him skirts the complexities it seeks to engage. A more radical and sophisticated thinking through of the ironies of identity appears in the *Epistle to a Lady* to come.

II

In the *Epistle to a Lady,* Pope discovers the most subtle and far-reaching uses for his skeptical view of character, satirizing the women in the poem and the society they represent, ironically establishing his superiority to them by elaborating on ways that he and men in general resemble, reflect, or create them and their characters. Again, his skepticism enables him to perform this maneuver, overtly insisting on an equality or parity between the genders to invisibly support the hierarchy between them. Like *Cobham, To a Lady* insists on human inconstancy but now declines to offer a sense of resolution with the notion of a ruling passion, which effectively vanishes as an explanatory device even as the poem's "Argument" reasserts it: "But tho' the *Particular Characters* of this Sex are more various than those of Men, the *General Characteristick,* as to the *Ruling Passion,* is more uniform and confin'd" (*TE*, vol. 3:2, 45). (Pope here alludes to the poem's assertion that women only have two possible ruling passions, "The Love of Pleasure, and the Love of Sway" [210], neither of which can therefore function as a principium individuationis.) The "Argument" distinguishes between men and women to suggest hierarchy, however confusingly: women's characters "are yet more inconsistent and incomprehensible than those of Men"—though men in *To Cobham,* even including Wharton, are presented as incomprehensibility itself. Pope still plays against the Stoic's paradox that asserts that all instances of inconstancy have, in a certain sense, the same status. Women epitomize the order of (masculine) inconstancy even as they exceed it.

This special status of women leads Pope to ascend to what he views as an elevated mode of poetic representation. Women, as particularly sublime objects, call upon Pope to refine his own attitude toward the poetic practice of the sublime, developed in the poem's dominant portraiture motif and Pope's references to himself as an artist and to men as connoisseurs. While *Cobham* verges on this territory, expanding character beyond flatness of literary type, it remains in a public, historical mode, using examples like Caesar alongside famous contemporaries like Goldophin, Wharton, and Cobham. *To a Lady,* on the contrary, associates protoaesthetic concerns with the private world of women and uses skepticism to elaborate the complexities of each. Pope's ironies in this poem work to unify a sympathy for the inconstancy of this feminized, private world with the satirical distance from it that he would always wish to maintain—a unity generating something like what will become Kantian disinterestedness toward objects of aesthetic judgment.

The poem works not by separating public from private, masculine from feminine, economic from aesthetic, but by showing their interdependence. Before *To a Lady* introduces its dominant metaphor of morally evaluating women according to the methods of judging fine art, Pope considers them in relation to another form of representation, the coining of precious metals. As has often been noticed,[26] the poem's opening lines implicitly compare women to gold:

NOTHING so true as what you once let fall,
'Most Women have no Characters at all.'
Matter too soft a lasting mark to bear,
And best distinguish'd by black, brown, or fair.

Gold is too malleable to bear characters (the stamped figures denominating different values), and this condition makes it unusable as money. Some have found the comparison of women to gold a compliment, some an insult, and both are right. In one of the better discussions of this aspect of the passage, Ellen Pollak speaks of Pope's "simultaneous assertion and denial of intrinsic female worth" (123) in the metaphor of women as gold:

> they are identified with gold in its primitive, inactive state and are thereby associated with unfruitful, decadent wealth (domestic treasure) and useless art. . . . They are a sort of filthy lucre unmediated by industrious or rational enterprise, a storehouse of unrealized possibility turned in upon itself, that, like the uncreated matter of Milton's cosmos, is recognizable by its formlessness and made manifest by its anticreative force. (125)

But this interpretation seems incomplete. Gold, in all its malleability and fungibility, represents the very practice, "industrious or rational enterprise," or rather the system of public economic exchange and credit, for which its softness disqualifies it. The allegorical figure of Lady Credit, used famously both by Defoe (*Review*, vol. 3, numbers 5 and 6) and Addison (*Spectator*, number 3), elaborates on the feminine nature of the economic speculation that is coming to dominate British finance.[27] In Addison's fantasy, the "beautiful Virgin, seated on a Throne of Gold" who represents Public Credit[28] presides over the ceaseless, restless exchange of gold and currency: "the great Heaps of Gold, on either side of the Throne, now appeared to be only Heaps of Paper"; the economy then improves, and the "Heaps of Paper [are] changed into Pyramids of Guineas" (vol. 1, 17). For Pope, too, such skittish exchange is essentially feminine, but his metaphor's logic goes one step further, noting not only women's (and gold's) figurative centrality in economic activity but also their actual absence from it. Like that of gold, women's softness necessitates their removal from the system they epitomize, becoming useless to society through their excess of the very property, inconstancy, that the ever-shifting, financially fluid social world requires to operate—literally true, if, as Pocock notes, a feminine whimsicality is seen to drive the economy.[29] The opening comparison of Pope's poem implicitly bears out the truth of Nancy Armstrong's assertion that "the modern individual was first and foremost a female."[30] Women's centrality to the modern social world, like that of gold to the system of money, renders them useless but only insofar as they are precious within that world's economy of values. On this reading, the two contrasting attitudes that Pollak attributes to Pope are identical: the denial of women's worth is inseparable from the affirmation of it, metaphorically denying and supporting the entire money-based economy.

The excess of social reality that women represent as unusable money will help define the finer sphere of taste later in the poem, especially when it elicits a sublime response. Slavoj Žižek has argued that money and the aesthetics of sublimity may be seen as closely linked. Following Alfred Sohn-Rethel, he notes that the form of the commodity, with money as its arch example, resembles the peculiar ontological status of the sublime object: "we know very well that money, like all other material objects, suffers the effects of use, that its material body changes through time, but in the social *effectivity* of the market we none the less *treat* coins as if they consist 'of an immutable substance, a substance over which time has no power, and which stands in antithetic contrast to any matter found in nature.' "[31] For Žižek, this defines the problem of "the *material* character of money: not of the empirical, material stuff money is made of, but of the *sublime* material, of that other 'indestructible and immutable' body which persists beyond the corruption of the body physical" (18).

Pope's opening gambit here invokes a related logic, reminding us that the circulation of money in public exchange is after all a physical process: therefore even coins in circulation are made of actual metals that will lose their "lasting mark[s]" when passed about. But gold, by epitomizing this changeability so much as to demand its removal from exchange, expresses a sublime form of the commodity distinct from that remarked by Žižek: it attains sublimity not by denying but by revealing its excessive, "empirical," mutable materiality, rising above the physical processes of exchange not figuratively, like the "*sublime* material" of money in use, but literally, representing cash value in its physical removal from the cash system. Women, "Fine by defect, and delicately weak," similarly attain a sublime status, not by being " 'indestructible and immutable' " but by their very mutability, which requires men to withdraw, protect, and frame them fetishistically as special objects: the very empirical materiality of women's bodies is the basis of their sublimity.

Such a system of reflection through removal also enables the practice of valuing works of art. By according a special ontological status to certain unique, often delicate material objects, rendering them priceless—objects appealing to taste only by their evocation of a je ne sais quoi—society lends backhanded support to the system wherein everything has its price in relation to everything else. The emphasis on the sublime materiality of a painting, its every delicate brushstroke unique, presents the obverse image of the sublime material of exchanged commodities wherein actual materiality is ignored or abstracted away: the fetishization of particularity in fine art (or poetry) happily complements the system of abstract values animating the market economy. For Adorno, elaborating on Marx's idea of commodity fetishism in a manner similar to Frankfurt-school "fellow-traveler" Sohn-Rethel,[32] art does ideological work for the world of capitalistic exchange by its very critical aloofness from it: art

> epitomizes the unsubsumable and as such challenges the prevailing principle of reality: that of exchangeability . . . if in empirical reality everything has become fungible, art holds up to the world of everything-for-something-else images of what it itself would be if it were emancipated from the schemata of imposed identification. Yet art plays over into ideology in that, as the image of what is beyond exchange, it suggests that not everything in the world is exchangeable.[33]

This suggestion, of course, is false: the market in art or gold, or the marriage market in women, may at any moment retrieve such priceless commodities to common exchange even as they are ideologically placed above it, and without this possibility of retrieval their elevation from exchange would be meaningless. Thus women's sublime inconstancy as Pope depicts it always refers back to the world of exchange for which their softness supposedly renders them unsuitable.

And as many contemporary works affirm, a primary faculty driving this inconstancy of economic desire is taste—a faculty in which moral, aesthetic, and economic appreciation converge. As one of the two anonymously published poems entitled *The Woman of Taste* (1733) puts it, "It shews a want of taste, as well as sense, / To be debarr'd from pleasure by expence,"[34] ironically conflating spending money and having taste in a manner typical in contemporary discourses about femininity. Throughout the two poems under this title, taste in clothes and makeup rises to taste in drama, literature, architecture, and painting: the addressee is instructed to "Spare no expence to make your *Villa* fine, / O'er the gay walls let *Holben's* pictures shine" (Epistle II, 21). Fine art serves the imperatives of display and expenditure that Pope mocks in *To Burlington*, and the whimsical tastes of women in these poems are similarly seen as engaged in economic activity.

The *Epistle to a Lady*'s portraiture motif emphasizes the male observer's ironic participation in this economy, a role played by oscillating between skeptical puzzlement and satirical disapproval, allowing the two impulses to sharpen and define each other, anticipatory of the Kantian aesthetic stance articulated later in the century. In this way, women best occasion the disinterested engagement that helps Pope define himself, both morally and as a poet. He masterfully achieves an "equal mind" not by renouncing but by admitting his share in inconstancy that women so risibly exemplify. When confronted with inconstant women, the male observer does not step back from them to assert his fixity. Rather he leans forward, using his fascination with their instability as a way to acknowledge and so master his own:

Ladies, like variegated Tulips, show,
'Tis to their Changes that their charms they owe;
Their happy Spots the nice admirer take,
Fine by defect, and delicately weak. (41–4)

Such appreciation depends not on overcoming a moral disapproval of women as objects but on cultivating it. Their charms stem from their inconsistency, "their Changes": like Pope's own "Spots" that prove the clarity of his "impartial Glass" in *Satire II, 1*, women's "happy Spots" here paradoxically enhance their value. The "nice admirer" finds himself "taken" by these spots as if against his will, his admiration for them, like the shifting admirations of the nil admirari, revealing his own inconstancy. But (presumably unlike the feminine objects), he discovers in his inconstancy a self-stabilizing pleasure, an amusement distinguished from the misery shared by the women in the poem.

Pope next asserts a connection (" 'Twas thus") between the fussy admiration of the connoisseur, who perceives beauty in flaws, and an alarmed reaction suggestive of sublime experience—and this second attitude even more strongly implies a reflection of the observer's own moral status in the object:

'Twas thus Calypso once each heart alarm'd,
Aw'd without Virtue, without Beauty charm'd;
Her Tongue bewitch'd as odly as her Eyes,
Less Wit than Mimic, more a Wit than wise:
Strange graces still, and stranger flights she had,
Was just not ugly, and was just not mad;
Yet ne'er so sure our passion to create,
As when she touch'd the brink of all we hate. (45–51)

The "strange" combination of charms and flaws here typifies the effect of sublime art. As Pope's friend Jonathan Richardson (the elder) puts it in his *Essay on the Theory of Painting* (1715), "the *Sublime* where-ever 'tis found, though in Company with a thousand Imperfections, transports and captivates the Soul";[35] or, in a later treatise (1719), "the Sublime is consistent with great Irregularity; nay that very Irregularity may produce that Noble effect."[36] Given Pope's assimilation of women's pictorial manifestations to their moral natures, Richardson's notion of painterly "Imperfections" and "Irregularity" must translate in the poem into their moral equivalents.

Calypso here teeters on the brink not just of her male admirers' hatred but of objectivity itself. Not only is she defined mostly with negatives ("without Virtue," "without Beauty"), her stimulating effect arises from her near approach, but avoidance, of the labels to be applied to her—"just not ugly," "just not mad." Her reflection of those around her also effects her curious recession from objective status, "Less Wit than Mimic, more a Wit than wise," presumably mimicking the male wits attracted to her, "Her Tongue" reproducing their own wit, and unconsciously satirizing, at a fascinating remove, their own wit's lack of wisdom—as "her Eyes" would reflect their images back to them. This objective mysteriousness, throwing the male observer back upon himself and his own powers of judgment, further connects the experience of Calypso with that of the sublime, which occasions a failure of the perceiving subject facing "the conjunction of excess and abyss" of meaning, as Stanley Cavell puts it.[37] Calypso, godlike, creates passion out of this abyss, at the brink of the male power of observation or objectification. "Our" inability to fix stable truths in the world has eudaemonistic implications, destabilizing the self in its struggle for moral coherence. The brink of all that men cannot entirely know or grasp is the same brink of moral repugnance that Calypso touches. The "Pyrrhonism" that Pope elaborates on in Cobham here concretely returns as a blurring of the distinction between moral and epistemological evaluation, and in Calypso's case, at least, this blurring becomes the focus of a kind of specialized aesthetic judgment.

The poem further complicates this connection between male observer and feminine object because Pope is not just observing women but also painting them. At first, this seems mostly just a problem of technique, a challenge for the masterful painter confronting especially elusive models, though he emphasizes the airiness of his materials and skills appropriate to the task:

Come then, the colours and the ground prepare!
Dip in the Rainbow, trick her off in Air,
Chuse a firm Cloud, before it fall, and in it
Catch, ere she change, the Cynthia of this minute. (17–20)

A similar passage stressing even more strongly how his models force him technically to imitate their own lack of firmness comes immediately after the long portrait of Atossa, a rhetorical climax halfway through the poem. Here he also acknowledges his own role as the designer[38] of those whom he represents:

Pictures like these, dear Madam, to design,
Asks no firm hand, and no unerring line;
Some wand'ring touch, or some reflected light,
Some flying stroke alone can hit'em right:
For how should equal Colours do the knack?
Chameleons who can paint in white and black? (151–6)

Here "no[t] unerring" means "wand'ring" but also "deviating from the truth," deviations that Pope's art ironically requires to be "true"; in rejecting "equal Colours" he means primary or unmixed ones but also suggests the incapacity of such colors to represent anything but the æquus animus, inadequate to the essentially equivocal or unstable objects confronting him. The word order of the last line produces what seems an intentionally confusing effect, as if the chameleons were not the objects of representation but the subjects of the clause, the ones "who can paint"—reminding us of chameleons' own curious ability to paint themselves to match their surroundings, further obscuring the line between representer and represented, subject and object. Pope encourages his readers to recognize ways that his representing the women redounds back to him, a middle-voiced action on an object that entails the subject's action on himself.

Such redounding hence signals a loss or attenuation of ordinary, full-bodied agency. The call here for "Some flying stroke" recalls the incident from antiquity when Apelles the artist finds a kind of success at representation by relinquishing the *techne* of design that he had mastered. In the *Outlines of Pyrrhonism* (again, which Pope could have read in his copy of Thomas Stanley's *Encyclopedia of Philosophy*), Sextus Empiricus draws a moral from the story illustrative of skepticism's procedure and goals:

> Thus it happens to the *Sceptick,* as to *Apelles* the Painter, who having drawn a Horse, and trying to Paint his Fome, it succeeded so ill, that in Despair he threw the Spunge, wherewith he used to blot out the Colours, at the Picture; which lighting upon the place, made an exact representation of Fome. In like manner the *Scepticks* hoped to obtain Indisturbance by judging of the Unsetledness in *Phænomena's* and Intelligibles: which not being able to do, they suspended, and whilst they were in Suspence, as it were accidentally, Indisturbance overtook them, as a Shadow follows the Body. (477b)

In Sextus's analogy, Apelles's goal of representational accuracy coincides with the skeptical desire for tranquillity not just because both are satisfied (as if) by accident, beyond our powers as willing agents, but also because both specifically find success in a kind of failure. This inversion in both Pope and Sextus establishes a connection between skepticism and the sublime: the artist comes to represent nature successfully not by standing back from it but by becoming its unknowing instrument, relinquishing his power to it in a way that Pope himself remarked was characteristic of Shakespeare—"not so much an Imitator, as an Instrument, of Nature; and 'tis not so just to say that he speaks from her, as that she speaks thro' him."[39] Skepticism hence provides a model for certain kinds of art that are successful insofar as they escape the intellect's inevitably self-defeating attempts at representational mastery. Pope thereby relinquishes control as an artist in order to assert a more elusive order of control as a satirical moralist. Acknowledging the perplexing disorder of women, their power to defeat masculine judgment, only enhances Pope's prestige as a representer of them.

The portrait that precedes and motivates Pope's commentary on his artistic methods is that of Atossa, "Scarce once herself, by turns all Womankind" (116), who has often been seen as a kind of reflection of Pope himself, a cognate figure of Wharton in *To Cobham*: as Pope says of himself in an earlier letter, she "Finds all her life one warfare upon earth" (118). Her self-reflexive satirical exertions again have been seen to evoke the similar dynamics of Pope's own satire: "Shines, in exposing Knaves, and painting Fools, / Yet is, whate'er she hates and ridicules" (119–20). If she reflects what she ridicules, some critics have reasoned, we are led to the thought that Pope, in ridiculing her, reflects her without being aware of it—especially since he names her vocation as "painting Fools" in a poem that refers again and again to his own painterly techniques. "*Madame Atossa, c'est moi,*" S. L. Goldberg comments.[40] But as inclined as we may be to read such reflections as unconscious, as signs of the richness of Pope's imagination leading him unawares into identifying with what he overtly despises, they can also be seen to be part of a strategy. Pope often shows himself to reflect the madness around him, eager to admit his own share of inconstancy—to deny it, after all, would show him to be a pompous dogmatist, a falsely inflated Stoic "Sage." He may thus admit himself to be like Atossa, like Wharton, without fearing the madness or treason into which their inconstancies have driven them. He identifies with them, again, as a way of distinguishing himself from them.

The ubiquity of inconstancy asserted in *Epistle to a Lady* prevents Pope from turning to the concept of the ruling passion to resolve his own "Pyrrhonism" about women's characters, to view their contradictions as only apparent and to conclude with an extended portrait of a figure like Wharton who may finally be seen as consistent by the keen observer. Instead, he finds feminine self-contradiction even in the positive, concluding character of Martha Blount, "The Picture of an estimable Woman, with the best kinds of contrarieties" (269n). His correspondence occasionally places her in the complex feminine world of mingled virtue and inconstancy described by the poem: for instance, his remark about her to Bethel written after the *Epistle to a Lady* was published, that "her Virtues & her Weakness go hand in hand" (vol. 4, 40). But he is most often disposed to assert her distinctive virtue, as when he applies Elizabeth I's motto to her in a letter to Swift written as he was working on the poem: "Your Lady friend is *Semper Eadem,* and I have written an Epistle to her on that qualification in a female character" (vol. 3, 349). The facetiousness here—the poem in fact *denies* all women "that qualification" of constancy—should not obscure the fact that Pope habitually referred to Martha in his letters as "always the same."

It is all the more striking, therefore, that he resolutely moves from praising the "unclouded ray" of her "Temper" (257) and the fact that she is "Mistress of herself" to a final assertion of her "contrariety":

And yet, believe me, good as well as ill,
Woman's at best a Contradiction still.
Heav'n, when it strives to polish all it can
Its last best work, but forms a softer Man;
Picks from each sex, to make its Fav'rite blest,
Your love of Pleasure, our desire of Rest,
Blends, in exception to all gen'ral rules,
Your taste of Follies, with our Scorn of Fools,
Reserve with Frankness, Art with Truth ally'd,
Courage with Softness, Modesty with Pride,
Fix'd Principles, with Fancy ever new;
Shakes all together, and produces—You. (269–80)

Pope perpetuates this view in part as a response to the "Stoic's paradox" described by Montaigne in "Of Drunkenness." Though "Contradiction" has been seen as the source of vice, here and in *Cobham,* he concludes now that contradiction characterizes "good as well as ill." We find virtue mysteriously: we may neither resolve contradiction by a Stoic act of will nor simply condone it in all its forms. Disapproval of women's inconstancy lingers throughout the passage: it begins with "And yet," as if qualifying his former praise of Martha by reminding her of her contradictory status, and there is at once praise and a sense of masculine superiority in his view of her as "but . . . a softer Man." Pope's sincerity in exalting Martha as Heaven's "last best work" and his sense of the inferiority of the softness and contrariety that characterize her ironically complement one another, just as the value of gold symbolically represents the system of money in which it cannot practically be used. Martha discovers her virtue in a kind of androgyny, but one that is blended "in exception to all gen'ral rules," essentially mysterious and impossible to duplicate exactly, like a work of art, sublime in its anomaly. In this Pope differs from Young, whose two satires on women in the collection *The Love of Fame: the Universal Passion* (1728) present a preponderance of ridiculously whimsical figures while occasionally proposing models of rational behavior to give his female readership something to emulate,[41] for instance, the one designated by a blank in Satire V, who is blessed with both good taste and "native force of mind" (V, 345): "When such her mind, why will the fair express / Their emulation only in their *dress?*" (V, 363–4).[42] Pope ends his passage about Martha on the second personal pronoun as if to assert that she is so exceptional that she cannot be a model for emulation. Of course the discourse of art as a je ne sais quoi supports such a valorization of the unsubsumable (to use Adorno's word), the "exception to all gen'ral rules." But the key to Pope's management of such a discourse here lies in his simultaneous praise and suspicion of contradiction, his discovery of praise in suspicion, and vice versa.

This view of Martha's ambiguous character complements rather than conflicts with the readings of her by the most prominent feminist critics of the poem, who tend to see her as implicitly supporting the hierarchy of gender even as she seems to rescue women from the imputation of necessary inferiority. For Felicity Nussbaum, in *The Brink of All We Hate* (1984), she is the exception that finally proves the rule: "the unexampled portrait of Martha Blount does not ease or negate the moral earnestness of the earlier portraits; it intensifies the disdain the narrator affects toward the sex."[43] Pope's condemnation of "Most Women" stands, even finding support from Martha's exceptional status. Ellen Pollak insists that despite Pope's description of Martha as heaven's "last best work," he subtly places her in the hierarchical position of inferiority—passive, obedient, tractable to the commands and imperious gaze of the aloof, critical male: "indeed in his very reverence for her 'difference' from the inferior sameness of 'other women,' he reinscribes her status both as object and inferior" (110). Valerie Rumbold notices how her positive traits rest on certain fallacies, for instance, his figurative assertion that glaring sunsets (dazzling unchaste women) are "unobserv'd" when the "Moon's more sober light" (Martha) appears in "Virgin Modesty":

> The simile is typical of those proscriptions that seek to keep women out of male preserves by claiming that the limited sphere ordained for women is really the more valuable. But if the world does not behave according to such "real" values, the justification is effectively an empty one. We can imagine a world in which people instinctively stare at the pale rising moon and habitually ignore flaming sunsets, but we know we do not live in it. In these lines it has apparently been Pope's achievement to obscure the fact.[44]

These recognitions of Pope's reassertion of gender hierarchy as he appears to revise it powerfully describe the meaning of the poem's ending and may be extended along lines argued here. Pope's praise of Martha indeed sets her among the women whose virtue he had mocked, as an object, as passive, as contradictory, as soft, and most significantly, as another portrait, another product of his own feminized art.

But we may allow Pope's praise to stand as such (despite the unrealistic element noted by Rumbold) if it is seen as part of his larger effort to discover a value in inconstancy even as he sees in it the source of all vice. He does so in order to see the inconstant world as it is—both sunsets and the moon are traditional symbols of inconstancy, after all—and through such a vision he reasserts his own worldly, undogmatic, sophisticated persona, superior to the inconstancy around him but only because he lets it define his values and affections as well as his authority to attack the vicious. This is the most subtle imaginable recuperation of the superiority of the male position. He himself is a gift to Martha from "ascendant Phoebus"; she reflects him and indirectly discovers his own invisible purity as a poet. Instead of disowning or implicitly disdaining the female sphere, he must actively promote its virtues to perform his act of ideological self-authorization. Our recognition of this interdependence also enables a more comprehensive view of social relations in the period than the critics cited earlier allow. Far from being dismissed as insignificant, the "limited sphere ordained for women" defines the public sphere of men, motivating not just its economic activities but its ethical and intellectual ones: the fashioning of valued feminine softness proves indispensable for nascent bourgeois ideology in its definitions of a society composed of a complementary opposition of public and private spheres. As the metaphor of gold and its attendant associations suggest, women confine themselves to privacy because they exemplify to excess the very values and properties that make public life possible and so function to determine its meaning. Pope's ambivalence about this larger social structure does not lead him to reject it outright but to mix with it, to identify with it, though in the process of noting its moral inferiority.

Thus Pope's feminism, or his sympathetic identification with the feminine and with inconstancy or contrariety, derives from his antifeminism, or his recognition that immorality consists in inconstancy that is essentially feminine and feminizing[45]—and his blending of these two attitudes into a potently contradictory one constitutes his most subtle work not just regarding women but as a moralist in general. His sympathy with skeptical writers like Montaigne makes him reluctant to resolve such a contradiction, in these two poems at least, to suggest that inconstancy is ever escapable or that humans can live like Stoic "demigods." Other moments in the *Epistle to a Lady* reflect other kinds of feminism, analytical accounts of women's subjection in society, explaining the two ruling passions of women, "The Love of Pleasure, and the Love of Sway":

That, Nature gives; and where the lesson taught
Is still to please, can Pleasure seem a fault?
Experience, this: by Man's oppression curst,
They seek the second not to lose the first. (211–4)

A fuller and even more explicit discussion of "Man's oppression" appears in an earlier poem to Martha's sister, the *Epistle to Miss Blount, With the Works of Voiture* (1712): "Still in Constraint your suff'ring Sex remains / Or bound in formal, or in real Chains" (41–2). Such sentiments were not unique. Young, in his Satire V, writes that men "scorn [women] for those ills [men] themselves create" (552): "Most hard! in pleasing your chief glory lies; / And yet from pleasing your chief dangers rise" (555–6). But such clichés hardly make Young a feminist, inasmuch as his two satires are also filled with the lamest, most oppressive insults imaginable ("If you resent, and wish a *woman* ill, / But turn her o'er one moment to her *will*" [V, 421–22]).

It is not Pope's endorsements of or dissent from such pronouncements that have exclusively determined the significance of his gender politics. Pope has elicited positive responses from women writers and readers following him in part because many recognize, and assume for themselves, the power of his double view of inconstancy, as a feminine failing linked to a universal (often economic) reality, that we must adopt to see the world accurately.[46] Unlike a set of propositions, the significance of this double perspective appears ironically in his poems of selfhood in the 1730s, all the more potent for being unstated and unstatable. Such ironies neither absolve nor condemn him of misogyny, and that is their point: Pope can hover, and many of those sentiments expressive of distaste for women derive their meaning from his identifications with them. The ideological power of this position lies not just in its entangling of gender differences in the conundrums of epistemology and Hellenistic ethics but in its invocation of the new standards of taste, the sublime, and the je ne sais quoi, that themselves will help order the arts and civil society as the century moves forward.

7

Modernity and the Skeptical Sublime
in the Final *Dunciad*

The power of skeptical doubt more than any other factor generates Pope's ambivalent perspective on the apocalyptic course of British cultural history charted in the final *Dunciad* (1743). Critics for some time have seen evidence of his mixed feelings in the poem: while obviously attacking the dunces' literary endeavors, Pope seems fascinated by Dulness's surreal, disorienting effects; he also takes the dunces seriously as representatives of potent intellectual tendencies, despite his dismissals of them as mere fools and bad stylists.[1] The concluding acceptance of Dulness's triumph makes the poem seem like less an act of satirical resistance than one of surrender—to forces that are somehow superior to his own good sense. Emrys Jones's classic essay "Pope and Dulness" (1968) reads Pope's evident delight in the dunces' activities as an oblique rebellion against the "imaginative depletion"[2] of his times: "what Pope as a deliberate satirist rejects as dully lifeless his imagination communicates as obscurely energetic" (637). G. Douglas Atkins proposes another sort of explanation in his *Quests of Difference: Reading Pope's Poems* (1986), arguing that "*The Dunciad* parallels (aspects of) deconstruction, its teaching, and its effects,"[3] and finds that the power of Dulness derives from the ceaseless play of signifiers that Pope unwittingly initiates in his text. But a focus on the historical presence of skepticism in the poem, and Pope's association of it to the sublime, develops both sorts of readings, addressing both his uniquely imaginative manipulation of philosophical ideas and literary techniques of his day and the generally radical epistemological implications that many readers now perceive in the poem. Pope with great sophistication portrays skeptical doubt as at once irresistible and intolerable, which thereby accounts for both his identifications with and hatred for the dunces who promote it.

I have argued throughout this book that writers from the Restoration onward had similarly discovered that their encounters with skepticism produced ambivalence. They espouse a moderate doubt concerning the capacity of reason and evidence to establish certainty on important questions to fend off the distressing, radical doubts occasioned by the unwarranted claims of dogmatists, enthusiasts, and charlatans. But many ironic consequences arise from this acceptance of (some) doubt to achieve intellectual stability. Perhaps none are more subtle than Pope's own skeptical attitudes, struck fitfully in his philosophical poetry of the 1730s—meditations that contribute to his enhancement of the first *Dunciad*'s scope (1728) in its revisions of the 1740s. The daring of the final *Dunciad* lies in its revelation of how our very efforts at epistemological moderation, directed against dogmatic, irresponsible ideologues, ironically infect all society with the inescapable power of global doubt. Even more dramatically than Swift, Pope depicts his own incorporation into the forces he opposes, announcing skepticism as a historical event overtaking British culture, a *"total oblivion of all Obligations, divine, civil, moral or rational"* ("Book the Fourth, Argument," *TE*, vol. 5, 338). While the skeptical sublime tradition originated ideologically to critique the clashing dogmatisms that destabilized British politics, religion, and society in the seventeenth century, Pope now portrays the practices of eighteenth-century civil culture as themselves conjuring a future of skeptical oblivion. The kinetic, unthinking factors driving the culture of the 1730s and 1740s may no longer be ironically accepted and mastered by the detached, critical poet: the *Dunciad*'s poet attains his special rhetorical force by allowing the forces he critiques to overtake him.

Pope's submission to the forces of Dulness against his own apparent wishes, furthermore, itself constitutes his most nuanced depiction of the sublime—which, as Longinus tells us (in Welsted's translation) "rather ravishes than persuades" (3). Skepticism seizes Pope (as if) against his will, unpersuaded, without his intellectual endorsement or sympathy—a prime instance of sublime experience, which itself has come to seem a kind of skeptically destructive parody or perversion of voluntary, enlightened, purposeful, rational thought. The *Dunciad* makes the most powerful use imaginable of the skepticism that sublimity engenders and brings it to its final, conscious, satirical end. Theories of the sublime typically distinguish themselves by their accounts of how the experience of overwhelming power is rendered pleasing or otherwise useful to its subject, usually by his learning ideologically to accept and enjoy his subjection, his position of weakness or servitude. The dunces in the *Dunciad* parody one type of such sublime thralldom, fatuously embracing the power that renders them passive idiots. Pope also insists on his own helplessness before the skeptical tide that Dulness brings forth, but in order to achieve his own satirical power: his heightened depictions of the threat of skepticism, which he understands far better than the dunces, testify to his poetic authority. He thus manages to be the victim of Dulness's doubt-inducing sublimity without quite being its butt. Of course such access to poetic power ironically demands that the humanistic values Pope ostensibly upholds must be presented as no match for the force that destroys them. But in undertaking poetically to represent the gravity of the threat to such values by indicating the impossibility of their survival, Pope himself lays hold of the power that he admits must destroy his own moralism, defying the promptings of epistemological perversion even as they are spoken through him.

I

The predicament of the "gloomy Clerk" (459) near the end of book IV, "Sworn foe to Myst'ry, yet divinely dark" (460), strikingly exemplifies skepticism's characteristically equivocal attendance upon Dulness, as a note by Pope and Warburton suggests: "The Epithet gloomy in this line may seem the same with that of dark in the next. But *gloomy* relates to the uncomfortable and disastrous condition of an irreligious Sceptic, whereas *dark* alludes only to his puzzled and embroiled Systems" (459n). The note oddly observes a similarity between two aspects of the Clerk's condition to insist on its dividedness: "gloomy" paints him as the unhappy, disillusioned victim of skeptical doubt, while "dark" refers to his own crabbed works, which, as "Systems," still hopefully seek some sort of metaphysical or "divine" truth. The Clerk's deistic philosophy is anything but skeptical, insofar as it claims to establish the existence and nature of God by reason. He is in fact "fond to dogmatize" (464) about religion:

Let others creep by timid steps, and slow,
On plain Experience lay foundations low,
By common sense to common knowledge bred,
And last, to Nature's Cause thro' Nature led.
All-seeing in thy mists, we want no guide,
Mother of Arrogance, and Source of Pride!
We nobly take the high Priori Road,
And reason downward, till we doubt of God . . . (465–72)

He does not want to "doubt of God," according to his announced agenda. His reasonings however land him in skepticism all the same, even if he does not realize it, even if he finds himself merely "uncomfortable" in the face of his "disastrous" circumstances, as the note says—another odd splitting of a single condition. (The phrasing recalls the letter to Pope from Atterbury on Huet's skepticism: if Huet's "doubting" could even be entertained without contradiction, "we should then be in the most uncomfortable and wretched state in the world" [*Correspondence*, vol. 2, 75].) The note's term "Sceptic" does not exactly mean someone who professes disbelief in God but rather someone who tries to believe in God in the wrong way and thence becomes an atheist without intending it, or intending it very peculiarly. This misfiring of intention is definitive of skepticism's main function in the poem: the dunces "explain a thing till all men doubt it, / And write about it, Goddess, and about it" (book IV, 251–2).

A charge of atheism is not quite fair to Samuel Clarke, author of *A Demonstration of the Being and Attributes of God* (1705), to whom the Clerk seems to refer, as Sutherland says in the Twickenham edition: "Clarke certainly used the *a priori* method to demonstrate the existence of God, but he also argues from Nature to Nature's cause. Nor do his *a priori* arguments lead him to 'doubt of God'" (459n). In a more subtle sense, however, Clarke's "demonstrations" exactly instantiate the skeptical dynamic that informs Pope's diagnosis of the world of the dunces: the attempt to shore up faith in God by rationalistic methods produces the effect opposite to the intended one. As one commentator on Clarke's appearance in the *Dunciad* puts it, "The danger perceived in such works was that they could all too easily lead to unbelief, so flimsy was their logical argumentation, and so distant were they from a necessary sense of mystery. Clarkean rationalism was considered as a dangerously insecure half-way house between the mysteries of true religion and the literally self-satisfied delusions of deism."[4] In fact, this slippage of dogmatism into doubt is explicitly thematized in the controversy of the period. Clarke's *Demonstration* begins by addressing "all those who either are or pretend to be atheists"[5] and goes on to prove God's existence, using primarily a version of the cosmological argument. But Francis Gastrell, a frequent responder to Clarke, writes *The Principles of Deism Truly represented and set in a clear Light, in Two Dialogues between a Sceptick and a Deist* (1708, 4th ed., 1726), in which the "Sceptick" proves that the "Deist" actually agrees with him on the main points. Pope's accusing Clarke of skepticism and atheism despite his professions of theism presents a common view of how the intentions of rationalists treacherously reverse themselves.

The broader contexts of such modern epistemological reversals have been explored in Stanley Cavell's readings of the tradition inaugurated by Descartes[6]—who began his project by doubting everything ultimately to erect a fully certain system. The rationalistic, Cartesian obsession with certainty, according to Cavell, creates a philosophical mode in which (as Wittgenstein puts it) "language is like an engine idling,"[7] alienated from its stabilizing, everyday usages and contexts and so made functionally dubious in a way that its users cannot intend: their every appeal to some "indubitable" bit of reasoning or evidence always must unintentionally invite further skeptical questions. Skepticism hangs over discourse after Descartes like a sword of Damocles, a perpetual threat, wielded by no one with full control. Though few if any profess it, all must address its unexpected and distressing eruptions, created by their own demands for an inhumanly high degree of certainty as much as anything. In this sense Cavell maintains that "the effort to deny skepticism is itself an expression of skepticism"[8] and thereby understands both skepticism and philosophical solutions of it as departures from ordinary intention. And this is precisely how Pope characterizes the "doubt" unintentionally generated by the dunces' "explanations."

The Clerk's religious doubts may seem remote from the more fundamental skepticism about the existence of the external world and other minds that Cavell discusses—a treatment derived from Wittgenstein's immensely subtle exposition of the concept of language-games in the *Philosophical Investigations*. However, Pope presents skepticism's influence as rather broader than a mere tendency toward atheism. The Clerk's hyperphilosophical language alienates us not just from the divine but from the entire culture that God was thought to inform and amounts to losing a sense of moral action, selfhood, and will. The a priori process that causes the trouble specifically operates at the expense of "common sense" and "common knowledge." The Clerk's arguments alienate us not only from God but from a sense of the worth of ordinary practices and "plain Experience," vitiating the power of common sense to tell us what we need to know. Of course for Pope this would finally include an ability to build out of experience a proof from design of the existence of God—itself a philosophical urge that, if pursued in rigorously rational detail, would perhaps eventuate in a philosophical excursion from "common knowledge." But here (as in the *Essay on Man*) Pope merely alludes to some comforting series of steps that will lead us to nature's cause, tactfully suppressing them so as to preserve his apparent allegiance to common sense.

Pope's coupling of the loss of God with the loss of common sense fairly exactly matches Cavell's discussion of the role of skepticism in bringing on the crisis of modernity, seen in Descartes's initiation of his project:

> In Descartes' thinking, the ground, one gathers, still exists, in the assurance of God. But Descartes' very clarity about the necessity of God's assurance in establishing a rough adequation or collaboration between our everyday judgments and the world (however the matter may stand in natural science) means that if the assurance in God will be shaken, the ground of the everyday is thereby shaken.[9]

Cavell is referring specifically here to Descartes's idea that we need to know that a benevolent God exists in order to guarantee the accuracy of our impressions of ourselves and the world, while simultaneously needing to be sure of the accuracy of these impressions in order to construct a proof that a benevolent God exists—the notorious "Cartesian circle."[10] Pope's evocation of "reasoning downward" captures something of this vertiginous circularity. We perhaps expect that the "high Priori Road" takes us into the realm of pure reason and thereby alienates us from the world before our eyes: we have faith more in our proofs than in "plain Experience." But curiously, when we reason downward from a priori truths (either the cosmological argument favored by Clarke or Descartes's ontological proof, which Clarke also mentions in *A Demonstration*),[11] we lose both abstract and concrete alike: Pope surprisingly finishes the line by noting the tendency of such thought toward a "doubt of God." Our reasoning along the high priori road not only overtly flouts "common knowledge" but also undermines the very abstract knowledge it seemed to promote, leaving us hovering in a rather more uncomfortable "middle state" that the one staked out in the *Essay on Man*.

The effects of the Clerk's methods reach far beyond religion and attack various intellectual principles that common sense seems to demand:

at one bound o'er-leaping all his laws,
Make God Man's Image, Man the final Cause,
Find Virtue local, all Relation scorn,
See all in *Self*, and but for self be born:
Of nought so certain as our *Reason* still,
Of nought so doubtful as of *Soul* and *Will*. (477–82)

Pope and Warburton supply rather odd glosses in the notes here:

> the Poet, from the errors relating to a Deity in Natural Philosophy, descends to those in Moral. Man was made according to *God's Image;* this false Theology, measuring his Attributes by ours, makes God after *Man's Image*. This proceeds from the imperfection of his *Reason*. The next, of imagining himself the Final Cause, is the effect of *Pride:* as the making Virtue and Vice arbitrary, and Morality the imposition of the Magistrate, is of the *Corruption* of his *heart*. Hence he centers everything in *himself.* The Progress of Dulness herein differing from that of Madness; one ends in *seeing all in God*, the other in seeing *all in Self.* (478n)

This confusing passage again suggests a similarity, now between madness and (theological) Dulness, while overtly insisting on a difference. Part of

Pope's point must be that *"seeing all in God"* is like *"seeing all in Self"*: the former means to include human frailties in God's nature by defining it reductively according to human reasoning's (necessarily imperfect) demands—to "Make God Man's Image"—while the latter means to madly assert these frailties and demands as the sole measures of truth and virtue. Bad theology itself is a kind of madness, here defined as a self-absorption that passes itself off as absorption in the divine. Still the note *contrasts* madness and Dulness to underscore the dividedness at the heart of the modern condition that has been presented in other ways: Dulness's efforts to "Make God Man's Image," as bad as they appear to sober critics, do not seem as dangerous as Mandevillean attempts to "Find Virtue local" or as demented as a madman's inability to find external standards for his beliefs. But in fact they are. Pope's diagnosis finds all on the same continuum, thereby presenting an account of both why bad theology looks different from madness and why the two come to mean the same thing. The loss of God results in the insanity of being "Of nought so doubtful as of *Soul* and *Will*"—and though these may themselves seem like philosophical abstractions, they are commonsensical enough for Pope and Warburton: "two things the most self-evident" (481n).

On one reading, this self-evidence creates the absurdity of the dunces' position. Pope may expect us to see the dunces confuting themselves: if we are "Of nought so certain as our *Reason,*" then we cannot by definition doubt of our souls and wills because our very act of reasoning confirms that they exist and function properly. The joke here perhaps depends on an implicit reminiscence of Descartes's cogito: Pope accords the highest degree of "self-evidence" to soul and will presumably on the Cartesian grounds that all can be justifiably doubted except the subject doing the doubting. In any case, the tension between faith in reason and doubt of ourselves may be taken to demonstrate skepticism's triviality. The dunces' reasonings really place nothing at risk because what they render dubious is simply self-evident. It is difficult to take this as the final word on the matter, however, in part because it raises the nontrivial question of how something "the most self-evident" could ever be rendered dubious to anybody. Descartes does not find himself indubitable for want of trying: the force of his argument rests on our intuition that doubting soul and will, what the dunces are doing here, literally cannot be done. The mere fact that the dunces really are doubtful, no matter how extravagantly or eccentrically, demonstrates on Descartes's own terms that his grounds are not quite what he thinks they are. In fact, a skeptic after Descartes like Huet "dissected the beginning of the Second Meditation so deftly," in Richard Popkin's words, "that he finally transformed *I think, therefore I am* into *I thought, then perhaps I was.*"[12] The dunces' finding "nought so doubtful" as the "two things the most self-evident" bespeaks on this reading not so much a simple contradiction as a kind of rationalistic perversity that cannot be cured by reason alone.

The copresence of certainty and doubtfulness in the Clerk's thinking is the purest form of the split condition of the modern subject in Pope's account. But again the fact of this division itself does not constitute a refutation or end of doubt. Skepticism's most compelling and distressing feature is that an absolute faith in reason in the end produces doubts about not only what reason seeks to prove but also reason itself. As Hume remarks in the *Treatise of Human Nature* (1739), "the understanding, when it acts alone, and according to its most general principles, entirely subverts itself, and leaves not the lowest degree of evidence in any proposition."[13] As it happens, the philosophers and theologians Pope mocks as duncesare not professed skeptics but metaphysical dogmatists. What he is decrying, then, is not the attempt to render soul and will doubtful but rather the fact that such doubt is the unintended consequence of any embrace of an exaggerated standard of reason. Skepticism is not, on this interpretation, the simple philosophical blunder made by people who fail to recognize that rationally discovered doubt presupposes an unskeptical dependence on rational procedures. It is the inevitable outcome of any discourse that cannot recognize the self-evidence of things like soul and will and uses the understanding "alone" (in Hume's sense) to prove them. The lines read this way present the ultimate alienation of intention, the loss of soul and will, selfhood and agency, as the condition of modern thought, not merely as one of its philosophical mistakes.

This depiction of Dulness's intellectual character does not challenge so much as complement Aubrey Williams's analysis in *Pope's Dunciad: A Study of Its Meaning* (1955), which in many ways remains the standard study of the poem's intellectual investments. Williams argues that "the most helpful approach to this problem, in light of both the contemporary educational situation and the poem itself, may be made, perhaps, through the medium of two parts of the *trivium*—rhetoric and dialectic."[14] He places Pope in the longstanding rhetorical, humanist tradition that views abstract philosophizing, scholastic theological inquiry, and other "dialectical" pursuits as disastrous because they drive a wedge between the objects of knowledge and expression, *res* and *verba*. These pursuits reveal their iniquity principally in the public sphere, where the divorce of matter from expression most obviously impedes purposeful communication. Though Williams does not specifically describe the role of skeptical doubt in determining the intellectual character of the dunces, he would probably argue that Cartesianism is another socially alienating, "dialectical" endeavor, and he would perhaps see the poem's dividednesses noted here as results of the dialectician's basic alienation of words from things.

But Williams's model does not account for several important features of Dulness's ascendancy. First, the virulence and the contagiousness of the dunces' intellectual practices suggest something far worse than a mere passion for dialectic. Like a general, broad-based skepticism, the reasonings of the dunces constitute a tangible threat to "all men," even those like Pope who are not disposed to think dialectically yet who know or fear (far more vividly than the dunces) that once begun, such thought cannot be checked, dismissed, or ignored. Pope does not stand detached upon some inviolable humanist ground in his poem, but rather stylistically and intellectually acknowledges the inevitability of Dulness's triumph—not only at the end of book IV but in the Bentleyan textual apparatus and paradoxical logic of the poem's narrative, as my next section will suggest. He surrenders so completely to Dulness because he recognizes that its skeptical tendencies really do threaten his own cherished beliefs in God, virtue, decorum, and order. They do so paradoxically, rendering dubious what all philosophers seek to prove, but this paradoxicality only makes it worse. Williams's model falls short because it fails to explain Pope's intense reluctance to indicate any hope that rhetorical values could ever prevail.

This lack of confidence appears most acutely in the specific historical dimension of the poem—a dimension that Williams must downplay if his portrait of Pope's engagement in an "enduring struggle" is to be convincing. At the root of this struggle for Williams is "a cleavage in the thought and attitude which extends through the whole of Western civilization," and he seeks to demonstrate that "the labels applied to the opposing parties change, but the parties contend about the same issues" (104). This reading implies that Pope is simply exaggerating to make a point: "one may not accept," Williams writes, "Pope's notion of a special or accelerated assault of duncical rhetoric in his own time, but one can still appreciate the validity of his concern for a certain rhetorical ideal" (113). Williams in short leaves out any attempt to characterize the intellectual traits of modernity. He does acknowledge that Pope portrays man "as having lost his traditional orientation," and he even suggests that Pope chronicles a historically real shift in the terms of the debate, noting the growing influence of "the 'raptur'd vision' of a Shaftesbury—or in the times to come, of a Wordsworth" (130). But he does not offer any convincing intellectual or historical reasons why such a shift is happening now.

The idea that the rise of skepticism produces the shift is on the face of it almost tautological: in its blandest sense, skepticism simply *means* the "loss of orientation" that Williams says is the result of dialectic's victory—the destruction of beliefs in God, virtue, justice, truth that is the fruit of the dunces' labors. The case has been made, especially by Richard Popkin, that skepticism rather more precisely initiates the discourses that we usually consider to be modern: Popkin argues that Montaigne's *Apology for Raimond de Sebond* (copiously annotated by Pope), with its reintroduction of Sextus Empiricus's Pyrrhonistic writings into European philosophical debate, is "the womb of modern thought, in that it led to the attempt either to refute the new Pyrrhonism, or to find a way of living with it" (54). In the wake of Popkin's work, many intellectual and literary historians have described in more specific detail the "way of living with it" developed in England in the seventeenth and eighteenth centuries, emphasizing the rise of nondogmatic, fallibilistic forms of natural science, of probabilistic rhetoric that helps us navigate the world while not pronouncing with certainty on it, or various other important strands of nondogmatic, provisional discourse like neo-Epicureanism. The *Dunciad* testifies, however, not to the success of these methods of living with uncertainty but to the way uncertainty erodes the very practices designed to contain it, which finally inspire rather than assuage doubt. Popkin's metaphor of skepticism as a womb resonates with the threatening maternal aspect of Dulness, her power to bring forth monstrous births that no one controls or quite knows what to do with.[15] The *Dunciad* articulates not the confidence generated by a new world of probable signs but a general anxiety about the questionable status of previously unquestionable truths. The poem seriously documents its claim that the duces represent something new, not merely another dip toward scholasticism on the seesaw of Western tradition—and the rise of skepticism characterized by Popkin as a historical factor broadly answers to this sense of seriousness.

The conclusion of the Clerk's speech again illustrates how skepticism's essentially unintended influence appears in the duces' production of effects contrary to what they recognize or expect—and Pope here significantly associates this division with a kind of poetic inspiration:

Oh hide the God still more! and make us see
Such as Lucretius drew, a God like Thee:
Wrapt up in Self, a God without a Thought,
Regardless of our merit or default.
Or that bright Image to our fancy draw,
Which Theocles in raptur'd vision saw,
While thro' Poetic scenes the Genius roves,
Or wanders wild in Academic Groves;
That NATURE our society adores,
Where Tindal dictates, and Silenus snores. (483–92)

In a note glossing "Academic groves," Pope and Warburton quote from Shaftesbury's *Moralists* to identify his philosophy with the Hellenistic ("Academic") tradition of skepticism: "Above all things I lov'd *Ease*, and of all Philosophers those who reason'd most *at their Ease*, and were never angry or disturb'd, as those call'd *Sceptics* never were. I look'd upon this kind of Philosophy as the *prettiest, agreeablest, roving Exercise of the Mind*, possible to be imagined."[16]

This quote's inclusion in the notes without further comment indicates that Pope and Warburton expected Shaftesbury's approval of skepticism to be read as patently self-damning. To complicate matters, however, the interlocutor in *The Moralists* who says this is not the "Theocles" mentioned in the passage, the beholder of the "raptur'd vision," but a character called Philocles, who in fact opposes his skepticism to Theocles' sublime philosophy: Philocles says, "[Theocles] heard everything with mildness and delight, and bore with me when I treated all his thoughts as visionary, and when, sceptic-like, I unravelled all his systems" (25). Shaftesbury intends, of course, this admission of skepticism into the debate to be seen as more innocent than the Pyrrhonism or Academic doubt often execrated in the period and as complementing a more sublimely assured view that he will explore later. His polemical success in general often depends on his persuading his readers to take usually suspect terms, like *enthusiasm, skepticism,* or *Deism,*[17] in special, positive senses. A sympathetic reading of Shaftesbury's dialogic method must recognize that Philocles' skepticism is only a preliminary move, to detach us from politics[18] and other unpleasant, worldly discourses, preparing us for Theocles' truly philosophical apprehension of God in "mighty Nature!" (vol. 2, 98).

But Pope's unsympathetic, highly condensed insinuation is that Theocles' visions represent a tendency somehow equivalent to the unprincipled skepticism of Philocles: both tend toward freethinking ("Tindal") and self-indulgent poetry, among other things, all of which maintain an unbroken affiliation with skeptical doubt. Though Shaftesbury will come to insist later in *The Moralists* that Theocles' rapture "proves" or at least offers assurances of a God compatible with the Christian one, Pope suggests that Philocles' initial skepticism persists to poison every subsequent effort to assure or inspire us: Shaftesburyan visions can never ascend above the Academic doubt where they began. The couplet, "While thro' Poetic scenes the Genius roves, / Or wanders wild in Academic Groves," again sees a similarity in a difference: the aestheticizing visions of Theocles ultimately are grounded no more firmly than the wanderings of a skeptical intellect amid uncertainties. Pope probably catches "Academic Groves" from the epigraph of *The Moralists,* Horace's *Epistle II, 2,* 45: "Inter silvas Academi quaerere verum," a line that Shaftesbury intends to refer not specifically to Academic skepticism but to a general search for truth, but that doubtless refers for Pope to Shaftesbury's persistent affiliation to unsavory doubts.

Pope's own imitation of that epistle (1737) supports a very different, moralized style of Horatian intellectual exploration: "my Father taught me from a Lad, / The better Art to know the good from bad: / (And little sure imported to remove, / To hunt for Truth in *Maudlin's* learned Grove)" (*II, 2,* 53–5). It is true that at other moments in the *Imitations,* Pope's Horatian attitude seems similar to Shaftesbury's agreeable intellectual roving: his reasoning at ease and shunning disturbance reflects the worldly skeptical poise of Pope's own version of the nil admirari. But here he criticizes the attitude, perhaps dimly recognizing in Shaftesbury the danger of his own Montaignean, unprejudiced intellectual fluidity. Once the skeptical intellect begins to "wander wild," it may never find the visionary assurances it seeks.

Pope's critical conflation of Theocles' visions and Philocles' doubt thus also sets him against the positive sublime vision that helps Shaftesbury and others of the period construct a social model of civility and politeness through taste. For Shaftesbury, after we cleanse our minds of prejudice by skeptically challenging all illiberal enthusiasms, we discover our "natural," higher destiny, our true spiritual vocation, through intimations of transcendent grandeur in nature and by reflecting on our own souls' inborn responsiveness to it. The position implied in the *Dunciad* is at once less and more skeptical than Shaftesbury's—less because it insists on the danger inherent in indulging in skeptical doubt, however preliminary, and more because of its acceptance of this danger's power: doubt, once begun, cannot be resolved, and nothing could be more dubious than the self-congratulatory delusions that arise in its wake. In this instance of the skeptical sublime, like many others, Pope expresses a conservatism opposed to the sublime justifications of what would be called liberal society, the claim to discover a universal, providential order in nature and humanity, ineffable, recalcitrant to manipulation or co-optation by religious or political zealots yet discernible through various sublime media: heightened feeling, peculiar sensory impressions, or poetic visions. While the *Essay on Man's* Shaftesburyan musings do assume the existence of such an order, that poem's peculiar lack of an account of sublime mediation and its many attendant contradictions signify his own skeptical reluctance to establish a positive link between human culture and providence. An unknowing, conservative view of virtue is all that remains: as Pope says to Caryll in an early letter, "the greater number of arts to which we apply ourselves, are mere groping in the dark. . . . 'Tis not our business to be guessing what the state of souls is, but doing what may make our own happy. We cannot be knowing, but we can be virtuous" (vol. 1, 190–1). The final *Dunciad,* at the end of his career, insists not just on the gulf between absolute knowledge and virtue but on the cultural collapse that must attend the sublime attempts of philosophers of civil society like Shaftesbury to bridge it.

II

The sublime character of the dunces' inducement of doubt appears not only in the linkage of "Poetic scenes" and "Genius" to the groves of Shaftesburyan "Academic" skepticism but throughout the poem, as specifically literary practices pour "*Oblivion*" into all regions of culture. Book IV magnifies the first three books' more limited attack on Pope's literary enemies, their bad poetry and criticism, and the enormities of the book trade. It is not immediately apparent how these are implicated in the atheism, valuelessness, and alienation from common sense that apocalyptically conclude the final version of the poem. But while the last *Dunciad* is more far-reaching in its diagnosis of modern culture than the earlier versions, Pope does not relinquish his insistence that poetry sets the terms and course of the decline: he does not replace Theobald in the 1743 edition of the poem with a philosopher like Mandeville or Clarke or a political figure like Walpole or George II but with the laureate Cibber. As has been often pointed out, the *Dunciad's* message becomes inclusive through the analogies it suggests between the literary men and women at the front of the action and historical, political, and cultural figures of more obviously national importance.[19] The emphasis on the literary nature of British cultural decline extends beyond such analogizing, however: the decline itself is realized as a quasi-aesthetic, sublime engulfment of a range of cultural endeavors.

Though Pope most fully realizes the connection between literary power and the skeptical decay of all truth and value in his last revisions, the versions of the poem from 1728 on anticipate the domination of all perception and thought by aesthetic modes: Dulness's power appears most impressively by its rendering of reality itself as a bad poem or a sensationally theatrical play. In book III of the *Dunciad Variorum* (1729), after the philosophical work of Toland, Tindal, and Woolston obliterates the enlightenment of Bacon, Locke, and Newton (208–220), Theobald (later Cibber) observes Dulness's "charms," which are "Not touch'd by Nature, and not reach'd by Art" (228), as if scientific departures from nature and the breaking of poetic rules were equivalent abuses. The imagery that follows does not merely violate the Horatian rules of decorum set down in *Ars Poetica* but inverts them—and more significantly projects the literary-pictorial images that Horace forbids onto the "real" world:

Thence a new world, to Nature's laws unknown,
Breaks out refulgent, with a heav'n its own:
Another Cynthia her new journey runs,
And other planets circle other suns:
The forests dance, the rivers upward rise,
Whales sport in woods, and dolphins in the skies. (237–42)

As Sutherland notes, line 242 in particular refers to Horace's *Delphinium silvis appingit, fluctibus aprum* (30). The implication of this movement from Newtonian and Lockean science to extravagant, fantastic excursions into "a new world" is that bad theatrical poetry contaminates not only literary taste but also our perceptions of reality. Theatrical representation takes the place of the "intellectual light" shed on the world by true religion and philosophy. Even in the 1729 edition, then, Pope implies that Dulness's debasing of taste operates specifically at the expense of a shared reality independent of our perceptions of it, anticipating Dulness's command in the final version to "MAKE ONE MIGHTY DUNCIAD OF THE LAND!" (IV, 604): "land becomes poem," as Howard Erskine-Hill comments, at the poem's climax.[20]

The final version goes even further than those of 1728 and 1729 to emphasize the power of aesthetics to pervert other modes of thinking and perception, when the "Harlot" of opera appears onstage first, to triumph over not only the muses but *"Science," "Wit," "Logic," "Rhet'ric,"* and *"Morality"* (21–30), all bound by Dulness. Bad art supplants not only good art but the whole range of human endeavor, especially those disciplines that offer knowledge and secure virtue. Though the Harlot vexes the muses in particular, Pope intends her attack on order and sense to be seen as a threat extending well beyond the realm of taste:

"O *Cara! Cara!* silence all that train:
Joy to great Chaos! let Division reign:
Chromatic tortures soon shall drive them hence,
Break all their nerves, and fritter all their sense:
One Trill shall harmonize joy, grief, and rage,
Wake the dull Church, and lull the ranting Stage. . . ." (IV, 53–8)

Once chaos and "Chromatic tortures" begin to be valued as aesthetic effects, they infect and desacralize the "dull Church"'s music. Here and elsewhere in the poem, bizarrely inverted tastes are vehicles of culture-wide devaluation, not merely analogues to the failure of value in putatively more serious spheres.

The *Dunciad* tends to figure such convergences of degraded arts and a broad skeptical destabilization as manifestations of the sublime, an aesthetic and cognitive field of experience marking the limits of our capacity to experience and to know, associated with the rapture and wildness of the Shaftesburyan vision. The sublime seductively appears as a mode of thought when true knowledge of reality fails, as Bolingbroke puts it in his *Letters, or Essays addressed to Alexander Pope, Esq.*: we "see just enough to tempt us with the hope of making better and more discoveries . . . every glittering apparition that is pointed out to them, in the vast wild of imagination, passes for a reality: the more distant, the more confused, the more incomprehensible it is, the more sublime it is esteemed."[21] This delusory sublime aesthetically dominates the poem as a whole, from the "vast profound" (I, 118) of Theobald/Cibber's thoughts in book I to the "Universal Darkness" of the final line of book IV. Poetic sublimity resonates with skepticism throughout, in Pope's quasi-metaphorical conflations of darkness with doubt, of sensory with intellectual failure. The poem repeatedly defines the skeptical sublime as the darkening of understanding at its horizon, or "that intellectual light which dies before the face of Dulness" (IV, 111). Such associations of sublimity with the death of light indicate a shift in Pope's attitude toward elevated poetic power. While *Peri Bathous* maintains the notion of a "true sublime" with which to contrast the poetic failures of Blackmore and the rest, the final *Dunciad* describes the inverting power of the duntes as its own species of limit experience, with its own destructive power: as complex as *Peri Bathous*'s accounts of bad poetry are, they tend invariably to emphasize the reduction and enfeeblement of language.

One striking instance of Pope's distrust of the sublime is the ambiguous role played by Milton throughout book IV.[22] By the time the *Dunciad* appears, Dryden's description of *Paradise Lost* as the "greatest, most noble, and most sublime P O E M"[23] in English was commonplace, as was Addison's assessment of Milton in "An Account of the Greatest English Poets" (1694): the poem, "Bold, and sublime, my whole attention draws, / And seems above the critick's nicer laws" (66–7). Others, however, vehemently resisted the absorption of their critical attention and the overriding of law in *Paradise Lost,* which, Rymer mocks, "some are pleas'd to call a Poem."[24] Perhaps more troubling to Pope would be the terms in which Milton was celebrated. Pope's longtime enemy Leonard Welsted writes in "Remarks on Longinus In a Letter to a Friend" (appended to his 1712 translation of Boileau's translation of *On the Sublime*):

> It is undoubtedly true of *Milton,* that no Man ever had a Genius so happily form'd for the Sublime: He found one only Theme capable enough to employ his Thoughts, but he could find no Language copious enough to express them. . . . When I view him thus, in his most exalted Flights, piercing beyond the Boundaries of the Universe, he appears to me as a vast Comet, that for want of room is ready to burst its Orb and grow eccentrick. (157)

While Pope admires Milton, he also recognizes the source of his greatness in his challenging the limits of thought and especially of language. In its own sublime practice, the *Dunciad* unites both attitudes: on the one hand, it complains that the dunces violate Milton's poetry and pervert its grandeur for their own petty purposes, but on the other it points out how Milton himself participates in exactly the same obscurantist cultivation of poetic mystery, lawlessness, and ambiguity that Pope suspects, itself sublimely violent like Welsted's Milton, "ready to burst its Orb." The Miltonic note sounded by the invocation indicates the ties between poetic sublimity and skeptically divided intellects of the dunces:

YET, yet a moment, one dim Ray of Light
Indulge, dread Chaos, and eternal Night!
Of darkness visible so much be lent,
As half to shew, half veil the deep Intent.
Ye Pow'rs! whose Mysteries restor'd I sing,
To whom Time bears me on his rapid wing,
Suspend a while your Force inertly strong,
Then take at once the Poet and the Song. (1–8)

Initially the request for a ray of light to be indulged seems heroic, if misguided. The ray would originate presumably with Pope himself, the poetic speaker—it cannot come, of course, out of "eternal Night"—and thus represent his last stand against the encroaching forces of chaos. But it seems odd of Pope to submissively ask permission to make such a stand. This equivocation between submission and defiance quickly modulates, however, to a more thorough acknowledgment of Dulness's control: he changes his request that a "dim Ray of Light" be "indulged" to one that a ray "Of darkness visible . . . be lent"—that is, he no longer seeks to provide his own light but rather borrows darkness from the force he ostensibly opposes. The invocation announces Dulness's absolute sway rather than resists it.

Of course "darkness visible" is already by Pope's time a touchstone for the Miltonic sublime, another way of presenting the dividedness of Dulness: the oxymoronic phrase's sublimity lies not merely in its evocation of obscurity, a lack of light,[25] but also of this lack's positive charge, its visibility. This effect provides empirical epistemologists like Boyle and Locke a crucial model of the "peculiar" impression by which we may recognize sublime objects otherwise utterly beyond our capacities: as Boyle puts it in *A Discourse of Things Above Reason,*

the eye sees both light and darkness: which expression, though somewhat odd, may be defended by saying that though, since darkness is a privation, not a being, it cannot properly be the object of sight, yet it may be perceived by means of the eye, by the very differing affection which that organ resents, when it is impressed on by luminous or enlightened objects, and when it is made useless to us by darkness.[26]

The uselessness of darkness for Boyle is in a sense the most useful of things: its visibility awakens "an inward sense that some things surpass [the soul's] forces," allowing it to "discern the limits of that sphere of activity within which nature had bounded it" (229)—hence it becomes a most prized conduit of sublime awareness.

In Pope's hands the phrase attains a broader, more immediate significance, showing the "deep Intent" of the language on the page before us, not something on the outskirts of experience (Hell, chaos, the infinite universe) or the limits of our rational capacities. Darkness's power to "shew" something else—as in *Paradise Lost* itself, where "darkness visible / Serv'd only to discover sights of woe" (I, 63–4)—is exactly what Richard Bentley objects to, in a notorious note in his edition of *Paradise Lost*,[27] but Pope, defying him, plays with Milton's paradoxical ascription of a power of discovery to darkness. The half-shown, half-veiled intent presents not two different things but a single thing's dual aspect: the intent reveals itself, as it were, by being veiled. Like the skeptic's certainty that produces doubt at the end of the Clerk's speech, the visibility of the intent ironically underscores its obscurity. This duality itself figures Longinus's own remarks on the relation between the sublime and reason: as an orator employs sublime effects, we are "drawn from the *Argumentative* part to a *smiting phantasie,* whereby the other is both *hid* and *enlightened*" (Hall, 36). The modern or post-Miltonic poet, whom the speaker of book IV's invocation exemplifies, derives his sublime power to initiate his poem by partaking of the skeptic's split condition.

Part of this dividedness issues from a heightened ambiguity concerning the poet's intentions: it is obscure whether the "deep Intent" is that of the poet or of Chaos and Night. The grammar of the passage suggests that Dulness ventriloquizes intentions through the poet, but the notes interpret otherwise. One remark, attributed to "Scriblerus," treats the lines as characteristic of "a dull Poet" who "can never express himself otherwise than by *halves,* or imperfectly." The mysterious dividedness of the "Intent" is a poetic misstep, and the lines function as simple parody. A second comment, attributed to "Bentley," compares the lines' "*Mysteries*" to those characteristic of Milton, quoting *Il Penseroso*'s notion that in a sublime poem "*more is meant than meets the ear*"—a distinction between matter and expression characteristic of poetic greatness. Pope's point is that the "imperfection" can be read as ineptitude or sublimity, according to taste. The aesthetic effects valued by Dulness encourage such a double reading, and even though the notes lay the blame or praise at the poet's feet, this doubling wrests his words' meaning from them by showing that they can be taken in opposite ways. Dulness's sway over the intentions of the poet manifests itself in the capacity of sublime utterances to affect different readers differently.

The invocation maintains an ambiguity concerning the poet's agency that parallels the doubling effects of the skeptical dynamic described earlier: Pope purposefully blurs the distinction between his control and Dulness's control over book IV. He asks the "Powers" to "Suspend a while your Force inertly strong," so that he himself can "sing," presumably with his own voice, according to his own intentions (and perhaps his own satirical agenda of criticism and even resistance). Yet now he writes of Dulness's "Mysteries restor'd" in the past tense as if her triumph has already occurred. While the invocation seems to beg time of the Goddess before "the Poet and the Song" are "at once" taken, it simultaneously suggests that time has already run out—almost as if the suspension of her powers "a while" and the taking of Pope "at once" were impossibly simultaneous aspects of a single moment of sublime, poetic composition. This temporal ambiguity is reinforced by Pope's acknowledgment that "Time bears [him] on his rapid wing" to Chaos and Night, working in concert with Dulness's "Pow'rs." Thus her force is not in suspension but already in effect, "the Poet and the Song" already taken on the wings of time. The invocation presents an impossibly divided picture of Pope's brief, hard-won control over his poem and Dulness's absolute dictation of it.

This doubling is, of course, intentional in a wider sense. The confusions between Pope's and Dulness's agencies, between Pope's resistance and his capitulation, are not mere mistakes or imperfections of expression—though they necessarily court the possibility of being read that way. Pope wants Scriblerus's criticisms in note 4, his attribution of the confusions of the passage to the dullness and clumsiness of the poet, to remain viable. By illustrating the sublime power of skeptical doubt with the ambiguities raised by his own utterance and turning them to his own satirical purpose, Pope has seized the skeptical sublime as a mode of ridicule. But this power is inherently unstable because it depends on the possibility of its being misread as mere stupidity. The *Dunciad* presents the interpreter with an instance of undecidability in something like Atkins's deconstructive sense: the invocation is both an example of bad writing and an orchestration of sublime techniques, and must be read as one to be read as the other. Since this attitude entails a contradiction, it cannot in a sense be intended, if intention implies the projection of a coherent or univocal message, meaning, or effect. Yet Pope does manifestly cultivate the contradictions and the temporal and volitional confusions that introduce book IV—and thus presents a picture of intentionality more complex and equivocal than one implied in the standard notion of "having a meaning." By illustrating the sublime power of skeptical doubt with the ambiguities raised by his own utterance and using them for his own satirical purpose, Pope turns the sublime into a mode of mockery—though ironically it is ridicule that must portray its failure, its misguidedness, in order to succeed.

This enriched depiction of intention is itself explicitly thematized as book IV unfolds. To be a dunce is to compromise one's own agency:

The gath'ring number, as it moves along,
Involves a vast involuntary throng,
Who gently drawn, and struggling less and less,
Roll in her Vortex, and her pow'r confess.
Not those alone who passive own her laws,
But who, weak rebels, more advance her cause. (81–6)

Here the agency of the "throng" again displays the curious division that the skeptical obliteration of knowledge exacts. The crowd of dunces seems both to assemble itself and to be assembled by Dulness: that is, the "gath-'ring number" demonstrates activity, moving along and involving (whirling in) "a throng"—yet the "number" apparently is or is coming to be identical to the "throng," which Pope calls "involuntary" and which responds to Dulness's will. The dunces here are not merely simultaneously active and passive but active by being passive: they act upon themselves, as it were—the "number" acting on the "throng"—so as to render themselves incapable of action. At one level, Pope intends the clumsiness of these and other "imperfect expressions." They instantiate one of the *Dunciad*'s explicit themes, that poets' propagation of Dulness is out of their control, even contrary to their wishes. The "weak rebels" hence anticipate the gloomy Clerk: their attempts not to be dull backfire just as the rationalists' attempts to "prove" God result in atheism. Like skepticism itself, Dulness prevails by gaining not only adherents but also foes, and it is through these dual means, intentional and "involuntary," that it succeeds in blotting out "intellectual light."

This blurred agency has political implications, inasmuch as it seems to render its subjects incapable of politics. When Pope sees Dulness's program as supported by "Not those alone who passive own her laws, / But who, weak rebels, more advance her cause," he alludes to the extreme, opposite positions in seventeenth-century political debate, the passive obedience to the monarch of the High Churchmen and Royalists and the rebellion threatened by radical elements in Parliament, Puritans, and Republicans. Pope insinuates that in the Britain of the 1730s and 1740s, both these traditional political extremes have been subsumed by cultural forces that turn them to the same end and so render them essentially apolitical.[28] Brooks-Davies, in *Pope's Dunciad and the Queen of Night: A Study in Emotional Jacobitism* (1985), argues that the poem expresses, by means of an elaborate submerged symbolism, a sympathy with the political sentiments if not the actions of the Jacobites. Following him, Howard Erskine-Hill has contended that "Pope's poetry of opposition is poetry of a Jacobite vision" and that "The *Dunciad* will be found the most significant work from this point of view" (95). But most of Brooks-Davies's references are to the 1728 and 1729 versions of the poem, and when he addresses elements of book IV, he recognizes its expressions of disillusionment with and criticism of aspects of Jacobite political views: he says, for instance, "For all his Stuart sympathies, Pope will never condone 'the right divine of kings to govern wrong'" (104, quoting IV, 188).[29] Erskine-Hill's references to book IV also concern Pope's ambivalence about politics by 1743, though he maintains the idea of Pope's nostalgic (if hopeless) attachment to the Jacobite cause.

But Dulness's exact political alliances and opponents by the 1743 version seem too vague and inclusive to be read as an allegory of any particular political struggle—and surely that is part of what Pope finds distressing about it. Dulness's bipartisan nature in fact appears even in the earlier versions: "Diff'rent our parties, but with equal grace / The Goddess smiles on Whig and Tory race, / 'Tis the same rope at sev'ral ends they twist, / To Dulness, Ridpath [Whig journalist] is as dear as Mist [Tory journalist]" (book III, 283–6). Such lines seem to insist that no one particular party nor even any concrete political philosophy serves Dulness exclusively: the system of opposing parties itself enhances her power. By 1743, as opposition and obedience produce the same effect, Pope indicates that the possibility of true politics has lapsed. The negation of politics by the paradoxical union of opposites again signals the aesthetic power of the new world of Dulness, which harmonizes conflict in a parody of a *discordia concors*. Pope thus ironically accepts the apolitical world of Shaftesbury's raptures in *The Moralists*. It is this ideology of ideology, not of any particular ideological position within political struggle, that the final *Dunciad* projects—not a covert Jacobitism but a critique of a debased, fantastic world of discourse that co-opts all attempts to articulate opposition to it.

One of the leading literary practices described in the poem that fractures intention is the editorial efforts of Bentley and his fellow philologists. Pope frames the entire section of book IV on modern education and the universities, from line 119 to Bentley's remarks ending at line 275, with discussions of the attenuations of authorial intention by textual editors. The section begins by asserting a quasi-mystical equivalence between the preservation and destruction of meaning:

When Dulness smiling—"Thus revive the Wits!
But murder first, and mince them all to bits;
As erst Medea (cruel, so to save!)
A new Edition of old Æson gave,
Let standard-Authors, thus, like trophies born,
Appear more glorious as more hack'd and torn,
And you, my Critics! in the chequer'd shade,

Admire new light thro' holes yourselves have made.
 "Leave not a foot of verse, a foot of stone,
A Page, a Grave, that they can call their own;
But spread, my sons, your glory thin or thick,
On passive paper, or on solid brick . . . " (119–30)

Perhaps the leading example of a "standard-Author" in Pope's mind now is Milton, whom *"bold* Benson" (110) revived "By erecting monuments, striking coins, setting up heads, and procuring translations" (110n). In Bentley's preface to his edition of *Paradise Lost,* he glorifies his own heroic willingness to "risque his own Character, while he labour'd to exalt Milton's," but the irony for Pope lies not just in the edition's revelation of Bentley's own shortcomings but its degradation of Milton in the effort to exalt him. Milton's admiring editors are not his fault, yet Pope suggests some illicit if unintended commerce between them when Dulness designates Milton and other "standard-Authors" as "Wits." While sometimes charging Bentley with vitiating the poetic power of sublime authors—"Thy mighty Scholiast, whose unweary'd pains / Made Horace dull, and humbled Milton's strains" (211–2)—Pope is equally interested in the aesthetic transformations wrought by textual editing. Bentley here does not disenchant literature but like Medea enlivens his victims with his own unnatural power, replacing a Horatian aesthetic of decorum, balance, and wholeness with an aesthetic of the sublimely mysterious fragment: "In ancient Sense if any needs will deal, / Be sure I give them Fragments, not a Meal" (229–30). Later, a note to four lines of asterisks dropped from editions subsequent to 1742 reads "Hiatus, but not *valdè deflendus,* since the learned Aristarchus loves a Fragment" (249–54n): Bentley produces fragmented editions not out of dry, philological scrupulosity but out of love.

Still, Pope often allows us to differentiate between poetic greatness and the mystifications of critics. The disfiguration of their heroes' texts, Pope implies, can be seen for what it is: the critics "Admire new light thro' holes [them]selves have made," and presumably better readers can tell the author's intent, at this point, from the critic's perforations. Yet the imagery of "holes" implies that meanings become irretrievably lost in the process: though the right-thinking people whom Pope's satire addresses can see them as editorial intrusions, we lose what was there in the first place. The poem deplores the obfuscation of "intellectual light" even as it implies that nothing can be done about it. Pope furthermore hints that the nature of authorship itself, and not merely the work of a few ill-willed editors, renders intention dubious. He insists that the critics "Leave not a foot of verse, a foot of stone, / A Page, a Grave, that they can call their own, / Turn what they will to Verse, their toil is vain, / Critics like me shall make it Prose again" (211–4). But these lines suggest not just that Bentley vexes a few passages but that he renders the meaning of every element of a text questionable. The comparison of editing with monument-building registers the severity and irreversibility of the problem, as writing is necessarily severed from the intentions that gave it life. Dead writers of course cannot "call" anything their own, and the speech-verb underscores their incapacity to guarantee their intentions after they are gone. Insofar as the works of even a great writer like Milton survive on "passive paper," he will be whirled into the throng following Dulness. Herein lies yet another source of modern sublimity: the mere fact that writing seems to invite interpretation and editorial parasitism offers a more totalizing dimension of the Miltonic, sublime effect of producing more meaning than meets the ear.[30]

Despite the various ways in which Pope allows us satirical distance from the Bentleyans' obscurantist efforts, he equally insists that they cannot but involve us sublimely in crises of interpretation:

See! still thy [Dulness's] own, the heavy Canon roll,
And Metaphysic smokes involve the Pole.
For thee we dim the eyes, and stuff the head
With all such reading as was never read:
For thee explain a thing till all men doubt it,
And write about it, Goddess, and about it:
So spins the silk-worm small its slender store,
And labours till it clouds itself all o'er. (247–54)

The puns here themselves equivocate, coupling the sublime excesses of rolling "Canon" (artillery) and metaphysical "smokes" with the bathetic images of the canons of University colleges and at their heads, the Poll of each—puns to which a note (247n) from Scriblerus torturously draws attention. Beyond that, the note introduces Milton again as an equivocal source of sublimity in the poem:

> It may be objected, that this is a mere *Paranomasia* or *Pun*. But what of that? Is any figure of Speech more apposite to our gentle Goddess, or more frequently used by her, and her Children, especially of the University? Doubtless it better suits the Character of Dulness, yea of a Doctor, than that of an Angel; yet *Milton* fear'd not to put a considerable quantity into the mouths of his. It hath indeed been observed, that they were the Devil's Angels, as if he did it to suggest the Devil was the Author as well of false Wit, as of false Religion, and that the Father of Lies was also the Father of Puns. But this is idle: It must be own'd a Christian practice, used

in primitive times by some of the Fathers, and in later by most of the Sons of the Church; till the debauch'd reign of Charles the second, when the shameful Passion for *Wit* overthrew every thing: and even then the best Writers admitted it, provided it was obscene, under the name of the *Double entendre.* (247n)

Among other things, this offers an example of explaining a thing until all men doubt it. The note's rambling quality (like others throughout the textual apparatus) is obviously meant to parody senseless annotations. But beyond this, it somewhat less playfully reintroduces Milton as a source of interpretive instability. Earlier, we heard that Bentley "humbled Milton's strains" (212), but here, when Scriblerus notes that "*Milton* fear'd not to put a considerable quantity [of puns] into the mouths of his [angels]," Pope suggests that Milton himself rather too recklessly employs indecorous effects. We may wish to defend Milton's use of puns along the lines presented at the second moment of Scriblerus's considerations: that is, only Satan's followers use them in *Paradise Lost.* But Scriblerus retracts this defense because such speculations are "idle," says that puns are "a Christian practice," then backtracks again by associating them with "the debauch'd reign of Charles the second." The note thus engenders genuine confusion concerning Pope's own "official" attitude toward puns. Of course he uses them all the time, but does he understand them as part of an illicit commerce with Dulness or a legitimate practice of true wit? The problem is most acute insofar as the puns here issue from Bentley's mouth in a quasi-accidental way and so cannot be seen to parody his self-conscious attempts to be clever. Instead we associate the joke of "heavy Canon," the mockery of collegial stupidity, with the perspective of the "author," Pope, now indulging himself by crossing his own boundary between false wit and true.

Like other moments in Pope's oeuvre that thematize doubt, the skeptical implications of the *Dunciad*'s attitudes toward interpretation, commentary, and textual criticism are anticipated by his favorite author, Montaigne—especially in his last essay, "Of Experience":

Experience makes it manifest, that so many interpretations dissipate the Truth, and break it. . . . Who will not say that *Glosses* augment Doubts and Ignorance, since there's no one Book to be found, either Humane or Divine, which the World busies it self about the Difficulties of, which are clear'd by Interpretation. The hundreth *Commentator* still refers you to the next, more knotty and perplext than he. When were we ever agreed amongst our selves, that a Book had enow, and that there was now no more to be said? (vol. 3, 481–2)

Montaigne captures the sense in which Bentley's focus on local textual difficulties expands into a generalized skeptical doubt, an undermining of the possibility of finding a book's truth. He uses a standard image for such activity: "Men do not know the natural Disease of the Mind, it does nothing but ferret and enquire, and is eternally wheeling, jugling, and perplexing it self; and like Silk-worms, suffocates it self with its own Web" (482)—perhaps consciously echoed by Pope's couplet, "So spins the silk-worm small its slender store, / And labours till it clouds itself all o'er." The contradictory double aspect of modernity presents itself, here in the work that smothers the worker even as it spins out of his control.

This self-confusing procedure is yet another way that Dulness generates the sublime, a leading characteristic of which is a kind of self-involvement, as Pope himself had astutely noted long ago in his lines in the *Essay on Criticism* on Longinus: "Whose own *Example* strengthens all his Laws, / And *Is Himself* that great *Sublime* he draws" (679–80). Bentley's labors similarly confuse poetry and criticism, involving all in the same cloudy vortex of himself. The theme of the dunces' self-involvement has been announced throughout the poem, as in book I: "What then remains? Ourself. Still, still remain / Cibberian forehead, and Cibberian brain" (217–8). Later, toward the poem's culmination, the gloomy Clerk urges us to "See all in *Self*, and but for self be born" (IV, 480). Sublimity's tendency to throw its subject back on himself, to grant him a sense of his own power or destiny instead of an objective sense of the state of affairs in the world (or the text) that causes his response, has been stressed throughout the aesthetic tradition and receives its most providentially comforting treatment at the hands of Kant in the third *Critique*—who argues that in confronting physically superior forces in nature, we discover our own moral superiority to them.[31] Pope's less self-affirming view in the *Dunciad* is that sublimity entraps the self solipsistically in its own peculiar judgments. While his skeptical sublime's emphasis on the subjective power generated by divisions among the mind's faculties may be seen to anticipate Kant's more sophisticated account—the failure of imagination compensated by the elevation of reason—instances like these in the *Dunciad* and elsewhere demonstrate the definitive difference between them: the skeptical sublime insists on the unbridgeable gulf between the self and whatever higher power it attempts to contemplate and recuperate, only entangling itself further in delusion as it claims narcissistically to recognize its own exaltation in the "sublime it draws." The critical self-involvement of Longinus celebrated in the *Essay on Criticism* here is precisely what arouses suspicion.

"Of Experience" presents a divided attitude toward such criticism similar to that of Pope's poem: the essay deplores the self-suffocations of textual critics as it recognizes (and even comes to celebrate) the inevitability of their efforts. Montaigne emphasizes the dangerous ways explanation produces doubt: "In sowing and retailing Questions, they make the World to fructifie and increase in uncertainties and disputes" (vol. 3, 481). With a characteristic disregard for consistency, however, he forgets these negative aspects of interpretation a few passages later:

> there is no end of our Inquisitions, our end is in the other World. 'Tis a sign either that Wit is grown shorter sighted when it is satisfied, or that it is grown weary. No generous Mind can stop in it self . . . it has *Sallies* beyond its *Effects* . . . its pursuits are without Bound or Method, its aliment is Admiration, ambiguity the Chace; which *Apollo* sufficiently declared, in always speaking to us in a double, obscure, and oblique Sence; not feeding, but amusing and puzzling us. 'Tis an irregular and perpetual motion, without Example, and without Aim. (vol. 3, 483–4)

This passage valorizes elements that have come to be characteristic of sublimity, in the *Dunciad* and elsewhere—obscurity, boundlessness, formlessness, irregularity—and one commentator, at least, has made a case that Montaigne's skepticism contributes in a historically precise way to the development of the sublime in the centuries following him.[32]

Nonetheless, the split attitude in "Of Experience" differs from the more vexed one of the *Dunciad*. Montaigne vacillates from unambiguous disapproval of textual wrangling to unambiguous celebration of interpretation, while Pope seems simultaneously appalled and fascinated by the sublime effects he presents. This distinction offers nothing less than a way of conceptualizing the difference between modernity's intellectual attitudes and those of premodernity. In Montaigne, interpretation takes on something of the measured, ambiguous variations of a becalmed if bemused personality, enhanced by its very failures to discover coherence: at times our insatiable curiosity frustrates, at others stimulates us. His doubts are motivated by the ancient tradition of Hellenistic eudaemonism: as the Pyrrhonist claimed to do, he recognizes the frustrations inherent in experience only in order to win his way to a perspective of passive tranquillity—a view enhanced here, perhaps, by his personal sense of impending death. The essay assumes a pacified, detached attitude toward the interminability of study and intellectual exploration as old as Ecclesiastes: "of making many books there is no end; and much study is a weariness of the flesh" (12:12). Pope himself explored the possibilities of such self-transcending immersion in inconstancy after Montaigne's literary example in the Horatian poems of the 1730s, asserting his own pleasurable integrity by succumbing to the fragmentary quality of life around and within him.

But in the world of the final *Dunciad* such detachment is impossible. The

Montaignian tendency to admit inconstancy and doubt in order to master them has been transformed into a Cartesian discovery of the intolerability of such a divided attitude toward knowledge. Division in the *Dunciad* persists, but only insofar as the poem obliquely registers the attraction of skeptical sublimity as an illicit, resisted seduction, not as the full, pleasurable, and masterful surrender of the self to doubt. The *Dunciad's* sublimity traps us in the vertiginous, threatening astonishment undergone by Descartes at the skeptical initiation of his project, forestalling the possibility of controlled detachment, admitting the power of doubt simply by feeling all our resistances to it fail. Pope's concluding appeals to the muse have all the irony of resignation. As in the invocation of book IV, he admits Dulness's dominance even as he begs the muse to allow him to remain independent:

O Muse! relate (for you can tell alone,
Wits have short Memories, and Dunces none)
Relate, who first, who last resign'd to rest;
Whose Heads she partly, whose completely blest;
What Charms could Faction, what Ambition lull,
The Venal quiet, and intrance the Dull;
'Till drown'd was Sense, and Shame, and Right, and Wrong—
O sing, and hush the Nations with thy Song! (619–26)

Pope here sets the muse in opposition to Dulness only obliquely. That is, he asks the muse not to block Dulness's triumph but to narrate it in detail, "who first, who last resign'd to rest," to "relate" what the wits and dunces cannot remember, which implies that the event from Pope's and the muse's standpoint has already happened. The *New Dunciad* of 1742 then concludes the poem with the couplet, "While the Great Mother bids Britannia sleep, / And pours her Spirit o'er the Land and Deep," after which two rows of asterisks declare the rest of the poem lost—as if some possibility may remain that the muse had memorialized the end of civilization in poetry now lost in the dulness of time.

But Pope does not permit even this small degree of separation between the muse and Dulness to stand in the 1743 version. After a single row of asterisks, he immediately exclaims, "In vain, in vain,—the all-composing Hour / Resistless falls: The Muse obeys the Pow'r" (627–8). Dulness does not banish or destroy the muse but gains her obedience. The colon in this couplet indicates that the falling of the all-composing hour consists in the enlisting of the muse under Dulness's banner. The term *all-composing* portrays the triumph of Dulness as an essentially poetic one: assuming the muse's prerogatives, Dulness will henceforth compose all intellectual endeavors as if they were sublime poetry. The *Dunciad* finally depicts not merely the destruction of culture but its destructive production: a view of culture as ideology, now overtaking all who struggle to be independent of it, whether heroically or ironically. Like Swift's recognition of elements of the enthusiast's reversal in civil society's more enlightened appeals to taste, the final *Dunciad* testifies to the compulsive power of cultural representations infused with the divisive, ambiguous energy of epistemology, creating doubt with every claim to certainty, reversing every rapturous effort to ascend to higher truth, alienating every intention in the sublime, impersonal, inertia of the subject's "own" thought. The final *Dunciad* expresses Pope's awareness that sublimity is a destructive effect that cannot be contained in the aesthetic realm—and must overcome every discourse requiring a commitment to truth and the possibility of certainty. The poem's modernity consists in its portrayal of an all-involving skeptical alienation that can only be intensified by conservative nostalgia for our previously undoubted condition and by every attempt to ground discourse anew.

Notes

1: Introduction

1. *Le Traité du Sublime ou du merveilleux dans le discours, Traduit du grec de Longin* (Paris, 1674), 73.

2. *Dionysius Longinus on the Sublime,* trans. William Smith (London, 1739), 14.

3. R. S. Crane's distinction between the "rhetorical sublime" and the "natural sublime" in his review (*Philological Quarterly* 15 [1936]: 165–7) of Samuel Holt Monk's classic study *The Sublime: A Study of Critical Theories in XVIIIth-Century England* (1935, 2d ed. Ann Arbor: University of Michigan Press, 1960) still well accounts for the historical change that turned attention from linguistic effects to the "aesthetic" mechanisms of human psychology, but David B. Morris rightly insists in *The Religious Sublime* (Lexington: University of Kentucky Press, 1972) that critics have applied it misleadingly to distinguish responses to sublimity in nature from sublime language: "To the integrated vision of many eighteenth-century Englishmen, nature and art did not occupy separate realms but often appeared as aspects of a single object of consciousness" (6).

4. *The End of the Line: Essays on Psychoanalysis and the Sublime* (New York: Columbia University Press, 1985), 1. Hertz alludes to the preceding passage quoted from Longinus and Pope's comment in the *Essay on Criticism* that Longinus "*Is himself* that great *Sublime* he draws" (680).

5. *Thoughts on Religion and Other Curious Subjects* (1704), 4th ed. (London, 1749), trans. Basil Kennet, 212.

6. *Poems on Several Occasions* ("Antwerp" [probably London], 1680), facsimile ed. by James Thorpe (Princeton: Princeton University Press, 1950), 7. While I cite the text of this edition throughout, I also consult *The Complete Poems of John Wilmot, Earl of Rochester,* ed. David Vieth (New Haven: Yale University Press, 1968), and *The Works of John Wilmot, Earl of Rochester,* ed. Harold Love (Oxford: Oxford University Press, 1999).

7. *Solid Philosophy Asserted, Against the Fancies of the Ideists: . . . with Reflexions on Mr Locke's Essay concerning Human Understanding* (London, 1697), preface.

8. Mark Akenside, *The Pleasures of the Imagination. A Poem. In Three Books.* (London, 1744), book I, 210–1. Lines 151 to 270 paraphrase Longinus's section 35, which Akenside freely translates in a footnote (p. 17).

9. *The Works of Dionysius Longinus On the Sublime: Or a Treatise Concerning the* Sovereign Perfection of Writing *Translated from the* Greek. *With Some Remarks on the English Poets* (London, 1712), 98.

10. *Peri Hupsous, or Dionysius Longinus on the Height of Eloquence* (London, 1652). Hall's translation was not widely known, and Boileau is credited with popularizing the word *sublime* to describe the Longinian effect, which Johnson in his *Dictionary of the English Language* (New York: Arno Press, 1979) calls "a Gallicism, but now naturalized." But Hall does use the word throughout his translation, for example, "For these Sublimities do not only *win*, but *astonish* their Hearers" (2); "Thus in *Sublimities* as in *vast* estates, there must be somewhat to *contemn* and throw away" (40).

11. *A Discourse of Logomachys, or Controversys about Words, so common among Learned Men* and *A Dissertation Concerning Meteors of Style, or False Sublimity* (London, 1711), 220.

12. *Personification and the Sublime: Milton to Coleridge* (Cambridge: Harvard University Press, 1985), 3.

13. "To these Disputes [about words] were undoubtedly owing the different Sects of the *Academicks, Scepticks,* or *Seekers,* who withheld their Assent from all Propositions, under pretence of the Intricacy, Perplexity, and Incomprehensibility of Things: and it's too probable, that our modern *Libertines, Deists,* and *Atheists* took occasion from the scandalous Contentions of Christians about many things, to disbelieve all" (59).

14. *A Tale of a Tub,* ed. A. C. Guthkelch and D. Nichol Smith (Oxford: Oxford University Press, 1920), 44. Unless otherwise noted, I cite this edition.

15. For a different account of the satirical response to sublimity, see Allen Dunn, "The Mechanics of Transport: Sublimity and the Imagery of Abjection in Rochester, Swift, and Burke," in *Cutting Edges: Postmodern Critical Essays on Eighteenth-Century Satire,* ed. James E. Gill (Knoxville: University of Tennessee Press, 1995), 94–109, which focuses more narrowly on tensions surrounding the epideictic mode, the "sublime" poetry of praise for patrons, lovers, and so on, undermined by the satirists' turn to the grossly material—a turn made sublime itself, Dunn thinks, later in Burke's theory. While Dunn's argument resonates with mine, his idea that the panegyrists promote and the satirists reject "an egalitarian vision of the world" (103) reads the ideological stakes of sublimity very differently from the way I do.

16. *Essays of Michael, Seigneur de Montaigne,* 3 vols., trans. Charles Cotton (London, 1685–87), vol. 2, 273. The copy Pope owned and extensively annotated is at Yale University. His characteristic marking is a hook (') in the margins, sometimes using a double hook (") for emphasis. This passage continues to develop the theme of reversal typical in Augustan satire: "from the rare and quick Agitations of our Souls, proceed the most wonderful and most deprav'd Frenzies; 'tis but a half turn of the Toe from one to the other" (273).

17. *Philosophical Investigations,* trans. G. E. M. Anscombe, 2d ed. (Oxford: Blackwell, 1958), 46.

18. Cavell undertakes this "quest" in *The Claim of Reason* (Oxford: Oxford University Press, 1979), 129–243.

19. See *This New Yet Unapproachable America: Lectures after Emerson after Wittgenstein* (Albuquerque: Living Batch Press, 1989): "Kant's conjunction of excess

and abyss [in the *Critique of Judgment*] seems to me to match Wittgenstein's sense of the conjunction of the hyperbolic (super-connections, super-concepts, etc.) with the groundless as the ideal which philosophy finds at once forbidding or terrible, and attractive. . . . But whereas in Kant the psychic strain is between intellect and sensibility, in Wittgenstein the straining is of language against itself, against the commonality of criteria which are its conditions" (58). See also my essay "The Wittgensteinian Sublime," *New Literary History* 27, 4 (1996): 605–619.

20. *This New Yet Unapproachable America,* 56.

21. See Rorty, "Keeping Philosophy Pure: An Essay on Wittgenstein," in *Consequences of Pragmatism* (Minneapolis: University of Minnesota Press, 1982), 19–36: "When Wittgenstein is at his best, he resolutely avoids such constructive criticism and sticks to pure satire. He just shows, by examples, how hopeless the traditional problems are—how they are based on a terminology which is as if designed expressly for the purpose of making solution impossible, how the questions which generate the traditional problems cannot be posed except in this terminology, how pathetic it is to think that the old gaps will be closed by constructing new gimmicks" (34).

22. Here and throughout (unless otherwise noted), I cite Pope's poems as they appear in the *Twickenham Edition of the Poems of Alexander Pope,* 11 vols., John Butt, gen. ed. (London: Methuen; New Haven: Yale University Press, 1951–1969), abbreviated *TE* as necessary.

23. "Preface: Introducing Cavell," in *Pursuits of Reason: Essays in Honor of Stanley Cavell,* ed. Ted Cohen, Paul Guyer, and Hilary Putnam (Lubbock: Texas Tech University Press, 1993), vii–viii.

24. *The Works of Lord Bolingbroke,* 4 vols. (Philadelphia: Carey and Hart, 1841), vol. 3, 52.

25. David L. Sedley, "Sublimity and Skepticism in Montaigne," *PMLA* 113, 5 (1998): 1079.

26. Immanuel Kant, *Critique of Judgment,* trans. Werner S. Pluhar (Indianapolis: Hackett , 1987), 120–1.

27. Thomas Weiskel, *The Romantic Sublime: Studies in the Structure and Psychology of Transcendence* (Baltimore: Johns Hopkins University Press, 1976), 93–4.

28. *Aesthetic Ideology* (Minneapolis: University of Minnesota Press, 1996), 115.

29. In *Of the Sublime: Presence in Question,* ed. Jeffrey S. Librett (Albany: State University of New York Press, 1993), 47.

30. "Longinus, the Dialectic, and the Practice of Mastery," *English Literary History* 60 (1993): 550–1.

31. Other prominent accounts that have influenced my discussion include Slavoj Žižek, *The Sublime Object of Ideology* (London: Verso, 1989), Frances Ferguson, *Solitude and the Sublime: Romanticism and the Aesthetics of Individuation* (New York: Routledge, 1992), Peter de Bolla, *The Discourse of the Sublime: Readings in History, Aesthetics, and the Subject* (Oxford: Blackwell, 1989), and Jean-François Lyotard's work, especially *Lessons on the Analytic of the Sublime,* trans. Elizabeth Rottenberg (Stanford: Stanford University Press, 1994), and "The Sublime and the Avant-Garde," in *The Inhuman: Reflections on Time* (Stanford: Stanford University Press, 1991).

32. *Prose Works of Jonathan Swift,* 14 vols., Herbert Davis, gen. ed. (Oxford: Blackwell, 1939–68), vol. 9, 166.

33. *A Treatise of Human Nature,* ed. L. A. Selby-Bigge, 2d ed. (Oxford: Oxford University Press, 1979), 186–7.

34. See Popkin, *The History of Scepticism from Erasmus to Spinoza* (1960), 3d ed. (Berkeley: University of California Press, 1979), chapter 7, "Constructive or Mitigated Scepticism," 129–50. Henry G. Van Leeuwen, a student of Popkin, applies his term "constructive skepticism" to a specifically English context in *The Problem of Certainty in English Thought 1630–1690* (The Hague: Nijhoff, 1963). For the eighteenth century's inheritance of this tradition, especially Hume's, see Popkin's collection *The High Road to Pyrrhonism,* ed. Richard A. Watson and James E. Force (San Diego: Austin Hill Press, 1980), particularly 181–95.

35. Throughout I use the California edition, *The Works of John Dryden,* 20 vols., Edward Niles Hooker, H. T. Swedenberg, Jr., and Vinton Dearing, gen. eds. (Berkeley: University of California Press, 1956–), vol. 2, 98.

36. *Scepsis Scientifica* (London, 1665), facsimile reprint (New York: Garland, 1978), preface, vii (unnumbered).

37. As Henry More writes in his *Antidote Against Atheism* (1653), "it is possible that *Mathematicall evidence* it self, may be but a constant undiscoverable delusion, which our nature is necessarily and perpetually obnoxious unto, and that either fatelly or fortuitiously there has been in the world time out of minde such a Being as we call *Man,* whose essentiall property is most of all to be mistaken, when he conceives a thing most evidently" (in *The Cambridge Platonists,* ed. C. A. Patrides [Cambridge: Harvard University Press, 1970], 214).

38. Antoine Arnauld and Pierre Nicole, *Logic or the Art of Thinking* (1662, 5th ed. 1683), trans. Jill Vance Buroker (Cambridge: Cambridge University Press, 1996), 7.

39. *Remarks Upon the Letter to a Lord Concerning Enthusiasm In a Letter to a Gentleman* (London, 1708), 88.

40. See White's attack on Glanvill's *Vanity of Dogmatizing,* published in English as *An Exclusion of Scepticks from all Title to Dispute* (London, 1665).

41. As Popkin says, "From Spinoza onward one of the main functions of scepticism has been to oppose traditional religion" (*History of Scepticism,* xviii).

42. *Probability and Literary Form* (Cambridge: Cambridge University Press, 1984): see especially "Humanism and the Revival of Ciceronian Skepticism," 13–9, which claims that "Carneades introduced as well a practical method (*ratio argumentandi*) for establishing probabilities" (15).

43. *Probability and Certainty in Seventeenth-Century England: A Study of the Relationships between Natural Science, Religion, History, Law, and Literature* (Princeton: Princeton University Press, 1983).

44. *The Material Word: Literate Culture in the Restoration and Early Eighteenth Century* (Baltimore: Johns Hopkins University Press, 1991), 50.

45. *A Social History of Truth: Civility and Science in Seventeenth-Century England* (Chicago: University of Chicago Press, 1994), 42.

46. Van Leeuwen begins with the liberal Anglicanism of Chillingworth in the 1630s, while Ian Hacking asserts, in *The Emergence of Probability: A Philosophical Study of Early Ideas about Probability, Induction, and Statistical Inference* (Cambridge: Cambridge University Press, 1975), that "probability began about 1660" (18). Patey and Shapiro note continuities between Restoration ideas of probability and ancient and Renaissance rhetoric, while Richard Kroll detects

"a coherent (if not universal) set of epistemological pressures in formation and operation between 1640 and 1660" (50).

47. Shapin argues that skepticism should not be seen as fundamentally calling trust into question (19), referring to Wittgenstein's notion that "All testing, all confirmation and disconfirmation of a hypothesis takes place already within a system" (*On Certainty*, trans. G. E. M. Anscombe and Denis Paul [New York: Harper, 1969], sec. 105).

48. Patey sometimes seems unnecessarily concerned to prove that the period's literary theory could not tolerate any improbability at all. He comments, for instance, that Pope's idea of *"Grace"* "is 'beyond the reach of *Art*' in that no rule has as yet been formulated to cover it. . . . (Only in this limited and temporary sense can Pope be said to defend any version of the so-called *je ne scais quoi*.)" (131). Patey's evidence for the "temporary" character of the *je ne scais quoi* for Pope is only the line "Some Beauties yet, no Precepts can declare" (141), taken to imply that the precepts *are* declarable, only not yet. But it seems more natural to read "yet" as meaning "however," as if Pope were making room for deviation from hierarchy in his system, marking a turn from the previous passage (88–140) on how rules may be learned with "Care."

49. *Historical and Critical Dictionary: Selections,* trans. Richard H. Popkin (Indianapolis: Hackett, 1991), 194–5 (remark B). Bayle then describes an argument between two *abbés,* the more philosophically astute insisting that Pyrrhonism is conformable even to orthodox theology (205).

50. Thomas Stanley, *The History of Philosophy, Containing the Lives, Opinions, Actions and Discourses of the Philosophers of Every Sect,* 3d ed. (London, 1701), 476b.

51. See Popkin, *History of Scepticism,* 129–50, and Shapiro, *Probability and Certainty,* 39.

52. See Harry M. Solomon, *The Rape of the Text: Reading and Misreading Pope's Essay on Man* (Tuscaloosa: University of Alabama Press, 1993), which situates Pope within Academic discourse. It remains customary to distinguish Academic skepticism from Pyrrhonism by seeing the former as "probabilistic" and the latter as more radical, though scholars of ancient philosophy challenge this: Myles Burnyeat, following Pierre Coussin, insists that Academic doctrines "do not . . . constitute anything that could be called a probabilistic theory of knowledge" (introduction to *The Skeptical Tradition* [Berkeley: University of California Press, 1983]), 7; see also Coussin's essay in the same volume, "The Stoicism of the New Academy," 31–63). For further debate, see Michael Frede, "The Sceptic's Two Kinds of Assent and the Question of the Possibility of Knowledge," in *The Original Sceptics: A Controversy,* ed. Myles Burnyeat and Michael Frede (Indianapolis: Hackett, 1997), which argues for an essential similarity between Academic and Pyrrhonian skepticism, distinguishing both from the "dogmatic scepticism" that claims that we know that nothing can be known for certain (127–8).

53. "For, his part being but to propose doubts and scruples, he does enough, if he shews that his adversaries arguments are not strongly concluding, though his own be not so neither. . . . And our Carneades by holding the negative, has this advantage, that if among all the instances he brings to invalidate the vulgar doctrine of those he disputes with, any one be irrefragable, that alone is

sufficient to overthrow a doctrine which universally asserts what he opposes" (*The Sceptical Chymist* [London: Dent, 1911], 4–5). In a later addition, Boyle backs away from any skeptical implications: "For though sometimes I have had occasion to discourse like a Sceptick, yet I am far from being one of that sect; which I take to have been little less prejudicial to natural philosophy than to divinity itself" (quoted in Van Leeuwen, *Problem of Certainty*, 96).

54. Wilkins, *Of the Principles and Duties of Natural Religion*, 4th ed. (London, 1699), 30. For an account of Wilkins as feeding the Humean naturalistic tradition, see M. Jamie Ferreira, *Scepticism and Reasonable Doubt: the British Naturalist Tradition in Wilkins, Hume, Reid, and Newman* (Oxford: Oxford University Press, 1986), 10–40. Ferreira argues that Wilkins employs "moral certainty" as a "threshold concept" (23–5) that obtains with the same "necessity" as infallible certainty as far as our assent is concerned—at least if we are not insane. Insanity is hence more a failure to be natural than a failure to be rational.

55. In *Three Restoration Divines: Barrow, South, Tillotson*, ed. Irène Simon (Paris: Société d'edition "Les Belles Lettres," 1967–), vol. 1:3, 408.

56. *Claim of Reason*, 242. Cavell sees Wittgenstein's work as not so much a refutation of skepticism as a placement of it at the extreme of a continuum of human responses to the world (with the hope that the pain of finding oneself at that extreme may be assuaged by recognizing it as such): "Wittgenstein's motive . . . is to put the human animal back into language and therewith back into philosophy. But he never, I think, underestimated the power of the motive to reject the human: nothing could be more human" (207).

57. *Some Passages of the Life and Death of John Earl of Rochester* (1680), in *Rochester: the Critical Heritage*, ed. David Farley-Hills (London: Routledge and Kegan Paul, 1972), 68. The meaning of "all this" is ambiguous: Rochester could mean simply that Burnet's putting common sense on a par with probable religious conviction begs the question because common sense is invulnerable to doubt while Christianity is not. Or he could mean that even the argument that a person simply knows that he is awake, when he is, begs the question: Rochester knew his Descartes, and earlier Burnet quotes him as saying unequivocally that "believing was at highest but a probable Opinion" (66) and is hence open to doubt in any given instance.

58. *The Sceptical Muse: Or, a Paradox on Humane Understanding, a Poem* (London, Cambridge: 1699), 204–9, published anonymously but included in collections of Pomfret's work.

59. *Miscellany Poems* (London, 1691).

60. *Correspondence of Alexander Pope*, 5 vols., ed. George Sherburn (Oxford: Clarendon Press, 1956), vol. 3, 445. This edition is cited throughout.

61. In *Selected Philosophical Papers of Robert Boyle*, ed. M. A. Stewart (Indianapolis: Hackett, 1991), 210.

62. Quoted in Shapiro, *Probability and Certainty*, 50. Theodore E. B. Wood, in *The Word "Sublime" and Its Context* (The Hague: Mouton, 1972), catalogues rhetorical and protoaesthetic usages without commenting much on the word's general scientific, philosophical, and theological ones.

63. In vol. 2, 1, by the title, marked with an *x*. Maynard Mack, "A Finding List of Books Surviving from Pope's Library . . . ," appendix A of *Collected in Himself*

(Newark: University of Delaware Press, 1982), 394–460, transcribes Pope's marginal remarks (not his markings) but omits this and some other important ones.

64. *TE*, vol. 3:2, xx. F. W. Bateson reproduces Spence's rough notes of Pope's table-talk (xx–xxii) during the week of 1–7 May 1730, where Pope affirms that he finds Montaigne's essay "Of the Inconstancy . . . " to be "The best in his whole book" (xx).

65. *Correspondence*, vol. 3, 81.

66. Phillip Harth argues, in *Contexts of Dryden's Thought*, that the Tory Dryden espoused the non-Pyrrhonistic skeptical attitudes of the Latitudinarians and Royal Society, and, in *Swift and Anglican Rationalism* (Chicago: University of Chicago Press, 1961), that Swift accepted the theological attitudes of Tillotson and mainstream Anglicanism. Pope's mitigated, "Academic" skepticism has been widely seen, for example by Solomon, as aligning him with the eschewal of dogmatism informing the science, theology, and philosophy of his time.

67. Pocock, *Virtue, Commerce, and History* (Cambridge: Cambridge University Press, 1985), 107. Pocock's dichotomy has proved durable and suggestive especially to literary scholars. For a qualification or nuancing of his view, see, for example, Shelley Burtt, *Virtue Transformed: Political Argument in England, 1688–1740* (Cambridge: Cambridge University Press, 1992), which elaborates, between Pocock's "civic virtue" and "civilization of the passions," a third category, "privately oriented public virtue" (13), taking religious impulses more fully into account. See also Joyce Oldham Appleby, *Economic Thought and Ideology in Seventeenth-Century England* (Princeton: Princeton University Press, 1978), which finds in the seventeenth century anxieties about the market similar to those in the eighteenth discussed by Pocock.

68. For a Pocockian view of commercial "feminization" in the specifically literary marketplace, see Catherine Ingrassia, *Authorship, Commerce and Gender in Early Eighteenth-Century England: A Culture of Paper Credit* (Cambridge: Cambridge University Press, 1998). For the ideological reactions to feminization in the public sphere pertaining to the problem of taste, see Robert W. Jones, *Gender and the Formation of Taste in Eighteenth-Century Britain* (Cambridge: Cambridge University Press, 1998), especially 27–36.

69. See Albert O. Hirschman, *The Passions and the Interests: Political Arguments for Capitalism before Its Triumph* (Princeton: Princeton University Press, 1977), for a long, pan-European view of ideas about the passions' economic, political, and social efficacy.

70. As Pocock puts it, in *The Machiavellian Moment: Florentine Political Thought and the Atlantic Republican Tradition* (Princeton: Princeton University Press, 1975), "the individual engaged in exchange could discern only particular values—that of the commodity which was his, that of the commodity for which he exchanged it. His activity did not oblige or even permit him to contemplate the universal good as he acted upon it, and he consequently continued to lack classical rationality" (464).

71. *Virtue, Commerce, and History*, 145.

72. Terry Eagleton, *The Ideology of the Aesthetic* (Oxford: Blackwell, 1990), 90.

73. See, for instance, Jonathan Lamb's distinction between Whig and Tory sublimes in "Longinus, the Dialectic, and the Practice of Mastery," which is

fairly straightforward: "Among the modernist Whigs in England," sublimity "consists not in submitting stoically to inherited forms or paradigms but in the ardent pursuit of liberty and resistance to tyranny" (553)—with the Tory sublime being all about submission and worship of authority. See also Jonathan Lamb, *The Rhetoric of Suffering: Reading the Book of Job in the Eighteenth Century* (Oxford: Oxford University Press, 1995).

74. *Art of Judgement* (Oxford: Blackwell, 1989), 39.

75. *Characteristics of Men, Manners, Opinions, and Times*, 2 vols., ed. John M. Robertson (London: Grant Richards, 1900), vol. 1, 38.

76. For a view of Burke's sublime as a more skeptical phenomenon, see Ferguson, *Solitude and the Sublime* 55–96. See also Dunn, "The Mechanics of Transport," which asserts that for Burke, "as a token of the sublime, the broken body becomes the most potent sign of a higher power" (102)—not the body's "natural," nonrational, sensitive reactions to greatness, as argued here.

77. Edmund Burke, *A Philosophical Enquiry into the Origin of Our Ideas of the Sublime and the Beautiful,* ed. James T. Boulton (Notre Dame: University of Notre Dame Press, 1968), 107.

78. "The Subject of the Subject and the Sublimities of Self-Reference," *Huntington Library Quarterly* 56, 2 (1993): 205.

79. *Characteristics,* vol. 1, 141.

80. The phrase applies to Hume's psychology in *Practicing Enlightenment: Hume and the Formation of a Literary Career* (Madison: University of Wisconsin Press, 1987), 35.

81. De Bolla's distinction unfolds in two chapters of *The Discourse of the Sublime,* "The Discourse on the Sublime" (27–58) and "The Discourse of the Sublime" (59–102).

82. *Virtue, Commerce, and History,* 112.

83. Michael McKeon, "Cultural Crisis and Dialectical Method: Destabilizing Augustan Literature," in *The Profession of Eighteenth-Century Literature: Reflections on a Institution,* ed. Leo Damrosch (Madison: University of Wisconsin Press, 1992), 44.

84. Louis I. Bredvold, "The Gloom of the Tory Satirists," in *Eighteenth-Century English Literature: Modern Essays in Criticism,* ed. James L. Clifford (Oxford: Oxford University Press, 1959), 3–20.

85. *Liberty,* part 1, 31, in *Liberty, The Castle of Indolence, and Other Poems,* ed. James Sambrook (Oxford: Oxford University Press, 1986).

86. See Douglas Brooks-Davies, *Pope's Dunciad and the Queen of Night: A Study in Emotional Jacobitism* (Manchester, England: Manchester University Press, 1985).

2: The Abyss of Reason

1. Dated by Vieth in *The Complete Poems of John Wilmot, Earl of Rochester.*

2. See *Works,* vol. 12, ed. Vinton A. Dearing.

3. *Works,* vol. 2, 98.

4. An often-cited account of the birth of the aesthetic out of epistemological-religious tensions that is very different from this one is Michael McKeon, "The Politics of Discourses and the Rise of the Aesthetic in Seventeenth-Century England," in *Politics of Discourse: the Literature and History of Seventeenth-Century*

England, ed. Kevin Sharpe and Steven N. Zwicker (Berkeley: University of California Press, 1987): 35–51.

5. See the introduction to Dustin Griffin, *Satires against Man: The Poems of Rochester* (Berkeley: University of California Press, 1973), "The Mind of a Skeptic," 1–20.

6. Here and throughout, I cite the text of *Poems on Several Occasions,* 16–9.

7. Harold Bloom, "Freud and the Poetic Sublime: A Catastrophe Theory of Creativity," in *Freud: A Collection of Critical Essays,* ed. Perry Meisel (Englewood Cliffs: Prentice-Hall, 1981), 224.

8. See, for example, his imitation, "Seneca's Troas, *Act.* 2. Chorus," "After Death, nothing is, and Nothing, Death" (*Poems on Several Occasions,* 50–1).

9. In the words of the anonymous translation of Longinus, *An Essay Upon Sublime* (Oxford, 1698), 70.

10. In *Scepsis Scientifica* (1665), Glanvill adds "An Address to the Royal Society," in which he affirms his *"regarding Your* Society *as the strongest* Argument *to perswade a* modest *and* reserved diffidence *in opinions"* (iii).

11. *The Vanity of Dogmatizing or Confidence in Opinions Manifested in a Discourse of the Shortness and Uncertainty of our Knowledge, and its Causes; with Some Reflexions on Peripateticism; and an Apology for Philosophy* (London, 1661), 102–3.

12. David Trotter discusses how Rochester's intellectual extravagance opposes him to Latitude men and Royal Society figures in "Wanton Expressions," in *Spirit of Wit: Reconsiderations of Rochester,* ed. Jeremy Treglown (Hamden, Conn.: Archon Press, 1982), 111–32.

13. The attack, *An Answer to the Satyr Against Mankind,* is often bound with Rochester's *Satyr,* as is the Houghton Library's 1679 edition (no title page). The poem, after initial cynicism, chooses "to converse, / (Although alone) with the whole Universe" (56–7) and embrace "Sacred knowledge most remote from Sense" (60). See *The Works of John Wilmot, Earl of Rochester,* 56, and Love's arguments for his attributions, 380–3.

14. "A level plain of a vast extent on land, is certainly no mean idea; the prospect of such a plain may be as extensive as a prospect of the ocean; but can it ever fill the mind with any thing so great as the ocean itself? This is owing to several causes, but it is owing to none more than this, that the ocean is an object of no small terror" (*A Philosophical Enquiry,* 58).

15. *Critique of Judgment,* 120.

16. Quoted in Marjorie Hope Nicholson, *Mountain Gloom and Mountain Glory: The Development of the Aesthetics of the Infinite* (Ithaca: Cornell University Press, 1959), 226. In *The Sublime,* Monk illustrates a similar point with the passage (206).

17. See, for instance, the echo of *The Discourse on the Method . . .* in *An Epistolary Essay from M. G. to O. B. upon Their Mutual Poems,* noted by Vieth (146).

18. Commenting on the passage's sources, Griffin says that "doubt as drowning . . . may have been a traditional metaphor" (215) but does not mention Descartes. See also Montaigne's exclamation in the *Apology for Raimond de Sebonde:* "how soon she [human reason] loses, confounds and fetters her self tumbling and floating in this vast, turbulent and waving Sea of Human Opinions, without restraint, and without any determinate end" (vol. 2, 326)—a passage marked by Pope. Another helpful study less focused on skepticism than that of Griffin is Marianne Thormählen, *Rochester: The Poems in Context* (Cam-

bridge: Cambridge University Press, 1993), also with two chapters on the *Satyr* that comprehensively survey the source-work done on it.

19. *Six Metaphysical Meditations,* trans. William Molyneux (London, 1680), 11—the first English translation.

20. In Tillotson et al., *Eighteenth Century English Literature* (San Diego: Harcourt Brace, 1969), 879a.

21. *Personification and the Sublime,* 79.

22. That is, *"flammantia moenia mundi,"* *De Rerum Natura* (book I, 73), rendered in Lucy Hutchinson's mid–seventeenth–century translation as "those flaming walls which are / Bounds to the Universe" (book I, 72–3, *Lucy Hutchinson's Translation of Lucretius: De Rerum Natura,* ed. Hugh de Quehen [Ann Arbor: University of Michigan Press, 1996]). The 1698 Oxford translation of Longinus runs: "Our ambitious fancies range farther than the flaming limits of the Heavens, and the most distant prospects of the Universe" (74–5)—infusing Longinus with a Lucretian vocabulary by gratuitously adding the word *flaming* to Boileau's version, which it otherwise follows.

23. For the popularity of Lucretius and Epicureanism in the Restoration, see Kroll, *The Material Word,* especially 85-111.

24. See Catherine Gimelli Martin, " 'Boundless the Deep': Milton, Pascal, and the Theology of Relative Space," *English Literary History* 63, 1 (1996): 45–78. The classic history of the idea is Alexandre Koyré, *From the Closed World to the Infinite Universe* (Baltimore: Johns Hopkins University Press, 1957). Ernest Tuveson relates spatial infinity to the sublime in "Space, Deity, and the Natural Sublime," *Modern Language Quarterly* 12, 1 (1951): 20–38.

25. See Thormählen's helpful survey of the discussion of this crux, *Rochester,* 223–7. She herself finds no contradiction in Rochester's embrace of animal virtues and disgust at perverse human excesses.

26. *Selected Philosophical Papers,* 216.

27. For discussions of this tendency, see David Farley-Hills, *Rochester's Poetry* (Totowa, N.J.: Rowman and Littlefield, 1978), 160–8; David Vieth, "Divided Consciousness: the Trauma and Triumph of Restoration Culture," *Tennessee Studies in Literature* 22 (1977): 46; and Kevin L. Cope's chapter "Rochester: Confrontational Systems," in *Criteria of Certainty: Truth and Judgment in the English Enlightenment* (Lexington: University of Kentucky Press, 1990), 21–42.

28. *The Letters of John Wilmot, Earl of Rochester,* ed. Jeremy Treglown (Chicago: University of Chicago Press, 1980), 123.

29. Later Sophronius admits, like Dryden and Burnet, that we have no really absolute knowledge of anything: "I must confess that we have no good notions of privileged things in particular; but then I must add that I fear we have few or none even of many things that we think ourselves very knowing in" (238).

30. See the section so titled in *A Social History of Truth,* 95–101.

31. In *Rochester: The Critical Heritage,* 49.

32. See Robert Parsons, *A Sermon preached at the Earl of Rochester's Funeral* (1680), also in *Rochester: The Critical Heritage:* "He seem'd to affect something singular and paradoxical in his Impieties, as well as in his Writings, above the reach and thought of other men" (46).

33. *Rochester: The Critical Heritage,* 214.

34. Shapin quotes Burnet's account of testimony as an illustration of Boylean principles: "I answered to all this, that, believing a thing upon the testimony of another . . . where there was no reason to suspect the testimony . . . was not only a reasonable thing, but it was the hinge on which all the government and justice of the world depended" (*A Social History of Truth*, 204). Shapin considers the "cynical" Rochester an opponent of this tendency—but the very exchange, with its candid testing of rational arguments, as well as Rochester's ultimate conversion, testify to his susceptibility to its gentling authority.

35. *The Letters of John Wilmot Earl of Rochester*, 216.

36. John Crowne, *City Politiques* (London, 1683), act 2, p. 18. Florio goes on: "When all that the most hot-brain'd Fellow in the world can do, is to make a smoak to darken things, he can't strike Fire enough out of himself to light him in the nature of a Fly. But 'tis time we went to Prayers."

37. *Solid Philosophy*, preface.

38. For instance, Steven Zwicker, in *Politics and Language in Dryden's Poetry: The Arts of Disguise* (Princeton: Princeton University Press, 1984), sees "the abrupt shift of loyalties from *Heroick Stanza's* [*Consecrated to the Glorious Memory of His most Serene and Renowned Highnesse Oliver Late Lord Protector*, 1659] to *Astraea Redux* [1660]" (71) as enabled by his cultivation of "Ambiguities and Uncertainties" (70–84), though for Zwicker this is a move in a game of political disguise, not a sign of epistemological crisis.

39. *Works*, vol. 1, 43–4. Kroll argues that the poem expresses "a Restoration insistence on the exclusion of tyranny from society, science, and politics" (35) and the connection of this insistence to mitigated skepticism, in "The Restoration as Cultural Moment" and "'Moments of Verisimility': The Neoclassical Discourse of Contingency" (33–79), in *The Material Word*.

40. See Louis I. Bredvold, *The Intellectual Milieu of John Dryden: Studies in Some Aspects of Seventeenth-Century Thought* (Ann Arbor: University of Michigan Press, 1934), especially 121–9, arguing that "*Religio Laici* and *The Hind and the Panther* are so closely allied in their philosophy that the earlier poem might be regarded as a sort of prelude or introduction to the later; both are basically skeptical and fideistic" (121).

41. *Works*, vol. 2, 100.

42. Harth's qualification in *Contexts of Dryden's Thought* of Bredvold's view itself must be qualified in terms of Richard Popkin's perception that Sextus Empiricus's Pyrrhonism helped develop the "scientific outlook": "The *crise pyrrhonienne* fundamentally could not be resolved, but, at least, it could be ignored or abided with, if one could relegate the doubts to the problems of dogmatic philosophy, while pursuing scientific knowledge as the guide to practical living" (*History of Scepticism*, 148).

43. *Works*, vol. 12, ed. Vinton A. Dearing, 86.

44. *Lives of the English Poets*, ed. George Birkbeck Hill, 3 vols. (Oxford: Clarendon Press, 1905), vol. 1, 459. Johnson links Dryden's love of argument to his tendency to depart from common sense into sublime heights that risk absurdity: "Next to argument, his delight was in wild and daring sallies of sentiment, in the irregular and excentrick violence of wit. He delighted to tread upon the

brink of meaning, where light and darkness begin to mingle; to approach the precipice of absurdity, and hover over the abyss of unideal vacancy" (vol. 1, 460).

45. *John Dryden and His World* (New Haven: Yale University Press, 1987), 269.

46. For a contrary argument, that Dryden's staging of *Paradise Lost* represents a covert but pointed royalist attack on Milton's principles, see Marcie Franck, "Staging Criticism, Staging Milton: Dryden's *The State of Innocence*," in *The Eighteenth Century: Theory and Interpretation* 34, 1 (1993): 45–64: "the changes [Dryden] makes to Milton's text retroactively create a 'literary' Milton who made aesthetic choices rather than political or theological ones" (56); it may be enough to add that Dryden's forestalling of political or theological resolution in the opera makes a "literary" Dryden of himself as well.

47. "The evidence of Cartesian influence in Dryden's work is small," writes Sanford Budick in *Dryden and the Abyss of Light* (New Haven: Yale University Press, 1970), 46, while Bruce King suggests that Dryden's dislike of Cartesian works like Cudworth's *True Intellectual System of the Universe* could mean that his attitude toward Adam's speech is satirical: "the tone of Adam's speech, over-positive and slickly concise, sounds mocking to me, as does the humour of Adam's first words and thought being an already formed philosophy" (*Dryden's Major Plays* [Edinburgh: Oliver and Boyd, 1966], 102).

48. *Vanity of Dogmatizing*, 73–4.

49. Book V, 860–1. I use the *Complete Poems and Major Prose* of Milton, ed. Merritt Hughes (New York: Macmillan, 1957), unless otherwise noted.

50. In the third *Meditation*, Descartes elaborates: "But first, If I were from myself, I should neither *doubt*, nor *desire*, nor *want* any thing, for I should have given my self all those *perfections*, of which I have any *Idea*, and consequently I my self should be *God*" (48). Stanley Cavell comments, "Apparently it is the very sense of my need for a human proof of my human existence—some authentication—that is the source of the idea that I need an author" (*In Quest of the Ordinary: Lines of Skepticism and Romanticism* [Chicago: University of Chicago Press, 1988], 110).

51. *Six Metaphysical Meditations*, preface, x–xi (unnumbered).

52. *Philosophical Works of Descartes*, 2 vols., trans. Elizabeth Haldane and G. R. T. Ross (Cambridge: Cambridge University Press, 1935), vol. 1, 87.

53. In book V, Raphael comments on how human reason's "discursive" operations distinguish it from the "intuitive" knowledge of angels but also asserts that human and angelic reasons fall on a single continuum, differing not in kind but in degree of perfection, and explicitly links this epistemological point with a monistic ontological view placing matter and spirit on the same scale. See Stephen Fallon's account of how Milton's monism distinguishes him from Cartesian dualism in *Milton among the Philosophers: Poetry and Materialism in Seventeenth-Century England* (Ithaca: Cornell University Press, 1991), 19–30 and 203–16.

54. J. Hintikka discusses the cogito as performative in "*Cogito, Ergo Sum*: Inference or Performance?" reprinted in *Descartes: A Collection of Critical Essays*, ed. Willis Doney (Notre Dame, Ind.: University of Notre Dame Press, 1968): 108–40—a view that Bernard Williams qualifies in *Descartes: the Project of Pure Inquiry* (Harmondsworth, England: Penguin, 1978), 75–7.

55. *In Quest of the Ordinary*, 130.

56. For an astute unfolding of Cavell's discussion of the cogito as a performative utterance (in J. L. Austin's sense) and as a performance (in a theatrical

sense), see Stephen Mulhall, *Stanley Cavell: Philosophy's Recounting of the Ordinary* (Oxford: Oxford University Press, 1994): "if," according to Cavell, "my inner life can find its full reality only through my giving expression to it to, and receiving acknowledgement from, others, then my full or genuine existence as a human individual is doubly dependent upon my capacity to declare my existence—to lay claim to it by actively making it manifest and passively waiting to be acknowledged" (169). Adam's performance of course indicates the obstacles inherent in the Cartesian attempt to meet this difficulty.

57. In *English Drama: 1660–1700* (Oxford: Clarendon, 1996), Derek Hughes offers a similar view of the "scepticism" (179) evolving from Adam's Cartesianism in the play, though his emphasis falls not on the sublime but on paradoxes of self-knowledge and self-representation (179–84).

58. See *Absorption and Theatricality: Painting and Beholder in the Age of Diderot* (Chicago: University of Chicago Press, 1980). Adam's initial, theatrical reasoning out of the cogito especially resonates with Fried's discussion of the absorptive figure: "a figure entirely engrossed or absorbed in an action, activity, or state of mind and therefore oblivious to the beholder's presence may be described as *alone* relative to the beholder" (100).

59. See Melissa Cowansage, "The Libertine-Libertarian Dichotomy in Dryden's *State of Innocence*," *English Language Notes* 21, 3 (1984): 38–44.

60. Dedication, *Peri Hupsous, or Dionysius Longinus on the Height of Eloquence*, unnumbered.

61. "But how [God's] certain foreknowledge can be had of contingent things, and such as depend upon the free will of man, is that which many great wits that have solicitously tried have found themselves unable clearly to comprehend" (*Selected Philosophical Papers*, 213).

62. Cowansage notes the similarity between Descartes's view of excessive will and Dryden's (43) but does not mention the additional parallel in their designations of human will as godlike.

63. *Works*, vol. 8, 96–7.

64. *Dryden and the Problem of Freedom* (New Haven: Yale University Press, 1997), 3. As important as Haley sees Adam's question "Why am I not tied from doing ill?" to Dryden's exposition of the problem of freedom, he also sees the opera (like the heroic plays in general) as presenting something of an impasse in the development of Dryden's political attitudes: "In Dryden's version of the fall, our will rebels against obedience with the help of the imagination, which gives substance to our dream of masterless sovereignty. The *State of Innocence*, like *Mac Fleckno*, works to curb individual subjectivity by exposing the falsehood of heroic decorum, but it does little to build up a genuinely political reflexivity" (206).

65. *Works*, vol. 2, 18.

66. *Lives of the English Poets*, vol. 1, 174.

67. See Dearing's commentary on the possibility of producing the play in the *Works*, vol. 12, 322–5. Winn in *John Dryden and His World* argues that the stage directions indicate that Dryden was thinking of particular stage effects but that the opera's great expense probably kept it off the stage (261–4).

68. Robert D. Hume, *Dryden's Criticism* (Ithaca: Cornell University Press, 1970), 211.

69. Sublime imaging is often thus praised for its capacity to mimic and sup-

plant "proper" sensory power, for example, by Joseph Trapp, who in "Of Beauty of Thought in Poetry; or of Elegance and Sublimity" (lecture VIII, delivered 1711–9, trans. 1742) praises (e.g.) Vergil's depiction of Dido's dreams of Aeneas, which "contains a mere intellectual idea not subject to the senses, which yet is as clearly impressed as if it were the proper object of them" (*Eighteenth-Century Critical Essays*, 2 vols., ed. Scott Elledge [Ithaca: Cornell University Press, 1961], vol. 1, 249).

70. This contrasts with more daring celebrations of departures from common sense in his earliest critical works, for instance, in the dedication of *Tyrannic Love* (1669): "He who creeps after plain, dull, common sense is safe from committing absurdities; but can never reach any height or excellence of wit" (*Works*, vol. 8, 96–7).

71. For an account of Prior's familiarity with the Kennet translation of the *Pensées*, see John Barker, *Strange Contrarieties: Pascal in England during the Age of Reason* (Montreal: McGill-Queens University Press, 1975), 114–6.

72. *The Literary Works of Matthew Prior*, 2 vols., eds. H. Bunker Wright and Monroe K. Spears (Oxford: Oxford University Press, 1959), vol. 1, *Solomon on the Vanity of the World*, book I, 508–12.

73. Cudworth's argument in *The True Intellectual System of the Universe* is typical: "And nature itself plainly intimates to us that there is some such absolutely perfect Being, which, though not inconceivable yet is incomprehensible to our finite understandings, by certain passions which it hath implanted in us, that otherwise would want an object to display themselves upon; namely those of devout veneration, adoration, and admiration, together with a kind of pleasing horror; which, in the silent language of nature, seem to speak thus much to us" (in *The Cambridge Platonists*, ed. Gerald R. Cragg [Oxford: Oxford University Press, 1968], 222).

74. Arguing for his right to debauch the wife of the mayor of Naples, Florio remarks: "our Principles are, he is not to be regarded who has a right to Govern, but he who can best serve the ends of Government. I can better serve the ends of your Lady, than you can, so I lay claim to your Lady" (*City Politiques*, act 5, p. 74).

75. In *Probability and Literary Form* (274–80), Patey argues that the contribution of Longinus to Dennis's critical theory is slight, though it is hard to deny that references to Longinus like this one are substantial and interesting.

76. *The Critical Works of John Dennis*, 2 vols., ed. Edward Niles Hooker (Baltimore: Johns Hopkins University Press, 1939), vol. 1, 218.

77. Joseph Addison, Richard Steele, et al., *The Spectator*, 5 vols., ed. Donald F. Bond (Oxford: Oxford University Press, 1965), vol. 3, 540.

78. *An Essay Concerning Human Understanding*, ed. Peter Nidditch (Oxford: Oxford University Press, 1975), 369.

3: Civil Enthusiasm in *A Tale of a Tub*

1. *A Tale of a Tub*, 162.
2. *The Material Word*, 44.
3. See Eilon, *Factions' Fictions: Ideological Closure in Swift's Satire* (Newark: University of Delaware Press, 1991), 113; Phiddian, *Swift's Parody* (Cambridge: Cambridge University Press, 1995), 86–94; Higgins, *Swift's Politics: A Study in Disaffection* (Cambridge: Cambridge University Press, 1994), especially 38–95;

and Montag, *The Unthinkable Swift: The Spontaneous Philosophy of a Church-of-England Man* (London: Verso, 1994), especially 1–41.

4. For a recent version of this argument referring specifically to Popkin's work on the history of skepticism, see J. T. Parnell, "Swift, Sterne, and the Skeptical Tradition," in *Studies in Eighteenth-Century Culture* 23 (1994): 221–42. Other prominent studies of Swift have already remarked the *Tale's* mitigated skepticism. Kathleen Williams, *Jonathan Swift and the Age of Compromise* (Lawrence: University of Kansas Press, 1958), declares, "Like Dryden, he finds a modified scepticism a useful tool, though neither writer could be classified as a sceptic" (49). In *Theme and Structure in Swift's "Tale of a Tub"* (New Haven: Yale University Press, 1960), Ronald Paulson finds that "The view of the nature of man that is expressed in the actions of Peter, Jack, and the Hack is a part of the skeptical tradition, whether in religious or secular thought" (177). Phillip Harth, in *Swift and Anglican Rationalism,* argues against the propriety of applying the terms *skeptic* or *fideist* to Swift, but still defines Swift's position as based almost entirely on faith: "Once we accept this definition of faith as a persuasion of the mind concerning anything, it becomes clear that faith in fact comprehends every kind of knowledge" (48)—a position that sounds radically fideist. But he stresses what he thinks of as Swift's rationalist position, which depends on Descartes's proof that God cannot be a deceiver (49). In *Swift's Narrative Satires: Author and Authority* (Ithaca: Cornell University Press, 1983), Everett Zimmerman says, "The epistemology represented in Swift's satires is negative: Swift explores the limitations of the human understanding that are imposed by the condition of being body and soul-spirit-mind. . . . The satires do . . . sometimes appear to be skeptical, because the very different perspectives of Hobbes, Descartes, Burnet, physico-theology, and even religious enthusiasm are allowed to shade into each other as examples of similar errors" (108).

5. *Gulliver and the Gentle Reader,* 2d ed. (Atlantic Highlands, N.J.: Humanities Press International, 1991), 32.

6. *Prose Works of Jonathan Swift,* vol. 9, 159–68. The composition of "On the Trinity," published with other sermons before Swift's death, is not dated by Louis Landa, editor of this volume.

7. In *Critical Essays of the Seventeenth Century,* 3 vols., ed. J. E. Spingarn (Oxford: Clarendon Press, 1908–9), vol. 3, 61–2.

8. *Longinus on the Sublime,* trans. A. O. Prickard (Oxford: Clarendon Press, 1906), 3.

9. *"Longinus" on the Sublime,* ed. D. A. Russell (Oxford: Oxford University Press, 1964), 63.

10. See E. L. Steeves, *The Art of Sinking in Poetry: Martinus Scriblerus' "Peri Bathous": A Critical Edition* (New York: King's Crown Press, 1952), liv–lvii.

11. "There is a different manner of contact of spirit with body, which produces a living being; and that conjunction is utterly amazing and beyond our powers of comprehension" (*City of God,* trans. Henry Bettenson [Harmondsworth, England: Penguin, 1984], 986).

12. As Kathleen Williams puts it, "The primary error of the Æolists is that in their anxiety to escape from a world of sense into pure spirituality they have only sunk deeper into the power of the body, the passions, and the deceiving senses" (*Swift and the Age of Compromise,* 139). Williams sees this descent into the body as

counterbalanced by Swift's implicit endorsement of epistemological compromise, but his own uncompromising insistence on the inescapable interplay of high and low make ascribing such a settled position to him unsatisfying. See also Dunn, "The Mechanics of Transport," 100–1, for an argument that Swift's general emphasis on the grossly physical is a retort to sublime self-inflation.

13. *Enthusiasmus Triumphatus* (London, 1662), 5.

14. Citing "On the Trinity," Zimmerman approaches this view in his chapter on "Epistemological Foundations" of the *Tale* but takes Swift as showing that "Matter and spirit are necessary counterbalances to each other" (*Swift's Narrative Satires*, 109), not that each tends to revert violently into its opposite whenever it is examined.

15. Contrast the following from More: "But men of a purer blood and finer spirits are not so obnoxious to this distemper: For this is the most natural seat of sublimer Reason; whenas that more Mechanical kind of *Genius* that loves to be tumbling of and trying tricks with the *Matter* (which they call *making Experiments*) when *desire of knowledge* has so heated it that it takes upon it to become *Architectonical* and flie above its sphere, it commits the wildest hallucinations imaginable, that material or corporeal fancie egregiously fumbling in more subtile and spiritual speculations." (36) Unlike the *Tale*, More's work presents a clear alternative to enthusiasm, here "sublimer Reason," an expression of confidence that Swift skeptically discourages.

16. See A. H. de Quehen, "Lucretius and Swift's *Tale of a Tub*," *University of Toronto Quarterly* 63, 2 (1993/94): 287–307: Swift "agrees [with Lucretius] that the ultimate realities are deeper than the senses, yet he [also like Lucretius] repeatedly images the search for those realities as absurd or repellent" (301). Swift calls Lucretius's work "a compleat System of Atheism" in "Mr Collins's Discourse of Free-Thinking" (vol. 4, 37) and elsewhere vigorously denounces Epicurus (*Prose Works*, vol. 9, 247), but as Irvin Ehrenpreis notes in *Swift: The Man, His Works, and the Age*, 3 vols. (Cambridge: Harvard University Press, 1962–83), his attitudes toward Lucretius as a poet are mixed (vol. 3, 88).

17. *The Sublime Object of Ideology*, 206.

18. The *Tale*'s sublimity may also be illuminated by being seen as an astringent anticipation of Wittgenstein's aphorism, "the human body is the best picture of the human soul" (*Philosophical Investigations*, 178—itself emphatically not a statement of materialist or behaviorist doctrine but rather an account of how the unrepresentable gets represented by what would seem to be its opposite). In Swift's view, what is best in this case must always seem inadequate.

19. See W. B. Carnochan's classic essay "Swift's *Tale*: On Satire, Negation, and the Uses of Irony," *Eighteenth-Century Studies* 5 (1971): 122–44, which concludes that the *Tale* moves radically beyond the negations offered in Hegelian dialectic—though Carnochan does not credit Hegel with the radicalism that Žižek finds in him.

20. *Prose Works*, vol. 9, 262.

21. For this passage's resonance in a long modernist tradition, see Rawson, "'Tis Only Infinite Below: Swift, with Reflections on Yeats, Wallace Stevens and R. D. Laing," in *Gulliver and the Gentle Reader*, 64–83.

22. *Pursuits of Reason*, viii.

23. *The Romantic Sublime*, 93.

24. De Man sees this tendency represented at large in what he calls a "closely familial romance," that is, "the American interpretation of Romanticism in Wimsatt, Abrams, Bloom, Hartman, and Weiskel" (*Aesthetic Ideology*, 110).

25. Of course Swift often authoritatively aligns himself with a larger, more expansive "Reason": in a later *Examiner*, he describes how "the Genius of the Nation" eventually "will naturally fall to act from Principles of Reason and Religion" (*Prose Works*, vol. 3, 158–9 [no. 42, 24 May 1711]). But such rational authority often is pointedly unreflective, inactive, and antiintellectual.

26. What Swift fears ironically materializes in "Mr Collins's Discourse of Free-Thinking" (1714), in which disputes among divines, concerning "the Doctrine of the *Trinity*" and "the Nature of our Bodies after the Resurrection, and in what manner they shall be united to our Souls," seem to license general disbelief (*Prose Works*, vol. 4, 34–5).

27. In *The Eighteenth Century: Theory and Interpretation* 34, 2 (1993), 156.

28. See Eilon, *Factions' Fictions*, for a discussion of how "Swift accounted for differences of belief and culture in terms of power relations" (64)—which for Eilon as well merit the name "ideology."

29. See J. H. Plumb, *The Growth of Political Stability in England: 1675–1725* (London: Macmillan, 1967), 134–40.

30. For the ambiguities of Swift's portrayal of the "monied interest" in the *Examiner* compared and contrasted with Defoe's *Review* and Addison's *Spectator*, see Pocock, *The Machiavellian Moment*, 446–61.

31. *The Machiavellian Moment*, 466.

32. For a rare argument that the "Bookseller's Dedication" is intended wholly ironically, "a parody of a Whig dedication to Somers" (125), see Higgins, *Swift's Politics*, 122–8.

33. *Ideology of the Aesthetic*, 93–4.

34. *Outside Literature* (London: Routledge, 1990), 151.

35. In *Critical Essays of the Seventeenth Century*, vol. 3, 75.

36. For Swift's relation to Addison and his circle, see Ehrenpreis, *Swift: The Man, His Works, and the Age*, vol. 2, 230–51.

37. *The Spectator*, vol. 3, 529.

38. See *Prose Works*, vol. 4, 87–95: "Nature hath left every Man a Capacity of being agreeable, though not of shining in Company" (87–8)—an emphasis withholding Addison's sense that everyone's natural genius may be improved to appreciate fine wit.

39. *Swift: The Man, His Works, and the Age*, vol. 2, 238–9.

40. Judith C. Mueller, "Writing under Constraint: Swift's 'Apology' for *A Tale of a Tub*," *English Literary History*: 60 (1993): 112.

41. For Caygill in *Art of Judgement*, the key reconciliation performed by taste in Shaftesbury's work is between individual judgment and a providential social order: "it is hard to avoid the suspicion that their natural unity [individual interest and providence] has been discovered after the fact of their difference. This suspicion is reinforced by Shaftesbury's admission that the relation between the interest of the individual and the end to which it tends is unknowable . . . it is the work of a *je ne sais quoi* which directs the judgement of taste" (48).

42. For discussions of the "Apology"'s ironies, see Neil Saccamano, "Authority and Publication: the Works of 'Swift,'" *Eighteenth Century: Theory and Interpretation* 25 (1984): 241–62, and Veronica Kelly, "Following the Stage Itinerant: Perception, Doubt, and Death in Swift's *Tale of a Tub*," *Studies in Eighteenth-Century Culture* 17 (1987): 239–58.

43. See "A Proposal for Correcting the English Tongue," *Prose Works*, vol. 4, 7–9.

44. Quoted in Ehrenpreis, *Swift: the Man, His Works, and the Age*, vol. 2, 331.

45. Of course it is common for writers of both sides to extol the taste of their leaders, but Addison's praise of Somers's taste in his eulogy for him in number 49 of *The Freeholder*, ed. James Leheny (Oxford: Oxford University Press, 1979) confirms the contrast between Swift's tendency to see taste as setting people apart and Addison's to see it as drawing them together: "If he [Somers] delivered his Opinion of a Piece of Poetry, a Statue, or a Picture, there was something so just and delicate in his Observations, as naturally produced Pleasure and Assent in those who heard him" (212).

46. The "Modest Defense" (*Prose Works*, vol. 4, 205–10) replies to "Gods Revenge Against Punning," ascribed to Pope. Davis (*Prose Works*, vol. 4, xxxv–vi) entertains the idea that the two were written together as a Scriblerian prank: if so both testify to the love Pope and Swift shared of playing high and low against each other.

47. *Correspondence*, 5 vols., ed. Harold Williams (Oxford: Clarendon Press, 1963–5), vol. 1, 100.

48. See Phiddian, *Swift's Parody*, 86–94, on this similarity between Swift and Shaftesbury's *Letter*. While Phiddian is persuasive, the differences between them noted here seem equally important. For another discussion attuned to the similarities, see John Sitter, *Arguments of Augustan Wit* (Cambridge: Cambridge University Press, 1991), 132–7.

49. Shaftesbury, *Characteristics of Men, Manners, Opinions, and Times*, vol. 1, 12.

50. As F. P. Lock puts it in *Swift's Tory Politics* (Newark: University of Delaware Press, 1983), "Swift was never in favour of any unlimited freedom of the press" (52). For an assertion in the *Examiner* of the need to censor his rivals, see *Prose Works*, vol. 3, 152–7. For his distrust of freedom of thought in general, see "Mr Collins's Discourse of Free-Thinking" (1714): "It is again objected, that *Free-thinking* will produce endless Divisions in Opinion, and by consequence disorder Society. To which I answer, When every single Man comes to have a different Opinion every Day from the whole World, and from himself, by Virtue of *Free-thinking*, and thinks it his Duty to convert every Man to his own *Free-thinking* (as all we *Free-thinkers* do) how can that possibly create so great a Diversity of Opinions, as to have a Sett of Priests agree among themselves to teach the same Opinions in their several Parishes to all who will come to hear them?" (vol. 4, 38–9). Here free–thinking ironically stabilizes civil society better than the rigid adherence to a single set of doctrines, a concept that neatly captures Shaftesbury's paradoxical position. Swift objects not just because he thinks that toleration fosters wrong opinions but because he is skeptical of Shaftesbury's assurance that diversity of opinion will naturally produce social harmony.

51. The ideological implications of Shaftesbury's work have been read variously. For a brusque statement of the aristocratic snobbishness of Shaftesbury's notion of taste, see Robert Markley, "Sentimentality as Performance: Shaftesbury, Sterne and the Theatrics of Virtue," in *The New Eighteenth Century*, ed. Felicity Nussbaum and Laura Brown (New York: Methuen, 1987), 210–30. For another emphasis on Shaftesbury's aristocratic (and masculinist) dimensions, see Robert W. Jones, *Gender and the Formation of Taste in Eighteenth Century Britain*, 16–23. Still, these and other writers emphasize Shaftesbury's contribution, with whatever dialectical complications, to the rise of bourgeois taste. On Shaftesbury's development of a Whiggish attitude toward social freedoms, see Lawrence E. Klein, *Shaftesbury and the Culture of Politeness* (Cambridge: Cambridge University Press, 1994), 121–98. Klein's view that the *Characteristics* effects a "rehabilitation of the affections as foundations of moral agency" (165–6) allows Shaftesbury to be seen as part of Pocock's "anti-civic" tradition of the civilization of the passions, though Klein stresses that his roots in a neo-Harringtonian civic virtue were never severed, offering "a significant expansion on the cultural politics of the civic tradition": "one cannot help but regard Shaftesbury's concern with discursive and cultural liberty as a significant shift of emphasis, one that distanced liberty from its specifically civic setting" (198).

52. *The Life, Unpublished Letters, and Philosophical Regimen of Anthony, Earl of Shaftesbury*, ed. Benjamin Rand (London: S. Sonnenschein, 1900), 504.

4: The Public Universe

1. The poem's engagement of such issues also leads its defenders to praise its sublimity, as when Voltaire calls it "the most beautiful, most useful, most sublime didactic poem ever written in any language," in *Philosophical Letters*, trans. Ernest Dilworth (Indianapolis: Bobbs-Merrill, 1961), 147.

2. Crousaz principally objects to the *Essay* because of this contradiction: "If this Earth and the Objects that display themselves about it, presented nothing but what the Mind of Man might perfectly comprehend at first Sight, the Work would not sufficiently declare the Character of its infinite Author. But if every thing was obscure here, it would be so far from making him known, and assuring the human Mind, quite imperfect as it is, of his Existence and Perfections, that it would absolutely conceal him" (*A Commentary Upon Mr Pope's Four Ethic Epistles intituled An Essay on Man by Monsieur de Crousaz* [London, 1738], 7–8). Throughout Crousaz attacks the poem for alternating between the first, authoritative view and the second, skeptical one, as all attempts to prove God from the visible world must. Crousaz rejects both, himself firmly embracing the cosmological argument (8).

3. A. D. Nuttall, *Pope's "Essay on Man"* (London: Allen and Unwin, 1984), 54.

4. *An Inquiry Concerning Human Understanding*, ed. Charles Hendel (Indianapolis: Bobbs-Merrill, 1955), 170.

5. *Essay Concerning Human Understanding*, 7.

6. Robert J. Fogelin, "The Tendency of Hume's Skepticism," in Burnyeat, *The Skeptical Tradition*, 409–10.

7. See Thomas Nagel, *The View from Nowhere* (Oxford: Oxford University Press, 1986), who differentiates his views from the one he sees as currently dominant in analytic philosophy (attributed to Donald Davidson, as well as to Bishop Berkeley and others): "if we try to form the notion of something we could never conceive, or think about, or talk about, we find ourselves having to use ideas which imply that we could in principle think about it after all (even if we cannot do so now): because even the most general ideas of truth or existence we have carry that implication" (94).

8. *Selected Philosophical Papers*, 241.

9. *Critical Works*, vol. 1, 365.

10. As Locke says in the *Essay*, "For nothing finite bears any proportion to infinite; and therefore our *Ideas*, which are all finite, cannot bear any" (371).

11. For congenial arguments that the *Essay* succeeds as a compelling failure, see Thomas R. Edwards, *This Dark Estate: A Reading of Pope* (Berkeley: University of California Press, 1963): "No one could deny that the poem would be better if its argument were more consistently reasoned, if the didactic impulse were more cogently realized. But such 'intentional' success would have taken the *Essay* even further from the Augustan mode's complex adjustment of ideal and actual, and the poem's poetic failure is the curious measure of its human success" (45). See also Hilary Putnam, "Pope's *Essay on Man* and Those 'Happy Pieties,'" in *Pursuits of Reason*: "Pope could not put together a moral image of Man that can command our allegiance out of the materials that he selected to work with; but, in the words of Rabbi Tarphon, 'The task is not yours to finish, but neither are you free to desist from it'" (20).

12. See, for example, Dustin Griffin, *Alexander Pope: The Poet in the Poems* (Princeton: Princeton University Press, 1978), for a view of how Pope's careful rhetoric successfully manages the contradiction: "what needs emphasis . . . is the *care* Pope seems to have taken to see double, to balance two different ways of looking at man without favoring either" (163–4).

13. Tories had no monopoly on such imagery. The dedication of J. T. Desaguliers's pro-Hanoverian poem *The Newtonian System of the World, the Best Model of Government: An Allegorical Poem* (Westminster, 1728) thus praises George II's constitutional powers over his subjects: "He turns their Motion from its devious Course, / And bends their Orbits by Attractive Force" (128–9). Pope is said by Warburton to have told him that Desaguliers was an early candidate for the authorship of the *Essay* when it was unknown (see *TE*, vol. 3:1, xv). The notion that cosmic plenitude, optimism, and keeping one's place in the Great Chain are indices of conservative Tory nostalgia cannot survive a glance at Mack's notes to the *Essay* in *TE*, vol. 3:1. For a "progressive" Whig argument "that whatever the order of the world produces, is in the main both just and good," see Shaftesbury, *An Inquiry Concerning Virtue or Merit* (*Characteristics*, vol. 1, 278).

14. All of Pope's views are ideologically of a piece for Jonathan Lamb: "His theology, his politics, his criteria of literature and morals, even his retirement to Twickenham, all define his right to authority and justification" (*The Rhetoric of Suffering*, 71). See also Laura Brown, *Alexander Pope* (Oxford: Blackwell, 1985): "Pope's images of animals, though ostensibly meant as a caution against human

pride, clearly evoke this doctrine of power and acquisition" (74). Another prominent account of the *Essay* as contradictory in what I am calling the weak sense appears in Brean Hammond, *Pope* (Atlantic Highlands, N.J.: Humanities Press International, 1986), 38–50.

15. As Sherburn notes, in 1730 he is "more on friendly terms with the Court than in other years" (*Correspondence*, vol. 3, 85).

16. *Characteristics*, vol. 1, 38–9.

17. I use Steven Shankman's convenient edition, *The Iliad of Homer Translated by Alexander Pope* (London: Penguin, 1996), book XIII, 27–31.

18. See de Man, "Hegel on the Sublime" in *Aesthetic Ideology*, contrasting Hegel's references to Genesis 1:3 and Psalm 104. De Man sees the fiat lux as allowing the subject's recuperation of power through language—the transitive result of God's creative utterance—while the psalm ("light is your garment, that you wear") emphasizes the disjunction between human address and divine essence (112–5).

19. Pope owned the *Oeuvres de Mr. Boileau Despréaux avec des Éclaircissements Historiques*, 2 vols. (Geneva, 1716 [see Mack, *Collected in Himself*, 399]), which contains the full debate in French (with Boileau interpolating his responses into Huet's objections; vol. 2, 379–402). Pope also owned Boileau's *Oeuvres Diverses avec le traité du sublime ou de merveilleux dans le discourse* (Amsterdam, 1702),which contains Boileau's Longinus translation and "Reflexions," with "Remarques" by Monsieur Dacier and Boivin, but not the (later) Huet debate; Pope's copy, held by Harvard's Houghton Library, bears no marginalia. He also owned Huet's *Demonstratio Evangelica ad Serenissimum Delphinum* (3d ed., 1690 [see Mack, *Collected in Himself*, 419]), where the initial objection to Boileau appears, but it was a gift from Warburton, who did not attach himself to Pope until 1740.

20. For an early statement of this view of the debate, see Smith's sarcastic note in his translation of Longinus: Huet and Le Clerc "have examined, taken to Pieces, and sifted [Genesis 1:3] as long as they were able, yet they still cannot find it sublime. It is simple, say they, and therefore not grand" (128–9). Monk similarly sees this as the issue and adds that "the controversy grows very tiresome" (*The Sublime*, 33, 14n). For a more recent example, see Jean-François Lyotard's essay "The Sublime and the Avant-Garde," in *The Inhuman:* against Huet, Boileau refers the sublime to "matters of hidden meaning, of eloquent silence, of feeling that transcends all reason and finally of openness to the *Is it happening?*" (96). My argument here stresses that Huet is more committed to eloquent silence than Boileau is.

21. *The Posthumous Works of Monsieur Boileau* (London, 1713), 27.

22. For an English version of his characteristic position, see *A Philosophical Treatise Concerning the Weakness of Human Understanding* (London, 1728).

23. *Prose Works of Alexander Pope*, vol. 2, *The Major Works, 1725–1744*, ed. Rosemary Cowler (Hamden, Conn.: Archon, 1986), 194.

24. *The Rhetoric of Suffering*, 225.

25. For doubts about Pope's Jacobitism by the 1730s, see Christina Gerrard, *The Patriot Opposition to Walpole: Politics, Poetry, and National Myth, 1725–1742* (Oxford: Clarendon Press, 1994), 68–95, especially "Pope and Jacobitism?" 85–7. Howard Erskine-Hill more sympathetically addresses "Pope and the Question

of Jacobite Vision" in *The Poetry of Opposition and Revolution: Dryden to Words-worth* (Oxford: Clarendon Press, 1996), 57–108. Mack finds Pope's political mood as early as the '15 to be opposed to the violence of revolution and committed to civil society (*Alexander Pope: A Life* [New York: Norton, 1985], 261–6). Around the time of the *Essay's* publication, Opposition rhetoric is full of dismissals of (in Bolingbroke's words) "hereditary right, and all those exalted notions, concerning the power and prerogative of kings, and the sacredness of their persons. All together they composed such a system of absurdity as had never been heard of in this country, till that anointed pedant [James I] broached them" (*A Dissertation upon Parties*, 1733, in *Political Writings: Bolingbroke*, ed. David Armitage [Cambridge: Cambridge University Press, 1997], 13). Bolingbroke also compares the "ministerial tyranny" of Walpole with the "regal . . . tyranny" (8) of James II.

26. This is comparable to Žižek's less political idea of the "Christian sublime": "a ragged, miserable creature crucified between two common brigands . . . in this wretched 'little piece of the real' lies the necessary counterpart (form of appearance) of pure spirituality" (*Tarrying with the Negative: Kant, Hegel, and the Critique of Ideology* [Durham, N.C.: Duke University Press, 1993], 50).

27. For the process of centralization of the "fiscal-military state" after 1688 under William's authority and the (often Tory) parliamentary resistance to it, see John Brewer, *The Sinews of Power: War, Money, and the English State, 1688–1783* (New York: Knopf, 1989), especially 137–66.

28. *The Growth of Political Stability in England*, 134.

29. *Virtue, Commerce, and History*, 107.

30. *The Miscellaneous Works of Joseph Addison*, ed. A. C. Guthkelch (London: G. Bell, 1914), 209–11. David Morris hears an echo of Nahum 1:3: "the Lord hath his way in the whirlwind and in the storm" (*The Religious Sublime*, 113).

31. "Immortal Rich! how calm he sits at ease / Mid snows of paper, and fierce hail of pease; / And proud his mistress' orders to perform, / Rides in the whirlwind, and directs the storm" (*TE*, vol. 5, Book III, 257–60).

32. *The Tatler*, 3 vols., ed. Donald F. Bond (Oxford: Clarendon Press, 1987), vol. 1, 310–1.

33. For analysis of the poem's sources and their significance see (of course) Mack's edition of the poem, as well as Douglas White, *Pope and the Context of Controversy: The Manipulation of Ideas in the "Essay on Man"* (Chicago: University of Chicago Press, 1970), and Nuttall, *Pope's "Essay on Man."*

34. "The poem you writ me of prevails much in the opinion of the world and is better relished than at first. . . . I perceive the divines have no objection to it, tho' now 'tis agreed not [to] be written by one, Dr Croxall, Dr Secker, and some others having solemnly denied it" (*Correspondence*, vol. 3, 358, to Caryll). Secker was to be Archbishop of Canterbury.

35. *The Structural Transformation of the Public Sphere: An Inquiry into a Category of Bourgeois Society*, trans. Thomas Burger (Cambridge: MIT Press, 1989), 27. The crucial divide in Habermas's discussion of "the Model Case of British Development" (57–67) lies between Government and Opposition, a logic that opens the public sphere to writers of both sides: "Men like Pope, Gay, Arbuthnot, and Swift combined literature and politics in a peculiar fashion comparable to Addison's and Steele's combination of literature and journalism" (59).

36. Despite initial enthusiasm, many have emphasized shortcomings of *The Structural Transformation of the Public Sphere* since its 1989 translation, particularly because it has proven difficult to disentangle the "bourgeois public sphere" from the voices of "the public authorities themselves": the established government of England is usually seen as itself the product of the "bourgeois revolution" of 1688, and the financial one starting in 1694. For interesting recent scruples about Habermas's applicability, see Jones, *Gender and the Formation of Taste in Eighteenth-Century Britain*, 33–4, and Jonathan Brody Kramnick, *Making the English Canon* (Cambridge: Cambridge University Press, 1998), 4–6.

37. For Shaftesbury's influence on the poem, see the introduction to Mack's edition (*TE*, 3:1, xxvii–xxviii).

38. *The Spectator*, vol. 5, 177.

39. *Prose Works*, vol. 3, 3.

40. Alexander Pettit, *Illusory Consensus: Bolingbroke and the Polemical Response to Walpole, 1730–1737* (Newark: University of Delaware Press, 1997), 16.

41. *Patriot Opposition to Walpole*, 32.

42. As Brean Hammond puts it in *Pope and Bolingbroke: A Study of Friendship and Influence* (Columbia: University of Missouri Press, 1984), "in the early thirties, Pope was convinced by Bolingbroke that deism was the solution to the problem of sectarianism and as such was complementary to his own Erasmian stance" (114).

43. *Essays Moral, Political, and Philosophical*, ed. Eugene F. Miller (Indianapolis: Liberty Press, 1985), 254.

44. See Stallybrass and White, *The Politics and Poetics of Transgression* (Ithaca: Cornell University Press, 1986): "the very blandness and transparency of bourgeois reason is in fact nothing other than the critical negation of a social 'colorfulness,' of a heterogeneous diversity of specific contents, upon which it is, nonetheless, completely dependent" (199). It is not always clear if "colorfulness" equally depends on reason for its conceptual existence: though the "low" is "'situated' by the dominant," it still "carries the promise of politically transformative power" (201). A yet stronger assertion of particularity's independence appears in Elizabeth Bohls, "Disinterestedness and the Denial of the Particular," in *Eighteenth-Century Aesthetics and the Reconstruction of Art*, ed. Paul Mattick Jr. (Cambridge: Cambridge University Press, 1993), 16–51.

45. For an argument that makes this connection at length, see David Simpson, *The Academic Postmodern and the Rule of Literature: A Report on Half-Knowledge* (Chicago: University of Chicago Press, 1995).

46. *The Rhetoric of Suffering*, 70.

47. Though admitting that mixing abstract and concrete in this poem is "a thing above my capacity" (8) later in "the Design," Pope does anticipate that "the particular" will be "deduce[d]" from the general in later epistles (what will be called the *Moral Essays*). But these will only reassert "the Design"'s skepticism, as in *To Cobham*'s contention that "'There's some Peculiar in each leaf and grain, / Some unmark'd fibre, or some varying vein" (*TE*, vol. 3:2, 15–6), that always renders human nature baffling.

48. John Barrell and Harriet Guest, "On the Use of Contradiction: Economics and Morality in the Eighteenth-Century Long Poem," in Nussbaum

and Brown, *The New Eighteenth Century*, 143—an essay focusing primarily on *To Bathurst* and Young's *Night Thoughts*.

49. *An Essay on Man*, ed. William Warburton (Boston, 1787), 2.

50. Pascal, *Thoughts on Religion, and Other Curious Subjects*, 348. See Barker's argument that Pope knew Kennet's translation, in *Strange Contrarieties: Pascal in England during the Age of Reason*, 121–7.

51. As impressively documented as Solomon's book is, his argument that the *Essay* succeeds at a kind of discourse (called "Academic") brushes aside the persistent critical sense that the poem's contradictions have been oddly, uniquely unsatisfying, even to its admirers like Edwards—many of whom cannot be dismissed as either obtuse dogmatists or radical Pyrrhonists who refuse to or cannot enter the poem's discursive world. Solomon's praise of the *Essay* is often correspondingly unrealistic: "Thus, perhaps Pope's greatest genius is to have solved the task Richard Rorty says was Heidegger's: 'how to work within a final vocabulary while somehow simultaneously "bracketing" that vocabulary—to keep the seriousness of its finality while letting it itself express its own contingency'" (178); "Pope creates the most powerful and profound synoptic description of reality in English" (181).

52. "Academic" moderation ties the style and meaning of the poem together for Solomon: "Pope's *via media* methodology correlates with an epistemological moderation that characterizes 'ignorance' both as thinking 'too little' (those who 'blindly creep') and 'too much' (those who 'sightless soar')" (61–2). Later, he characterizes the *Essay's* "Academic discourse" as essentially different from "the Logocentric or the Aesthetic": "the third world of discourse lies between what Pope and his contemporaries understood as the Skeptic and Stoic extremes" (118).

53. *Aesthetic Ideology*, 113.

54. *The Romantic Sublime*, 59.

55. See Laura Brown: "Though the explicit purpose of this imperialist trope in the *Essay on Man* is to ridicule anthropocentrism, it carries with it all the attractions of acquisition and power that we can easily see in its other contemporary appearances. Pope's obvious irony cannot negate these attractions, especially since he has filled his poem with metaphors of submission from imperialist apologia" (*Alexander Pope*, 78).

56. *Probability and Literary Form*, 69.

57. *Essays of Michael, Seigneur de Montaigne*, vol. 2, 195.

58. Mack omits this remark in his transcription of the marginalia of Pope's copy of the *Essays* in *Collected in Himself.*

59. *The Great Chain of Being: A Study of the History of an Idea*, 2d ed. (New York: Harper, 1960), 129.

60. *Thoughts on Religion*, 193. As Lovejoy says, "the intellectual basis of the religious convictions in which he found escape from the pessimism and scepticism which the spectacle of mere nature bred, lay (apart from the argument of the wager) almost wholly in the belief in the reality of a supernatural revelation through the history of Judaism and Christianity and the documents in which that history is recorded" (*The Great Chain of Being*, 129).

61. See G. Douglas Atkins, "Pope and Deism": "surprisingly, considering the large number of works opting for deism in Pope, we find him clearly op-

posed to the deistic belief in the sufficiency of reason. . . . [T]he *Essay on Man* is strewn with passages dealing precisely with insufficiency of reason" (in *Recent Essays by Several Hands,* ed. Maynard Mack and James A. Winn [Hamden, Conn.: Archon Press, 1982], 405).

62. Stephen refers specifically to John Toland, *Christianity Not Mysterious* (1696), in *The History of English Thought in the Eighteenth Century,* 2 vols. (New York: Harcourt, Brace, 1962), vol. 1, 89–91.

63. *Literary Works,* book III, 644–8.

64. *The Complaint: or Night Thoughts on Life, Death, and Immortality to which is added A Paraphrase on Part of the Book of Job* (London, 1768), 310.

65. Even Pope's avowal of the *Essay's* Catholicism, in response to Louis Racine's attack a decade after the poem appeared, is less a statement of inner conviction than a sociable, submissive conformity to or imitation of others' views: "I have the pleasure to answer you in the manner you most desire, a Sincere Avowal that my Opinions are intirely different from those of Spinoza; or even of Leibnitz; but on the contrary conformable to those of Mons. Pascal & Mons. Fenelon: the latter of whom I would most readily imitate, in submitting all my Opinions to the Decision of the Church" (*Correspondence,* vol. 4, 416).

66. The proximate cause of such an assertion, written in September 1733, was the defection of Pope's friends, the Whig peers Bathurst, Burlington, Cobham, and others, to the Opposition after the Excise Tax fiasco in the spring of the year. But Pope's terms here far exceed any justifiable characterization of this new anti-Walpole coalition.

67. Lovejoy remarks, "It would hardly be excessive to say that much of Kant's cosmology is a prose amplification and extension of the 'philosophy' of the First Epistle of the *Essay on Man*" (*The Great Chain of Being,* 355, 24n).

68. Immanuel Kant, *Universal Natural History and Theory of the Heavens,* trans. Stanley L. Jaki (Edinburgh: Scottish Academic Press: 1981), 182.

69. I follow Jaki's translation of Kant's version, which helpfully preserves its awkwardness.

70. Hannah Arendt argues that Kant's account of aesthetic judgment performs just this function in her *Lectures on Kant's Political Philosophy,* ed. Ronald Beiner (Chicago: University of Chicago Press, 1982). See also Eagleton, *Ideology of the Aesthetic:* "Aesthetic intersubjectivity adumbrates a utopian community of subjects," "distinct from the political" for Kant, building a "non-coercive consensus" (97).

5: Pope's *Imitations of Horace*

1. *Prose Works,* vol. 2, 157.

2. *The Machiavellian Moment,* 483.

3. *The Garden and the City* (Toronto: University of Toronto Press, 1969), 116.

4. Goldberg's phrase appears in "Integrity and Life in Pope's Poetry," in Mack and Winn, *Pope: Recent Essays by Several Hands,* 31. Thomas Edwards cites a conflict between Pope's Augustan "amplitude and equanimity" and "an anxious, 'modern' concern about the workings of mutability" (*This Dark Estate,* 2). Reuben A. Brower contrasts the *Essay on Man* with the fluidity of his subsequent Horatian mode, by which he "won his way out of argument into a free-

dom which he exploited more happily and more seriously in poems where he felt less obliged to play the solemn philosopher" (*Alexander Pope: The Poetry of Allusion* [Oxford: Oxford University Press, 1959], 239). Patricia Meyer Spacks, *An Argument of Images: The Poetry of Alexander Pope* (Cambridge: Harvard University Press, 1971), analyzes Pope's imagery in terms of the complementary tension between "energy" and "restraint," which presents "a problem crucial to the thought of the early eighteenth century . . . energy demanded control while control became meaningless without energy" (2). Rebecca Ferguson discusses the dialectical tension between reason and passion in Pope's thought in *The Unbalanced Mind: Pope and the Rule of Passion* (Brighton, England: Harvester Press, 1986).

5. Introduction to *Critical Essays on Alexander Pope*, ed. Wallace Jackson and R. Paul Yoder (New York: Macmillan, 1993), 5. Jackson elaborates on points made by Robert Markley in this volume, "Beyond Consensus: *The Rape of the Lock* and the Fate of Reading Eighteenth-Century Literature," 69–83.

6. Goldberg fleshes out a meaning of "integrity" in Pope that "he could not quite express in the conceptual vocabulary available to him" ("Integrity and Life in Pope's Poetry," 34): "the word [integrity] now includes what is meant by the existentialists' term 'authenticity' " (32).

7. Brown's idea is that Pope's poetry encodes the ideological contradictions of his culture: "Pope has been the centre of the canon in traditional eighteenth-century literary history for good reason, it seems. This study keeps him there. But it keeps him as a subversive, as a lever against the whole canon of eighteenth-century studies" (*Alexander Pope*, 5).

8. *Works*, vol. 4, 278.

9. *Correspondence of Alexander Pope*, vol. 2, 74–5.

10. *Virtue, Commerce, and History*, 48.

11. Ian A. Bell's view in " 'Not Lucre's Madman': Pope, Money, and Independence," in *Alexander Pope: Essays for the Tercentenary*, ed. Colin Nicholson (Aberdeen, Scotland: Aberdeen University Press, 1988), 53–67, is not uncommon: in Pope's understanding of himself, "an image of the dignified satirist" sits uneasily with "his steady accumulation of cash" (66).

12. Locke, "Of Identity and Diversity" initiates the modern debate on personal identity taken up by Bishop Butler, Hume, Reid, and others. Locke concludes that reflection affords no unitary idea of self as substance and that our sense of personal identity instead arises from "unity of consciousness"—what later philosophers would characterize as a memory-based theory of personal identity. See Thomas Nagel, *The View from Nowhere* , 32–7, for an analytical account of the debate.

13. Butler's position is easily summarized: "consciousness presupposes, and therefore cannot constitute personal identity any more than knowledge, in any other case, can constitute truth, which it presupposes." See "Of Personal Identity," in *The Analogy of Religion, Natural and Revealed, to the Constitution and Course of Nature*, ed. Henry Morley, 3d ed. (London: Routledge, 1887), 286. See also chapter 1 of *The Analogy of Religion*, "Of a Future Life," 9–28.

14. Christopher Fox, *Locke and the Scriblerians: Identity and Consciousness in Early Eighteenth-Century Britain* (Berkeley: University of California Press, 1988), 122.

15. *Essay Concerning Human Understanding*, 345. For a characterization of this view as a form of skepticism, see Henry Lee, *Anti-Scepticism: Or, Notes upon Each Chapter of Mr Locke's Essay Concerning Humane Understanding* (London, 1711).

16. *Treatise of Human Nature*, 259.

17. Frank Stack, *Pope and Horace: Studies in Imitation* (Cambridge: Cambridge University Press, 1985), 75.

18. *Epistles to Lucilius*, CXX, quoted by Stack, *Pope and Horace*, 268.

19. The other epistles of the *Essay* lack such elaborate headpieces, and in the earlier editions of the *Essay* I have seen (London 1732–34), the tag is not present in Epistle I's headpiece either. See the facsimile of the 1734 *Essay* in Alexander Pope, *Poems in Facsimile* (Aldershot, England: Scolar Press, 1988).

20. Niall Rudd, *Satires of Horace: A Study* (Cambridge: Cambridge University Press, 1966), 19.

21. *Sylvæ: or, the Second Part of Poetical Miscellanies* (London, 1685), preface, xxv (unnumbered).

22. Pierre Charron, *Of Wisdome*, 2 vols., trans. George Stanhope, 3d ed. (London, 1729), vol. 2, 646–7.

23. Blaise Pascal, *Pensées and Other Writings*, trans. Honor Levi (Oxford: Oxford University Press, 1995), 28. This passage, crossed out by Pascal and copied and crossed out by the copyist of his notes, does not appear in the Port-Royal edition of the *Pensées* or in Kennet's translation. (Pascal misquotes the opening lines of Horace's *Epistle I, 6.*)

24. Stanley, *History of Philosophy*, 477a.

25. Here and throughout, I use the Latin text that Pope printed with his imitation, following its italicizations, as reproduced in *TE*, vol. 4.

26. M. J. McGann, *Studies in Horace's First Book of Epistles* (Brussels: Latomas, 1969), 47.

27. For Pope's detachment from the Opposition agenda that he seemed to endorse, see Gerrard, *The Patriot Opposition to Walpole*, 68–95.

28. See similar insistences on the precedence of passion over reason in the *Essay on Man* (II, 133–60) and the *Epistle to Cobham*'s pronouncement that "On human actions reason tho' you can, / It may be reason, but it is not man" (35–6).

29. *De Natura Deorum* & *Academica*, trans. H. Rackham (Cambridge: Harvard University Press, 1933): "the sole object of our discussions is by arguing on both sides to draw out and give shape to some result that may be either true or the nearest possible approximation to the truth" (475). For this practice in Renaissance humanism, see Victoria Kahn, *Rhetoric, Prudence, and Skepticism in the Renaissance* (Ithaca: Cornell University Press, 1985): "The activity of the Academic skeptic, who can argue on both sides of any philosophical question (*in utrumque partem*), is considered to be analogous to that of the orator and the prudent man: all three are concerned with efficacious action and, accordingly, for all three the criterion of truth is not theoretical reason but probability or 'practical certainty' " (20).

30. On Carneades, see David Sedley's essay "The Motivation of Greek Skepticism," in Burnyeat, *The Skeptical Tradition*, 9–29.

31. Burnyeat's formula occurs in his important essay "Can the Skeptic Live His Skepticism?" in *The Skeptical Tradition*, 140.

32. Spence, *Observations, Anecdotes, and Characters of Books and Men: Collected from Conversation*, 2 vols., ed. James M. Osborn (Oxford: Clarendon Press, 1966), vol. 1, 470.

33. See *This Dark Estate*, 2. Edwards notes that in *The Essay on Man* "a steady skeptical undercurrent qualifies Pope's dogmatism" (32) and generally comments on persisting "signs of some uncertainty about the Augustan synthesis" (48).

34. In *Acts of Knowledge: Pope's Later Poems* (Lewisburg, Pa.: Bucknell University Press, 1981), Bogel views skepticism as a phase through which Pope must pass as he achieves his greatest poetic successes: "in the *Epistles to Several Persons*, taken as a whole, the skeptical imagination brooding on trivial surfaces, is gradually led onward to a fuller humanity and a more fully humanized art" (45). Pope comes then to embrace a mitigated skepticism or fallibilism, "a form of positive skepticism, the skepticism of a Dryden rather than of a Pyrrhon [sic]. Such skepticism assumes that there is something significant in experience to be known, and that what is significant is knowable, but it also assumes that the proportion of misconception to true knowledge will be high" (222).

35. Shenstone, *Poems Upon Various Occasions* (London, 1737), 34–6.

36. See Caygill, *Art of Judgement*: "Mandeville replaces the *je ne sais quoi* with a cynical I know only too well; in place of providence he puts the manipulative politician. His exposure of the violence of the *je ne sais quoi* served to put Shaftesbury's successors on the defensive" (52).

37. See especially Barrell and Guest, "On the Use of Contradiction," in Nussbaum and Brown, *The New Eighteenth Century*, 121–43.

38. *The End of the Line*, 14.

39. Jonathan Lamb, "The Subject of the Subject and the Sublimities of Self-Reference," 204. This essay reviews Peter de Bolla's *Discourse of the Sublime* and distinguishes Lamb's views of Pitt's oratory from what he calls de Bolla's understanding of "the transaction of Pitt's eloquence solely at the level of the public space, articulating text and collectivity via a person that instances the subjective possibilities of public experience" (204). See de Bolla's account of Pitt, "The Voice of Liberty," in *Discourse of the Sublime*, 143–5.

40. *Disowning Knowledge in Six Plays of Shakespeare* (Cambridge: Cambridge University Press, 1987), 3.

41. Cavell qualifies this view in regard to other minds in the fourth section of *The Claim of Reason*: "My intuition that, on the contrary, I can live my skepticism with respect to other minds, is an intuition that there is no comparable, general alternative to the radical doubt of the existence of others. . . . To say I cannot 'live' material object skepticism is to say that there is an alternative to its conclusion that I am bound, as a normal human being, to take. Accordingly, to say I (can) live skepticism with respect to others is to say that there is no such alternative, or no such conclusion" (447–8).

42. See Hume, *Treatise of Human Nature*, which narrates his reentry into ordinary life after his skeptical reasonings: "Here then I find myself absolutely and necessarily determin'd to live, and talk, and act like other people in the common affairs of life . . . the course of my animal spirits and passions reduce me to this indolent belief in the general maxims of the world" (269).

43. For a detailed disagreement with Burnyeat's conclusion that ancient skepticism is impracticable, see R. J. Hankinson, *The Sceptics* (London: Routledge, 1995), 282–6.

44. The skeptic says, "You don't really see that apple on the table, you see only one side of it" or "You see only a sense-impression of it" or "You could be dreaming you see it": such remarks alienate us from our ordinary grasp of what it means to see an apple. See Stanley Cavell, *Must We Mean What We Say?* (Cambridge: Cambridge University Press, 1976), especially the title essay (1–43), and parts 1 and 2 of *The Claim of Reason,* for how epistemological perspectives on "generic objects" represent points of departure from ordinary life and language.

45. *Prose Works,* vol. 2, 152 (removed after 1st edition). The idea also appears in *Correspondence,* vol. 1 , 274. See also Addison's lines on the relation between Milton's poetry and his politics: "While the clean current, tho' serene and bright, / Betrays a bottom odious to the sight" ("An Account of the Greatest English Poets," 84–5).

46. See "Moderation Display'd" in *Poems on Affairs of State: Augustan Satirical Verse, 1660–1714,* 7 vols., ed. George deF. Lord et al. (New Haven: Yale University Press, 1963–75), vol. 7, 19–42. Frank H. Ellis, editor of this volume, cites Pope's attribution of the poem to Shippen (22), but Mack's *Collected in Himself* (434) shows that it was the poem "Faction Display'd" that Pope identified as Shippen's work in a marginal note in his copy of *Poems Relating to State Affairs.* It does seem that the two poems were thought of together, however.

47. That is, of course, the Roman Catholic one: see Erasmus, *Diatribe seu Collatio de Libero Arbitrario* (1524), in *Erasmus-Luther: Discourse on Free Will,* trans. Ernst F. Winter (New York: Unger, 1962), 6.

48. Jean Starobinski, *Montaigne in Motion,* trans. Arthur Goldhammer (Chicago: University of Chicago Press, 1985), 26–7.

49. For a similar view of the ambiguities of the poem's conclusion, see Howard D. Weinbrot's essay " 'Such as Sir Robert Would Approve'? Answers to Pope's Answer from Horace," in *Eighteenth-Century Satire: Essays on Text and Context from Dryden to Peter Pindar* (Cambridge: Cambridge University Press, 1988), 120–7.

50. As Leo Damrosch puts it, "St. Paul wanted to be 'all things to all men' . . . but this is nonetheless strange company to find him in." Damrosch next quotes Warton's *Essay on Pope:* " 'There is an impropriety and indecorum,' Warton objects, 'in joining the name of the most profligate parasite in the court of Dionysius with that of an apostle.' " See *The Imaginative World of Alexander Pope* (Berkeley: University of California Press, 1987), 169. Such an extreme contrast functions specifically to deny, in the spirit of ancient skepticism, that any given belief adheres to the self in a logically definitive way.

51. *Resemblance and Disgrace: Alexander Pope and the Deformation of Culture* (Cambridge: Harvard University Press, 1996), 146. Focusing on oppositions between Pope's mind and (deformed) body, Deutsch valuably emphasizes Pope's manipulation of divisions within the self, and the image of the self as an "impartial Glass" in *Satire II, 1,* is significant to her argument as well: "in the Horatian poems, the 'spots' which mar his medium enable it to be read as transparent self-exposure" (136).

52. Keats's famous letter to Richard Woodhouse (27 October 1818) defines "the poetical Character," "that sort distinguished from the wordsworthian or egotistical sublime," as chameleonlike: "it is a very fact that not one word I ever utter can be taken for granted as an opinion growing out of my identical nature—how can it, when I have no nature?" (*Letters,* ed. Maurice Buxton Forman [Oxford: Oxford University Press, 1952], 227–8). Eliot's impersonalist theory appears in "Tradition and the Individual Talent" (1919): "Poetry is not a turning loose of emotion, but an escape from emotion; it is not the expression of personality, but an escape from personality" (*Selected Essays: 1917–1932* [New York: Harcourt, 1950], 11–2). Deconstruction itself may be seen as a development of this long modernist tradition, as de Man suggests in *Allegories of Reading: Figural Language in Rousseau, Nietzsche, Rilke, and Proust* (New Haven: Yale University Press, 1979): "Within the epistemological labyrinth of figural structures, recuperation of selfhood would be accomplished by the rigor with which the discourse deconstructs the very notion of the self. The originator of this discourse is then no longer the dupe of his own wishes; he is as far beyond pleasure and pain as he is beyond good and evil or, for that matter, beyond strength and weakness. His consciousness is neither happy nor unhappy, nor does he possess any power. He remains however a center of authority to the extent that the very destructiveness of his ascetic reading testifies to the validity of his interpretation. The dialectical reversal that transfers the authority from experience into interpretation and transforms, by a hermeneutic process, the total insignificance, the nothingness of the self into a new center of meaning, is a very familiar gesture in contemporary thought, the ground of what is abusively called modernity" (173–4).

6: Knowing Ridicule and Skeptical Reflection in the *Moral Essays*

1. See David B. Morris, *Alexander Pope: The Genius of Sense* (Cambridge: Cambridge University Press, 1984): we must "distinguish between inconsistency and its more extreme counterpart, inconstancy. For Pope . . . all individuals . . . are inconsistent, but their fitful changes do not call in question their underlying nature as fools, rogues, or persons of virtue. Inconstancy, by contrast, involves a much more radical kind of change. It does not imply variation from or within a firm, centered, consistent character. Inconstancy suggests the absence of any center. Character becomes the focus of oppositions so extreme and changes so unceasing that there is a real question whether character still exists" (200–1).

2. As A. A. Long puts the paradoxes, "there are no degrees of virtue and vice; all men except the sage are insane; all acts of wrong-doing are equally wrong" (*Hellenistic Philosophy,* 2d ed. [Berkeley: University of California Press, 1986], 214). Such extremism and rigidity are alien to the ethics of Montaigne and Pope, but inasmuch as any inconsistency is as inconsistent as any other, it becomes logically difficult to rank them.

3. *Essays,* vol. 2, 14. I have not identified the translation of Horace; it perhaps is by Charles Cotton, translator of the edition of Montaigne in which it appears.

4. *The Poetics of Sexual Myth* (Chicago: University of Chicago Press, 1985), 118.

5. Many accounts link the modern psychology of ideas and the problem of other minds, especially given the (arguable) importance for Descartes of the "incorrigibility" of mental states—which opens up an absolute epistemological gap between my knowledge of my mental states and my knowledge of yours. On the distinction between Cartesian incorrigibility and ancient notions of the mind, see Richard Rorty, *Philosophy and the Mirror of Nature* (Princeton: Princeton University Press, 1979), 38–61. A classic discussion is John Wisdom, *Other Minds*, 3d ed. (Berkeley: University of California Press, 1968), inspired by Wittgenstein. Stanley Cavell's own Wittgensteinian reading of the problem unfolds in the fourth section of *The Claim of Reason*, "Skepticism and the Problem of Others: Between Acknowledgment and Avoidance," 327–496.

6. *Correspondence*, vol. 2, 23.

7. *Philosophical Works*, vol. 1, 155.

8. Montaigne, *Essays*, vol. 2, 4. Matthew Prior's "Essay on Opinion" takes Montaigne's maxim and, like Pope, relates it to the wider skeptical claim that we can know nothing about the world: "We judge of things according to the humour we are in and that very Humour is subject to infinite Variety. . . . So many things seem, I say, to contribute to the forming of our Opinion the least of which has Power in a great Measure to make Us change it; so that no Man is so different from another as the same Man is from Himself." Though the essay was not published until 1907 in *Dialogues of the Dead and Other Works in Prose and Verse*, ed. A. R. Waller (Cambridge: Cambridge University Press, 1907), 196, Pope knew it in manuscript: see *TE*, vol. 3:2, 16, l14n.

9. See *TE*, vol. 3:2, xx–xxii, for Bateson's account of the relationship between these conversations and the poem.

10. *History of Scepticism*, 59. Popkin's interpretation has been challenged by Maryanne Cline Horowitz, "Pierre Charron's View of the Source of Wisdom," in *Journal of the History of Philosophy* 9 (1971): 443–57, finding Stoic elements of Charron's thought. Charron also seems concerned to mitigate his skepticism by referring it to Academicism: his book, he says in his preface, is *"Argued and Disputed Problematically, and in the old Academick Way."* But at times he strikes a strongly skeptical note: "alas! Our utmost Attempts are short and insufficient; for Absolute Certainty is not a Prize allotted to us" (vol. 1, 159).

11. I follow the dating offered in *The Complete Essays of Montaigne*, trans. Donald M. Frame (Stanford: Stanford University Press, 1958).

12. See Christopher Fox, "Pope, Perhaps, and Sextus: Skeptical Modes in Moral Essay I," *English Language Notes* 29, 2 (1991): 37–48.

13. *History of Philosophy*, 477b. At other places in the *Outlines of Pyrrhonism*, Sextus invokes a sense of the problematic diversity among people to support his broader argument: under the *"second Common place,"* or trope, the argument from *"the Diversity of Men,"* he remarks, *"Indians* delight in some things, we in others; but to delight in several things, argueth a reception of different Phantasies from the same Objects. We differ also in *Constitution;* there are some who can digest Beef, easier than Anchovies" (480b), and so on. Sextus notices these differences not so much to argue that our various tastes or constitutions make each of us impossible to know as to suggest that they render certainty about "Objects" impossible.

14. I quote the English translation, *A Philosophical Treatise Concerning the Weakness of Human Understanding* (London, 1728), 26–7, which appeared after Atterbury's letter was written. (The translator is not identified, though Sherburn in Pope's *Correspondence* suggests Ozell.)

15. See *Correspondence*, vol. 2, 74–5n.

16. *The Machiavellian Moment*, 464.

17. *OED*, quoted in *TE*, vol. 3:2, 106n.

18. Brower says that "Wharton is a man of parts so various that the concluding strokes give an impression of dazzling conflicts . . . the lesson that remains with us is not Pope's short and easy method for understanding human nature, but his sense of its mystery and inscrutability" (*The Poetry of Allusion*, 264). Benjamin Boyce says that "the force of the picture is not in the paradoxical key, the ruling passion, but in the extravagant, all-inclusive, jarring self-contradictions" (*The Character Sketches in Pope's Poems* [Durham, N.C.: Duke University Press, 1962], 68).

19. For Richardson Jr.'s role in editing the poem, see *TE*, vol. 3:2, 4–12.

20. These particular lines appear only in versions of Epistle II from 1734 to 1735 as lines 148–9. See *TE*, vol. 3:1, 72.

21. *A Treatise of Human Nature*, 252.

22. *Poems on Affairs of State*, vol. 6.

23. *Poems on Affairs of State*, vol. 7.

24. See *TE*, vol. 3:2, 179n.

25. See *TE*, vol. 3:2, 262–5n.

26. The first to elaborate on the hidden metaphor of women as gold is J. G. Keogh, in "Pope's 'Epistle to a Lady' 1– 4," *Explicator* 31, 5 (1973), no. 37. The following discussion owes much to Keogh's brief paragraph as well as to Pollak's discussion in *The Poetics of Sexual Myth*, 123–7.

27. See Pocock, *The Machiavellian Moment*, 452–61, for what remains the most illuminating discussion of the feminization of credit in the contemporary political imagination.

28. *Spectator*, vol. 1, 15.

29. Pocock describes "the image of the woman who wants a new gown for thoroughly selfish and whimsical reasons . . . and instantly sets tradesmen and artisans to work in ways whose benefit to society is in no way commensurate with the triviality of her motivation" (*The Machiavellian Moment*, 465).

30. *Desire and Domestic Fiction* (Oxford: Oxford University Press, 1987), 66.

31. *The Sublime Object of Ideology*, 18. The quote is from Sohn-Rethel, *Intellectual and Manual Labor: A Critique of Epistemology* (London: Macmillan, 1978), 59.

32. As Žižek characterizes him in *The Sublime Object of Ideology*, 16.

33. *Aesthetic Theory*, trans. Robert Hullot-Kentor (Minneapolis: University of Minnesota Press, 1997), 83.

34. *The Woman of Taste. Occasioned by a late Poem, Entitled, The Man of Taste. By a Friend of the Author's. In two Epistles, from Clelia in Town to Sapho in the Country*, attributed to Thomas Newcomb (London, 1733), Epistle II, 9.

35. *An Essay on the Theory of Painting* (London, 1715), 214.

36. [*An Essay on the Whole Art of Criticism as it Relates to Painting.*] *Two Discourses* (London, 1719), 37. Richardson soon pulls back from the radical asser-

tion that artistic defects are good: "However 'tis not those Defects, but what is Excellent that is Sublime" (37).

37. *This New Yet Unapproachable America*, 58.

38. Of course *design* in the period does not primarily mean contrivance out of nothing, as we use it: in Richardson's words, "Drawing, or Designing signifies only the giving those Things their true Form, which implies an exact proportionable Magnifying, or Diminishing in every part alike" (*An Essay on the Theory of Painting*, 133). But Pope's rejection of "equal Colours" and the "proportionable" indicates his anticipation, as it were, of his models' inconsistency in the technique he brings to them.

39. *Prose Works* vol. 2, 13.

40. "Integrity and Life in Pope's Poetry," 38.

41. "To ———— turn, she never took the height / Of *Saturn*, yet is ever in the right," Satire V, *The Love of Fame: the Universal Passion*, 2d ed. (London, 1728), 343–4. See also his picture of wise old age in women: "O how unlike her is the sacred age / Of prudent *Portia*! Her gray hairs engage, / Whose thoughts are suited to her life's decline: / *Virtue*'s the paint that can make wrinkles shine" (V, 519–22).

42. Valerie Rumbold argues that Young's procedure is more representative of typical misogyny than Pope's and emphasizes that "the fascination with which female brilliance compelled Pope's divided imagination" (294) is a key to understanding what is distinctive about his poetic depictions of women. See *Women's Place in Pope's World* (Cambridge: Cambridge University Press, 1989), 268–9, for the contrast with Young.

43. Felicity Nussbaum, *The Brink of All We Hate: English Satires on Women, 1660–1750* (Lexington: University of Kentucky Press, 1984), 156.

44. "The Poetic Career of Judith Cowper: An Exemplary Failure?" in *Pope, Swift, and Women Writers*, ed. Donald C. Mell (Newark: University of Delaware Press, 1996), 53.

45. See Ingrassia, *Authorship, Commerce, and Gender*, for a linkage between specifically literary exchange and the feminizing tendency of commerce: "The participation of women, while seemingly peripheral, actually fueled the gendered characterization placed on the commercialization of the literary marketplace, the proliferations of speculative investment, and the readers and writers of the novel" (3)—a theme also stressed in Catherine Gallagher's account of women novelists in *Nobody Story: The Vanishing Acts of Women Writers in the Marketplace* (Berkeley: University of California Press, 1995).

46. For instance, Mary Leapor in *An Essay on Woman* (1751) begins, like Pope, by characterizing women as "Too soft for business and too weak for power" (2) but then develops her own version of the odd visual response that women provoke: "What numbers for her charming features pine, / If blooming acres round her temples twine!" (7–8)—cleverly rendering female beauty's relation to wealth as a recession of figure into ground ("charming features" into "blooming acres") in the masculine visual field. Leapor's poem appears in *Eighteenth Century Women's Poetry: An Oxford Anthology*, ed. Roger Lonsdale (Oxford: Oxford University Press, 1989). In *Alexander Pope and His Eighteenth Century Women Readers* (Carbondale: University of Southern Illinois Press, 1994),

Claudia Thomas presents a wide-ranging discussion to show that "a response to Pope was, for many women, a response to cultural issues ranging from women's emotional and intellectual qualities to their creative capacity" (3).

7: Modernity and the Skeptical Sublime in the Final *Dunciad*

1. On the surreal nature of the *Dunciad*'s imagery, see, among many, Tony Tanner, "Reason and the Grotesque: Pope's *Dunciad*," in *Essential Articles for the Study of Alexander Pope*, ed. Maynard Mack (Hamden, Conn.: Archon Press, 1968), 825–44. For the far-reaching destruction of the dunces, see Howard Erskine-Hill, "The 'New World' of Pope's *Dunciad*," also in Mack, *Essential Articles*, 803–24.

2. Emrys Jones, "Pope and Dulness," in Mack and Winn, *Pope: Recent Essays*, 622.

3. Atkins, *Quests of Difference: Reading Pope's Poems* (Lexington: University of Kentucky Press, 1986), 155.

4. B. W. Young, " 'See *Mystery* to *Mathematics* Fly!' Pope's *Dunciad* and the Critique of Religious Rationalism," *Eighteenth-Century Studies* 26, 3 (1993): 443.

5. *A Demonstration of the Being and Attributes of God and Other Writings*, ed. Ezio Vailati (Cambridge: Cambridge University Press, 1998), 3.

6. For Cavell's treatment of skepticism's relevance to the problem of intention, see especially the title essay of *Must We Mean What We Say?* 1–43.

7. *Philosophical Investigations*, 51.

8. *This New Yet Unapproachable America*, 38.

9. *Disowning Knowledge in Six Plays of Shakespeare*, 3.

10. On the Cartesian circle, see Bernard Williams, *Descartes: The Project of Pure Inquiry*, 189–204.

11. *A Demonstration*, 16–7.

12. *History of Scepticism*, 200.

13. *Treatise of Human Nature*, 267. Pope owned a copy of the *Treatise*, though it seems unlikely that he read it. See Mack's *Collected in Himself*, 420.

14. Aubrey Williams, *Pope's Dunciad: A Study of Its Meaning* (Baton Rouge: Louisiana State University Press, 1955), 105. R. G. Peterson also emphasizes Pope's humanism in "Renaissance Classicism in Pope's *Dunciad*," *Studies in English Literature* 15, 3 (1975): 431–45.

15. For cultural and economic implications of Dulness's femininity, see Ingrassia, *Authorship, Commerce, and Gender*, 40–76.

16. See 489n. Throughout I refer only to Pope's notes (labeled "P." in *TE*) and those attributed to Pope and Warburton ("P. W.")—not the notes Warburton wrote on his own ("W."). The passage cited is from *The Moralists* and appears in the *Characteristics*, vol. 2, 18.

17. "For as averse as I am to the cause of theism, or the name of Deist, when taken in a sense exclusive of revelation, I consider still that in strictness the root of all is theism, and that to be a settled Christian, it is necessary to be first of all a good theist; for theism can only be opposed to polytheism or atheism" (vol. 2, 19). Despite such special pleading, no doubt a controversialist like Warburton would take this as proof that Shaftesbury was a deist.

18. "I must own, indeed, 'tis become fashionable in our nation to talk politics in every company, and mix the discourses of State affairs with those of

pleasure and entertainment. However, 'tis certain we approve of no such free-dom in philosophy. Nor do we look upon politics to be of her province, or in the least related to her" (vol. 2, 4).

19. The most elaborate tracing of correspondences between the poem's satire of the literary world and politics is Brooks-Davies, *The Dunciad and the Queen of the Night*, though the parallels between (e.g.) Theobald/Cibber's ele-vation as King of the Dunces and other kings have long been obvious, for in-stance, "Still Dunce the second reigns like Dunce the first" (I, 6 in the 1728 ver-sion, published soon after George II's coronation in 1727).

20. *The Poetry of Opposition and Revolution*, 106.

21. *Works*, vol. 3, 52.

22. See Dustin Griffin, *Regaining Paradise: Milton in the Eighteenth Century* (Cambridge: Cambridge University Press, 1986) for a survey of Miltonic infl-uence on eighteenth-century writing. Chapter 3 of Martin Battestin, *The Prov-idence of Wit: Aspects of Form in Augustan Literature and the Arts* (Oxford: Claren-don Press, 1974), analyzes relations between *Paradise Lost* and the *Dunciad*, especially parallel passages concerning creation. In addition, Brooks-Davies, *Pope's Dunciad and the Queen of Night*, analyzes some of the *Dunciad*'s allusions to *Paradise Lost* in political terms, especially the 1728 version, though the exact political force of Pope's attitude toward Milton's antimonarchical language is left a little vague: "Politically and theologically Milton, Dryden and Pope could not have held more divergent views. What they shared was a commitment to human freedom and the values of Christian civilisation" (66).

23. *Works*, vol. 12, 86.

24. "The Tragedies of the Last Age," in *Critical Essays of the Seventeenth Cen-tury*, vol. 2, 208.

25. Burke gives perhaps the most play to the sublimity of obscurity, partic-ularly in regard to Milton, in the famous discussions of *Paradise Lost* in sections III–IV of *A Philosophical Inquiry into the Origins of Our Ideas of the Sublime and the Beautiful*, 58–64, but inasmuch as it evokes a sense of human limitation be-fore the boundless, it appears a commonplace attribute of sublime objects from at least Dennis and Addison.

26. *Selected Philosophical Papers of Robert Boyle*, 229–30.

27. "*Darkness visible* and *Darkness palpable* are in due place very good Expres-sions: but the next Line makes *visible* here a flat Contradiction. *Darkness visible* will not serve to *discover Sights of Woe* through it, but to cover and hide them. . . . To come up to the Author's Idea, we may say thus, *No Light, but rather a* TRAN-SPICUOUS GLOOM. *Gloom* is equivalent to Darkness; yet so as to be in some measure *transparent*" (*Paradise Lost*, ed. Richard Bentley [London, 1732], 4).

28. In *Poetry of Opposition and Revolution*, Erskine-Hill sees not just the ref-erence to Passive Obedience but also the one to "weak rebels" as swipes at the Jacobites and their failed rebellions against the Hanoverians: the lines are "a good analysis of the Jacobite failure in practice: the cause had only been com-promised by weak rebellion, and enfeebled by the doctrine of Passive Obedi-ence which had originally enjoined loyally to James II and his heirs" (105). But the picture to my mind alludes to a more general, theoretical opposition per-taining to monarchy itself, between absolutist obedience and republican rebel-

lion, only to find, yet again, no difference between the opposites as far as Dulness is concerned. The contrastive phrases—"Not those alone," "But who"—make it seem unlikely that Pope refers only to the Jacobite faction.

29. Brooks-Davies also remarks, "After all, James and his Jacobites can be dunces as well as Hanoverians" (65); he also frequently mentions "Pope's reservations about absolutism" (83).

30. The resonance of my discussion here and throughout with standard themes of deconstruction does not escape me. See Hugh J. Silverman, introduction to *The Textual Sublime: Deconstruction and Its Differences,* ed. Hugh J. Silverman and Gary E. Aylesworth (Albany: State University of New York Press, 1990), especially Silverman's definition of "the textual sublime": "as the text opens itself to what is other than itself, it marks the differential spaces of the text" (xii–xiii).

31. "Hence if in judging nature aesthetically we call it sublime, we do not so because nature arouses fear, but because it calls forth our strength (which does not belong to nature [within us]), to regard as small the [objects] of our [natural] concerns: property, health, and life, and because of this we regard nature's might (to which we are indeed subjected in these [natural] concerns) as yet not having such dominance over us, as persons, that we should have to bow to it if our highest principles were at stake, and we had to choose between upholding or abandoning them" (*Critique of Judgment,* 121).

32. See David L. Sedley, "Sublimity and Skepticism in Montaigne," which argues that Montaigne's contemplation of Roman ruins leads to an aesthetic of the fragment that surpasses the rhetorical category of *admiratio.* While not offering any direct link between Longinus and Montaigne, he does describe how Montaigne's skepticism allowed him to appreciate ruined grandeur in a new way—not as a part suggestive of a lost whole but a trace indicative of sublime lack or loss.

Bibliography

Anonymous. *Remarks Upon the Letter to a Lord Concerning Enthusiasm, In a Letter to a Gentleman.* London, 1708.

Addison, Joseph. *The Freeholder.* Edited by James Leheny. Oxford: Oxford University Press, 1979.

———. *The Miscellaneous Works of Joseph Addison.* Edited by A. C. Guthkelch. London: G. Bell, 1914.

Addison, Joseph, Richard Steele, et al. *The Spectator.* Edited by Donald F. Bond. 5 vols. Oxford: Oxford University Press, 1965.

———. *The Tatler.* Edited by Donald F. Bond. 3 vols. Oxford: Clarendon Press, 1987.

Adorno, Theodor. *Aesthetic Theory.* Translated by Robert Hullot-Kentor. Minneapolis: University of Minnesota Press, 1997.

Akenside, Mark. *The Pleasures of the Imagination. A Poem. In Three Books.* London, 1744.

Appleby, Joyce Oldham. *Economic Thought and Ideology in Seventeenth-Century England.* Princeton: Princeton University Press, 1978.

Arendt, Hannah. *Lectures on Kant's Political Philosophy.* Edited by Ronald Beiner. Chicago: University of Chicago Press, 1982.

Armstrong, Nancy. *Desire and Domestic Fiction: A Political History of the Novel.* Oxford: Oxford University Press, 1987.

Arnauld, Antoine, and Pierre Nicole. *Logic or the Art of Thinking.* Edited and translated by Jill Vance Buroker. Cambridge: Cambridge University Press, 1996.

Atkins, G. Douglas. "Pope and Deism: a New Analysis." In *Pope: Recent Essays by Several Hands.* Edited by Maynard Mack and James A. Winn, 392–415. Hamden, Conn.: Archon Press, 1980.

———. *Quests of Difference: Reading Pope's Poems.* Lexington: University Press of Kentucky, 1986.

Augustine. *The City of God*. Translated by Henry Bettenson. Harmondsworth, England: Penguin, 1984.

Barker, John. *Strange Contrarieties: Pascal in England during the Age of Reason*. Montreal: McGill-Queens University Press, 1975.

Barrell, John, and Harriet Guest. "On the Use of Contradiction: Economics and Morality in the Eighteenth-Century Long Poem." In *The New Eighteenth Century*. Edited by Felicity Nussbaum and Laura Brown, 121–143. New York: Methuen, 1987.

Battestin, Martin. *The Providence of Wit: Aspects of Form in Augustan Literature and the Arts*. Oxford: Clarendon Press, 1974.

Bayle, Pierre. *Historical and Critical Dictionary: Selections*. Translated by Richard H. Popkin. Indianapolis: Hackett, 1991.

Bell, Ian A. "'Not Lucre's Madman': Pope, Money, and Independence." In *Alexander Pope: Essays for the Tercentenary*. Edited by Colin Nicholson, 53–67. Aberdeen, Scotland: Aberdeen University Press, 1988.

Bennett, Tony. *Outside Literature*. London: Routledge, 1990.

Blackmore, Richard. *Paraphrase on the Book of Job*. 2d ed. London, 1716.

Bloom, Harold. "Freud and the Poetic Sublime: A Catastrophe Theory of Creativity." In *Freud: A Collection of Critical Essays*. Edited by Perry Meisel, 211–31. Englewood Cliffs, N.J.: Prentice-Hall, 1981.

Bogel, Fredric. *Acts of Knowledge: Pope's Later Poems*. Lewisburg, Pa.: Bucknell University Press, 1981.

Bohls, Elizabeth. "Disinterestedness and the Denial of the Particular." In *Eighteenth-Century Aesthetics and the Reconstruction of Art*. Edited by Paul Mattick Jr., 16–51. Cambridge: Cambridge University Press, 1993.

Boileau Despréaux, Nicolas. *Oeuvres de Mr. Boileau Despréaux avec des Éclaircissements Historiques*. 2 vols. Geneva, 1716.

———. *Oeuvres Diverses avec le traité du sublime ou de merveilleux dans le discourse*. Amsterdam, 1702.

———. *The Posthumous Works of Monsieur Boileau*. London, 1713.

Bolingbroke, Henry St. John, Viscount of. *Political Writings: Bolingbroke*. Edited by David Armitage. Cambridge: Cambridge University Press, 1997.

———. *The Works of Lord Bolingbroke*. Philadelphia: Carey and Hart, 1841.

Boyce, Benjamin. *The Character Sketches in Pope's Poems*. Durham, N.C.: Duke University Press, 1962.

Boyle, Robert. *The Sceptical Chymist*. Dent: London, 1911.

———. *Selected Philosophical Papers of Robert Boyle*. Edited by M. A. Stewart. Indianapolis: Hackett, 1991.

Bredvold, Louis I. "The Gloom of the Tory Satirists." In *Eighteenth-Century English Literature: Modern Essays in Criticism*. Edited by James L. Clifford, 3–20. Oxford: Oxford University Press, 1959.

——. *The Intellectual Milieu of John Dryden: Studies in Some Aspects of Seventeenth-Century Thought*. Ann Arbor: University of Michigan Press, 1934.

Brewer, John. *The Sinews of Power: War, Money, and the English State, 1688–1783*. New York: Knopf, 1989.

Brooks-Davies, Douglas. *Pope's Dunciad and the Queen of Night: A Study in Emotional Jacobitism*. Manchester, England: Manchester University Press, 1985.

Brower, Reuben A. *Alexander Pope: The Poetry of Allusion*. Oxford: Oxford University Press, 1959.

Brown, Laura. *Alexander Pope*. Oxford: Blackwell, 1985.

Budick, Sanford. *Dryden and the Abyss of Light: A Study of Religio Laici and the Hind and the Panther*. New Haven: Yale University Press, 1970.

Burke, Edmund. *A Philosophical Enquiry into the Origin of Our Ideas of the Sublime and the Beautiful*. Edited by James T. Boulton. Notre Dame: University of Notre Dame Press, 1968.

Burnet, Gilbert. *Some Passages of the Life and Death of John Earl of Rochester*. In *Rochester: The Critical Heritage*. Edited by David Farley-Hills, 47–92. London: Routledge and Kegan Paul, 1972.

Burnyeat, Myles. Introduction and "Can the Skeptic Live His Skepticism?" In *The Skeptical Tradition*. Edited by Myles Burnyeat, 1–8, 117–48. Berkeley: University of California Press, 1983.

Burtt, Shelley. *Virtue Transformed: Political Argument in England, 1688–1740*. Cambridge: Cambridge University Press, 1992.

Butler, Joseph. *The Analogy of Religion, Natural and Revealed, to the Constitution and Course of Nature*. Edited by Henry Morley. 3d ed. London: Routledge, 1887.

Carnochan, W. B. "*Swift's Tale*: On Satire, Negation, and the Uses of Irony." *Eighteenth-Century Studies* 5 (1971):122–44.

Cavell, Stanley. *The Claim of Reason*. Oxford: Oxford University Press, 1979.

——. *Disowning Knowledge in Six Plays of Shakespeare*. Cambridge: Cambridge University Press, 1987.

——. *In Quest of the Ordinary: Lines of Skepticism and Romanticism*. Chicago: University of Chicago Press, 1988.

——. *Must We Mean What We Say?* Cambridge: Cambridge University Press, 1976.

——. *This New Yet Unapproachable America: Lectures after Emerson after Wittgenstein*. Albuquerque: Living Batch Press, 1989.

Caygill, Howard. *Art of Judgement*. Oxford: Blackwell, 1989.

Charron, Pierre. *Of Wisdome*. 2 vols. Translated by George Stanhope. 3d ed. London, 1729.

Christensen, Jerome. *Practicing Enlightenment: Hume and the Formation of a Literary Career*. Madison: University of Wisconsin Press, 1987.

Cicero. *De Natura Deorum* & *Academica*. Translated by H. Rackham. Cambridge: Harvard University Press, 1933.

Clarke, Samuel. *A Demonstration of the Being and Attributes of God and Other Writings*. Edited by Ezio Vailati. Cambridge: Cambridge University Press, 1998.

Cope, Kevin L. *Criteria of Certainty: Truth and Judgment in the English Enlightenment*. Lexington: University Press of Kentucky, 1990.

Coussin, Pierre. "The Stoicism of the New Academy." In *The Skeptical Tradition*. Edited by Miles Burnyeat, 31–63. Berkeley: University of California Press, 1983.

Cowansage, Melissa. "The Libertine-Libertarian Dichotomy in Dryden's *State of Innocence*." *English Language Notes* 32, 3 (1984): 38–44.

Crane, R. S. Review of *The Sublime: A Study of Critical Theories in XVIIIth-Century England* by Samuel Holt Monk. *Philological Quarterly* 15 (1936): 165–7.

Crowne, John. *City Politiques*. London, 1683.

Crousaz, Jean Pierre de. *A Commentary Upon Mr Pope's Four Ethic Epistles intituled An Essay on Man by Monsieur de Crousaz*. London, 1738.

Cudworth, Ralph. *The True Intellectual System of the Universe*. Selections in *The Cambridge Platonists*. Edited by Gerald R. Cragg, 195–257. Oxford: Oxford University Press, 1968.

Damrosch, Leo. *The Imaginative World of Alexander Pope*. Berkeley: University of California Press, 1987.

de Bolla, Peter. *The Discourse of the Sublime: Readings in History, Aesthetics, and the Subject*. Oxford: Blackwell, 1989.

Defoe, Daniel. *The Review*. Facsimile edited by Arthur Wellesley Secord. 22 vols. New York: Columbia University Press, 1938.

de Man, Paul. *Aesthetic Ideology*. Minneapolis: University of Minnesota Press, 1996.

———. *Allegories of Reading: Figural Language in Rousseau, Nietszche, Rilke, and Proust*. New Haven: Yale University Press, 1979.

Dennis, John. *The Critical Works of John Dennis*. Edited by Edward Niles Hooker. 2 vols. Baltimore: Johns Hopkins University Press, 1939.

de Quehen, A. H. "Lucretius and Swift's *Tale of a Tub*." *University of Toronto Quarterly* 63, 2 (1993–94): 287–307.

Desaguliers, J. T. *The Newtonian System of the World, the Best Model of Government: An Allegorical Poem*. Westminster, 1728.

Descartes, René. *Philosophical Works of Descartes*. Translated by Elizabeth Haldane and G. R. T. Ross. 2 vols. Cambridge: Cambridge University Press, 1935.

———. *Six Metaphysical Meditations*. Translated and introduced by William Molyneux. London, 1680.

Deutsch, Helen. *Resemblance and Disgrace: Alexander Pope and the Deformation of Culture*. Cambridge: Harvard University Press, 1996.

Dryden, John. *Sylvæ: or, the Second Part of Poetical Miscellanies*. London, 1685.

————. *The Works of John Dryden.* Edward Niles Hooker, H. T. Swedenberg, Jr., and Vinton A. Dearing, general editors. 20 vols. Berkeley: University of California Press, 1956–.

Dunn, Allen. "The Mechanics of Transport: Sublimity and the Imagery of Abjection in Rochester, Swift, and Burke." In *Cutting Edges: Postmodern Critical Essays on Eighteenth-Century Satire.* Edited by James E. Gill, 94–109. Knoxville: University of Tennessee Press, 1995.

Eagleton, Terry. *The Ideology of the Aesthetic.* Oxford: Blackwell, 1990.

Edwards, Thomas R. *This Dark Estate: A Reading of Pope.* Berkeley: University of California Press, 1963.

Ehrenpreis, Irvin. *Swift: The Man, His Works, and the Age.* 3 vols. Cambridge: Harvard University Press: 1962–83.

Eilon, Daniel. *Factions' Fictions: Ideological Closure in Swift's Satire.* Newark: University of Delaware Press, 1991.

Eliot, T. S. *Selected Essays: 1917–1932.* New York: Harcourt, 1950.

Erasmus, Desideratus. *Diatribe seu Collatio de Libero Arbitrario.* In *Erasmus-Luther: Discourse on Free Will.* Translated by Ernst F. Winter. New York: Unger, 1962.

Erskine-Hill, Howard. "The 'New World' of Pope's *Dunciad.*" In *Essential Articles for the Study of Alexander Pope.* Edited by Maynard Mack, 803–24. Hamden, Conn.: Archon Press, 1968.

————. *The Poetry of Opposition and Revolution: Dryden to Wordsworth.* Oxford: Clarendon Press, 1996.

Fallon, Stephen. *Milton among the Philosophers: Poetry and Materialism in Seventeenth-Century England.* Ithaca: Cornell University Press, 1991.

Farley-Hills, David. *Rochester's Poetry.* Totowa, N.J.: Rowman and Littlefield, 1978.

Ferguson, Frances. *Solitude and the Sublime: Romanticism and the Aesthetics of Individuation.* New York: Routledge, 1992.

Ferguson, Rebecca. *The Unbalanced Mind: Pope and the Rule of Passion.* Brighton, England: Harvester Press, 1986.

Ferreira, M. Jamie. *Scepticism and Reasonable Doubt: The British Naturalist Tradition in Wilkins, Hume, Reid, and Newman.* Oxford: Oxford University Press, 1986.

Fogelin, Robert J. "The Tendency of Hume's Skepticism." In *The Skeptical Tradition.* Edited by Myles Burnyeat, 397–412. Berkeley: University of California Press, 1983.

Fox, Christopher. *Locke and the Scriblerians: Identity and Consciousness in Early Eighteenth-Century Britain.* Berkeley: University of California Press, 1988.

————. "Pope, Perhaps, and Sextus: Skeptical Modes in Moral Essay I." *English Language Notes* 29, 2 (1991): 37–48.

Franck, Marcie. "Staging Criticism, Staging Milton: Dryden's *The State of Innocence.*" *The Eighteenth Century: Theory and Interpretation* 34, 1 (1993): 45–64.

Frede, Michael. "The Sceptic's Two Kinds of Assent and the Question of the Possibility of Knowledge." In *The Original Sceptics: A Controversy*. Edited by Myles Burnyeat and Michael Frede, 127–51. Indianapolis: Hackett, 1997.

Fried, Michael. *Absorption and Theatricality: Painting and Beholder in the Age of Diderot*. Chicago: University of Chicago Press, 1980.

Gallagher, Catherine. *Nobody Story: The Vanishing Acts of Women Writers in the Marketplace*. Berkeley: University of California Press, 1995.

Gastrell, Francis. *The Principles of Deism Truly Represented and Set in a Clear Light, in Two Dialogues Between a Sceptick and a Deist*. London, 1708.

Gerrard, Christine. *The Patriot Opposition to Walpole: Politics, Poetry, and National Myth, 1725–1742*. Oxford: Clarendon Press, 1994.

Glanvill, Joseph. *Scepsis Scientifica*. London, 1665. Facsimile reprint. New York: Garland, 1978.

———. *The Vanity of Dogmatizing or Confidence in Opinions Manifested in a Discourse of the Shortness and Uncertainty of our Knowledge, and its Causes; with Some Reflexions on Peripateticism; and an Apology for Philosophy*. London, 1661.

Goldberg, S. L. "Integrity and Life in Pope's Poetry." In *Pope: Recent Essays by Several Hands*. Edited by Maynard Mack and James A. Winn, 15–44. Hamden, Conn.: Archon Press, 1980.

Griffin, Dustin H. *Alexander Pope: The Poet in the Poems*. Princeton: Princeton University Press, 1978.

———. "Interpretation and Power: Swift's *Tale of a Tub*." *The Eighteenth Century: Theory and Interpretation* 34,2 (1993): 151–68.

———. *Regaining Paradise: Milton in the Eighteenth Century*. Cambridge: Cambridge University Press, 1986.

———. *Satires against Man: The Poems of Rochester*. Berkeley: University of California Press, 1973.

Habermas, Jürgen. *The Structural Transformation of the Public Sphere: An Inquiry into a Category of Bourgeois Society*. Translated by Thomas Burger, with the assistance of Frederick Lawrence. Cambridge: MIT Press, 1989.

Hacking, Ian. *The Emergence of Probability: A Philosophical Study of Early Ideas about Probability, Induction, and Statistical Inference*. Cambridge: Cambridge University Press, 1975.

Haley, David B. *Dryden and the Problem of Freedom*. New Haven: Yale University Press, 1997.

Hammond, Brean. *Pope*. Atlantic Highlands, N.J.: Humanities Press International, 1986.

———. *Pope and Bolingbroke: A Study of Friendship and Influence*. Columbia: University of Missouri Press, 1984.

Hankinson, R. J. *The Sceptics*. London: Routledge, 1995.

Harte, Walter. *An Essay on Reason*. London, 1734.

Harth, Phillip. *Contexts of Dryden's Thought*. Chicago: University of Chicago Press, 1968.

——. *Swift and Anglican Rationalism*. Chicago: University of Chicago Press, 1961.

Hertz, Neil. *The End of the Line: Essays on Psychoanalysis and the Sublime*. New York: Columbia University Press, 1985.

Heyrick, Thomas. *Miscellany Poems*. London, 1691.

Higgins, Ian. *Swift's Politics: A Study in Disaffection*. Cambridge: Cambridge University Press, 1994.

Hintikka, Jaakko. "Cogito, Ergo Sum: Inference or Performance?" In *Descartes: A Collection of Critical Essays*. Edited by Willis Doney, 108–40. Notre Dame, Ind.: University of Notre Dame Press, 1967.

Hirschman, Albert O. *The Passions and the Interests: Political Arguments for Capitalism Before Its Triumph*. Princeton: Princeton University Press, 1977.

Horowitz, Maryanne Cline. "Pierre Charron's View of the Source of Wisdom." *Journal of the History of Philosophy* 9 (1971): 443–57.

Huet, Pierre-Daniel. *Demonstratio Evangelica ad Serenissimum Delphinum*. 3d ed. Paris, 1690.

——. *A Philosophical Treatise Concerning the Weakness of Human Understanding*. Translator unknown. London, 1728.

Hughes, Derek. *English Drama: 1660–1700*. Oxford: Clarendon Press, 1996.

Hume, David. *Essays Moral, Political, and Philosophical*. Edited by Eugene F. Miller. Indianapolis: Liberty Fund, 1985.

——. *An Inquiry Concerning Human Understanding*. Edited by Charles W. Hendel. Indianapolis: Bobbs-Merrill, 1955.

——. *A Treatise of Human Nature*. Edited by L. A. Selby-Bigge. 2d ed. revised by P. H. Nidditch. Oxford: Oxford University Press, 1979.

Hume, Robert D. *Dryden's Criticism*. Ithaca: Cornell University Press, 1970.

Hutchinson, Lucy. *Lucy Hutchinson's Translation of Lucretius: De Rerum Natura*. Edited by Hugh de Quehen. Ann Arbor: University of Michigan Press, 1996.

Ingrassia, Catherine. *Authorship, Commerce, and Gender in Early Eighteenth-Century England: A Culture of Paper Credit*. Cambridge: Cambridge University Press, 1998.

Jackson, Wallace. Introduction to *Critical Essays on Alexander Pope*. Edited by Wallace Jackson and R. Paul Yoder, 1–6. New York: Macmillan, 1993.

Johnson, Samuel. *A Dictionary of the English Language*. Facsimile of London, 1755 ed. New York: Arno Press, 1979.

——. *Lives of the English Poets*. Edited by George Birkbeck Hill. 3 vols. Oxford: Clarendon Press, 1905.

Jones, Emrys. "Pope and Dulness." In *Pope: Recent Essays by Several Hands*. Edited by Maynard Mack and James A. Winn, 612–51. Hamden, Conn.: Archon Press, 1982.

Jones, Robert W. *Gender and the Formation of Taste in Eighteenth-Century Britain*. Cambridge: Cambridge University Press, 1998.

Kahn, Victoria. *Rhetoric, Prudence, and Skepticism in the Renaissance*. Ithaca: Cornell University Press, 1985.

Kant, Immanuel. *Critique of Judgment*. Translated by Werner S. Pluhar. Indianapolis: Hackett, 1987.

———. *Universal Natural History and Theory of the Heavens*. Translated by Stanley L. Jaki. Edinburgh: Scottish Academic Press, 1981.

Keats, John. *Letters*. Edited by Maurice Buxton Forman. 4th ed. Oxford: Oxford University Press, 1952.

Kelly, Veronica. "Following the Stage Itinerant: Perception, Doubt, and Death in Swift's *Tale of a Tub*." *Studies in Eighteenth-Century Culture* 17 (1987): 239–58.

Keogh, J. G. "Pope's 'Epistle to a Lady' 1–4." *Explicator* 31, 5 (1973): no. 37.

King, Bruce. *Dryden's Major Plays*. Edinburgh: Oliver and Boyd, 1966.

Klein, Lawrence E. *Shaftesbury and the Culture of Politeness*. Cambridge: Cambridge University Press, 1994.

Knapp, Steven. *Personification and the Sublime: Milton to Coleridge*. Cambridge: Harvard University Press, 1985.

Koyré, Alexandre. *From the Closed World to the Infinite Universe*. Baltimore: Johns Hopkins University Press, 1957.

Kramnick, Jonathan Brody. *Making the English Canon*. Cambridge: Cambridge University Press, 1998.

Kroll, Richard W. F. *The Material Word: Literate Culture in the Restoration and Early Eighteenth Century*. Baltimore: Johns Hopkins University Press, 1991.

Lamb, Jonathan. "Longinus, the Dialectic, and the Practice of Mastery." *English Literary History* 60 (1993): 545–67.

———. *The Rhetoric of Suffering: Reading the Book of Job in the Eighteenth Century*. Oxford: Oxford University Press, 1995.

———. "The Subject of the Subject and the Sublimities of Self-Reference." Review of *The Discourse of the Sublime*, by Peter de Bolla, and *Words of Eternity: Blake and the Poetics of the Sublime*, by Vincent de Luca. *Huntington Library Quarterly* 56, 2 (1993): 191–205.

Leapor, Mary. *An Essay on Woman*. In *Eighteenth Century Women's Poetry: An Oxford Anthology*. Edited by Roger Lonsdale, 207–8. Oxford: Oxford University Press, 1989.

Lee, Henry. *Anti-Scepticism: Or, Notes upon Each Chapter of Mr Locke's Essay Concerning Humane Understanding*. London, 1711.

Lock, F. P. *Swift's Tory Politics*. Newark: University of Delaware Press, 1983.

Locke, John. *An Essay Concerning Human Understanding*. Edited by Peter Nidditch. Oxford: Oxford University Press, 1975.

Long, A. A. *Hellenistic Philosophy: Stoics, Epicureans, Sceptics*. 2d ed. Berkeley: University of California Press, 1986.

Longinus. *On the Sublime*. First-century Greek text edited by D. A. Russell. Oxford: Oxford University Press, 1964.

———. Translated anonymously as *An Essay Upon Sublime, translated from the Greek of Dionysius Longinus Cassius; compar'd with the French of the Sieur Despreaux Boileau*. Oxford, 1698.

―――. Translated by Nicolas Boileau Despréaux as *Le Traité du Sublime ou du merveilleux dans le discours, Traduit du grec de Longin*. Paris, 1674.

―――. Translated by John Hall as *Peri Hupsous, or Dionysius Longinus on the Height of Eloquence*. London, 1652.

―――. Translated by A. O. Prickard. Oxford: Clarendon Press, 1906.

―――. Translated by William Smith as *Dionysius Longinus on the Sublime*. London, 1739.

―――. Translated by Leonard Welsted as *The Works of Dionysius Longinus On the Sublime: Or a Treatise Concerning the* Sovereign Perfection of Writing *Translated from the* Greek. *With Some Remarks on the English Poets*. London, 1712.

Lovejoy, A. O. *The Great Chain of Being: A Study of the History of an Idea*. 2d ed. New York: Harper, 1960.

Lyotard, Jean-François. *The Inhuman: Reflections on Time*. Stanford: Stanford University Press, 1991.

―――. *Lessons on the Analytic of the Sublime*. Translated by Elizabeth Rottenberg. Stanford: Stanford University Press, 1994.

Mack, Maynard. *Alexander Pope: A Life*. New York: Norton, 1985.

―――. *Collected in Himself: Essays Critical, Biographical, and Bibliographical on Pope and Some of His Contemporaries*. Newark: University of Delaware Press, 1982.

―――. *The Garden and the City: Retirement and Politics in the Later Poetry of Pope, 1731–1743*. Toronto: University of Toronto Press, 1969.

Markley, Robert. "Beyond Consensus: *The Rape of the Lock* and the Fate of Reading Eighteenth-Century Literature." In *Critical Essays on Alexander Pope*. Edited by Wallace Jackson and R. Paul Yoder, 69–83. New York: Macmillan, 1993.

―――. "Sentimentality as Performance: Shaftesbury, Sterne and the Theatrics of Virtue." In *The New Eighteenth Century*. Edited by Felicity Nussbaum and Laura Brown, 210–30. New York: Methuen, 1987.

Martin, Catherine Gimelli. " 'Boundless the Deep': Milton, Pascal, and the Theology of Relative Space." *English Literary History* 63, 1 (1996): 45–78.

McGann, M. J. *Studies in Horace's First Book of Epistles*. Brussels: Latomas, 1969.

McKeon, Michael. "Cultural Crisis and Dialectical Method: Destabilizing Augustan Literature." In *The Profession of Eighteenth-Century Literature: Reflections on an Institution*. Edited by Leo Damrosch, 42–61. Madison: University of Wisconsin Press, 1992.

―――. "Politics of Discourses and the Rise of the Aesthetic in Seventeenth-Century England." In *Politics of Discourse: The Literature and History of Seventeenth-Century England*. Edited by Kevin Sharpe and Steven N. Zwicker, 35–51. Berkeley: University of California, 1987.

Milton, John. *Complete Poems and Major Prose*. Edited by Merritt Hughes. New York: Macmillan, 1957.

————. *Paradise Lost.* Edited by Richard Bentley. London, 1732.

Monk, Samuel Holt. *The Sublime: A Study of Critical Theories in XVIIIth-Century England.* 1935. 2d ed. Ann Arbor: University of Michigan Press, 1960.

Montag, Warren. *The Unthinkable Swift: The Spontaneous Philosophy of a Church-of-England Man.* London: Verso, 1994.

Montaigne, Michel de. *The Complete Essays of Montaigne.* Translated by Donald M. Frame. Stanford: Stanford University Press, 1958.

————. *Essays of Michael, Seigneur de Montaigne.* Translated by Charles Cotton. 3 vols. London, 1685–86. (Copy owned and annotated by Alexander Pope, held by the Beinecke Library, Yale University.)

More, Henry. *Antidote Against Atheism.* London, 1653. Selections in *The Cambridge Platonists.* Edited by C. A. Patrides, 213–87. Cambridge: Harvard University Press, 1970.

————. *Enthusiasmus Triumphatus. or, A brief discourse of the nature, causes, kinds, and cure of enthusiasm.* London, 1662.

Morris, David B. *Alexander Pope: The Genius of Sense.* Cambridge: Cambridge University Press, 1984.

————. *The Religious Sublime: Christian Poetry and Critical Tradition in Eighteenth-Century England.* Lexington: University of Kentucky Press, 1972.

Mueller, Judith C. "Writing under Constraint: Swift's 'Apology' for *A Tale of a Tub*," *English Literary History* 60 (1993): 101–15.

Mulhall, Stephen. *Stanley Cavell: Philosophy's Recounting of the Ordinary.* Oxford: Oxford University Press, 1994.

Nagel, Thomas. *The View from Nowhere.* New York: Oxford University Press, 1986.

Nancy, Jean-Luc. "The Sublime Offering." In *Of the Sublime: Presence in Question.* Edited by Jeffrey S. Librett, 25–53. Albany: State University of New York Press, 1993.

[Newcomb, Thomas.] *The Woman of Taste. Occasioned by a late Poem, Entitled, The Man of Taste. By a Friend of the Author's. In two Epistles, from Clelia in Town to Sapho in the Country.* London, 1733.

Nicholson, Marjorie Hope. *Mountain Gloom and Mountain Glory: The Development of the Aesthetics of the Infinite.* Ithaca: Cornell University Press, 1959.

Noggle, James. "The Wittgensteinian Sublime." *New Literary History* 27, 4 (1996): 605–19.

Nussbaum, Felicity. *The Brink of All We Hate: English Satires on Women, 1660–1750.* Lexington: University of Kentucky Press, 1984.

Nuttall, A. D. *Pope's "Essay on Man."* London: Allen and Unwin, 1984.

Parnell, J. T. "Swift, Sterne, and the Skeptical Tradition." *Studies in Eighteenth Century Culture* 23 (1994): 221–42.

Parsons, Robert. *A Sermon preached at the Earl of Rochester's Funeral.* In *Rochester: The Critical Heritage.* Edited by David Farley-Hills, 45–6. London: Routledge and Kegan Paul, 1972.

Pascal, Blaise. *Pensées and Other Writings*. Translated by Honor Levi. Oxford: Oxford University Press, 1995.

———. *Thoughts on Religion and Other Curious Subjects*. Translated by Basil Kennet.1704, 4th ed. London, 1749.

Patey, Douglas Lane. *Probability and Literary Form: Philosophic Theory and Literary Practice in the Augustan Age*. Cambridge: Cambridge University Press, 1984.

Paulson, Ronald. *Theme and Structure in Swift's "Tale of a Tub."* New Haven: Yale University Press, 1960.

Peterson, R. G. "Renaissance Classicism in Pope's *Dunciad*," *Studies in English Literature* 15, 3 (1975): 431–45.

Pettit, Alexander. *Illusory Consensus: Bolingbroke and the Polemical Response to Walpole, 1730–1737*. Newark: University of Delaware Press, 1997.

Phiddian, Robert. *Swift's Parody*. Cambridge: Cambridge University Press, 1995.

Plumb, J. H. *The Growth of Political Stability in England: 1675–1725*. London: Macmillan, 1967.

Pocock, J. G. A. *The Machiavellian Moment: Florentine Political Thought and the Atlantic Republican Tradition*. Princeton: Princeton University Press, 1975.

———. *Virtue, Commerce, and History: Essays on Political Thought and History, Chiefly in the Eighteenth Century*. Cambridge: Cambridge University Press, 1985.

Pollak, Ellen. *The Poetics of Sexual Myth: Gender and Ideology in the Verse of Swift and Pope*. Chicago: University of Chicago Press, 1985.

Pomfret, John. *The Sceptical Muse: or, A Paradox on Humane Understanding, a Poem*. London, Cambridge, 1699.

Pope, Alexander. *The Correspondence of Alexander Pope*. 5 vols. Edited by George Sherburn. Oxford: Clarendon Press, 1956.

———. *An Essay on Man*. London, 1732–34.

———. *An Essay on Man*. Edited by William Warburton. Boston, 1787.

———. *The Iliad of Homer Translated by Alexander Pope*. Edited by Steven Shankman. Harmondsworth, England: Penguin, 1996.

———. *Poems in Facsimile*. Aldershot, England: Scolar Press, 1988.

———. *Prose Works of Alexander Pope*. Vol. 2. *The Major Works, 1725–1744*. Edited by Rosemary Cowler. Hamden, Conn.: Archon Press, 1986.

———. *The Twickenham Edition of the Poems of Alexander Pope*. John Butt, general editor. 11 vols. London: Methuen; New Haven: Yale University Press, 1951–1969.

Popkin, Richard H. *The High Road to Pyrrhonism*. Edited by Richard A. Watson and James E. Force. San Diego: Austin Hill Press, 1980.

———.*The History of Scepticism from Erasmus to Spinoza*. 3d ed. Berkeley: University of California Press, 1979.

Prior, Matthew. *Dialogues of the Dead and Other Works in Prose and Verse*. Edited by A. R. Waller. Cambridge: Cambridge University Press, 1907.

————. *The Literary Works of Matthew Prior.* Edited by H. Bunker Wright and Monroe K. Spears. 2 vols. Oxford: Oxford University Press, 1959.

Putnam, Hilary. "Preface: Introducing Cavell" and "Pope's *Essay on Man* and Those 'Happy Pieties.'" In *Pursuits of Reason: Essays in Honor of Stanley Cavell.* Edited by Ted Cohen, Paul Guyer, and Hilary Putnam, vii–xii, 13–20. Lubbock: Texas Tech University Press, 1993.

Rawson, Claude. *Gulliver and the Gentle Reader: Studies in Swift and Our Time.* 2d ed. Atlantic Highlands, N.J.: Humanities Press International, 1991.

Richardson, Jonathan. *An Essay on the Theory of Painting.* London, 1715.

————. [*An Essay on the Whole Art of Criticism as it Relates to Painting.*] *Two Discourses.* London, 1719.

Rochester, John Wilmot, Earl of. *The Complete Poems of John Wilmot, Earl of Rochester.* Edited by David Vieth. New Haven: Yale University Press, 1968.

————. *The Letters of John Wilmot, Earl of Rochester.* Edited by Jeremy Treglown. Chicago: University of Chicago Press, 1980.

————. *Poems on Several Occasions.* Facsimile of 1680 "Antwerp" (probably London) ed. Edited by James Thorpe. Princeton: Princeton University Press, 1950.

————. *The Works of John Wilmot, Earl of Rochester.* Edited by Harold Love. Oxford: Oxford University Press, 1999.

Rochester, John Wilmot, Earl of, et al. *A Satyr Against Mankind, An Answer to the Satyr Against Mankind* [by Joseph Glanvill?], *& On Man: A Satyr.* [no title page: London? 1679].

Rorty, Richard. *Consequences of Pragmatism.* Minneapolis: University of Minnesota Press, 1982.

————. *Philosophy and the Mirror of Nature.* Princeton: Princeton University Press, 1979.

Rudd, Niall. *Satires of Horace: A Study.* Cambridge: Cambridge University Press, 1966.

Rumbold, Valerie. "The Poetic Career of Judith Cowper: An Exemplary Failure?" In *Pope, Swift, and Women Writers.* Edited by Donald C. Mell, 48–66. Newark: University of Delaware Press, 1996.

————. *Women's Place in Pope's World.* Cambridge: Cambridge University Press, 1989.

Rymer, Thomas. "The Tragedies of the Last Age." In *Critical Essays of the Seventeenth Century.* Edited by J. E. Spingarn, vol. 2, 181–208. 3 vols. Oxford: Clarendon Press, 1908–9.

Saccamano, Neil. "Authority and Publication: The Works of 'Swift.'" *The Eighteenth Century: Theory and Interpretation* 25 (1984): 241–62.

Sedley, David. "The Motivation of Greek Skepticism." In *The Skeptical Tradition.* Edited by Myles Burnyeat, 9–29. Berkeley: University of California Press, 1983.

Sedley, David L. "Sublimity and Skepticism in Montaigne." *PMLA* 113, 5 (1998): 1079–82.

Sergeant, John. *Solid Philosophy Asserted, Against the Fancies of the Ideists: . . . with Reflexions on Mr Locke's Essay concerning Human Understanding.* London, 1697.

Sextus Empiricus. *Pyrrhoneæ Hypotyposes.* Translated by Thomas Stanley. In *The History of Philosophy, Containing the Lives, Opinions, Actions and Discourses of the Philosophers of Every Sect.* 3d ed. London, 1701.

Shaftesbury, Anthony Ashley Cooper, Third Earl of. *Characteristics of Men, Manners, Opinions, and Times.* Edited by John M. Robertson. London: Grant Richards, 1900.

———. *The Life, Unpublished Letters, and Philosophical Regimen of Anthony, Earl of Shaftesbury.* Edited by Benjamin Rand. London: S. Sonnenschein, 1900.

Shapin, Steven. *A Social History of Truth: Civility and Science in Seventeenth-Century England.* Chicago: University of Chicago Press, 1994.

Shapiro, Barbara J. *Probability and Certainty in Seventeenth-Century England: A Study of the Relationships between Natural Science, Religion, History, Law, and Literature.* Princeton: Princeton University Press, 1983.

Shenstone, William. *Poems Upon Various Occasions.* London, 1737.

Shippen, William. "Moderation Display'd." In *Poems on Affairs of State: Augustan Satirical Verse, 1660–1714.* Edited by George deF. Lord et al., vol. 7, 19–42. 7 vols. New Haven: Yale University Press, 1963–75.

Silverman, Hugh J. Introduction to *The Textual Sublime: Deconstruction and Its Differences.* Edited by Hugh J. Silverman and Gary E. Aylesworth, xi–xix. Albany: State University of New York Press, 1990.

Simpson, David. *The Academic Postmodern and the Rule of Literature: A Report on Half-Knowledge.* Chicago: University of Chicago Press, 1995.

Sitter, John. *Arguments of Augustan Wit.* Cambridge: Cambridge University Press, 1991.

Solomon, Harry M. *The Rape of the Text: Reading and Misreading Pope's "Essay on Man."* Tuscaloosa: University of Alabama Press, 1993.

Spacks, Patricia Meyer. *An Argument of Images: The Poetry of Alexander Pope.* Cambridge: Harvard University Press, 1971.

Spence, Joseph. *Observations, Anecdotes, and Characters of Books and Men: Collected from Conversation.* Edited by James M. Osborn. 2 vols. Oxford: Clarendon Press, 1966.

Stack, Frank. *Pope and Horace: Studies in Imitation.* Cambridge: Cambridge University Press, 1985.

Stallybrass, Peter, and Allon White. *The Politics and Poetics of Transgression.* Ithaca: Cornell University Press, 1986.

Stanley, Thomas. *The History of Philosophy, Containing the Lives, Opinions, Actions and Discourses of the Philosophers of Every Sect.* 3d ed. London, 1701.

Starobinski, Jean. *Montaigne in Motion*. Translated by Arthur Goldhammer. Chicago: University of Chicago Press, 1985.

Steeves, E. L., ed. *The Art of Sinking in Poetry: Martinus Scriblerus' "Peri Bathous": A Critical Edition*. New York: King's Crown Press, 1952.

Stephen, Leslie. *The History of English Thought in the Eighteenth Century*. 2 vols. New York: Harcourt, Brace, 1962.

Swift, Jonathan. *Le Conte de Tonneau Contenant tout ce que les Arts, & les Sciences Ont de plus Sublime, Et de plus Mysterieux*. Translated by Justus van Effen. La Haye, 1720.

———. *Correspondence*. Edited by Harold Williams. 5 vols. Oxford: Clarendon Press, 1963–65.

———. *Prose Works of Jonathan Swift*. Herbert Davis, general editor. 14 vols. Oxford: Blackwell, 1939–68.

———. *A Tale of a Tub to which is added The battle of the books, and the Mechanical operation of the spirit*. Edited by A. C. Guthkelch and D. Nichol Smith. Oxford: Clarendon Press, 1920.

Tanner, Tony. "Reason and the Grotesque: Pope's *Dunciad*," in *Essential Articles for the Study of Alexander Pope*. Edited by Maynard Mack, 825–44. Hamden, Conn.: Archon Press, 1968.

Temple, William. "Essay Upon the Ancient and Modern Learning" and "Of Poetry." In *Critical Essays of the Seventeenth Century*. Edited by J. E. Spingarn, vol. 3, 32–109. 3 vols. Oxford: Clarendon Press, 1908–9.

Thomas, Claudia N. *Alexander Pope and His Eighteenth Century Women Readers*. Carbondale: Southern Illinois University Press, 1994.

Thomson, James. *Liberty, The Castle of Indolence, and Other Poems*. Edited by James Sambrook. Oxford: Oxford University Press, 1986.

Thormählen, Marianne. *Rochester: The Poems in Context*. Cambridge: Cambridge University Press, 1993.

Tillotson, John. *The Wisdom of Being Religious Preach'd at Saint Paul's, March 1663/4*. In *Three Restoration Divines: Barrow, South, Tillotson*. Edited by Irène Simon. Paris: Société d'edition "Les Belles Lettres," 1967–.

Trapp, Joseph. "Of Beauty of Thought in Poetry; or of Elegance and Sublimity." Lecture VIII, *Lectures on Poetry*. In *Eighteenth-Century Critical Essays*. Edited by Scott Elledge, vol. 1, 229–50. 2 vols. Ithaca: Cornell University Press, 1961.

Trotter, David. "Wanton Expressions." In *Spirit of Wit: Reconsiderations of Rochester*. Edited by Jeremy Treglown, 111–32. Hamden, Conn.: Archon Press, 1982.

Tuveson, Ernest. "Space, Deity, and the Natural Sublime." *Modern Language Quarterly* 12, 1 (1951): 20–38.

Van Leeuwen, Henry G. *The Problem of Certainty in English Thought 1630–1690*. The Hague: Nijhoff, 1963.

Vieth, David. "Divided Consciousness: The Trauma and Triumph of Restoration Culture." *Tennessee Studies in Literature* 22 (1977): 46–62.

Voltaire. *Philosophical Letters.* Translated by Ernest Dilworth. Indianapolis: Bobbs-Merrill, 1961.

Weinbrot, Howard D. *Eighteenth-Century Satire: Essays on Text and Context from Dryden to Peter Pindar.* Cambridge: Cambridge University Press, 1988.

Weiskel, Thomas. *The Romantic Sublime: Studies in the Structure and Psychology of Transcendence.* Baltimore: Johns Hopkins University Press, 1976.

Werenfels, Samuel. *A Discourse of Logomachys, or Controversys about Words, so common among Learned Men* and *A Dissertation Concerning Meteors of Stile, or False Sublimity.* London, 1711.

White, Douglas. *Pope and the Context of Controversy: The Manipulation of Ideas in the "Essay on Man."* Chicago: University of Chicago Press, 1970.

White, Thomas. *An Exclusion of Scepticks from All Title to Dispute.* London, 1665.

Wilkins, John. *Of the Principles and Duties of Natural Religion.* 4th ed. London, 1699.

Williams, Aubrey. *Pope's Dunciad: A Study of its Meaning.* Baton Rouge: Louisiana State University Press, 1955.

Williams, Bernard. *Descartes: The Project of Pure Inquiry.* Harmondsworth, England: Penguin, 1978.

Williams, Kathleen. *Jonathan Swift and the Age of Compromise.* Lawrence: University of Kansas Press, 1958.

Winn, James Anderson. *John Dryden and His World.* New Haven: Yale University Press, 1987.

Wisdom, John. *Other Minds.* 3d ed. Berkeley: University of California Press, 1968.

Wittgenstein, Ludwig. *On Certainty.* Translated by G. E. M. Anscombe and Denis Paul. New York: Harper, 1969.

———. *Philosophical Investigations.* Translated by G. E. M. Anscombe. 2d ed. Oxford: Blackwell, 1958.

Wood, Theodore E. B. *The Word "Sublime" and Its Context, 1650–1760.* The Hague: Mouton, 1972.

Young, B. W. " 'See *Mystery* to *Mathematics* Fly!' Pope's *Dunciad* and the Critique of Religious Rationalism." *Eighteenth-Century Studies* 26, 3 (1993): 435–48.

Young, Edward. *The Complaint: or Night Thoughts on Life, Death, and Immortality to which is added A Paraphrase on Part of the Book of Job.* London, 1768.

———. "Conjectures on Original Composition." In *Eighteenth Century English Literature.* Edited by Geoffrey Tillotson, Paul Fussell, Jr., and Marshall Waingrow, 871–89. San Diego: Harcourt Brace, 1969.

———. *The Love of Fame: The Universal Passion. In Seven Characteristical Satires.* 2d ed. London, 1728.

Zimmerman, Everett. *Swift's Narrative Satires: Author and Authority*. Ithaca: Cornell University Press, 1983.

Žižek, Slavoj. *The Sublime Object of Ideology*. London: Verso, 1989.

———. *Tarrying with the Negative: Kant, Hegel, and the Critique of Ideology*. Durham, N.C.: Duke University Press, 1993.

Zwicker, Steven. *Politics and Language in Dryden's Poetry: The Arts of Disguise*. Princeton: Princeton University Press, 1984.

Index

Abrams, M. H., 225

Academic skepticism. *See* skepticism, Academic

Addison, Joseph, 26, 29, 65, 72, 143, 170, 230, 243
  "An Account of the Greatest English Poets," 195, 237
  "The Campaign," 106–7
  The Freeholder, 226
  The Spectator, 67–9, 86–8, 90, 108, 170, 225

Adorno, Theodor, 172, 178

æquus animus, 134, 149, 154–5, 157, 160, 165, 173, 175

Akenside, Mark, 5, 209

Anne, Queen of England, 29, 64, 82

apatheia, 24, 135

Apelles, 175–6

Appleby, Joyce Oldham, 215

Arbuthnot, John, 74, 230

Arendt, Hannah, 233

Aristippus, 151–2, 166

Aristophanes, 6

Aristotle, 16, 47, 49, 137

Armstrong, Nancy, 170

ataraxia, 131, 135–41, 150

atheism, 15, 20, 184–5, 193, 199, 212, 224, 242

Atkins, G. Douglas, 181, 198, 232–3

Atterbury, Francis, 121, 131, 161–2, 166–8, 183, 240

Augustine, 74, 223

Austin, J. L., 220

Bacon, Francis, 193

Banks, John, 58

Barker, John, 222

Barrell, John, 111–2, 231–2

Barry, Elizabeth, 43

Bateson, F. W., 161, 215, 239

Bathurst, Allen, First Earl of, 233

Battestin, Martin, 243

Bayle, Pierre, 17–8, 213

Bell, Ian A., 234

Bennett, Tony, 85

Benson, William, 201

Bentley, Richard, 86, 189, 197, 200–4, 243

Berkeley, George, 121, 228

Bethel, Hugh, 177

Blackmore, Richard, 26, 104–7, 120–1, 195

Bloom, Harold, 34, 53, 225

Blount, Charles, 47

Blount, Edward, 122

Blount, Martha, 176–9

Blount, Teresa, 180

Bogel, Fredric, 142, 236

Bohls, Elizabeth, 231
Boileau Despréaux, Nicolas, 3, 4, 33, 39,
    44, 50, 62, 65, 81, 102–4, 195, 210,
    218, 229
Boivin, Jean, 229
Bolingbroke, Henry St. John, Viscount
    of, 89, 93, 135, 151, 153–4, 155, 160
    A Dissertation upon Parties, 108–9, 230
    Fragments or Minutes of Essays, 15,
        131–2, 140
    Letters, or Essays Address'd to Alexan-
        der Pope, 8, 13, 194–5
Boyce, Benjamin, 240
Boyle, Henry, 108
Boyle, Robert, 16, 18, 26, 66, 219
    A Discourse of Things Above Reason,
        21, 41–4, 46, 56, 64, 68, 98, 124,
        196–7, 218, 221
    The Sceptical Chymist, 18, 213–4
Bredvold, Louis, 32, 49, 219
Brewer, John, 230
Brooks-Davies, Douglas, 199, 243–4
Brower, Reuben A., 233–4, 240
Brown, Laura, 130, 132, 228–9, 232, 234
Buckingham, George Villiers, Duke of,
    29, 64
Budick, Sanford, 220
Burke, Edmund, 3, 6, 11, 26, 27–8, 36–
    7, 210, 216–7, 243
Burlington, Richard Boyle, Earl of, 233
Burnet, Gilbert, 20, 26, 37, 44–6, 48,
    63–4, 70, 73, 214, 218–9
Burnyeat, Myles, 141, 145, 147, 152, 213,
    235, 237
Burtt, Shelley, 215
Butler, Joseph, 133, 234

Carneades, 16, 18, 140, 212–3, 235
Carnochan, W. B., 224
Cartesianism. *See* Descartes, René
Caryll, John, 108, 118
Catholicism, 4, 6, 15, 17, 22, 42, 47, 49,
    50, 63, 71, 105, 109, 121, 129, 148,
    166–7, 233, 237
Catullus, 153

Cavell, Stanley, 7–9, 20, 54, 144–5, 147,
    174, 184–6, 210–1, 214, 220, 236–7,
    239, 242
Caygill, Howard, 26, 69, 143, 225, 236
Charles II, 49
Charleton, Walter, 21, 49
Charron, Pierre, 22, 137, 156, 161, 239
Christensen, Jerome, 31
Cibber, Colley, 193, 204, 243
Cicero, 16, 140, 235
civic humanism. *See* ideology, civic
    humanist
civil humanism. *See* ideology, civil
    humanist
Civil War, English, 3, 22
Clarke, Samuel, 184, 186, 193
Clitomachus, 18
Cobham, Richard Temple, Viscount
    of, 139, 168–9, 232
cogito, 50–4, 59, 187, 220–1
conservatism, 26, 29, 31–2, 64, 72, 84–5,
    99, 127, 131–2, 192, 207, 228
Cope, Kevin L., 218
Corinthians, 166
Cornbury, Henry Hyde, Viscount of, 138
Coste, Pierre, 95
Cotton, Charles, 238
Country party. *See* ideology, Country
Court party. *See* ideology, Court
Coussin, Pierre, 213
Cowansage, Melissa, 221
Craftsman, 108–9, 155
Craggs, James, 121
Crane, R.S., 209
credit, public, 23–4, 129, 132, 163, 170, 240
Crousaz, Jean Pierre de, 113, 227
Crowne, John, 47, 64, 219, 222
Cudworth, Ralph, 64, 220, 222
Curll, Edmund, 102
Cyrenaicism, 136, 152, 156, 166

Dacier, André, 136, 229
Damrosch, Leo, 237
Dartmouth, William Legge, First Earl
    of, 89

Davidson, Donald, 228
Davis, Herbert, 226
Dearing, Vinton, 221
de Bolla, Peter, 31, 211, 236
debt, national, 24, 83, 129
Defoe, Daniel, 24, 83, 170, 225
deism, 15, 79, 109, 118–9, 183–4, 191,
  231–3, 242
de Man, Paul, 10–1, 79, 115, 117, 155, 225,
  229, 238
Dennis, John, 26, 65–7, 86, 98, 143, 222,
  243
de Quehen, A. H., 224
Desaguliers, J. T., 228
Descartes, René, 13, 15–6, 20, 36, 50,
  63–4, 68, 82, 144, 159, 184–8, 206,
  214, 217, 221, 223, 239, 242
  Discourse on the Method..., 53, 160, 217
  Meditations, 6, 37, 46, 51–2, 55, 57, 187,
  220
d'Este, Mary Beatrice, 50
Deutsch, Helen, 154, 237
Dissenters, 6, 15, 22, 71, 75, 80, 82–4
Dryden, John, 3, 9, 13, 21, 28–9, 64–5,
  69–70, 88, 102, 129, 144, 217, 219–
  20, 236, 243
  Absalom and Achitophel, 62, 166
  "The Authors Apology for
    Heroique Poetry; and Poetic
    License," 49–50, 59–63, 195
  The Hind and the Panther, 64
  Marriage à la Mode, 62
  Religio Laici, 14, 21, 49, 58
  The Rival Ladies, 58
  The State of Innocence and Fall of Man,
    21, 33, 49–63, 70
  Sylvæ, 136
  To My Honor'd Friend, Dr Charleton...,
    48–9
  *To My Honored Friend, Sir Robert
    Howard*, 61
  Tyrannic Love, 222
  The Unhappy Favourite, prologue,
    58
Dunn, Allen, 210, 216, 224

Eagleton, Terry, 25, 84, 110, 233
Ecclesiastes, 205
Edwards, Thomas R., 130, 142, 228, 231,
  233, 236
Ehrenpreis, Irvin, 87, 89, 224
Eilon, Daniel, 72, 225
Eliot, T. S., 155, 230
Elizabeth I, 177
Ellis, Frank H., 237
enthusiasm, 13, 16, 25, 27, 31, 33, 45–7,
  60, 63–6, 69–72, 75, 82, 84–6, 91,
  94–5, 100, 182, 191–2, 207, 223–4
Epictetus, 136
Epicureanism, 15–6, 40, 75, 85, 95, 135–
  6, 156, 190, 218, 224
Erasmus, 22, 121, 148, 237
Erskine-Hill, Howard, 194, 199–200,
  229–30, 242–3
Euclid, 43
Euripides, 65

Fallon, Stephen, 220
Farley-Hills, David, 218
femininity. *See* ideology and
  femininity
Fénelon, François de Salignac de la
  Mothe-, 233
Ferguson, Frances, 211, 216
Ferguson, Rebecca, 234
Ferreira, M. Jamie, 214
fiat lux, 28, 52–3, 101–2, 229
fideism, 47, 72, 103, 129, 219, 223
Fogelin, Robert J., 97
Fortescue, William, 121
Fox, Christopher, 133, 239
Frede, Michael, 213
Freud, Sigmund, 9
Fried, Michael, 54–5, 221

Gallagher, Catherine, 241
Garth, Samuel, 121
Gay, John, 64, 230
Gassendi, Pierre, 18
Gastrell, Francis, 79, 184
Genesis, 101–3, 119, 229

Gentlemen's Magazine, 108

George II, 163, 193, 228, 243

Gerrard, Christine, 109, 229, 235

Glanvill, Joseph, 14, 21, 35–6, 39, 47, 51, 53, 56, 212

Glorious Revolution, 3, 6, 22–3, 25–7, 166, 230–1

Goldberg, S. L., 130, 176, 233–4

Goldophin, Sidney, First Earl of, 82, 89, 169

great chain of being, 113, 116, 118, 228

Griffin, Dustin, 80–1, 217, 228, 243

Guest, Harriet, 111–2, 231–2

Habermas, Jürgen, 99, 107–8, 230–1

Hacking, Ian, 212

Haley, David B., 58, 221

Hall, John, 5, 55–6, 210

Hammond, Brean, 229, 231

Hankinson, R. J., 237

Harley, Robert, later First Earl of Oxford, 83, 89, 91, 93

Harte, Walter, 98, 119

Harth, Phillip, 49, 215, 219, 223

Hartman, Geoffrey, 225

Hazlitt, William, 45

Hegel, G. W. F., 10, 76, 79, 224, 229

Heidegger, Martin, 232

Hertz, Neil, 4, 9–11, 143, 209

Heyrick, Thomas, 20–1

Higgins, Ian, 72, 225

Hintikka, J., 220

Hippocrates, 47

Hirschman, Albert O., 215

Hobbes, Thomas, 55

Homer, 29, 100–1, 104, 132

Horace, 132, 134–9, 142, 145–6, 151, 154, 156, 158, 193–4, 201, 235, 238

Horowitz, Maryanne Cline, 239

Huet, Pierre-Daniel, 102–4, 107, 112–3, 127, 161–2, 183–4, 187, 229

Hughes, Derek, 221

humanism, 23, 30, 183, 188–9, 235–6, 242

Hume, David, 145, 212, 214, 216, 234
    "Of Commerce," 109–10

Enquiry Concerning Human Understanding, 97, 100

Treatise of Human Nature, 11–2, 38, 134, 165, 188, 236, 242

Hume, Robert D., 59

Hutcheson, Francis, 17

Hutchinson, Lucy, 218

ideology, 3, 23, 31, 81–3, 95, 98–9, 110–1, 130–1, 143, 155, 200, 206–7, 225, 227–9
    aesthetic, 3, 23, 25, 31, 33, 50, 64–5, 84–5, 87, 91, 96, 112, 126–7, 130, 155–6, 171–2, 182, 200, 210
    civic humanist, 23–4, 29–31, 132, 163–4, 215, 227
    civil humanist, 23, 29–31, 132, 182, 215, 227
    Country, 23–4, 83, 108–9
    Court, 23–4, 83, 109
    and femininity, 23, 108, 158–9, 165, 169–72, 179–80, 215, 240–2
    and mitigated skepticism, 23, 29–30, 98–9, 111, 143, 182
    and the sublime, 25–8, 64, 81–2, 97–9, 105, 127, 130, 207, 210, 215–6

Ingrassia, Catherine, 215, 241–2

intentionality. *See* skepticism and intentionality

Jackson, Wallace, 130–1, 234

Jacobitism, 32, 72, 99, 105, 158, 166–7, 199–200, 229–30, 243–4

Jaki, Stanley, 233

James I, 230

James II, 50, 230, 243–4

je ne sais quoi, 26–7, 87, 142–3, 171, 178, 180, 213, 225, 236

Jervas, Charles, 160

Job, 104–6, 119–21

Johnson, Esther, 89

Johnson, Samuel, 50, 59, 210, 219–20

Jones, Emrys, 181

Jones, Robert W., 215, 227, 231

Kahn, Victoria, 235
Kant, Immanuel, 3, 6, 11–2, 38, 76, 78–
    9, 112, 169, 172
    Critique of Judgment, 9, 36–7, 104, 106,
        122, 124–7, 204, 210–1, 244
    *Universal Natural History and Theory
        of the Heavens*, 122–5
Keats, John, 155, 238
Kelly, Veronica, 226
Kennet, Basil, 113, 222, 232, 235
Keogh, J. G., 240
King, Bruce, 220
Klein, Lawrence E., 227
Knapp, Steven, 6, 10–1, 27, 39, 106
Koyré, Alexandre, 218
Kramnick, Jonathan Brody, 231
Kroll, Richard, 16–7, 22, 71, 212–3,
    218–9

Lacan, Jacques, 76
Lamb, Jonathan, 10, 28, 81, 105, 111, 143–
    4, 146, 215–6, 228, 236
Landa, Louis, 223
Latitudinarianism, 8, 14–5, 20–2, 49,
    73, 82, 215, 217
Leapor, Mary, 241
Le Clerc, Jean, 102, 229
Lee, Henry, 235
Leibnitz, Gottfried Wilhelm, 233
liberalism, 3, 23, 26, 28–9, 70, 84, 98–9,
    121, 126–7, 192
Lock, F. P., 226
Locke, John, 68–9, 71, 94, 97–8, 132–4,
    152, 159, 165, 193–4, 196, 228
Long, A. A., 238
Longinus, 3–6, 28–9, 33, 35–6,
    39–40, 44, 52, 56, 58, 60, 62–3,
    65, 72, 74, 77, 80–1, 86–7, 100–4,
    115, 143, 182, 197, 204, 218, 222, 229,
    244
Love, Harold, 36, 217
Lovejoy, A. O., 118, 232–3
Lucretius, 39, 42, 112, 218
Lyotard, Jean-François, 211, 229
Lyttleton, George, 152

Mack, Maynard, 116, 130, 214–5, 230–2,
    237
Mandeville, Bernard, 143, 187, 193, 236
Markley, Robert, 227, 234
Marlborough, John Churchill, First
    Duke of, 83, 106–7
Marx, Karl, 172
McGann, M. J, 138
McKeon, Michael, 32, 216
Mersenne, Marin, 18
Milton, John, 59, 63, 170, 195–6, 202,
    237, 243
    The Christian Doctrine, 61
    Paradise Lost, 49–50, 52–4, 59, 61,
        195, 197, 201, 220, 243
    Il Penseroso, 197
Molyneux, William, 52–3, 218
Monk, Samuel Holt, 50, 209, 217,
    229
Montag, Warren, 72
Montagu, Mary Wortley, 160
Montaigne, Michel de, 30, 64, 118, 127,
    130, 132, 144, 146, 148–9, 151, 152,
    155–6, 163–4, 168, 179, 192, 238,
    244
    Apology for Raimond de Sebonde, 6, 18,
        117, 131, 136–7, 149, 152–3, 161, 210,
        217
    "Of Drunkenness," 157–8, 177
    "Of Experience," 203–5
    "Of the Inconstancy of Our
        Actions," 22, 24, 134, 153, 160, 215
    "Of Vanity," 149
More, Henry, 75, 212, 224
Morris, David, 157, 209, 230, 238
Moses, 101–2, 112
Mueller, Judith C., 87
Mulhall, Stephen, 220–1

Nagel, Thomas, 228, 234
Nahum, 230
Nancy, Jean-Luc, 10
Newton, Isaac, 193–4
Nussbaum, Felicity, 178
Nuttall, A. D., 97, 113, 230

Opposition (to Walpole), 29, 31, 109, 121, 139, 150, 152, 155, 163, 230, 233, 235
other minds, problem of, 159–60, 165, 185, 236, 239

Parnell, J. T., 223
Parsons, Robert, 218
Pascal, Blaise, 4, 22, 64, 112–5, 117–21, 129, 137, 156, 231, 235
Patey, Douglas Lane, 16–7, 116, 212–3, 222
Paul, 6, 82, 152, 166, 237
Paulson, Ronald, 223
Perrault, Charles, 86
personal identity, problem of, 132–5, 160, 165, 234
Peterson, R. G., 242
Pettit, Alexander, 109
Phiddian, Robert, 72, 226
Philips, Ambrose, 91
Pitt, William, 28, 143–4, 146, 236
Plato, 94
Plumb, J. H., 105, 225
Pocock, J. G. A., 23–4, 31, 83, 105–6, 129–30, 132, 170, 215, 225, 240
Pollak, Ellen, 158, 170, 178, 240
Pomfret, John, 20, 119
Pope, Alexander, 3, 13, 18, 24, 28, 31–2, 64, 226, 230, 238–40, 242–3
  annotations of Montaigne's *Essays*, 6, 22, 24–5, 117, 131, 137, 149, 153, 161, 190, 210, 214–5, 217, 232
  Correspondence, 21, 99, 107, 118–9, 121, 127, 131, 135, 160, 162, 176–7, 184–5, 192, 230, 232, 240
  Dunciad, 7–8, 13–4, 30–1, 156, 181–207, 230
  Epistle to Dr. Arbuthnot, 151
  Essay on Criticism, 29–30, 100, 142, 204, 213
  Essay on Man, 13, 30–1, 97–100, 107–27, 129–30, 135, 165, 185–6, 192, 228, 230, 232, 235

  Imitations of Horace, 127, 129–32, 142–3, 145, 149–50, 155–7, 163, 192
    Epistle I, 1, 25, 141, 151–5, 166
    Epistle I, 6, 134–42, 150
    Epistle II, 2, 151, 192
    Satire II, 1, 146–51, 158, 160, 166, 173, 237
    Satire II, 2, 156
  Iliad, 100–2, 127
  Moral Essays, 157–8, 160, 231
    Epistle to Bathurst, 143, 231
    Epistle to Burlington, 90, 172
    Epistle to Cobham, 133, 137, 158–69, 174, 231, 235
    Epistle to a Lady, 141, 157–9, 162, 168–80
  Odyssey, 100
  Peri Bathous, 29, 62, 74, 100, 104–7, 113, 127, 195
  "Preface to *Shakespear*," 176
  Thoughts on Various Subjects, 129, 148
Popkin, Richard, 14, 18, 161, 187, 189–90, 212, 219, 223, 239
Prior, Matthew, 22, 64, 222
  "Essay on Opinion," 239
  Solomon on the Vanity of the World, 64, 119
probabilism, 3, 14–7, 19–22, 25–7, 44, 59, 114, 190, 212–3
providence, 21, 24, 26–30, 64–7, 69–71, 84, 94, 98–9, 107, 112, 143, 192, 225
Psalms, 101–2, 229
public sphere, 22, 24, 93, 99–100, 107–8, 110, 121–2, 165, 179, 188, 215, 230
Putnam, Hilary, 8–9, 19, 78, 228
Pyrrhonism. *See* skepticism, Pyrrhonian
Pythagoras, 136–7

Racine, Louis, 233
Rawson, Claude, 72, 224
Reid, Thomas, 234

Richardson, Jonathan, the elder, 159,
    173–4, 240–1
Richardson, Jonathan, the younger,
    164, 240
Rochester, John Wilmot, Earl of, 4, 13,
    20–1, 28–9, 51, 62–5, 69–70, 73,
    141, 144, 214, 217
    Correspondence, 43, 47
    An Epistolary Essay from M. G. to O. B.
        upon Their Mutual Poems, 44, 217
    Satyr [Against Reason and
        Mankind], 4, 33–45, 47–8, 55–6,
        217
    "Seneca's Troas, Act 2, Chorus," 217
Romanticism, 7, 37, 50, 115, 117–8, 131,
    144, 225
Romans, Epistle to, 6
Rorty, Richard, 7, 9, 211, 232, 239
Royal Society, 8, 14–6, 21, 35, 47, 49, 51,
    215, 217
Rudd, Niall, 136
Rumbold, Valerie, 178–9, 241
Rymer, Thomas, 86, 195

Saccamano, Neil, 226
Sappho, 134
Secker, Thomas, 230
Sedley, David, 235
Sedley, David L., 8, 205, 244
selfhood, 9–10, 24–5, 132–5, 144–7,
    149–50, 152, 154–6, 158, 165, 168,
    180, 185, 188, 234, 238
Seneca, 134, 141
Sergeant, John, 4, 15, 47
Sextus Empiricus, 18, 137–9, 144–5, 161,
    175–6, 190, 219, 239
Shaftesbury, Anthony Ashley Cooper,
    Third Earl of, 15, 18, 26–7, 29–31,
    72, 108, 136, 143, 225–7, 231, 236
    Correspondence, 95
    An Inquiry Concerning Virtue or Merit,
        228
    Letter Concerning Enthusiasm, 25, 91–
        6, 99–100, 107, 226

    The Moralists, 31, 94, 190–2, 200,
        242–3
    Soliloquy, or Advice to an Author, 28
Shakespeare, Wiiliam, 7, 144, 176
Shapin, Steven, 16–7, 41, 44–5, 213, 219
Shapiro, Barbara, J., 16, 22, 212
Shenstone, William, 142–3
Sherburn, George, 121, 229, 240
Shippen, William, 146, 148, 166, 237
Silverman, Hugh J., 244
Simpson, David, 231
Sitter, John, 226
skeptical sublime
    defined, 11, 13, 17, 50, 63, 78, 103, 130,
        175–6, 181–2, 195, 198
skepticism
    Academic, 15–6, 18–9, 113–4, 129,
        131–2, 136–7, 140, 190–1, 213, 215,
        232, 235, 239
    ancient vs. modern, 6, 134, 144–5,
        147, 159–60, 205–6
    and conservatism, 29, 31, 64, 84, 99
    and intentionality, 6–8, 15–6, 37, 79–
        83, 147, 175–6, 183–5, 188, 198–
        200, 207, 242
    mitigated, 14, 16, 18–9, 21–3, 28, 33,
        69, 72, 76, 79, 83, 98, 113, 182, 212,
        219, 223, 236
    Pyrrhonian, 15, 17–8, 22, 49, 113–4, 118,
        129, 131–2, 136–7, 144, 160–2, 164, 168,
        174–6, 190, 205, 213, 232, 236, 239
    and selfhood, 140–1, 145–9, 152, 154–5
    subject-object relation, 4–5, 113, 175–
        6, 204
Smith, William, 74, 229
Sohn-Rethel, Alfred, 171–2, 240
Solomon, Harry M., 113, 132, 213, 215, 232
Somers, John, 29, 83, 91, 225–6
Spacks, Patricia Meyer, 234
Spence, Joseph, 22, 141, 160–1, 215
Spinoza, Benedict de, 233
Stack, Frank, 134–5
Stallybrass, Peter, 110, 231
standing army, 24, 106

Stanley, Thomas, 18, 137–40, 175
Steele, Richard, 26, 106–7, 230
Stephen, Leslie, 118, 233
stoicism, 24, 30, 114, 129, 134–8, 141, 145,
 149, 156–7, 162, 169, 176–7, 232,
 238–9
sublime
 and power, 4–5, 8–14, 27–9, 31–4, 36–
  9, 41, 44–5, 47–8, 60, 64–7, 78–9,
  81, 84, 101, 103, 107, 130, 144, 176,
  182–3, 193, 195, 197–8, 204, 221, 229
 as satiric reversal, 5–7, 29, 35, 37–8,
  63, 73–4, 77–9, 84, 91, 182, 207
 subject-object relation, 4–5, 9, 14,
  52–53, 60, 102–3, 174, 204
 as tension between reason and
  imagination, 5–6, 8, 12, 21, 27–8,
  35–6, 42, 56–8, 65–9, 80, 100, 204
Sutherland, James, 184, 194
Swift, Jonathan, 3, 7, 9, 12, 21, 24, 28,
 30–1, 101, 107, 121, 127, 129, 132, 134,
 141, 144, 177, 182, 207, 215, 225, 230
 Correspondence, 91
 Examiner, 29, 82–3, 108, 225–6
 "Hints towards an Essay on
  Conversation," 87, 225
 Gulliver's Travels, 72
 Journal to Stella, 89
 "Modest Defense of Punning," 90,
  226
 "Mr. Collins's Discourse of Free-
  Thinking," 224–6
 "On the Trinity," 11, 21, 73–4, 76, 79,
  223
 "A Proposal for Correcting the
  English Tongue," 226
 A Tale of a Tub, 6, 8, 13, 21, 25, 29, 31,
  72–96, 100, 130, 223
 "Thoughts on Religion," 77

Tanner, Tony, 242
taste, 26–7, 30, 72, 84–9, 95–6, 100, 143,
 159, 172, 180, 194, 207, 215, 225–7

Temple, William, 73, 85
Theobald, Lewis, 193, 243
Thomas, Claudia, 241
Thomson, James, 32
Thormählen, Marianne, 217–8
Tillotson, John, 19–20, 215
Tindal, Matthew, 191, 193
Toland, John, 193, 233
Tories, 3, 23–4, 29, 64, 72, 82, 89–90,
 108–9, 139, 167, 215–6, 228,
 230
Trapp, Joseph, 221–2
Trotter, David, 217
Tuveson, Ernest, 218

Van Leeuwen, Henry G., 211
Vieth, David, 44, 218
Voltaire, 227

Walpole, Robert, 23, 109, 129, 150, 156,
 163, 193, 230, 233
Warburton, William, 112, 161, 183, 186–
 7, 190–1, 228–9, 242
Warton, Thomas, 237
Weinbrot, Howard D., 237
Weiskel, Thomas, 9–11, 14, 28, 78–9,
 115–6, 225
Welsted, Leonard, 5, 107–8, 182,
 195–6
Werenfels, Samuel, 5–6, 210
Wharton, Philip, Duke of, 164–9
Wharton, Thomas, Marquis of, 166
Whigs, 3, 21, 24, 26–9, 31, 64, 72–3,
 81–2, 84–5, 98, 105–6, 108–9,
 139, 152, 166–7, 215–6, 225,
 227–8
White, Allon, 110
White, Douglas, 230
White, Thomas, 15, 47, 212
Wilkins, John, 19–20, 214
William III, 104–5, 230
Williams, Aubrey, 188–9
Williams, Bernard, 200, 242

Williams, Kathleen, 223–4
Wimsatt, W. K., 225
Winn, James A., 50
Wisdom, John, 239
Wittgenstein, Ludwig, 9, 11, 20, 211,
    214, 239
  On Certainty, 213
  Philosophical Investigations, 7, 184–5,
    224
Wood, Theodore E. B., 214
Woolston, Thomas, 193
Wordsworth, William, 115–6, 189
Wotton, William, 86–7

Young, B. W., 184
Young, Edward
  "Conjectures on Original
    Composition," 37
  The Love of Fame: the Universal
    Passion, 178, 180, 241
  Night Thoughts, 232
  Paraphrase on Part of the Book of Job,
    120

Zimmerman, Everett, 223–4
Žižek, Slavoj, 76, 82, 171, 211, 224, 230
Zwicker, Steven, 219, 240